THE MIRACLES IN THE GOSPELS

THE MIRACLES IN THE GOSPELS

What do they teach us about Jesus?

KEITH WARRINGTON

The Miracles in the Gospels

Hendrickson Publishers Marketing, LLC
P. O. Box 3473
Peabody, Massachusetts 01961-3473

ISBN 978-1-61970-832-7

Originally published in Great Britain in 2015
Society for Promoting Christian Knowledge
36 Causton Street
London SW1P 4ST
www.spck.org.uk

Printed in the United States of America

First Hendrickson Edition Printing — June 2016

Contents

Contents

Contents

Tables

List of tables

Preface

This book has provided me with the very pleasant opportunity of exploring the Gospels and, in particular, focusing on Jesus and his supernatural ministry. Although I believe that Christians today have the privilege of functioning supernaturally through the power of God, the Gospels provide another reason for emphasizing the miraculous ministry of Jesus that is more to do with offering truth about him and the revelation of God that he imparts as God incarnate.

However, this book offers another purpose – which is to discover truth in the Bible by asking questions of the text and engaging with it dynamically. I am aware that for many believers today, the Bible is being read considerably less than it was just a few decades ago. There are a variety of reasons for this, but one danger is that, to a significant degree, where the Bible is silent in the lives of people, so is God, who speaks through its pages. One of the challenges facing Christian leaders today is to encourage people to recognize that the Bible is more accessible than they may fear, more relevant, and has a greater potential to transform their lives than they may anticipate.

With these facts in mind, I have sought to keep central key concepts in my quest to explore the miracles of Jesus in the Gospels, concepts that relate to exploration, discovery and application. This is a sacred journey, not merely an analytical and academic one, as we explore aspects of the life of God who became a man to reveal aspects of his character, and for our benefit – so that we could appreciate the remarkable nature of his grace to us.

At the same time, this is intended to be an adventure of discovery that will result in fresh lessons being learnt about Jesus. The writers of the Gospels function as literary wordsmiths, creatively and artistically displaying truths concerning Jesus. The more one recognizes the value of examining the text carefully, the more one will anticipate the remarkable potential of engaging not just with truth but with the God of truth, who chooses to encounter people through his words. The Bible does not function primarily as a database of dogma or a theological dictionary but as an opportunity to encounter the divine author. It is an altar of sacrifice to which we bring ourselves in full anticipation that the God of the universe, who has chosen to dwell with us, will meet with us in the text.

Undergirding this book has been the desire to remind readers that with our gifts of curiosity and careful imagination, and the help of the Holy Spirit, messages of the authors can be identified and applied by any believer. God wishes to speak to us more than we may realize, and my desire is that this will be your experience as you explore the miracles through the Gospels; if this book helps whet your appetite for further exploration, so much the better.

My appreciation goes to all those in seminaries and churches who have spurred me on in my quest to make the Bible more accessible to believers. My wife Judy has been my partner in this journey . . . and some of her observations have crept into these pages; she is of inestimable value to me.

Acknowledgements

This book is dedicated to my wife Judy, who has inspired me to discover the motivations of the Gospel writers who recorded the miracles of Jesus, by her dedicated desire to explore those same miracles.

Abbreviations

ABPR	Association of Baptist Professors of Religion
ACS	*African Christian Studies*
AfricEcclRev	*African Ecclesiastical Review*
AJBS	*African Journal of Biblical Studies*
AJET	*African Journal of Evangelical Theology*
AJPS	*Asian Journal of Pentecostal Studies*
BBR	*Bulletin for Biblical Research*
BibS	*Bibliotheca Sacra*
BibT	*Bible Today*
BR	*Bible Review*
BTB	*Biblical Theology Bulletin*
BZ	*Biblische Zeitschrift*
CBQ	*Catholic Bible Quarterly*
CC	*Christian Century*
CurTM	*Currents in Theology and Mission*
DR	*Downside Review*
ESV	English Standard Version
ETR	*Études Théologiques et Religieuses*
EvQ	*Evangelical Quarterly*
ExpTim	*Expository Times*
FT	*Faith and Thought*
FV	*Foi et Vie*
HBT	*Horizons in Biblical Theology*
HeyJ	*Heythrop Journal*
HTR	*Harvard Theological Review*
HW	*Healing and Wholeness*
IJP	*International Journal of Psychiatry*
IRM	*International Review of Mission*
ITQ	*Irish Theological Quarterly*
JAAR	*Journal of the American Academy of Religion*
JBL	*Journal of Biblical Literature*
JETS	*Journal of the Evangelical Theological Society*
JEPTA	*Journal of the European Pentecostal Theological Association*
JJS	*Journal of Jewish Studies*
JP	*Journal of Psychohistory*

JPC	*Journal of Pastoral Care*
JPT	*Journal of Pentecostal Theology*
JRHlth	*Journal of Religion and Health*
JSHJ	*Journal for the Study of the Historical Jesus*
JSJ	*Journal for the Study of Judaism*
JSNT	*Journal for the Study of the New Testament*
JSP	*Journal for the Study of the Pseudepigrapha*
JTS	*Journal of Theological Studies*
KJV	King James Version
LV	*Lumen Vitae*
LXX	Septuagint
MelTheol	*Melbourne Journal of Theology*
NASB	New American Standard Bible
NEB	New English Bible
NovT	*Novum Testamentum*
NRT	*Nouvelle Revue Théologique*
NT	New Testament
NTS	*New Testament Studies*
OT	Old Testament
PGM	*Greek Magical Papyri*
PP	*Pastoral Psychology*
PRS	*Perspectives in Religious Studies*
RB	*Revue Biblique*
RevExp	*Review and Expositor*
RevSciRel	*Review of Science and Religion*
RSV	Revised Standard Version
SB	Sources Bibliques
SBL	Society of Biblical Literature
SE	*Studia Evangelica*
SJT	*Scottish Journal of Theology*
SLJT	*St. Luke's Journal of Theology*
ST	*Studia Theologica*
StudRel	*Studies in Religion*
SWC	*Studies in World Christianity*
SwJT	*Southwestern Journal of Theology*
TD	*Theology Digest*
TrinJourn	*Trinity Journal*
TynBul	*Tyndale Bulletin*
TZ	*Theologische Zeitschrift*
UBS	United Bible Societies

VoxScrip	*Vox Scripturae*
WW	Word and World
ZNT	*Zeitschrift für Neues Testament*
ZNW	*Zeitschrift für die neutestamentliche Wissenschaft*
ZTK	*Zeitschrift für Theologie und Kirche*

Ancient sources

Dead Sea Scrolls

1QapGen	*Genesis Apocryphon*
1QH	*Thanksgiving Hymns*
1QM	*War Scroll*
1QS	*Rule of the Congregation*
4Q159	*Ordinances*
4QNab	*Prayer of Nabonidus*
11QTemp	*Temple Scroll*
CD	Cairo Genizah copy of the *Damascus Document*

Graeco-Roman sources

Abr.	Philo, *On the Life of Abraham*
Ag. Ap.	Josephus, *Against Apion*
Ant.	Josephus, *Jewish Antiquities*
De Mig. Abr.	Philo, *On the Migration of Abraham*
De Vit. Mos.	Philo, *On the Life of Moses*
Dial.	Justin, *Dialogue with Trypho*
Disc.	Dio Chrysostom, *Discourses*
Diss.	Epictetus, *Dissertations*
Ep.	*Epistles*
Haer.	Irenaeus, *Against Heresies*
Hist.	Tacitus, *Histories*
Mor.	Plutarch, *Moralia*
Nat. Hist.	Pliny, *Natural History*
Prov.	Seneca, *On Providence*
Wars	Josephus, *Jewish Wars*

Pseudepigrapha

2 Bar.	*2 Baruch*
Jub.	*Jubilees*
Pss. Sol.	*Psalms of Solomon*
Sib. Oracles	*Sibylline Oracles*

Test. Ben.	*Testament of Benjamin*
Test. Dan	*Testament of Dan*
Test. Gad	*Testament of Gad*
Test. Jud.	*Testament of Judah*
Test. Levi	*Testament of Levi*
Test. Mos.	*Testament of Moses*
Test. Naph.	*Testament of Naphtali*
Test. Reu.	*Testament of Reuben*
Test. Sim.	*Testament of Simeon*
Test. Sol.	*Testament of Solomon*
Test. Zeb.	*Testament of Zebulun*

Rabbinic literature

'Abod. Zar.	*'Abodah Zarah*
Arak.	*Arakhin*
b.	Babylonian Talmud
Bek.	*Bekhorot*
Ber.	*Berakhot*
Deut. Rab.	*Deuteronomy Rabbah*
Erub.	*Erubin*
Git.	*Gittin*
Hor.	*Horayot*
Hull.	*Hullin*
j.	Jerusalem Talmud
Kel.	*Kelim*
Ket.	*Kettubot*
Kidd.	*Kiddushin*
Lev. Rab.	*Leviticus Rabbah*
m.	Mishnah
Meg.	*Megillah*
Me'il.	*Me'ilah*
Mid. Gen.	*Midrash Genesis*
Ned.	*Nedarim*
Neg.	*Nega'im*
Nid.	*Niddah*
Num. Rab.	*Numbers Rabbah*
Ohal.	*Ohalot*
Pes.	*Pesahim*
Pesik.	*Pesikta*

List of abbreviations

Sanh.	*Sanhedrin*
Seqal.	*Sheqalim*
Shab.	*Shabbat*
Song of Sol. Rab.	*Song of Solomon Rabbah*
Ta'an.	*Ta'anit*
Yeb.	*Yebamot*
Zeb.	*Zebahim*

1

Purposes, structure and methodology

Purposes

The intention of this book is to explore the miracles of Jesus as they are located in the Gospels in order to understand the reason for their inclusion. Although one may learn from them for one's involvement in a healing or exorcistic ministry, it is not clear that the Gospels or Jesus intended to provide such a methodology to be imitated by believers. Rather, the miracle narratives have been carefully crafted by the authors to demonstrate that God has become man in the person of Jesus. To miss this portrait of God as he is radiated in Jesus through the writings of the Gospels is to rob oneself of extraordinary opportunities to discover significant truth.

This book is dedicated to readers who believe that the Gospels are accurate records and that the miracles therein are historical acts that were achieved by Jesus and who are interested in identifying the reasons why the authors chose to record them.

Structure

The structure of this book is as follows: in Chapter 2, the social and religious context of the miraculous mission of Jesus will be briefly explored. Chapter 3 will answer the question 'Why were miracles performed by Jesus?' The following chapters (4–7) comprise a survey of every miracle of Jesus recorded in the Gospels. Miracles of healing are followed by exorcisms and nature miracles. As far as the Synoptics are concerned, multiple accounts are explored in canonical order before parallel accounts offered by two authors, concluding with narratives recorded by only one author.[1]

The setting of each narrative in its literary context is an important element in determining reasons for the stories being included by the authors and so each of these is analysed. Identifying the prior and following narratives can be very helpful in identifying themes that the author may be developing.

---

[1] The ESV is used throughout.

Some repetition is inevitable in this explorative process, and, on some occasions, is deliberate, given that many will use this book as a resource for the study of individual miracles rather than reading it from start to finish.

Each passage is then analysed, focusing on the purpose of the miracles as they have been presented in order to identify the reasons for their inclusion; where the same story is recorded by more than one Gospel writer, they will each be examined in order to determine supplementary lessons. In order to make this a viable exercise, a number of supernatural events concerning Jesus, including the virgin birth, his resurrection and Ascension, have not been explored.

Methodology

Time has not been expended on critical enquiries of the biblical text in which that which is perceived to be authentic is separated from the inauthentic. The miracles of Jesus have been explored by many, and conclusions drawn concerning their authenticity have been as varied.[2]

Critical evaluations of the healings and exorcisms of Jesus that lead to their rejection as being pre-scientific explanations of psychosomatic problems

---

[2] In 1965, Glasswell (M. E., 'The Use of Miracles in the Markan Gospel', in *Miracles*. (ed.) Moule, C. F. D., Mowbray, London, 1965, p. 151) wrote, 'With the decline in emphasis on miracles in the presentation of religious belief has gone a similar decline in emphasis on the gospel miracles in studies of Jesus.' On both counts, rapid change has occurred in the last few decades. These issues have been dealt with by others with varying results: Blomberg (C. L., *The Historical Reliability of John's Gospel*. IVP, Leicester, 2001) argues for their authenticity as do Mussner, F., *The Miracles of Jesus*. (tr.) Wimmer, A., Ecclesia Press, Shannon, 1970, pp. 18–39, 55–65, 81–7; Hoffman, D. S., 'The Historical Jesus of Ancient Belief', *JETS*. 40.4, 1997, pp. 551–62; Loader, W. R. G., 'The Historical Jesus Puzzle', *Colloquium*. 29.2, 1997, pp. 131–50; Bauckham, R., *Jesus and the Eyewitnesses: The Gospels as Eyewitness Testimony*. Eerdmans, Grand Rapids, 2006; Keener, C. S., *The Historical Jesus of the Gospels*. Eerdmans, Grand Rapids, 2009; and Kee, H. C., *Miracles in the Early Christian World: A Study in Socio-Historical Method*. Cambridge University Press, Cambridge, 1983, pp. 1–41. Blackburn (B. L., 'The Miracles of Jesus', in *Studying the Historical Jesus*. (eds) Chilton, B., Evans, C. A., Brill, Leiden, 1994, pp. 353–94) questions the historicity of the miracles. Bultmann (R., *The History of the Synoptic Tradition*. Harper & Row, New York, 1963), Meier (J. P., *A Marginal Jew*. Doubleday, Garden City, 1991, Vol. 1, pp. 220–5), Sanders (E. P., *The Historical Figure of Jesus*. Penguin, New York, 1993), and Heiligenthal, R., Wohlers, M., Riesner, R. ('Wunder im frühen Christentum – Wirklichkeit oder Propaganda?', *ZNT*. 4.7, 2001, pp. 46–58) pursue a policy of demythologization based on a form-critical methodology (and an epistemology that excludes miracles) to show that they were the product of the later Christian community, and are unrelated to the activity of the historical Jesus; Fossum (J., 'Understanding Jesus' Miracles', *BR*. 10 Feb. 1994, p. 18), examining the theological import of the healings, assumes that a theological emphasis necessitates inauthenticity; also Davies, S., *Jesus the Healer*. SCM, London, 1995, pp. 69–77 and Gnilka, J., *Jesus of Nazareth*. Hendrickson, Peabody, 1997, pp. 120–1. Keller (E. and M., *Miracles in Dispute*. Fortress Press, Philadelphia, 1968, pp. 227–39) assumes that they were intended to show that with God difficult situations can be overcome.

or psychologically induced ailments are not engaged with.[3] Discussions relating to the healings and exorcisms of Jesus from a psychotherapeutic viewpoint have also not been included.[4] Parallels with alleged miracle workers in the ancient world have not been undertaken unless they shed light on the Gospel narratives.[5] It will be assumed that the miracle narratives reflect authentic occurrences of interest for a better appreciation of the historical Jesus, and, in particular, of his mission and status.

It is an examination of the final composition of the Gospels as they have been presented that will be the focus of this book, on the basis of which the priorities of the authors will be traced in order to determine the message they sought to transmit to their ancient readers. Of course, attempting to identify the motivation of the original authors is a complex process and to do full justice to this would involve a great deal of critical examination of the original texts and a variety of hermeneutical considerations. Such an intensive procedure is not possible in this book that is based on a choice to work with the most reliable manuscripts available to us. The hermeneutic tools that undergird this examination are redaction criticism (in that the distinct emphases of the authors are highlighted and explored, though this does not presume a creative exercise on the part of the authors that has resulted in historically suspect contents) and narrative criticism in which the literary aspects of the Gospel records are examined and rooted in their social and historical contexts.[6]

---

[3] Horsley (R. A., *Jesus and the Spiral of Violence*. Harper & Row, San Francisco, 1987, pp. 181–5) and Crossan (J. D., *The Historical Jesus: The Life of a Mediterranean Peasant*. T. & T. Clark, Edinburgh, 1991, pp. 303–32) view the miracles as intended to act as catalysts to set people free from the social, religious and economic privations of the first century. Van Aarde (A., 'Understanding Jesus' Healings', *Scriptura*. 74, 2000, pp. 223–36) understands the healings of Jesus, not as miracles, but as means to empower people to cope with their stressful situations; also Dormandy, R., 'The Expulsion of Legion: A Political Reading of Mark 5.1–20', *ExpTim* 111.10, 2000, pp. 335–7; Capps, D., *Jesus the Village Psychiatrist*. John Knox Press, London, 2008.

[4] See Sanford, J. A., *Healing Body and Soul*. Gracewing, Leominster, 1992; Hankoff, L. D., 'Religious Healing in First-Century Christianity', *JP*. 19.4, Spring 1992, pp. 387–407; Applebaum, S., 'Psychoanalytic Therapy: A Subset of Healing', *Psychotherapy*. 25.2, 1988, pp. 202–13; Calestro, K. M., 'Psychotherapy, Faith Healing and Suggestion', *IJP*. 10.2, 1972, pp. 83–113; Chordas, T. J., Gross, S. J., 'The Healing of Memories: Psychotherapeutic Ritual among Catholic Pentecostals', *JPC*. 30.4, 1976, pp. 245–57.

[5] Blackburn (B. L., *Theios Aner and the Markan Miracle Traditions: A Critique of the Theios Aner Concept as an Interpretative Background of the Miracle Traditions*. Mohr Siebeck, Tübingen, 1990, pp. 13–96, 188–93) provides a survey of Hellenistic miracle workers. However, although he claims an impressive number of parallels between Jesus and the Hellenistic figures examined, the quality and regularity of the alleged parallels are to be questioned. Many dissimilarities are evident and the alleged parallels are between Jesus and others living up to seven centuries distant from the life of Jesus.

[6] For a helpful and brief overview of the key hermeneutical methods available for the modern exegete, see Bock, D. L., *Studying the Historical Jesus: A Guide to Sources and Methods*. Baker Academic, Grand Rapids, 2002, pp. 153–216.

A prime purpose of the examination of the miracle narratives is to identify the intention of the author in writing in his particular historical context before drawing any lessons for the modern reader. It is assumed from the start, and demonstrated thereafter, that the Gospels are carefully crafted documents, intended to teach the readers rather than merely recording historical facts, to be sermonic rather than journalistic, offering guidance concerning key aspects of Jesus rather than existing as biographies of him. Rather than viewing the Gospels as sources for modern sermons, they will be treated as sermons in their own right, each of the miracle narratives being set in particular literary contexts in order to teach particular lessons to their readers. Thus, on occasion, the same story will be presented by different authors in different chronological settings; the reader is encouraged to notice this and ask 'Why?', resulting in a better appreciation of the author's purposes.

Markan priority is assumed throughout; this assumes that Matthew and Luke used Mark as a valuable source for their Gospels. Many of the narratives explored are presented in more than one Gospel. Often, there is considerable agreement, though there are also significant differences in content. As well as identifying these similarities and dissimilarities, the more difficult task will be to respond to the question 'Why do they exist?' With due caution, suggested answers will be offered in the hope that the process will take us deeper into the values and emphases of the individual authors. A basic deduction would be that if each of the Synoptics records the same story or the same wording, it is probable that this indicates that the data is of fundamental value to each of the authors. Similarly, reductions or additions by one or more author provide the intriguing possibility of identifying key issues of foundational importance to each of them.

Throughout, the focus is intentionally maintained on the issue of what the narratives reveal about Jesus. This is not only a textual analysis but also an opportunity to explore the status and mission of Jesus, and, insofar as he is God incarnate, to examine aspects of God.

2

Historical context

Suffering

Suffering was the basis of a great deal of discussion in the ancient world, especially due to the fact that illness, particularly in urban settings, was much more common than today. Suffering was viewed as being inherent to life, while death was the only certain release from it. The assumption that suffering forms and tests character is common in the writings of ancient philosophers,[1] and the wise and self-disciplined person was expected to face suffering fearlessly.[2] Some even considered suffering to be a sign of a god's love for, and approval of, a sufferer rather than his hostility or negligence.[3] As a result of these beliefs, most people accepted their lot in life and even if they did not, there was very little opportunity to amend their situations, let alone transform them.

Suffering was also a central element of first-century Jewish life. However, the sick were often deemed to be ceremonially impure[4] and a stigma was attached to them.[5] This was largely due to the belief that sickness was caused by sin.[6] The challenge to be faced was how to cope with sickness when it remained even after prayer and repentance. Given the assumption that God had sent it, the easily drawn conclusion was that he had chosen not to remove it, though often no reason was provided.

The issue of miracles of healing, and in particular, in the Old Testament (OT) has been explored in depth by a number of scholars.[7] A belief that was basic to the issue of healing and suffering for Jews was that God was

---

[1] Epictetus, *Diss.* 3.10.11; 3.12.11; Seneca, *Prov.* 4.2–3; *Ep.* 13.1; 26.6; 71.26; Pseudo-Crates, *Ep.* 19; Pseudo-Diogenes, *Ep.* 31.

[2] Dio Chrysostom, *Disc.* 8.15; Plutarch, *Mor.* 476.D.

[3] Seneca, *Prov.* 1.5, 4.5, 7, 8, 12, 16; Epictetus, *Diss.* 1.29.47–9; 2.1.39; 4.8.30, 32.

[4] Lev. 13—14.

[5] Ps. 38.11–12; John 9.2.

[6] Num. 12.11–13, 15; 21.7–9; b. *Ned.* 41b, 'A sick man does not recover from his sickness until all his sins are forgiven him'.

[7] Brown, M. L., *Israel's Divine Healer*. Paternoster Press, Carlisle, 1995; Hogan, L. P., *Healing in the Second Tempel (sic) Period*. Vandenhoeck & Ruprecht, Göttingen, 1992; Seybold, K., Mueller, U. B., *Sickness and Healing*. Broadman, Nashville, 1981; Kottek, S. S., *Medicine and Hygiene in the Works of Flavius Josephus*. Brill, Leiden, 1994.

their healer,[8] while it was believed that he also initiated suffering, including sickness.[9] The OT does not teach that God was the only one who caused suffering; rather he is designated as the only divine being who did so. Rather than expend too much time on the largely fruitless task of removing suffering, the Jews identified a number of mainly religious reasons for its existence:

- It was believed that divine chastisement due to sin resulted in sickness,[10] plague, poverty, famine, drought and oppression.[11] When it was the result of sin, it was believed that it helped people to strengthen their resolve to fight against sin. It was also believed to be proof of their being God's people and evidence of God's affection for them; thus, he disciplined them when they sinned and used suffering in his refining of their characters, thus enhancing their potential.[12]
- According to the rabbis,[13] healing was not always to be expected, nor were attempts to heal always encouraged. Anyone who was healed of an illness was deemed to be very fortunate and encouraged to thank God.[14] There was also the notion of inherited sickness,[15] the possibility of contracting illness, the recognition of the importance of

---

[8] Exod. 15.26; 23.25–26; Deut. 7.13–15; 32.39; Pss. 6.1–2; 30.2–3; 38.3–7; 41.3–4; 103.3; 2 Macc. 9.5–29; *Jub.* 23.30; Wisd. 16.12.

[9] Exod. 4.11; Deut. 28.18, 27–29, 35, 59–61; 1 Sam. 2.6; Job 2.10; Ps. 38.2, 3; Isa. 45.7; Lam. 3.38; Hos. 6.1.

[10] Deut. 28.22; 2 Kings 20.1–4; Job 33.19; Ps. 103.3; Isa. 33.24; Wisd. 11.16; Philo, *De Mig. Abr.* 206; *De Vit. Mos.* 2.235; Josephus, *Ant.* 18.325; *Test. Reu.* 1.7; *Test. Sim.* 2.12; *Test. Gad* 5.10; *Test. Ben.* 3.6; *Mid. Gen.* 33.3; b. *Shab.* 132a, *Ber.* 5a; *Sanh.* 101a; *Ned.* 41a; 1QS 1.23–7; 1QH 2.8; Horsley, G. H. R., *New Documents Illustrating Early Christianity* (*NDIEC*). The Ancient History Documentary Research Centre, MacQuarie University, 1987–, 2.23; 3.6, 15, 27; Schürer (E., *The History of the Jewish People in the Age of Christ*. T. & T. Clark, London, 1986) discusses the connection between sin and suffering (Vol. 2, pp. 540–6).

[11] Gen. 19.11; Exod. 23.20–23; Lev. 26.14–16; Num. 12.10–15; 21.4–6; 25.4–8; Deut. 28.1–13, 27–29; 1 Sam. 5.1–12; 2 Sam. 6.7–10; 1 Kings 8.37–38; 14.10–14; 2 Chron. 26.16–23; Pss. 38.1, 2, 17, 18; 73.14; Isa. 48.16; 53.4; Zech. 7.12; Josephus, *Ant.* 17.168–71 (concerning Herod); *Wars* 7.451–3; Philo, *Abr.* 92–8; b. *Shab.* 31b, 32b, 33a; *Ber.* 5a; *Sanh.* 101a; *Baba Mezia* 85a (lack of compassion); because of sin, longevity was deemed to have been reduced.

[12] Job 5.17–18; Jer. 29.10–13; Tobit 11.13–15; Di Lella, A. A., 'Health and Healing in Tobit', *BibT.* 37.2, 1999, pp. 69–73.

[13] Rabbinic resources relate, in the main, to the Talmud, of which there are two, identified as the Jerusalem and the Babylonian Talmuds, the latter of which is the more authoritative and fuller. However, both were written centuries after the time of Jesus, the Babylonian Talmud being transcribed 400 to 500 years after the Gospels were written. Given the oral and accurate way of transmitting the deliberations of the rabbis over the centuries, much of it reflects first-century beliefs and practices. Nevertheless, because of the time-gap, it should be used cautiously when seeking to identify what Jews believed and did in the time of Jesus.

[14] b. *Ber.* 54b.

[15] b. *Yeb.* 64b.

cleanliness and nutrition to one's health[16] and the inevitability of sickness in old age.[17]

- Persecution was an obvious cause of suffering.[18]
- Satanic/demonic activity was believed by some to result in personal suffering, though this was always under the sovereign rule of God (Job 2.4–7).[19]
- The Jews accepted that some suffering was inexplicable and even indiscriminate.[20]
- They also believed that they were living in the end times, a period associated with suffering (Dan. 8.23), but that God would vindicate them and deliver them from their suffering in the eschatological age.[21] Suffering was, therefore, always to be viewed in the context of a future hope (Mic. 4.4).
- It was believed that some suffering could be removed as a result of prayer,[22] while the Jews also believed that the Holy Spirit strengthened people in times of suffering (Isa. 11.1–4), offering hope after the suffering (Isa. 43.19; Ezek. 37.11–14).

At first sight, it may be assumed that a basic aspect of the ministry of Jesus was to remove suffering. However, not all suffering was remedied by Jesus, nor is there evidence to suggest that this was the most important part of his agenda. In the ministry of Jesus, there is, for example, no reference to the removal of slavery, the oppression of the Roman Empire, the crippling poverty of the people caused by the taxation burden, or the many other aspects of life that called for a radical solution to establish justice. Indeed, rather than cause all suffering to flee with a flick of his fingers, he forecast suffering for his followers (Mark 10.38–45). However, what is significant is that whereas God healed in the OT, it is Jesus who does so in the Gospels. He is identified by the writers as emulating God, not merely the prophets of God.

---

[16] Deut. 14.3–21; 23.13–14; b. *Erub.* 65a, 83b.
[17] Gen. 27.1; Deut. 31.2; 1 Sam. 4.15, 18; 2 Sam. 19.35; 1 Kings 14.4; Eccles. 12.5; 3 Macc. 4.5.
[18] Exod. 4.25; Deut. 25.11–12; Judg. 1.6; 2 Sam. 4.4; 18.14; Jer. 20.2.
[19] b. *Hull.* 43a describes the whole treatment of Job by God as miraculous.
[20] Gen. 16.2; 30.2; Exod. 4.11; 1 Sam. 1.5; Eccles. 7.15.
[21] Ps. 35.24; Isa. 35.4–6; 42.7; 50.8, 9.
[22] Gen. 25.21; 30.6, 17, 22; Exod. 14.10–14; 1 Sam. 1.10, 12, 17; Ps. 30.2; *The Lives of the Prophets* 2.1–7 (dated first century AD) refers to Jeremiah praying for Egyptians who were subsequently healed. As a result of prayer, Jacob heals Reuben (*Test. Reu.* 1.7) while Daniel heals the king, the latter healing involving the removal of Behemoth, believed to be a demon (*Life of Daniel* 4.12–17, see also *1 Enoch* 60.25).

Miracles

Outside the Gospels, there are few reports of the miracles of Jesus (or those of so-called 'divine men').[23] Indeed, evidence for miracle workers in the ancient world is not as common as some have claimed.[24] However, the possibility of miraculous activity was generally accepted in the ancient world.[25] Much of quality has been written on this topic and thus space is not given to it here.[26] A basic identification of a miracle that I will adopt is that it is a supernatural action that transforms a previously dire and humanly insoluble situation; it is used by the Gospel writers to define a supernatural action of God, Jesus or someone whom they have delegated to function thus. It is intended to draw from the observer the question 'Who or what has enabled this person to function thus?' If God causes a miracle, the biblical writers do not subscribe to the notion that God has broken his own laws; rather, he has achieved what is his right to do.

Most ancient Jewish literature, outside the OT, also concentrates on the OT prophets when referring to miracles.[27] Similarly, when Josephus refers to miracles, they relate to the OT prophets,[28] though he also believes that some occurred in his lifetime,[29] referring to Onias (*Ant.* 14.22–4) who, on one occasion, apparently prayed successfully that a drought would end. Actual evidence for Jewish miracle workers is largely restricted to Honi

---

[23] This is largely a construction of relatively modern scholarship to refer to ancient (mainly Greek) people who claimed (or of whom claims were made) to be able to function miraculously.

[24] Theissen (G., *Miracle Stories of the Early Christian Tradition*. T. & T. Clark, Edinburgh, 1983, pp. 271–2) claims that during the 300 years prior to Jesus, 'we hear nothing of charismatic miracle-workers', and the lack of evidence to the contrary supports this claim.

[25] Garland, R., 'Miracle in the Greek and Roman World', *The Cambridge Companion to Miracles*. (ed.) Twelftree, G. H., Cambridge University Press, Cambridge, 2011, pp. 73–94.

[26] Brown, C., *Miracles and the Critical Mind*. Eerdmans, Grand Rapids, 1984; Craig, W. L., 'The Problem of Miracles: A Historical and Philosophical Perspective', pp. 9–48 and Blomberg, C. L., 'The Miracles as Parables', in *Gospel Perspectives, Vol. 6: The Miracles of Jesus*. (eds) Wenham, D., Blomberg, C. L., JSOT Press, Sheffield, 1986, pp. 327–59; Garland, 'Miracles in the Greek and Roman World', pp. 75–94; Nicklas, T., Spittler, J. E., *Credible, Incredible: The Miraculous in the Ancient Mediterranean*. Mohr Siebeck, Tübingen, 2013.

[27] Moses (*Jub.* 48.13–14; Sir. 39.17; Wisd. 10.18–19; 19.7–8; 4 Ezra 13.39–45; Philo, *De Vit. Mos.* 1.91–146, 196–206); Elijah (*Lives of the Prophets* 21.14); Elisha (*Lives of the Prophets* 22.5); Isaiah (*Lives of the Prophets* 1.2–4); Jeremiah (*Lives of the Prophets* 2.2–7); Ezekiel (*Lives of the Prophets* 3.8–9).

[28] Moses (*Ant.* 2.274, 286, 339; 3.7, 35; 4.52, 55), Samuel (*Ant.* 6.27, 92), Elijah (*Ant.* 8.337–43), Elisha (*Ant.* 9.48–50).

[29] Twelftree (G. H., *Paul and the Miraculous*. Baker, Grand Rapids, 2013, pp. 39–42, 49–104) explores the place of the miraculous in the beliefs of the Pharisees, concluding that there was a widespread belief in the possibility of such phenomena, though with limited references to healings.

(first century BC) and Hanina ben Dosa (first century AD), while the number of miracles is very limited in contrast to the narratives in the Gospels about Jesus.

To the Jews, miracles demonstrated the sovereignty of God and his provision for them,[30] including food,[31] water,[32] fire (1 Kings 18.16–40), rain (1 Kings 18.41–45), miraculous escape and protection,[33] and guidance (Num. 17.1–8; b. *Shab.* 97a), or judgement[34] and retribution for their enemies.[35] In the Talmud, miracles are alluded to, but there is little expectation that they should occur[36] and people are advised not to expect miraculous intervention even when in danger;[37] indeed, b. *Yoma* 29a records that the story of Esther signalled the end of all miracles.

Healing

The Graeco-Roman world

In this era, there was a variety of means whereby healing could be sought. These included several gods (especially Asclepius[38] and Apollonius), as

---

[30] Exod. 34.10; Pss. 72.18; 78.4; 86.10; 96.3; 106.21–22; 107.8, 15, 21, 31; 136.4.

[31] 1 Kings 17.4 (daily bread and meat), 7–24; 2 Kings 4.42–44 (the multiplication of bread with some left over); Jos., *Ant.* 9.47–50 (inexhaustible flour and oil).

[32] Exod. 17.5–6; Num. 20.8–11; Judg. 15.19; 2 Kings 3.15–20.

[33] E.g. of Herod (Jos., *Wars* 1.331–2; 340.7); of a man who needs to cross a river (b. *Git.* 45a–b); safe passage across water (Exod. 14.21–22); protection (Dan. 3.19–30; 6.16–23).

[34] Num. 11.1 (fire); Num. 21.6 (snakes); 1 Kings 17.1–7 (drought); 2 Kings 2.23–25 (bears); 2 Kings 5.19–27 (leprosy); 1 Chron. 21.7–14 (plague); Jos., *Wars* 1.657–8 (terminal illness of Herod).

[35] Exod. 14.23–28; 17.8–13; Judg. 14.19; 15.14–15; 16.28–31; 2 Kings 1.10–14; Jos., *Ant.* 1.14.

[36] b. *Ber.* 54a, 58a; *Baba Mezia* 106a.

[37] b. *Shab.* 32a; *Pes.* 64b; *Yoma* 37b–8a.

[38] Asclepius was originally a doctor (c. fifth century BC), who, according to the myth, was elevated to being a god after his death. Temples were erected to him throughout the ancient world and people would make pilgrimage and stay the night, in the hope that he would visit them in their dreams and heal them of their sicknesses (testimonies refer to occasions when he apparently performed operations on their bodies which they saw in their dreams). The dissimilarities between the followers of Jesus and Asclepius in belief and practice are significant: snakes in the temples as symbols of Asclepius which people were encouraged to touch in order to receive healing, the presence of and ministration by priests, therapies involving exercise (walking barefoot, running) or other practices (pouring wine over oneself before bathing), payment or sacrifices to the Asclepius cult prior to any ministry, and a written declaration or (clay) object left that related to the part of the body healed. At the same time, although popular throughout the Roman world prior to Jesus, there is little evidence to indicate a significant presence in Palestine; see Edelstein, L. and Edelstein, E. J., *Asclepius: A Collection and Interpretation of the Testimonies*, 2 vols. Baltimore, Hopkins, 1945; Aleshire, S. B., *Asklepios at Athens: Epigraphic and Prosopographic Essays on the Athenian Cults.* J. C. Gieben, Amsterdam, 1991; Klauck, H-J., *The Religious Context of Early Christianity.* Edinburgh, T. & T. Clark, 2000, 154–68.

well as doctors[39] and magic.[40] Although magic was widely practised in the ancient Jewish[41] and Graeco-Roman world,[42] it has not been proven that Jesus functioned as a magician,[43] nor was he accused of such in his life.[44] Indeed, the OT condemns magical practices,[45] as does the Talmud.[46]

The Jewish world

The healing narratives of the OT mainly relate to the activities of the prophets,[47] while answers to prayer for restoration, in contexts of sickness, are occasionally noted in the OT.[48] Jewish literature of the New

---

[39] This, to a large extent, commenced as a result of the work of Hippocrates, whose beliefs and methodologies were recorded by Galen, much now lost. Celsus, a Roman, writing in AD 14–37 explores medical treatments for illness (*De Medecina*). The Greeks were the first to take seriously the identification of causes of illness as not necessarily sent by gods or evil spirits. However, although medical treatments had developed by the time of Jesus, in reality, the majority of people relied on supernatural forces to alleviate their illnesses. This was partly due to the danger and esoteric materials and practices of some medical therapies, its limitations and the fees often charged.

[40] Although belief in magic was rejected by many among the upper classes (Plut., *Mor.* 164b; Pliny, *Nat. Hist.* 28.48), the lower classes accepted its value without question. The *Papyri Magicae Graecae* (in *The Greek Magical Papyri in Translation, Including the Demotic Spells, Vol. 1: Texts.* University of Chicago Press, Chicago, 1986) provides many examples of spells that were used to combat illness, though mainly dated from the second century to the fifth century AD, none of which originate in Palestine.

[41] b. *Sanh.* 17a; *Baba Mezia* 107b states that no one may be a member of the Sanhedrin without a knowledge of sorcery; cf. Tobit 6.1–8; 8.2–3; 11.7–14; Jos., *Ant.* 8.46–8; b. *Shab.* 66b, 129b; Trachtenberg, J., *Jewish Magic and Superstition: A Study in Folk Religion.* Atheneum, New York, 1987; Naveh, J., Shaked, S., *Amulets and Magic Bowls: Aramaic Incantations in Late Antiquity.* Magnes Press, Jerusalem, 1985; Bohak, G., *Ancient Jewish Magic: A History.* Cambridge University Press, Cambridge, 2011.

[42] Keener, C. S., *Miracles: The Credibility of the New Testament Accounts.* Baker, Grand Rapids, 2011, 1.46–51; Remus, H., *Pagan-Christian Conflict over Miracle in the Second Century.* Harvard University Press, Cambridge, 1983.

[43] For speculation that Jesus functioned magically, see Smith, M., *Jesus the Magician.* Harper & Row, San Francisco, 1978; Hull, J. M., *Hellenistic Magic and the Synoptic Tradition.* SCM, London, 1974; Aune, D., 'Magic in Early Christianity', in *Aufstieg und Niedergang der römischen Welt.* De Gruyter, Berlin, 1980; Klutz, T. (ed.), *Magic in the Biblical World.* T. & T. Clark, London, 2003. Craffert, P. F., *The Life of a Galilean Shaman: Jesus of Nazareth in Anthropological-Historical Perspective.* Cascade Books, Eugene, 2008.

[44] Though see later texts: b. *Ber.* 55b; *Shab.* 61a, 67a; *Kidd.* 73b; *Pes.* 110a, 112a; *Sanh.* 43a, 107b; *Sotah* 47a refer to Jesus practising magic and being executed because of sorcery and deceiving Israel. Celsus, in the second century, accused Jesus of having learnt magic in Egypt (Origen, *Contra Celsum*, 1.28). Justin Martyr (*Dial.*, 69.7) refers to such accusations in his day.

[45] Exod. 22.18; Lev. 19.31; Deut. 18.10–12; 2 Kings 9.22; Isa. 2.6; Jer. 27.9; Ezek. 13.17–18; Mal. 3.5.

[46] b. *Sanh.* 67a–b, 101a; *Shab.* 61a–b.

[47] Moses, Deut. 34.11; Elijah, 1 Kings 17.21–24; Elisha, 2 Kings 5.1–14; Isaiah, Isa. 38.1–8; Jewish miracle narratives became more popular by the third century (b. *Ber.* 6a; *Shab.* 67a, 110b; see also Margalioth, M. (ed.), *Sepher-ha-Razim: The Book of Mysteries.* Scholars Press, Atlanta, 1983; it is a third- to fourth-century document of purported Jewish miracles.

[48] Exod. 2.23; 3.7; 2 Kings 20.5; Ps. 6.8.

Testament (NT) era or earlier contains little reference to healings,[49] while Josephus records very few healing miracles.[50] The Jews looked forward to an eschatological era when sickness would be removed during the messianic age.[51] Until then, it was anticipated that when in trouble it was appropriate to pray and, on occasion, the prayer would be answered positively.

The OT demonstrates a limited appreciation of the value of physicians,[52] though healing remedies were generally not condemned.[53] Priests legislated concerning issues of purity (Lev. 13.6–17), though did not provide therapy. Debates about the value of the doctor are present in rabbinic sources,[54] while Sirach 38.1–15 provides an unusually positive insight into the role of the physician, defining the relationship between the physician and God.[55] In particular, as well as recording that Yahweh is the healer and that prayer to him may result in healing (38.8–9), Sirach also writes, 'Honour physicians for their services, for the Lord created them; for their gift of healing comes from the Most High' (38.1–2). He refers to the skill of the doctors (38.6), such expertise resulting in God being glorified. The best doctors are those who recognize the value of prayer (36.1–12; 38.9, 13–14; 46.2–3), repentance (38.10–11) and medicine (38.4–8).

The Mishnah, however, records a very negative opinion, identifying the best of physicians as destined for Gehenna,[56] while Tobit (2.10) records their limitations. The apparent competition between Yahweh and physicians is famously noted in 2 Chronicles 16.12 which records King Asa seeking the help of the latter instead of the former.

---

[49] 2 Macc. 3.31–34 refers to an apparent miraculous healing of a man, and some references to the healings of OT prophets are recorded in Sir. 48.23; Wisd. 18.20–25; *Jub.* 10.12; 25.14–31; 1QapGen; 4QNab. Tobit 3.16–17; 11.7–8 records that God's angel taught Tobit how to heal his elderly father.

[50] *Ant.* 8.325–7 (Elijah); 10.29 (Hezekiah); see similar disinterest in healing miracles in *Pseudo-Philo*, *1 Enoch*, *Jubilees* and Qumran; see also Eve, E., *The Jewish Context of Jesus' Miracles*. Sheffield Academic Press, Sheffield, 2002, pp. 117–216.

[51] *2 Bar.* 73.2.

[52] Exod. 21. 19; Job. 13.4; Isa. 1.6; 38.21; Jer. 8.22; Jos., *Ant.* 1.208; 6.166, 168; 8.45; 10.25b; b. *Ber.* 60a asserts that the healing skill of the physician is granted by God. In general, though, physicians are infrequently recorded in Jewish literature, and healing tends to occur via prayer (Gen. 20.17).

[53] Gen. 30.14–22; 2 Kings 20.1–11; Isa. 1.4–9; 38.21–22; Jer. 8.22. However, Wisd. 16.12 denies healing power to plants and *1 Enoch* 7.1 cautions against using herbs for therapeutic purposes because, apparently, fallen angels had introduced this notion to people; however, *Jub.* 10.10–15 reveals that angels instructed Noah concerning their therapeutic value, and Tobit (6.6, 9) uses fish gall.

[54] b. *Ber.* 60a.

[55] See McConvery, B., 'Ben Sira's "Praise of the Physician" (Sir. 38. 1–15) in the Light of Some Hippocratic Writings', *Proceedings of the Irish Biblical Association.* 21, 1998, pp. 62–87.

[56] m. *Kidd.* 82a.

Exorcism

Social scientific and anthropological theories concerning demonization are not discussed as they have been presented elsewhere.[57] Although there may be some similarities in behavioural manifestations, the remedies initiated by Jesus are different from successful, modern therapies for mental illness. The former involve Jesus speaking to the demonic force, not the human victim; there is an absence of the characteristic touch of the demonized sufferer by Jesus; and the remedies are concluded immediately, or at least in a matter of minutes, after the initial meeting.

Belief in the existence of evil spirits and their negative impact on people, mainly in causing physical suffering, was widespread in the worldviews of Jesus' contemporaries, Jews[58] and Graeco-Romans, and many attempts were made to mitigate their presence.[59] However, there is a limited amount

---

[57] Davies (S., *Jesus the Healer*. SCM, London, 1995, 79–83) suggests that those exorcized by Jesus were people who found themselves 'in intolerable circumstances of social subordination' in which 'becoming a demon is normally a mode of response, a coping mechanism and not a supernatural event per se' (86); see also Kiev, A. (ed.), *Magic, Faith and Healing: Studies in Primitive Psychiatry Today*. Free Press, New York, 1964, pp. 135–9, 204–5, 262–3; Bourguignon, E., *Possession*. Chandler and Sharp, San Francisco, 1976, pp. 53–4; Wink (W., *Unmasking the Powers: The Invisible Forces That Determine Human Existence*. Fortress Press, Philadelphia, 1986; *The Powers That Be: Theology for a New Millennium*. Doubleday, New York, 1998) recognizes the reality of evil in the world but refuses to see it as the result of supernatural demonic beings, rather blaming it on political and religious human authorities and individual and corporate organizations; Myers (C., *Binding the Strong Man: A Political Reading of Mark's Story of Jesus*. Orbis, New York, 1988, pp. 141–52, 191–4, 243–7) suggests a context of a repudiation of the Roman military oppression; see also Waetjen, H. C., *A Reordering of Power: A Socio-Political Reading of Mark's Gospel*. Fortress Press, Minneapolis, 1989, pp. 113–19; Klutz, T. E., *The Exorcism Stories in Luke-Acts: A Sociostylistic Reading*. Cambridge University Press, Cambridge, 2004; Wahlen, C., *Jesus and the Impurity of Spirits in the Synoptic Gospels*. Mohr Siebeck, Tübingen, 2004; Kay, W. K., Parry, R. (eds), *Exorcism and Deliverance: Multi-disciplinary Studies*. Paternoster Press, Milton Keynes, 2011, pp. 120–38.

[58] 1 Sam. 16.14–16; 18.10–12; 19.9 refers to a spirit that caused Saul to try to kill David and was partially dispelled by David playing the lyre (1 Sam. 16.23). Certain nights were associated with demonic attack (b. *Pes.* 112b). References to a spirit of jealousy (Num. 5.14–15), lying spirits (1 Kings 22.19–24), spirits sent by God to inspire the king of Assyria to leave Judah (Isa. 37.7) and a 'spirit of whoredom' (Hos. 5.4) hint at the possibility of malevolent presence of alien spiritual forces possessing the persons concerned; see also Miranda, V. A., 'A Cristogia dos Demonios', *VoxScrip* 10.1, 2000, pp. 3–18; see Novakovic, L., 'Miracles in Second Temple and Early Rabbinic Judaism', in *The Cambridge Companion to Miracles*. (ed.) Twelftree, G. H., Cambridge University Press, Cambridge, 2011, pp. 95–112.

[59] Yamauchi (E., 'Magic or Miracle? Diseases, Demons and Exorcisms', in *Gospel Perspectives, Vol. 6*. (eds) Wenham, D. et al., pp. 99–115) traces demonic beliefs and exorcistic practices from the empires of Mesopotamia, Egypt, Greece and Rome; Sorensen (E., *Possession and Exorcism in the New Testament and Early Christianity*. Mohr Siebeck, Tübingen, 2002) explores practices in the Ancient Near East (pp. 18–46) and Greece (pp. 75–117) and identifies the four main ways of treating demonized people – physically binding them in order to restrain them, medicine, cultic healing and purification, whereby any defilement that may have caused the condition is removed; Leeper, E. A., 'Exorcism in Early Christianity', unpubl. PhD, Duke University, 1991, pp. 8–73; see also *PGM*, esp. 4.11231–9 (dated after the first century) in which 'Jesus Chrestos, the Holy Spirit, the Son and the Father', among others, are incorporated into a spell to 'drive away this unclean demon Satan'.

of literary evidence for exorcisms prior to the life of Jesus in Jewish and especially in Graeco-Roman literature.[60] Most of it is much later than the first century, the *Magical Papyri*, which refers to such events, dating around AD 300 and later. Moreover, there is considerable dissimilarity between exorcism as reflected in the Gospels and the practice of other alleged exorcisms.[61]

There is limited information in the OT that would indicate a developed (or even basic) demonology[62] or satanology,[63] and scant evidence of exorcism.[64] Reference to demons is generally in the context of an assertion that the readers should not consult them or allow them to undermine their loyalty to God (Deut. 18.10–14).[65] Even the word 'Satan' is less of a proper name and more the description of an accusatory role undertaken by someone under the authority of God.[66] Evil spirits are referred to, though they

---

[60] Sorensen (*Possession*. p. 7) states that it 'is undocumented in Roman society until late in the first century Common Era'.

[61] Yamauchi ('Magic or Miracle?', pp. 131–40) provides very limited evidence of exorcistic praxis from the ancient world prior to the first century, including incantations, carefully spoken, with repetition and sometimes chants, nonsense language, reference to various gods, the name of the demon to be exorcized, the placing of the hands on the victim, and different tones of voice; Sorensen (*Possession*. p. 6) writes of 'the foreignness of the . . . Christian practices of exorcism to the Graeco-Roman world'.

[62] References to spirits occur in 2 Chron. 18.21, 22; in Isa. 34.14 Lillith, a Mesopotamian demon, is referred to; *1 Enoch* 15.8–12; 69.4–15; 86 and *Test. Sol.* record many apparent deeds of demons, including initiating fires, whirlwinds, battles, sickness and death of and sex with people; see Ma, W., 'The Presence of Evil and Exorcism in the Old Testament', in Kay, W., Parry, R., *Exorcism and Deliverance*. Paternoster Press, Milton Keynes, 2011, pp. 27–44; Wright, A. T., *The Origins of Evil Spirits: The Reception of Genesis 6.1–4 in Early Jewish Literature*. Mohr Siebeck, Tübingen, 2005.

[63] 'Satan' is only referred to 16 times in the OT (1 Chron. 21.18; Ps. 109.6; Zech. 3.1–2); Job 1—2 accounts for 12 of these occasions; b. *Kidd.* 81a refers to Satan recognizing the status of R. Meir and R. Akiba, though neither of the rabbis achieve an exorcism of Satan; see Day, P., *An Adversary in Heaven: Satan in the Hebrew Bible*. Scholars Press, Atlanta, 1988.

[64] b. *Me'il.* 17b provides a rare reference to an exorcism where R. Simeon casts a demon out of an emperor's daughter; see also *Num. Rab.* 19.8 where the burning of roots and the sprinkling of water are used in achieving an exorcism; Josephus refers to a root that effected the expulsion of demons (*Wars* 7.180, 185) and in *Wars* 6.3 states that some illnesses were caused by demons and eradicated through exorcism and magic, describing an exorcistic technique associated with Solomon's name conducted by Eleazar (*Ant.* 8.42–9). It is referred to in Qumran (4QNab 1.4; 1QapGen 20). In *Jub.* 10.1–9, Noah prays against demons while *1 Enoch* 40.7 describes a heavenly voice which dispels demons; Eve (*Jewish Context*. p. 258), after comprehensively exploring the relevant Jewish literature, concludes: 'although the defeat of the evil powers is described in a number of ways, exorcism is not one of them'; see also Twelftree, G. H., 'The Miracles of Jesus: Marginal or Mainstream?', *JSHJ*. 1, 2003, pp. 104–24.

[65] Lev. 17.7; Deut. 32.17; Ps. 106.36–38.

[66] He is not described as being the leader of evil spirits, though much later *Test. Sol.* 1.1–13 records that Satan ruled the demons, including Beelzebul. *1 Enoch* 16.6–13 (dating from the third century BC) records that the descent from heaven of evil spirits was due to their rebellion, suggesting that they derive from illegitimate sexual activity between heavenly beings and earthly women (or from the dead bodies of the rebellious giants recorded in Gen. 6.4 (*1 Enoch* 15.8—16.1)).

are often sent by God and thus operate with permission granted by and under the authority of God.[67] Demons or Satan were sometimes associated with harmful influences on people (1 Sam. 19.9; Job 1.12). The origin of the devil is also only obliquely referred to in the OT (Isa. 14.3–21; Ezek. 38.1–19), the demonic being largely marginalized in the OT.

Jewish[68] literature outside the OT (especially *1 Enoch*[69]) provides a more developed demonological structure than is evident in the OT, much of it related to the power,[70] location[71] and demise[72] of demons. The book of *Jubilees* (dated in the middle of the second century BC) also provides an elaborate demonology (10.1–10) in which such beings are described as subject to Satan, are called 'evil spirits' and 'demons', who lead astray, blind and kill the sons of Noah, and are bound by the good angels, though one tenth are left for Satan to use as he wishes; furthermore, an angel is told to teach the sons of Noah how to control the Satan.

Josephus[73] has limited references to exorcism and Philo has none. A highly developed demonology is provided in the Talmud, referring to the number of demons[74] and the means of protecting oneself from them, by water,[75] piety (including the study of the Torah),[76] magical incantations and amulets,[77] phylacteries,[78] medicine,[79] prayer,[80] not travelling on certain days and keeping away from certain places.[81] In this, demons are also associated with disease, though not exclusively.[82]

It is in the NT that demons are more clearly described in terms of their spiritual danger and malevolence. Many of Jesus' Jewish contemporaries tended to view demons as being at least mischievous and at worst

---

[67] Judg. 9.23; 1 Sam. 16.14–23; 1 Kings 22.17–23; Job 4.12–16.

[68] Some of this (*Testament of Solomon, Testaments of the Twelve Patriarchs*) post-dates the NT.

[69] 7.1—8.4; 14.3; 40.7; 69.12–15 refer to demons imparting illnesses to people and various forms of expulsion of demons.

[70] Power to encourage a variety of sins, including adultery, lies, witchcraft and anger (*Test. Jud.* 23.1; *Test. Dan.* 2.1, 5.5). *1 Enoch* 69.12 records how they attack people; see also Tobit 3.7; 6.7, 16; 8. 1–3; 11.8–12; Josephus (*Ant.* 6.166) believed that demons caused strangulation and suffocation.

[71] Among ruins (b. *Ber.* 3ab), graves (*Ber.* 18b) and clustered in the air (*Ber.* 6a).

[72] *1 Enoch* 9 and 10 record their denunciation and punishment by Michael, Gabriel and Raphael.

[73] *Wars* 7.180–5; *Ant.* 8.46–9.

[74] b. *Ber.* 6a.

[75] b. *'Abod. Zar.* 12b.

[76] b. *Sotah* 21a; *Pes.* 8b.

[77] b. *Shab.* 67a.

[78] b. *Ber.* 5a.

[79] *Jub.* 10.10–13; b. *Ber.* 6a.

[80] b. *Ber.* 9b; *Kidd.* 29b; *Pesik.* 187b.

[81] b. *Pes.* 111a–12b; b. *Ber.* 3ab.

[82] b. *Hor.* 10a, leprosy; *Yoma* 83b, rabies; *Bek.* 44b, asthma; *Hag.* 67a, epilepsy.

malicious – but rarely a moral or spiritual threat;[83] indeed, on occasion, it was believed that demons helped people.[84] Perhaps this is one reason why there is little expectation that they would be expelled in the messianic age.[85]

Furthermore, the Gospels record that Satan has a kingdom (Matt. 12.26) and that he claims to own the kingdoms of the world (Matt. 4.8–9). The NT does not record demons functioning on behalf of God or sent by God; instead, they are presented in a contest with Jesus. Neither does it explore reasons for possession, or blame the demonized person for some-how causing or encouraging the presence of the demon; on the contrary, the demonized are described as being passive victims. They play no part in the exorcism, Jesus requiring them to do nothing to effect the cure.

The origin of demons is not identified in the NT, though a common belief is that they are synonymous with fallen angels.[86] It is also in the Gospels that exorcism is often referred to, the most common terms used to expel the demons being *exerchomai*[87] ('I go out') and *ekballō* ('I throw out').[88] It is not clear that the Synoptists intended to offer guidelines for exorcistic practice, and such is also absent in the rest of the NT; the healing procedure in James 5.14–16 is not replicated for exorcisms. The exorcism narratives appear to be recorded to teach about Jesus' authority rather than to provide guidance for future exorcisms.

A number of motifs are common to the majority (or all) of the exorcism narratives. Thus, Jesus does not look for demons – they come to him (Mark 5.6) or their victims are presented to him (Mark 7.25). There is often a dramatic confrontation or a sense of consternation on the part of the demons, at least initially;[89] they are removed authoritatively and leave immediately (Mark 1.26), as a result of a command from Jesus (Mark 1.25).

---

[83] Satan accuses Abraham (b. *Sanh.* 89b) and seduces people (b. *Baba Bathra* 16a), including David (b. *Sanh.* 107a).

[84] b. *Meʿil.* 17b; *Git.* 66a; *Sanh.* 101a cautiously recognized that, although dangerous, taking advantage of their power was permissible. Some rabbis apparently benefited from their service (b. *Pes.* 110a; *Yeb.* 122a; *Hull.* 105b).

[85] Although there is some evidence that Messiah was expected to defeat Satan and demons (*Test. Levi* 18.12; *Test. Dan.* 5.10), these texts were edited by Christians and it is difficult to know how much they actually reflect Jewish thought. *1 Enoch* 10.4 and 55.4 reveal that Azazel and his demons were judged and condemned by God; Sanders (E. P., *Jesus and Judaism*. Fortress Press, Philadelphia, 1985, pp. 134–5) asserts, 'the view that the Messiah . . . was expected in Judaism to overcome the demonic world and to demonstrate this victory miraculously by exorcisms . . . is hard to find'.

[86] Matt. 25.41; 2 Pet. 2.4; Jude 6; Rev. 12.7–9.

[87] Matt. 8.31–32; Mark 1.25–28; 5.8, 13; Luke 4.41; 8.29.

[88] Matt. 7.22; 10.8; Mark 1.34, 39; 3.15; Luke 9.40, 49; 11.14–20.

[89] Mark 1.23, 24; 5.7; 9.20.

Although exorcisms are included in the Synoptics, it is significant to note that John's Gospel does not record any. The author chose to use a selection of signs to enforce his teaching and it appears that exorcisms did not achieve his purposes. The paucity of exorcisms in the Acts of the Apostles (16.16–23) and the absence of exorcisms in the rest of the NT are also of interest. It may be that exorcisms were more prominent in the ministry of Jesus, given the dynamic nature of his person and his radical message concerning the kingdom he was initiating, which resulted in a violent backlash from his demonic foes. In this regard, it may be appropriate to recognize exorcisms as offering the clearest evidence of Jesus' opposition to and rebuttal of Satan and his kingdom. Jesus' reign is legitimate; Satan's is not. Whereas Jesus is associated with light, life, transformation and goodness, demons are associated with darkness, death, suffering and evil.

Conclusion

Jesus exists in a context of significant and various manifestations of suffering experienced by people. In the Graeco-Roman world, this was addressed mainly with reference to various gods or medical therapies, though the prognosis for possible benefits was not hopeful. The Jews concluded that suffering occurred for a number of reasons, though God was not expected to intervene often and, if he did, it would generally be mediated through a prophet. The challenge for first-century Jews was that the era of the prophets appeared to have ended, individual prophecies being absent for centuries. The possibility of relief from suffering was thus relegated to the messianic era for which they longed but which did not appear close. Into this vacuum of uncertainty and helplessness came Jesus, manifesting an authority to help and transform beyond their wildest dreams.

3

The purposes of Jesus' miracles in the Gospels

Introduction

The miracles of Jesus are significant elements of the Gospels. Excluding summary accounts of miracles, the following data affirms this. In Matthew, 153 verses (out of 969) reflect miracle stories (15.79 per cent); in Mark, there are 196 verses (out of 643 – 30.48 per cent); in Luke, 140 verses (out of 938 – 14.92 per cent) and in John, 181 verses (out of 789 – 22.94 per cent). In total, 670 out of 3,339 verses relate to miracles of Jesus, 20.06 per cent of the Gospel narratives.

Although Heil[1] is right to describe miracles of Jesus as being 'multi-dimensional', the main reason for their inclusion in the Gospels is to teach the readers about Jesus. The writers present Jesus as someone who has no peer, the miracles being intended to result in the question being asked, 'Who is this man?', closely followed by the more spectacular question, 'Is he God?' Jesus' miracles are unique, not merely on the basis of his style or success rate, or because of the high numbers or their distinctiveness when contrasted to those of other healers, or even because of their association with the kingdom of God. Although they may indicate that he is a prophet and even the Messiah, there is more to be gleaned, for they are intended to declare his divine authority and status.[2]

Jesus' miraculous ministry was intended to establish truth about himself rather than to act as a healing model for others. The OT indicates that healing, control over evil spirits and power over nature are unique prerogatives of God. In presenting Jesus as a remarkable miracle worker, the writers of the Gospels identify him functioning as God.

---

[1] Heil, J. P., 'Significant Aspects of the Healing Miracles in Matthew', *CBQ*. 41, 1979, p. 279.

[2] The Gospel writers often use *exousia* (authority) with reference to Jesus (Matt. 9.6, 8; 21.23–24, 27; 28.18; Mark 1.22, 27; 2.10; 11.28–29, 33; Luke 4.32, 36; 5.24; 7.8; 20.2, 8; John 5.27; 10.18; 17.2; 19.11) and with reference to his ability to be able to delegate it to others (Matt. 10.1; Mark 3.15; 6.7; Luke 9.1; 10.19); see also Warrington, K., 'The Role of Jesus in the Healing Praxis and Teaching of British Pentecostalism: A Re-Examination', *Pneuma*. 25.1, 2003, pp. 66–92.

Lessons about Jesus from his miracles

Jesus resolves many varied problems authoritatively

Jesus is presented in the Gospels as having divine authority to heal sicknesses,[3] cast out demons[4] and raise the dead.[5] A number of summary accounts are also presented in the Gospels,[6] which affirm these central truths. Thus, Matthew (4.23–25) indicates that (i) Jesus healed all/every illness, demonstrating the comprehensive power of Jesus over all kinds of illnesses, and (ii) people came from Galilee and Syria (the Roman province which included Palestine), emphasizing the widespread effect of Jesus' ministry; his authority was such that even Syrians, and thus Gentiles also, came to Jesus for help. Thus, in his first summary account, Matthew emphasizes the comprehensive nature and success of Jesus' transformative mission, recording a multiplicity of problems needing resolution by Jesus.[7] (iii) The healings of Jesus occurred instantaneously. Thus, Matthew (8.16) records that Jesus dealt with the demons 'with a word' while Mark (1.34) records that Jesus did not allow the demons to speak, because they knew him, Luke (4.41) more clearly identifying the fact that it was because they knew he was the Christ and the Son of God.

Jesus delegates his supernatural restorative authority

The Synoptists record no specific healings by the disciples, identifying Jesus as the central figure in healing. However, Jesus anticipated a continuing preaching, healing and exorcistic ministry after his resurrection, and the writers refer to Jesus commissioning his disciples to heal and cast out demons.[8] The implication is that they are to do as their Master has done (see the very similar language between Matt. 10.1 and 4.23, the latter recording Jesus' restorative ministry). The commissioning of the Seventy

---

[3] Matt. 8.14–17//s; 12.15–21//s; 13.51–58//s; 14.34–36//s; 15.29–31; 19.2; 21.14; Mark 7.31–37; Luke 13.32; John 4.46–54; 5.2–47; 9.1–41.

[4] Matt. 8.16; 8.28–34//s; 9.32–34; 12.22–29//s; 15.21–28//s; 17.14–21//s; Mark 1.23–28//s; 1.39; 9.38–41//s; Luke 13.32.

[5] Matt. 9.18–19; 23–26//s; Luke 7.11–17; John 11.2–44.

[6] Matt. (4.23–24; 8.16–17; 9.35; 11.4–5; 12.15–21; 14.1–2, 35–36; 15.29–31; 19.2); Mark (1.32–34, 39; 3.7–12; 6.54–56); Luke (4.40–41; 6.17–19; 7.21–22); John (20.31).

[7] The terms used to describe the issues needing to be resolved are 'disease' (*nosos*, 4.23, 24; also 8.17; 9.35; 10.1); 'infirmity' (*malakia*, 4.23); 'sick' (*kakōs exontas*, 4.24); 'pain' (*basanos*, 4.24); 'demonized' (*daimonizomai*, 4.24); 'epileptic' (*selēniazomai*, 4.24), used only here and 12.15 in the NT; 'paralytic' (*paralutikos*, 4.24). The term often used to describe the restoration process, including the restoration of those afflicted with demons, is 'to heal' (*therapeuō*, 4.23, 24, used 16 times by Matthew with reference to Jesus' healing ministry).

[8] Matt. 10.1, 8//Mark 3.15; 6.7//Luke 9.1–2, 6.

(Luke 10.1, 9) also refers to healing, though they also discovered that they had authority over demons (Luke 10.17).

Mark 16.17–20 records that miraculous signs, including healings, will confirm the preaching of the gospel. Much has been written concerning the authenticity of these verses with most scholars concluding, on the basis of literary evidence in the main, that they are not Markan,[9] though still part of Scripture. The book of Acts confirms that miracles occurred through the hands of believers in the years following Jesus' Ascension.[10]

In John 14.12–14, Jesus promises that the works he performed will be achieved to a greater degree by those who believe in him, as a result of his returning to the Father. The clarification of 'greater works' has been the cause of some discussion. It is possible that 'works' (14.10) refers to the preaching of the gospel, though this is not reflected in the text itself and more clearly relates to Jesus' miracles, as also noted in the next verse (14.11). The use of the same term in 14.12, first referring to the same works mentioned in verse 11 as being achieved by Jesus and, second, as potential realities in the experience of the disciples, assumes a continuation of the same reference to miracles.

John identifies the prospect of the disciples benefiting from Jesus' authority even during his physical absence. The reference to the Spirit (14.15–17, 25–26) indicates that the presence of the latter is the distinguishing feature in this promise, the Church being the community of the Spirit in which he will dwell[11] and through whom he will minister.[12] Thus, the greatness of 'the works' is best understood in terms of the new context in which they are to be achieved, the new era of the Spirit now available through every member of the Church and no longer limited to the Twelve or the Seventy.

Jesus reinstates the marginalized

Matthew records the substantial nature of Jesus' miraculous ministry as being directed to people at the perimeters of society.[13] It is the consequential

---

[9] Cf. Kelhoffer, J. A., *Miracle and Mission*. Mohr Siebeck, Tübingen, 2000; France, R. T., *The Gospel of Mark*. Grand Rapids, Eerdmans, 2002, pp. 685–8; Evans, C. A., *Mark 8.27–16.20*. Word, Waco, 2001, pp. 540–51; Stein, R. H., *Mark*. Baker Academic, Grand Rapids, 2008, pp. 733–7.

[10] 2.43; 5.15–16; 6.8; 8.7; 9.18, 34, 36–41; 13.11–12; 14.3, 8–10; 16.16–18; 19.10–11; 20.9–10; 28.3–6; 8–9; see also Warrington, K., 'Acts and the Healing Narratives. Why?', *JPT*. 14.2, April 2006, pp. 189–218; Warrington, K., 'Healings by Jesus in Luke and in Acts: Pedagogical and Paradigmatic Explorations', *Evangelical Theological Society Conference*. Boston, MA, November 1999.

[11] Rom. 8.15–16; 1 Cor. 3.16–17, 6.18–19.

[12] Acts 1.8; 2.17–18; 1 Cor. 2.4.

[13] Gentiles (Mark 5.1–20//s; 7.24–30//; 7.31–37; 8.22–26); the ceremonially impure (1.40–45; 5.25–34); the poor (Mark 5.25–26//Luke 8.43–44). Luke, in particular, introduces Jesus' ministry to the marginalized sectors of Jewish society (4.16–30; 5.27–32; 7.36–50; 8.40–56//s; 12.32; 14.13–14, 21), especially Gentiles (7.1–10; 17.11–19) and those excluded from society (5.12–16; 8.26–39; 19.1–10).

issues of illness, including isolation, rejection and an inability to function in a corporate context, that are also of importance to Jesus. His desire is not just to heal but also to restore the sick person to a normal role in society. Schnackenburg[14] describes Jesus as the one who 'liberates people from their ostracism among the people and their guilt and redeems them from their misery . . . Jesus is the Savior in a comprehensive sense'.

This is a sign not simply of Jesus' compassion but also of his authority. In the OT, it is God who reintegrates the sick and the outcast;[15] in the Gospels, it is Jesus who takes on that responsibility. In fact, the Synoptists do not often refer to compassion as Jesus' motivation in healing.[16] Wacker[17] accurately writes, 'The principal purpose of Jesus' miracles was not compassion but revelation'. While Jesus' miracles are obviously acts of mercy, the Gospel writers demonstrate that such activity, especially dedicated to the poor and helpless, is to reveal that he has the authority to institute the kingdom of God and to welcome into it those who, at worst, were rejected by their communities, or, at best, were pitied by them. Jesus demonstrates that he had the authority to ensure that those who were excluded, and unable to participate in their communities, were transformed and incorporated.

Jesus is greater than Messiah

The OT does not provide a great deal of information concerning the messianic age and even less about the Messiah, especially with regard to any authority to achieve miracles.[18] Much more data concerning the Messiah is available in later Jewish literature[19] that explores, often speculatively, his

---

[14] Schnackenburg, R., *Jesus in the Gospels.* (tr.) Dean, O. C., Westminster Press, Louisville, 1995, p. 313; Percy, M., 'Christ the Healer: Modern Healing Movements and the Imperative for the Poor', *SWC.* 1.2, 1995, pp. 118, 120–1.

[15] Ps. 147.2; Isa. 25.8; 56.8; Jer. 30.17; Mic. 4.6–7; Zeph. 3.20.

[16] Matt. 14.14; 20.34; Mark 1.41 is uncertain; Matt. 5.19 refers to the mercy of Jesus with reference to a demonized person; Luke 7.13; John's Gospel excludes any association. Lewis (D., *Healing: Fiction, Fantasy or Fact?* Hodder & Stoughton, London, 1989, p. 268) speculates when he claims that God has 'a bias to the poor', as does Alana (O. E., 'Jesus' Healing Miracles: A Sign of His Loving Compassion for Humanity', *AfricEcclRev.* 42.3–4, 2000, pp. 106–13) and Bretherton (L., 'Pneumatology, Healing and Political Power: Sketching a Pentecostal Political Theology', in *The Holy Spirit in the World Today.* (ed.) Williams, J., Alpha, London, 2011, pp. 132–3) who, with limited textual evidence, suggests that 'Jesus is either moved to heal by compassion . . . or in response to a request for him to have compassion'.

[17] Wacker, G., 'Wimber and Wonders: What about Miracles Today?', *Reformed Journal.* 37, April 1987, p. 17.

[18] The term is referred to fewer than 40 times in the OT, most of which refer to the Jewish king, and only once to an eschatological figure (Dan. 9.25–26).

[19] *Pss. Sol.* 3.16; 13.9–11; 14.13–15; 18.7–10; 4 Esdras 7.12, 27–31; 8.53; Sir. 44.21; *Jub.* 17.3; 22.14; 32.19; *1 Enoch* 5.7; 96.3; *4 Ezra* 6.59; *2 Bar.* 14.13; 29.5–8; 51.3; 73.2—74.4; *Sib. Oracles* 3.373–80, 619–23, 744–59; *Test. Zeb.* 9.8; *Test. Jud.* 18.12.

roles, resulting in a keen expectation of his coming, especially from the times of the Maccabees.[20] It is this literature along with the deep desire for the coming of Messiah that fuelled such expectations in the time of Jesus. In particular, it anticipated that the establishment of the kingdom of God would be introduced by healings achieved by the Messiah.[21] The Synoptists often present Jesus as the Messiah[22] and the Son of David, a common messianic title,[23] though they also establish him as someone who functions with divine power and authority at a much higher level of authority than was expected of Messiah.[24]

Jesus fulfils Old Testament prophecy

It is of particular interest that Matthew expresses Jesus' authority by identifying the exorcisms and healings of Jesus as the fulfilment of OT prophecy concerning the Messiah. Thus, in 8.18, he presents Jesus fulfilling Isaiah 53.4. Matthew does not follow the Septuagintal (LXX) text of Isaiah 53.4a, or any other Greek versions, but instead provides a translation of the Hebrew that relates it more to physical illness, thus suiting his purpose to demonstrate that Jesus fulfils the Isaianic prophecy in his healing ministry.

---

[20] Oegema, G. S., *The Anointed and His People: Messianic Expectations from the Maccabees to Bar Kochba*. Sheffield Academic Press, Sheffield, 1998; Satterthwaite, P. E., Hess, R. S., Wenham, G. J. (eds), *The Lord's Anointed: Interpretation of Old Testament Messianic Texts*. Paternoster Press, Carlisle, 1995; Juel, D., *Messianic Exegesis: Christological Interpretation of the Old Testament in Early Christianity*. Fortress Press, Philadelphia, 1988.

[21] *Jub.* 23.29–30; *4 Ezra* 7.123; 8.53; *1 Enoch* 96.3; *2 Bar.* 73.2; b. *Sanh.* 91b; 1QS 4.6; 1QH 11.22.

[22] Matt. 1.16–7; 16.13–20//Mark 8.27–30//Luke 9.18–21 (John 20.31); Mark 14.61–62; Luke 2.11, 26.

[23] Matt. 22.41–46//Mark 12.35–37//Luke 20.41–44. Some rabbis sought to prove this of themselves (b. *Sanh.* 56a; *Ket.* 62b), including even R. Hillel (j. *Ta'an.* 4.2). For further reading, see Charlesworth (J. H., 'The Son of David: Solomon and Jesus (Mark 10.47)', in *The New Testament and Hellenistic Judaism*. (eds) Borgen, P., Giversen, S., Hendrickson, Peabody, 1997, pp. 72–87). Chae (Y. S., *Jesus as the Eschatological Davidic Shepherd*. Mohr Siebeck, Tübingen, 2006) and Baxter (W., 'Healing and the "Son of David": Matthew's Warrant', *NovT.* 98.1, 2006, pp. 36–50) associate the title with the Davidic shepherd of Ezek. 34. Ezekiel condemns 'the shepherds of Israel' (34.1) for many reasons but, in particular, because they have not strengthened the weak nor have they healed the sick (34.4). See also Duling, J., 'Matthew's Plurisignificant "Son of David" in Social Science Perspective: Kinship, Kingship, Magic, and Miracle', *BTB.* 22, 1992, pp. 99–116; Mullins, T. Y., 'Jesus, the "Son of David"', *Andrews University Seminary Studies.* 29, 1991, pp. 117–26; Loader, W., 'Son of David, Blindness, Possession, and Duality in Matthew', *CBQ.* 44, 1982, pp. 570–85; Kingsbury, J. D., 'The Title "Son of David" in Matthew's Gospel', *JBL.* 95, 1976, pp. 591–602.

[24] Although healing is anticipated in the messianic era, it is God who is identified as the healer (*Jub.* 23.26–30; *2 Bar.* 73.1–3), not Messiah. For a comprehensive overview and support for this conclusion, see Kvalbein, H., 'The Wonders of the End-Time: Metaphoric Language in 4Q251 and the Interpretation of Matthew 11.5 *par*', *JSP.* 18, 1998, pp. 101–6 (87–110). Charlesworth (J. H., 'Solomon and Jesus: The Son of David in Ante-Markan Traditions (Mark 10.47)', in *Biblical and Humane*. (eds) Elder, L. B., Barr, D. L., Malbon, E. S., Scholars Press, Atlanta, 1996, pp. 125–51) concludes, 'There is not one pre-70 Jewish writing that depicts the Messiah as one who will come and heal the sick' (150).

He records, 'He took (*lambanō*) our infirmities (*astheneia*) and bore (*bastadzō*, "I remove, carry away") our diseases (*nosos*)' instead of 'He has borne (*pherō*) our griefs (*hamartia*) and (carried) our sorrows (*odunaomai*)'.

So while Isaiah 53.4 presents the Messiah as carrying our sorrows, Matthew describes Jesus as *removing* our diseases. In Isaiah 53.4, the Servant[25] suffers vicariously, carrying the griefs and sorrows in himself, but this aspect is not repeated in Matthew 8.17; rather, Jesus authoritatively heals the sick by removing their diseases, but without becoming ill himself. Isaiah presents the Servant as a substitutionary sufferer, whereas Matthew identifies the Servant as Jesus, an authoritative healer, who transforms people and removes sickness and demons without himself being negatively affected.

Some have associated Matthew 8.17 with the death of Jesus and thus concluded that Matthew is indicating that Jesus removed people's sicknesses on the cross. However, Matthew clearly sees Jesus fulfilling Isaiah 53.4 in his life, through his healing activity. Although the death of the Servant is in view in Isaiah 53.4, in Matthew 8.17 it is Jesus' healing mission that is the focus for Matthew.

Indeed, Matthew's omission of Isaiah 53.4b ('yet we esteemed him stricken, smitten by God and afflicted') and especially 53.5 ('But he was wounded for our transgressions; he was crushed for our iniquities; upon him was the chastisement that brought us peace, and with his stripes we are healed') indicates that this reference in Matthew is not an anticipation of the Passion of Jesus by Matthew; the repetition of these verses by Matthew would have made such an association much more likely. The exclusion of these verses and the translation of the Hebrew that Matthew offers demonstrate that his desire was to emphasize Jesus as the supreme healer who heals throughout his life, not on the cross. He is the healer par excellence, who fulfils OT prophecy, but offers more than it promised.

Jesus is identified as the Son of God

Instead of demonstrating that Jesus' healings simply affirmed his messianic status, the authors prefer to use them also to indicate his deity. Of course, to define Jesus as being divine does not exclude the fact that he was also human; he is God incarnate. However, it is important to recognize that, in achieving miracles, he does not do so as did some of the OT prophets. Furthermore, in engaging in miraculous activity, he manifests not just the

---

[25] Identified with Moses (b. *Sotah* 14a), Elijah (Sir. 48.9–10) and an unnamed 'righteous person' (Sir. 11.12–3) while the majority view of the LXX is that it is the Jewish nation (Isa. 42.1).

power of God through him but also the presence of God in him and in time. Thus, in casting out demons, he does so with a different dynamic from that of a human exorcist; he offers a divine statement in that, in him, God has come to earth to demonstrate his antagonism towards and authority over evil. People were unable to combat such evil and it was into that kingdom of evil that Jesus came, as God, to break its power over people. Similarly, in manifesting miraculous actions on earth, Jesus demonstrates his divine credentials in that he achieves what God did, as recorded in the OT. If Jesus is demythologized or if his life and person are assumed to be historically suspect, these facts are significantly under-mined; to do that would be to call into question the purpose of the Incarnation and crucifixion, let alone the preaching of the kingdom of God and its manifestation in supernatural activity in Jesus' ministry.

In the miracle narratives, Jesus is often referred to as the Son of God whose authority is unrivalled and equal to that owned by God.[26] Mark (3.11) notes that the evil spirits confess Jesus as the Son of God. Although their identification of Jesus as the Son of God may indicate that they were attempting to control him by name magic, it is more likely that this was an honest, and perhaps surprised, outburst as they recognized his true status; as elsewhere, they are the first to recognize who Jesus truly was. In 1.24, demons identify Jesus as 'the holy one of God'; now, they more closely identify him as God's Son. Other than 1.1, this is the first reference to this title in Mark, and it is noticeable that it is demons (not people, or even disciples) that accurately define Jesus thus (see also 5.7). The only other one in Mark who accurately realizes that Jesus is the Son of God is a Roman centurion, at the cross (15.39).

The concept of 'son of God' was used of people who, by virtue of their being created by God, were defined as sons of God, including Adam (Luke 3.38) and the Israelites.[27] The term is also used of the Jewish king in the singular form,[28] and, in the plural, of angels[29] and believers.[30]

However, the Gospel writers indicate, by their use of the term, that a different quality of sonship is being anticipated with reference to Jesus. The synoptic authors build a number of features into the term that explicitly

---

[26] The title 'Son of God' is a favourite for Matthew with some unique references (14.33; 16.16), while he also refers to God being the Father of Jesus, 15 references being unique to Matthew (including 4.6; 8.29; 14.33; 16.16; 26.63).

[27] Deut. 14.1; 32.8; Isa. 1.2; Jer. 3.19.

[28] 2 Sam. 7.14; Pss. 2.7; 89.27.

[29] Gen. 6.2, 4; Job 1.6; 2.1; 38.7; Heb. 1.5.

[30] Matt. 5.9; Luke 20.36; Rom. 8.14, 19; Gal. 3.26.

demonstrate that it may not be understood to indicate that he owns an inferior status as a member of the Godhead. Rather, it is intended to define a most exalted status for Jesus. Thus, Jesus is described as knowing the Father as much as the Father knows the Son (Matt. 12.27). As the Son of God, Jesus partakes of the nature of God. Furthermore, this knowledge is exclusive and immediate. Others may only enter this relationship with the express permission of the Father and the Son. Most importantly, in the Ancient Near East, the one who best and most naturally reflected the character and aspirations of a father was his son. So also, Jesus in the flesh is presented as the most acutely accurate and authentic presence of God on earth that can be envisaged; he is the complete and unique revelation of God.

Thus, when John the Baptist enquired about the identity of Jesus, in particular if he was the Messiah,[31] Jesus responded by reporting his healings and preaching, alluding to a number of OT verses.[32] However, these Isaianic references refer to the supernatural acts of God, not Messiah, and Matthew presents Jesus as achieving them and thus fulfilling the OT prophecies concerning God. Similarly, Jesus is presented in the Gospels as functioning as God in healing people, establishing his authoritative control over envoys of Satan, and emulating God in his authority over nature.

Jesus initiates the kingdom of God

The healing ministry of Jesus provides evidence of the presence of the kingdom of God, the present-tense participles in Matthew 4.23 ('teaching', 'preaching' and 'healing') expressing an ongoing and holistic manifestation of the kingdom. A fundamental characteristic of Jesus' teaching was, 'The time is fulfilled, and the kingdom of God is at hand',[33] his miracles providing evidence of that truth. Every healing anticipated the final victory over death and thus authenticated the message of the kingdom. As such, the miracles indicated a new era being initiated by Jesus, functioning as signs of a kingdom promoted by hope that was to replace a kingdom plagued by fear.

Jesus manifests God's authority

As will be seen, the miracle narratives offer opportunities to highlight the deity of Jesus. Thus, the writers demonstrate that Jesus forgives sins, and

---

[31] The term used by John – *ho erchomenos* 'the coming one' – is used in the context of the expected Messiah elsewhere in Matthew (3.11; 21.9).
[32] Isa. 26.19; 29.18; 35.5–6; 42.7, 18; 61.1.
[33] Matt. 4.12–17//s; 10.1, 8//s; 11.4–6//s; 12.22–29//s; Mark 1.39; 6.7; Luke 4.40–43; 5.15, 17.

manifests authority over the law, touching lepers and the dead, over the Sabbath and over the Temple. He walks on water and feeds thousands, calms storms, creates objects out of nothing, and acts as the superlative judge of the Jews. He even achieves miracles not manifested by God in the OT but, most significantly, he offers a better relationship with God than that which God himself established with the Jews.

Jesus offers people opportunities to believe in him

Although the miracles of Jesus did not always lead to expressions of faith, they did provide people with the opportunity to gain a more accurate perception of his identity. Thus, for John, the healings are always identified as 'signs', the purpose of which is to provide an opportunity for faith in Jesus as the Son of God.[34] Although Jesus, in 20.29, exalts the faith of those who believe without the support of signs, he does not condemn signs as being an illegitimate means of encouraging faith in him. This purpose associated with miracles is also reflected in the OT where Naaman concludes, after being healed, 'there is no God in all the earth but in Israel' (2 Kings 5.15). In Jesus' ministry, they functioned as stepping stones to a more developed appreciation of his person and mission.[35] In this regard Melinsky's comment is helpful when he argues that Jesus 'did not heal people just to make them better'.[36] In following Jesus, people do not simply subscribe to the agenda of a rabbi, or even of the Messiah. They have the opportunity to engage with God, who chooses to touch them with human hands, even though he is God.

On only one occasion is it recorded that Jesus' ministry of healing was partially impeded in a context of unbelief by those present where that unbelief reflects an absence of faith, an unwillingness to believe, rather than an insufficient amount of faith. The literary context is identified in Table 3.1. Although the account is recorded in each of the Synoptists, they present their narratives differently and it is instructive to treat them separately. However, before the dissimilarities are commented on, agreements in each of the accounts will be identified as of central importance to the stories, so important that each of the writers includes them.

---

[34] 10.38; 14.11; 20.31.
[35] Matt. 4.23; 9.6–8, 35; 10.1, 7–8; 11.4–5, 20–30; Mark 1.39; 6.7, 12–13; Luke 4.18–19, 40–43; 5.15, 17; 6.17–18; 7.22; 9.6; 10.13–15; 13.32; John 11.47–48.
[36] Melinsky, M. A. H., *Healing Miracles.* Mowbray, London, 1968, p. 26.

Table 3.1 The effect of unbelief on Jesus' healing ministry – the literary context

	Matthew	*Mark*	*Luke*
Jesus restores a blind and dumb demoniac	12.22–23		(11.14)[37]
Jesus is accused of being empowered by Beelzebul	12.24–32	(3.22–27)	(11.15–23)
Jesus speaks about the importance of fruitful lives	12.33–37		(6.43–45)
Jesus denounces the Pharisees' request for signs	12.38–42	(8.11–12)	(11.29–32)
Jesus teaches about a returning unclean spirit	12.43–45		(11.24–26)
Jesus identifies his 'true' family as doing God's will	12.46–50	(3.31–35)	(8.19–21)
Parables of the kingdom	13.1–51	4.1–25, 30–34	(8.4–18)
Jesus calms the storm	(8.18, 23–27)	4.35–41	(8.22–25)
Jesus exorcizes a demon from the Gerasene	(8.28–34)	5.1–20	(8.26–39)
Jesus heals Jairus' daughter and the woman with the haemorrhage	(9.18–26)	5.21–43	(8.40–56)
Jesus is tempted in the wilderness	(4.1–11)	(1.12–13)	4.1–13
Jesus preaches in Galilee	(4.12–17)	(1.14–15)	4.14–15
Rejection of Jesus by his countrymen	**13.52–58**	**6.1–6**	**4.16–30**
Jesus commissions the Twelve	(10.1, 7–11, 14)	6.7–13	(9.1–6)
Herod's assessment of Jesus	14.1–2	6.14–16	(9.7–9)
Death of John the Baptist	14.3–12	6.17–29	(3.19–20)
Jesus feeds 5,000	14.13–21	6.30–44	(9.10–17)
Jesus teaches authoritatively in a synagogue		(1.21–22)	4.31–32
Jesus exorcizes a demon		(1.23–28)	4.33–37
Jesus heals Peter's mother-in-law	(8.14–15)	(1.29–31)	4.38–39
Jesus heals many and casts out many demons	(8.16–17)	(1.32–34)	4.40–41

Matthew and Mark record that Jesus left where he was in order to return 'to his country' or 'homeland', identified as Nazareth by Luke, where he taught in the synagogue, resulting in people being amazed and wondering about his message. It appears that their astonishment was initially favourable, although, because of their quick change of mind, it may actually refer

---

[37] Verses in brackets identify where the topics are presented elsewhere in the individual Gospels.

to perplexity on their part. However, because they knew him and his provenance, they rejected him. Each author records the maxim that prophets are welcome anywhere except in their own home, though it appears that the people were not even prepared to acknowledge that Jesus was a prophet. The fundamental message recorded by each of the authors is that Jesus was rejected by those who had known him the longest, the occasion of that rejection relating to his preaching in the synagogue.

Why does Matthew tell the story?

It appears that a chiasm is being offered by Matthew which identifies the people's rejection of Jesus as being due to elements of his humanity.[38]

> A. The people were astonished (54)
> > B. They ask, 'Where does this man get this?' (54)
> > > C. They question Jesus' wisdom and power (55)
> > > C1. They assert Jesus' humanity (55–56)
> > B1. They ask, 'Where does this man get all this?' (56)
> A1. The people were offended (57)

Matthew immediately precedes the narrative under consideration with a collection of six parables concerning the kingdom of God (13.1–51). Parables had the potential to enlighten, as confirmed by Matthew who notes that when Jesus asked the people 'Have you understood . . . ?', they replied in the affirmative (13.51). However, when Jesus then went to Nazareth, he was confronted by unbelief (*apistia*), the only occasion of this term in Matthew; those who had known him the longest still chose not to accept him.[39] Matthew records that their rejection was due to their being scandalized (*eskandalizontai*,[40] the imperfect tense indicating an ongoing assessment) by him (13.57).

Matthew records that Jesus' kinsfolk were astonished (*ekplēssesthai* (see also 7.28; 22.33), the present tense indicating a continuing amazement). However, their astonishment was not that which led to reverence but to rejection, their assertion based on the assumption that he was merely

---

[38] Chiasms are literary styles common in the ancient world that enabled writers to emphasize certain facts, generally in the middle of a narrative; see Davies, W. D., Allison, D. C., *Matthew 8–18*. T. & T. Clark, London, 1991, p. 451.

[39] The word *apistia* is the antonym of *pistis*; the latter is best translated as 'faith', the former as an absence of faith (see Mark 16.14); thus, the term is often associated with unbelievers (Luke 12.46; 1 Cor. 6.6; 7.14, 15; 2 Cor. 6.14; Rev. 21.8). Keener (C. S., *A Commentary on the Gospel of Matthew*. Eerdmans, Grand Rapids, 1999, p. 397) refers to it as 'anti-belief'.

[40] Jesus warns against those who are scandalized by him (11.6); in 15.12, the Pharisees are also scandalized by him.

a man (*toutō*, literally 'this one') (13.54). Matthew uniquely records their question 'Where then did this man get this wisdom?', indicating that it was lack of scholastic pedigree that partially caused their scepticism.

Their unwillingness to believe in Jesus is contrasted with the high opinion of Jesus held by Herod in the following narrative (14.2). He had heard about the fame of Jesus due to his supernatural power and concluded that Jesus was John the Baptist, raised from the dead. Even Herod, a despised despot, who had never met, let alone heard, Jesus, did not doubt the accuracy of those reports, while those who knew and listened to Jesus chose to reject him. Ominously, Matthew then records the death and burial of John the Baptist (14.3–12), as if to forecast that the rejection of Jesus was to have a similar result to that of his God-ordained forerunner.

Thereafter, Matthew refers to a great crowd (14.13, 14) who followed Jesus from their towns to a 'lonely place apart' (14.13, 15), Matthew replacing Mark's 'ran' with 'followed', a term that he often uses to indicate a positive assessment of Jesus.[41] Such was the assessment of some concerning Jesus that they were willing to travel far, and on foot (14.14), to be where he was. Jesus goes to Nazareth and is rejected by his people, while strangers go from their towns to him in the wilderness, and benefit from his supernatural power in healing and providing food (14.14–21).

Matthew records that Jesus 'did not do many mighty works there' in Nazareth; he did some but, unusually, they were fewer than may have been anticipated. This, for Matthew, is the last occasion relating to Jesus being in a synagogue, his final references to a synagogue identifying it as a place of persecution for his followers (23.34).

Why does Mark tell the story?

Mark records the rejection of Jesus following stories that describe the benefits of placing one's faith in Jesus, resulting in his authoritative restoration of them and their loved ones. In this narrative, Mark records the opportunity for those who knew Jesus best to also express their faith in him. However, while they acknowledge his wisdom and 'mighty works', as in Matthew, they are scandalized because they know his parents, his family and that he is a carpenter.[42] Mark inserts the reference to the miracles being achieved 'by his hands', followed immediately by their recognition that he is a carpenter (6.2–3). It is as if they cannot accept that someone

---

[41] 4.20, 22; 9.9, 27; 10.38; 12.15; 16.24; 19.2, 21, 27; 20.29, 34.

[42] b. *Shab.* 31a implies that Shammai the scribal scholar was also a carpenter but, unlike Jesus, he was defined as a rabbi whereas Jesus is merely refered to as a carpenter.

who used his hands to create objects from wood can also create wonders; the mystery of the Incarnation is still a stumbling block to those who choose not to believe.

Mark uniquely refers to the fact that 'his disciples followed him' to his home. The humiliation to Jesus is exacerbated by his rejection being exhibited publicly and by people who had known him longer than had the disciples. At the same time, it functions as a graphic lesson for their future missions which will also be rejected.[43] Ominously, he then refers to John the Baptist who was imprisoned and beheaded for his faith in Jesus (6.16–29); again the shadow of the cross hangs over the text as John walks a path of suffering, rejection, death and burial that will be also trodden by Jesus.

After his rejection in the synagogue, Mark, as Matthew, does not again record Jesus re-entering a synagogue, instead referring to them as places of religious hypocrisy (12.39) and persecution (13.9). As in Matthew, the rejection of Jesus is contrasted with Herod's attitude to him, though Mark includes extra information (6.14–16). Thereafter, Mark records that a great crowd ran (unique to Mark) from their towns to the desert, to Jesus, arriving at the location before even he did, such was their desire to be with him (6.30–33). This is then followed by the record of those at Gennesaret who also ran to bring their sick to Jesus, their belief being such that they anticipated that they would be restored if they simply touched 'the fringe of his garment' (6.53–56). For Mark, faith in Jesus is identified as making movement towards him, while lack of faith is identified as rejection of him.

A significant difference between the accounts of Matthew, Mark and Luke is that whereas Matthew records that Jesus 'did not do (*ouk epoiēsen* (aorist active)) many mighty works there', Mark states that 'he could do no (*ouk edunato* (imperfect) ... *poiēsai* (aorist infinitive)) mighty work there'[44] except to heal a few sick folk, while Luke excludes this data. Many explanations have been offered for this apparent contradiction between Matthew and Mark. Given that Mark was written prior to Matthew and was available to Matthew, it is clear that he has amended Mark's words, possibly because they imply Jesus' power was limited, a suggestion that Matthew would have been unwilling to affirm.[45]

---

[43] 6.11; 8.34; 10.21.

[44] Note the double negative *ouk ... oudemian*, indicating the certain absence of miracles.

[45] See Matt. 4.23 (also 8.16; 14.36) where he refers to Jesus healing 'every disease and every affliction', contrasted with Mark's 'he healed many' (1.34; 3.10).

Some have understood this passage to imply that Jesus needed an expression of faith on the part of those present in order to activate his healing power, and that lack of faith disabled him. Thus, Hooker[46] suggests, 'mighty works cannot be done except in a context of faith – and this faith (with a few exceptions) was lacking, for the people had rejected his teaching'. However, such a notion is nowhere articulated in the Gospels; indeed, on occasion Jesus restored people in the absence of even a request for healing.[47]

Melinsky[48] is closer to the truth, describing faith as being 'necessary for healing not because a cure was physically impossible without it, but because it would have been spiritually meaningless'. Similarly, rather than assume that Jesus lacked healing power in Nazareth, Lane[49] concludes that 'the performance of miracles in the absence of faith could have resulted only in the aggravation of human guilt'. The people had chosen to reject Jesus; to perform miracles there would have placed the people in a state of greater condemnation, accentuating their guilt, not just for rejecting Jesus but also for doing so in the context of his providing miracles on their behalf. Jesus had performed miracles in Chorazin, Bethsaida and Capernaum, and because they did not result in repentance, Jesus informed them that their punishment would be greater than that experienced by Sodom and Gomorrah because they had not benefited from his presence as had the former towns (Matt. 11.20–4; Luke 10.13–5).

This incident may not be used simplistically to assert that a lack of faith restricted Jesus. Rather, Jesus is presented as choosing not to heal because of an absence of faith. The identity of that unbelief is to be defined as unwillingness to accept him, a determination to oppose him, rejection, not doubt. The faith that brought a positive response from Jesus is the readiness simply to go to him for help. The people of Nazareth did not offer this, but instead expressed rejection – a tragic mistake.

Why does Luke tell the story?

In the narratives leading to Jesus' rejection in Nazareth, Luke records the affirmation of Jesus by Gabriel (1.32), the Holy Spirit (1.35), the Father

---

[46] Hooker, M. D., *A Commentary on the Gospel According to St. Mark*. Black, London, 1991, p. 154; also France, *Mark*. p. 244.

[47] Matt. 8.14//s; 12.9//s; Luke 7.11–15; 22.51; John 5.6–9; 11.38–44.

[48] Melinsky, *Healing*. pp. 23, 36.

[49] Lane, W. L., *The Gospel According to Mark*. Marshall, Morgan & Scott, London, 1974, p. 204; Turner (D. L., *Matthew*. Baker, Grand Rapids, 2000, p. 361) concludes that 'Jesus' lack of miracles in Nazareth should not be viewed as a matter of impotence but as a matter of choice'; also Guelich, R. A., *Mark 1–8.26*. Word, Dallas, 1989, p. 311; Stein, *Mark*. p. 284.

(3.22) and even the devil. Each recognizes his identity (4.9) and each affirms that Jesus is the Son of God. Earlier, Simeon, Anna, the angels and even the unborn John in Elizabeth's womb testified to the status of Jesus, and Luke also recorded that Jesus' ancestry goes back to Adam (3.38). The stage is set for others also to affirm him. Indeed, before his rejection, Jesus entered various Galilean synagogues and was welcomed by all (4.14–15), but his home synagogue does not welcome him. In the light of this positive data, it is surprising that, by contrast, people who had known him the longest are strident in their rejection of him. Luke alone records the rejection of Jesus in the context of the prophecy of Isaiah 61.1–2 with which Jesus identified his mission to socially and spiritually transform people's lives. The Redeemer is rejected by those he came to redeem.

Even though Luke records that a radical, societal, comprehensive and very positive mission is to be undertaken by Jesus, the initial appreciation for Jesus soon turns into anger, outright rebuttal and physical expulsion from the synagogue and the city, culminating in an attempt to murder him, even though it is the Sabbath. The people's original assessment of Jesus as speaking 'gracious words' (4.22) degenerates to 'wrath' (4.28) because he has incorporated non-Jews into the community of those who were to benefit from God's mercy (4.25–27). Whereas Matthew (13.57) and Mark (4.4) refer to a prophet being dishonoured when he returns home, Luke states that a prophet is not even 'welcomed'. The earlier use of this word is in 4.19, which refers to 'the *acceptable* year of the Lord'; the one who has brought a message of welcome is himself not welcomed by those to whom he has come. Their unbelief is graphically portrayed as a malevolent determination to kill him. As a result of his rejection, Jesus left the town and, although Luke records Jesus being in Nazareth earlier (2.39, 51), he does not record that Jesus ever went back.

Luke follows this narrative with a record of Jesus teaching in another synagogue, at Capernaum, where he receives the accolade of the people (4.31–32). He follows this with an exorcism (4.33–37) in which the demon identifies Jesus as 'the Holy One of God' (4.34). The tragic irony is that a dirty demon (*daimoniou akathartou*) perceived the true status of Jesus, while those who had known him from childhood failed to do so; while a demon got it right, his neighbours got it wrong. Thereafter, Luke records that, in contrast to the people of Nazareth who had watched him develop from childhood and yet rejected him, the people of Capernaum were amazed by his authoritative teaching (4.31), power and authority (4.36), and positive (implied) reports were transmitted from the town.

This emphasis on the misunderstanding of the people of Nazareth concerning Jesus may be affirmed when considering a possible chiastic structure that is located in this passage.[50]

A. the synagogue (4.16b)
  B. standing (4.16c)
    C. receiving the Scripture (4.17a)
      D. opening the Scripture (4.17b)
        E. preaching the good news (4.18c)
          F. proclaiming release to the captives (4.18d)
            G. giving sight to the blind (4.18e)
          F1. setting free the oppressed (4.18f)
        E1. proclaiming the acceptable year of the Lord (4.19a)
      D1. closing the Scripture (4.20a)
    C1. returning the Scripture (4.20b)
  B1. sitting (4.20c)
A1. the synagogue (4.20d)

In this chiasm, Luke's central point relates to the provision of sight by Jesus. However, these words are not located in Isaiah 61.1–2 and they replace 'he has sent me to bind up [heal] the broken-hearted'. Luke has chosen to insert a reference to sight, a feature that is important to this and future narratives.[51] Indeed, immediately after this, Luke records that 'the eyes of all in the synagogue were fixed on him'[52] but, tragically, those who saw Jesus the most failed to truly 'see' him. Unfortunately, the audience at Nazareth saw Jesus but rejected him and missed the beneficial consequences of understanding his true status.

Conclusion

The narratives concerning Jesus' miracles present invaluable lessons about Jesus.[53] In particular, they provide opportunities to teach about his authority

---

[50] Tiede, D. L., *Luke*. Augsburg, Minneapolis, 1988, p. 103.

[51] Positive consequences follow those who see, including the revelation of truth: 1.2, 12, 22; 2.9, 17, 20, 30; 3.6; 5.8, 12, 20, 27; 6.10; 7.13; 8.27, 36; 9.32, 36; 13.12; 15.20; 17.14; 18.43; 19.2–5; 21.1, 2; 23.47, 48–49, 55; 24.16, 23, 24, 31, 37, esp. 39.

[52] The term *atenidzō* ('fixed (on him)') is used 12 times in Luke-Acts and only twice elsewhere in the NT (2 Cor. 3.7, 13), appearing at key moments (Luke 22.56, the maid sees Peter; Acts 1.10, the Ascension of Jesus; 7.55, Stephen's trial (Acts 6.15) and vision of Jesus; Cornelius' vision (Acts 10.4); Peter's vision (Acts 11.6)); as well as other occasions where a significant aftermath is anticipated (Acts 3.4, 12; 13.9; 14.9; 23.1).

[53] Ellenburg, B. D., 'A Review of Selected Narrative-Critical Conventions in Mark's Use of Miracle Material', *JETS*. 38.2, 1995, pp. 171–80; Johnson, D. H., 'Preaching the Miracle Stories of the Synoptic Gospels', *TrinJourn*. 18.1, 1997, pp. 85–97; La Grand, J., 'The First of the Miracle Stories According to Mark (1.21–28)', *CurTM*. 20.6, 1993, pp. 479–84; Carroll, J. T., 'Sickness and Healing in the New Testament Gospels', *Interpretation*. 49.2, 1995, pp. 130–42.

and status while also demonstrating his authority to reinstate the outcast within society and provide them with a relationship with God. Furthermore, his miracles are signs that he has initiated the kingdom and created opportunities for belief that has the potential of a relationship with Jesus, sufficient to give access to eternal life.

4

The Synoptics: healings and resurrections

Jesus heals a leper (Matt. 8.1–4//Mark 1.40–45//Luke 5.12–16)

Table 4.1 Cleansing a leper – the literary context

	Matthew	Mark	Luke
Jesus calls his first four disciples	4.18–22	1.16–20	5.1–11
Jesus' teaching/preaching ministry	4.23–25		
Sermon on the Mount	5.1—7.29		
Exorcism of the synagogue demon		1.21–28	(4.31–37)
Healing of Simon's mother-in-law	(8.14–15)	1.29–31	(4.38–39)
Summary of healings	(8.16–17)	1.32–34	(4.40–41)
Jesus preaches elsewhere		1.35–39	(4.42–44)
Cleansing of the leper	8.1–4	1.40–45	5.12–16
Healing of a centurion's servant	8.5–13		(7.1–10)
Healing of a paralytic	(9.2–8)	2.1–12	5.17–26

Main messages from each of the narratives

There are a number of similarities in this narrative as it is presented in each of the Gospels. Each refers to a leper requesting to be cleansed (*katharizō*, 'I cleanse'), recognizing that Jesus had the authority so to do; each also notes that Jesus stretched out his hand and touched him, saying 'I will; be clean'. Thereafter, they each record that the leper was cleansed, Jesus offering a threefold instruction. The messages to be gleaned from the miracle relate to Jesus in the main and, in particular, to his authority to cleanse leprosy and, as importantly, to incorporate the outcast.

The authority of Jesus to cleanse leprosy

In transforming a leper, Jesus is doing more than simply performing a healing. The writers knew that such supernatural power had the potential of elevating Jesus in the estimation of their readers; indeed, 2 Kings 5.8 indicates that the cleansing of a leper indicated prophetic authority.

The specific identification of the leprosy is uncertain as the term was used to cover a wide variety of skin diseases,[1] including those that were relatively common.[2] However, Luke informs us that this man was 'full of leprosy' (5.12), which may indicate Hansen's disease,[3] which is the form often associated with leprosy today. Jesus was confronted with a serious, disfiguring condition that had no known cure; indeed, the rabbis considered such a restoration was as difficult to achieve as raising someone from the dead.

The words of Jesus, 'I will;[4] be clean', are recorded in each narrative, the healing initiated by a one-word command, '*katharisthēti*' (be clean), demonstrating the desire, ability and authority of Jesus to heal the man, each writer recording that the cleansing occurred immediately.[5] Given the visible manifestation of the disease, the picture presented is that, before the eyes of the watchers, the leprosy was exchanged for perfect, unscarred skin.

The leper

Although leprosy was physically troublesome, depending on its seriousness, it was the isolation that it caused which was particularly stigmatizing, the Jewish law demanding that lepers should live in isolation 'outside the camp'.[6] This was mainly due to the relationship of leprosy with ceremonial uncleanness, the uncleanness of the leper being associated with the uncleanness of death. Indeed, a leper was viewed as little better than a dead person,[7] his or her very clothes being also characterized as

---

[1] Browne, S. G., *Leprosy in the Bible*. Christian Medical Fellowship, London, 1970; Weissenrieder, A., *Images of Illness in the Gospel of Luke*. Mohr Siebeck, Tübingen, 2003, pp. 133–75.

[2] The Talmud contains a tractate (*Nega'im*) dedicated to the laws of leprosy; Josephus (*Ag. Ap.* 1.31, 281–2) records the rites of purification involved if a leper is cured, which include bathing in spring water, cutting off of all hair and offering a variety of sacrifices before entering Jerusalem.

[3] So van der Loos, H., *The Miracles of Jesus*. Brill, Leiden, 1965, pp. 464–79. For an alternative, and well-supported, view that identifies the illness as relating to the kind of leprosy referred to in Lev. 13—14 which was more of a skin complaint, albeit serious, see Cotter, W. J., *The Christ of the Miracle Stories: Portrait through Encounter*. Baker, Grand Rapids, 2010, pp. 23–9.

[4] Davies and Allison (W. D. and D. C., *Matthew 8–18*. T. & T. Clark, London, 1991, p. 14) note that the text does not read 'God wills' but 'I will', concluding 'Jesus himself is in control, and he is the source of healing power'.

[5] Although *euthus* (immediately) is a very common word in Mark, both Matthew and Luke record the feature here also.

[6] Lev. 13. 45, 46; Num. 5.2; 12.10; 11QTemple 45.12–13; 11QTemple 46.16–47.11 states that lepers should be confined to the east of Jerusalem; lepers were forbidden from entering Jerusalem so as to ensure that the city would not be defiled; see Neusner, J., 'The Idea of Purity in Ancient Judaism', *JAAR.* 43, 1975, p. 21; Neusner, J., *Purity in Rabbinic Judaism: A Systemic Account*. Scholars Press, Atlanta, 1994, pp. 64–5, 110–13; Davies, M. L., 'Levitical Leprosy: Uncleanness and the Psyche', *ExpTim.* 99.5, 1988, pp. 136–9; Garland, D. E., 'I Am the Lord Your Healer: Mark 1. 21–2. 12', *RevExp.* 85.2, 1988, pp. 336–7.

[7] Num. 12.12; 2 Kings 5.7; Job 18.13; Jos., *Ant.* 3.264; b. *Sanh.* 47a; *Ned.* 64b.

leprous.[8] Furthermore, the assumption that leprosy had been sent by God as judgement was a most upsetting perspective.[9] Because the OT records that leprosy was sometimes sent as a punishment by God, it was assumed by many in the time of Jesus that if someone suffered from leprosy, it must also be due to sin. The reason why lepers often wore torn clothes (Lev. 13.45) was not because they were poor but because they sought to demonstrate their repentance for the sins that they assumed they must have committed and that had caused their leprosy; similarly, they were told to let their hair hang loose and to cover their upper lips (Mic. 3.7), indicative of mourning and sorrow.[10] This must have psychologically damaged them insofar as they were never sure what was the identity of the sin that they had apparently committed and that had caused the leprosy, and therefore they were unsure as to whether they had confessed it. At the same time, it was believed that God alone had the authority to heal the disease. Not only were lepers doomed to a life of seclusion but also it was an existence that was apparently devoid of God, since his graphic mark of disapproval was on them. It is difficult to imagine a more traumatic life condition, some rabbis even suggesting that it was caused by demons (b. *Hor.* 10a), sent by God.

It was thus difficult for people to help lepers in the light of the above. If God had instructed the exclusion and punished them with leprosy, it put others in a quandary as to how much help and friendship they could offer them; thus, lepers often lived lonely lives, having to shout, 'Unclean, unclean' as a warning when people came close to them (Lev. 13.46), finding solace with others who were similarly affected (Luke 17.12), prevented from living in walled cities and, most importantly, from going to the Temple.[11] As such, leprosy was associated with a sense of repulsion, as a

---

[8] Lev. 13.47–59.

[9] Lev. 13.9; 2 Kings 5.25–27; 22.19; 2 Chron. 26.19–21; 34.27; Job 18.13; b. *Sanh.* 471; b. *Ned.* 64b; b. *Kel.* 1.4; b. *Neg.* 13.11; the term 'hyssop' was used in the context of cleansing from sin (2 Kings 5.27; 15.5; 2 Chron. 26.21; Ps. 51.7) and the fact that hyssop is part of the cleansing procedure of the leper (Lev. 14.4) suggests that leprosy was an illustration of sin; b. *Arak.* 15b–16b describes particularly serious sins (including idolatry, blasphemy, incest, murder, theft, false testimony and slander (*Lev. Rab.* 16.6–7; *Num. Rab.* 16.6; *Deut. Rab.* 6.8)) as being punished with leprosy; b. *Meg.* 12b speculates that Vashti did not go to the public banquet because she had contracted leprosy, sent to her by God because she undressed Jewish girls.

[10] Lev. 21.10 reports that priests were not to let their hair hang loose or to rend their clothes; similarly, Ezek. 24.17, 22–23 asserts that in order to demonstrate that he is not in sorrow, Ezekiel is told to wear a head covering and not to cover his lips.

[11] Lev. 5.3; 13.45–46; Num. 12.15; 2 Kings 7.3–10; Jos., *Ant.* 3.261; later rabbis offered their own definitions as to how isolated the leper ought to be; thus, *Lev. Rab.* 16.3 refers to a minimum of '100 cubits downwind'.

result of which lepers tried to remove the signs of their condition by anointing, scraping or burning their skin.

The authority of Jesus to touch the untouchable and incorporate the outcast

Each Synoptist records that Jesus touched the leper, demonstrating his lack of concern relating to any potential ceremonial contamination that he would have incurred.[12] It might have been expected that Jesus would have raised his hand to gesticulate and warn the leper not to come nearer, or perhaps, as with Elisha (2 Kings 5.11), waved his hand in his direction or raised it over him. Instead, Jesus touched the leper. Rather than view Jesus touching the leper as a deliberate act of provocation designed to undermine the sanctity of the Mosaic law, it is preferable to understand it as the commencement of a process of reintegration for the victim, a journey back into societal acceptance and a re-involvement with the corporate life of the community.

It is significant to note that although Moses (Num. 12.9–15) and Elisha (2 Kings 5.1–14) were involved in the healing of lepers, they did not touch them in the process. Although they touched others who were ill prior to their being healed,[13] they chose not to touch lepers before they were healed. This is not an incidental detail, and each of the Synoptists records the fact that Jesus not only touched the leper but stretched in order so to do. In this deliberate action, the writers indicate that Jesus did not accidentally touch the man. On the contrary, it is as if he is declaring without ambiguity that he is going to touch the leper, even if it means stretching out his arm in the process.

Given that Jesus could have healed the leper without touching him, it begs the question why he should do so. The Synoptists do not indicate that the touch of Jesus effected the healing, for they note that the words of Jesus ('I will; be clean') were stated after he touched the leper and immediately preceded the healing. It is probable that, in touching the leper, Jesus is demonstrating his authority.[14] Although leprosy ceremonially contaminated those who came into contact with it, Jesus is revealing that he is prepared to break the Mosaic law that marginalized such people,

---

[12] The Synoptists refer to the desire of the people to touch the fringe of Jesus' garment (Matt. 9.20; 14.34–36; Mark 5.28; 6.53–56; Luke 8.44), while on other occasions people request that he touch them (Matt. 9.18//Mark 5.23; Mark 7.32; 8.22).

[13] 1 Kings, 17.21; 2 Kings 4.35.

[14] See earlier discussion concerning touch as a symbol of authority.

in order to demonstrate that they are not to view themselves as outsiders, the healing providing the means whereby that truth can be facilitated. Such an action was unprecedented and highlights the authority of Jesus, for he may be seen to be reinterpreting God's law.[15] By reaching out to touch and heal this marginalized man, Jesus facilitates the leper's reintegration into his society.[16] He transmitted wholeness and cleansing without being troubled by any potential ceremonial contamination from the leper. In this action, Jesus introduces the unique[17] feature of touch that is regularly repeated in his healings[18] and was continued in the healing ministry of the early Church.[19]

It is possible that by touching this man (and others who were sick), Jesus is showing compassion, touch sometimes being viewed as a sign of friendship. However, neither Matthew nor Luke includes a reference to compassion in Jesus on this occasion; that is not to say that Jesus was not compassionate for those who were sick (9.36), but it at least should cause us to pause in order not to state that which the authors do not. Indeed, in the absence of a motif of compassion, it may be best to understand the touch of Jesus as indicating his influential power and authority. There are ancient Jewish precedents for viewing the hand as a personification of the power of God,[20] and also for God touching people in order to commission them, enable them to function miraculously, or do them good.[21] Jesus thus symbolized his identification with the most marginalized of people in a graphic and powerful way, providing them with hope even before they were restored to health and the community.

---

[15] Dunn (J. D. G., *Jesus and the Spirit*. SCM, London, 1975, p. 77) describes Jesus as being aware of a 'transcendent authority which set him above party and (at times) even the Law'; cf. Kazmierski, C.R., 'Evangelist and Leper: A Socio-Cultural Study of Mark 1.40–45', *NTS*. 38, 1992, pp. 37–42.

[16] So Ukpong, J. S., 'Leprosy: Untouchables of the Gospel of Today', *Concilium*. 1997/5, pp. 67–8; van Eck, E., van Aarde, A. G., 'Sickness and Healing in Mark: A Social Scientific Interpretation', *Neutestamentica*. 27.1, 1993, p. 46.

[17] There is only one reference to laying on of hands in Qumran in an exorcistic rite that relates to the healing of Pharoah as a result of the prayer of Abram (1QapGen. 20.21–3, 28–9). Rabbinic literature is devoid of the practice; b. *Ber.* 5b comes close in that it refers to the use of the hand in healing, although, here, the hand of the sick person is requested to be extended to the rabbi concerned.

[18] Matt. 8.3, 15; 9.29; 15.31; 20.34; Mark 1.41, 45; 5.41; 7.33; Luke 7.14 (Jesus touched a coffin); 13.13; 22.51; John 9.6.

[19] Acts 9.12–19; 14.3; 19.11; 20.10(?); 28.8; see Warrington, K., 'Acts and the Healing Narratives. Why?', *JPT*. 14.2, April 2006, pp. 189–218.

[20] Num. 11.23; Deut. 33.3; 1 Sam. 5.7; 1 Chron. 29.12; Job 5.18; 19.21; Pss. 20.12; 104.32; 144.5; Isa. 1.25; Jer. 16.21; Dan. 5.23; Zech. 13.7.

[21] Judg. 6.21; 1 Sam. 10.26; 1 Kings 19.7; Isa. 6.7; Jer. 1.9; Dan. 8.18; 10.10, 16, 18; Amos. 9.5.

The authority of Jesus indicates his superior status

In coming to Jesus, the leper is presented by the writers as recognizing that he is in the presence of someone who had at his disposal the power to reverse the judgement that had apparently resulted in leprosy and to restore him to full health. Matthew and Mark record that the leper knelt (*proskuneō*) before Jesus, a term that is earlier used by Matthew to more clearly indicate worship (4.10), while Mark only uses the term elsewhere on two occasions (10.17; 15.19). Luke asserts that the man fell on his face before Jesus, an action clearly associated with obeisance;[22] later, Luke records the only other occasion when a person falls on his face before Jesus, referring to another leper, after he had been healed by him (17.16).

The writers thus demonstrate that the leper had an elevated perception of Jesus, even before he was healed. The words of the leper, 'If you will, you can make me clean', indicated his belief that Jesus had supernatural authority;[23] he realizes that Jesus can heal him – the only obstacle to be overcome is whether he will. Given that the man is a leper and dis-enfranchised in society, and apparently by God, it is understandable that he should be cautious in coming to one who has supernatural authority available to him. Although Matthew and Luke add *kurios* ('lord') as a description of Jesus, it does not indicate an inferior perception of the leper in Mark, for the words of the leper indicate assumed authority. However, for Matthew and Luke, it may indicate more than a term of respect, given that the previous uses of the term with reference to Jesus are in a judg-mental capacity (Matt. 7.21–22; see also 3.3; Luke 5.8).[24]

The authority of Jesus merits obedience

Each Synoptist records Jesus' threefold instruction that the leper should tell no one about his healing but instead show himself to the priest and present the gift that would enable him to complete the process of ceremonial cleaning, as prescribed by Moses.[25]

The charge to tell no one of the healing. Each of the writers notes the terse nature of the first requirement to the healed man, Mark presenting

---

[22] 1 Cor. 14.25; Rev. 7.11; 11.16 (by implication, Luke 8.41; Acts 10.25).

[23] Wojciechowski (M., 'The Touching of the Leper (Mk. 1.40–45)', *BZ*. 33, 1989, pp. 114–19) asserts that the man identified Jesus' power with God's power; Kazmierski, 'Evangelist and Leper', pp. 44–6.

[24] Luz (U., *Matthew 8–20*. Fortress Press, Minneapolis, 2001, p. 5) describes it as 'the majestic title'; Hagner (D. A., *Matthew 1–13*. Word, Waco, 1993, p. 198) also views it as indicative of more than a respectful term and more akin to 'a confession of faith'; so also Nolland, J., *Luke 1–9.20*. Word, Dallas, 1989, p. 227.

[25] Lev. 13.2–37, 50–59; 14.1–57.

it most clearly by way of a double negative, repeating the adjective *mēdeni mēden* ('no one, nothing') – 'do not tell anyone anything'; Mark and Luke precede the instruction with words that indicate that this is a command, not a recommendation, from Jesus ('he sternly charged him (*embrimēsamenos*) and sent him away'). On a number of other occasions, Jesus also required those who had benefited from his ministry to tell no one about it.[26] Some have suggested that these recommendations by Jesus were the inventions of the early Church, fed back into the text of the Gospels (the so-called, and now largely discredited, 'Messianic Secret'). However, it was much more likely due to Jesus' concern that people would see him as merely a healer and worker of miracles, or an earthly king, beliefs that were amplified by popular expectations concerning the Messiah. At the same time, publicity was not always helpful for Jesus to fulfil his mission elsewhere, as crowds obstructed him (Mark 1.45) from doing that for which he had come to earth – the preaching of the gospel (Mark 1.15, 38).

The charge to show himself to the priest. The requirement that a priest should examine someone whose skin complaint had cleared up is carefully defined in Leviticus 13 and 14, involving an emptying, cleansing (and even destruction (14.45)) of the home (14.35–53), along with the cleansing of anyone who has entered it (14.46–47) and any clothing present in it (13.47–59). Such an examination process could take longer than seven days to be completed (Lev. 14.39).[27] It is thus possible that Jesus requires this of the leper as public proof of the cure. It is also possible that it was to demonstrate to the priests that Jesus respected the OT law, though this is unlikely as the Gospels nowhere else reflect this as a significant issue for Jesus. The first option is certainly a possibility, for by this action Jesus gives the priests an opportunity to accept him, though at the same time it will work against them if they reject him. Lane[28] asserts that it was a testimony against the priests or a particular priest, since each narrator refers to 'the priest'.[29]

---

[26] Matt. 9.30; 12.16; 16.20; 17.9; Mark 3.12; 5.43; 7.36; 9.9; Luke 9.36.

[27] See m. *Neg.* 14.

[28] France (R. T., *The Gospel of Mark.* Grand Rapids, Eerdmans, 2002, p. 120) notes that *eis marturion autois* ('in order to provide evidence for them') is only used on two other occasions in Mark (6.11; 13.9), both of which are in the context of opposition to Jesus or his followers.

[29] Lane, W. L., *The Gospel According to Mark.* Marshall, Morgan & Scott, London, 1974, p. 88; Cave, C. H., 'The Leper: Mk. 1.40–45', *NTS.* 25, 1978, p. 249; Mussner (F., *The Miracles of Jesus.* (tr.) Wimmer, A., Ecclesia Press, Shannon, 1970, p. 36) suggests 'against their self-righteousness'; Myers, C., *Binding the Strong Man: A Political Reading of Mark's Story of Jesus.* Orbis, New York, 1988, p. 153; Broadhead, E. K., 'Mark 1.44: The Witness of the Leper', *ZNW.* 83, 1992, pp. 260–8; Broadhead, E. K., 'Christology as Polemic and Apologetic: The Priestly Portrait of Jesus in the Gospel of Mark', *JSNT.* 47, 1992, pp. 24–32.

However, there is no evidence of antagonism against Jesus on the part of any priests in this narrative, or indeed earlier. It is more likely that Jesus was encouraging the leper to follow the protocols needed for him to be able legitimately to re-enter society.

The charge to present the prescribed offering. Leviticus notes that, as part of the cleansing procedure, two birds, two lambs, grain, flour and oil (in lesser quantities if the person concerned was poor) (14.4, 10, 21–22, 49) were to be offered to God with reference to atonement and the termination of the state of being unclean.[30] Thereafter, the leper would be eligible to participate fully in secular, religious and familial society.

In the previous passage, Matthew offers two narratives that affirm the importance of obedience (7.21–23, 24–28), while the following narrative highlights the authority of Jesus (8.5–12). For Matthew, the cleansing of the leper specifically links the themes of obedience with the authority of Jesus. Already, Jesus has been revealed by Matthew to his readers as the authoritative Son of God,[31] and later he will develop the motif of obedience by recording that wherever Jesus goes, people, given the opportunity, follow him.[32]

The emphasis on obedience to Jesus is also affirmed in Luke. Significantly, he records Jesus calling his first disciples immediately prior to this narrative, noting that they left everything in order to follow Jesus (5.11). Mark also affirms the importance of obedience but, as we shall see, he does it uniquely by highlighting the leper's disobedience.

The authority of Jesus as expressed by the individual writers

Thus, the central elements of the narrative are clear. A leper believes that Jesus can meet his need and, without an explicit request to Jesus, his leprosy is cleansed immediately by Jesus, who stretches out his hand in order to touch him in the process, and subsequently requests that he obey him. However, each writer offers extra lessons for his audience.

Messages from Matthew

Matthew provides the shortest account, omitting any references to the emotions of Jesus in encountering the leper and in charging him to go to the priest. There is no reference to the disobedience of the leper (as Mark) or details concerning the aftermath of the cleansing (as Luke). This story

---

[30] 14.18–20, 29, 31, 53.
[31] 1.23; 2.15; 3.17; 4.3, 6.
[32] 8.1, 10, 19, 22, 23; 9.9; see Kingsbury, J. D., 'The Verb *akolouthein* (to follow) as an Index of Matthew's View of His Community', *JBL*. 97, 1978, pp. 56–73.

is minimally told as an example of Jesus responding positively to the request of a man who believed he could help him.

The passage forms part of a distinct section in Matthew,[33] being introduced by *idou* ('behold'), which Hagner defines as Matthew's 'favorite device for calling attention to something extraordinary', being used 62 times.[34] Bruner[35] comments, 'Matthew is trying to say something', offering by way of explanation that 'we feel very unclean after the sermon' and hence, the story of the cleansing of the leper. Although Bruner is right to identify a significant purpose in the placing of this miracle at this juncture, it is for a more substantial reason than the one he offers.

Although the healing is sensational, the programme of Matthew has been to describe Jesus not merely as a healer but as a teacher who also achieves miracles. Thus, the Sermon on the Mount is offered before any miracles are recorded; similarly, the first reference to Jesus' ministry excludes a reference to healing (4.17), while the final commission to the disciples includes teaching but excludes healing and exorcisms (28.18–20). Indeed, this first miracle of Jesus is narrated nearly one third through Matthew's Gospel; he has other priorities besides presenting Jesus as a healer.

The authority of Jesus

In exploring the prior events in the Gospel, it is possible to identify issues that were particularly important to Matthew, which helps to set a context for this narrative (see Table 4.1). The major issue that is emphasized in the preceding data relates to the authority of Jesus. Matthew does this by preceding his narrative concerning Jesus' birth and childhood with a genealogical pedigree in which Jesus' messianic status is clear (1.1, 16, 17, 18), the messianic title 'Son of David' being used of him (1.1), and David being referred to him on four occasions (1.6, 17). He also affirms the superior person of Jesus by identifying the role of the Spirit in his life (1.18, 20) and demonstrates that he is the fulfilment of OT prophecies (1.22–23). Not only is he identified as Jesus (1.1, 16, 18, 25) but his name is explained – 'he will save his people from their sins' (1.21). Perhaps more importantly, he is identified as 'Immanuel' (1.23), the only reference to

---

[33] Gerharddson (B., *The Mighty Acts of Jesus According to Matthew.* (tr.) R. Dewsnap, CWK Gleerup, Lund, 1975, p. 41) notes that verses 14 and 15 are made up of 15 Greek words and 30 syllables for each verse, concluding that 'this does not suggest the work of an unreflective narrator'; Thompson, W. G., 'Reflections on the Composition of Matthew 8.1–9.34', *CBQ.* 33, 1971, pp. 368–87; Burger, C., 'Jesu Taten nach Matthaus 8, 9', *ZTK.* 70, 1973, pp. 272–87; Kingsbury, J. D., 'Observations on the "Miracle Chapters" in Matthew's Gospel', *CBQ.* 40, 1978, pp. 559–73.

[34] Hagner, *Matthew 1–13.* p. 18.

[35] Bruner, F. D., *Matthew: A Commentary, Vol. 1.* Word, Waco, 1987, pp. 299–300.

this name in the NT, again with an explanation of its meaning, 'God is with us'. Before chapter 2 is commenced, the readers have been introduced to a person with incredible credentials.

Chapter 2 then outlines events relating to the childhood of Jesus. His superior status is reflected in that wise men visit him, joyfully giving him costly gifts and worshipping him (2.10–11), while angels introduce him (2.13, 19). The king of Israel searches for him (2.8), but also 'his star' draws attention to his presence on the earth (2.2, 9). Again, Jesus is identified as fulfilling OT prophecy (2.5, 15, 18, 23).

In chapter 3, John the Baptist is introduced as a prophet, reminiscent of Elijah (3.4), who himself fulfils OT prophecy (3.3) and preaches a message that presages the mission of Jesus (3.1). Despite his authority and prestige (3.7–10), he identifies himself as being inferior to the one who is to come, Jesus (3.11–12). Moreover, he ascribes to Jesus the sensational ability of being able to 'baptize you with the Holy Spirit and with fire' (3.11). In Isaiah 4.4, God is described as cleansing Jerusalem by a 'spirit of judge-ment and by a spirit of burning'. However, here, John identifies Jesus as the one who baptizes 'with the Holy Spirit and with fire'. Furthermore, in the OT, it is God who is presented as authorizing the activity of the Spirit;[36] here, Matthew ascribes that role to Jesus. Similarly, the role of judge, previ-ously related to God, is here applied to Jesus (3.12).[37]

This exaltation of Jesus is followed by Matthew drawing attention to the affirmation of Jesus by the Father and the Spirit (3.16–17). Not only does the Spirit descend on Jesus, but Jesus is identified for the first time as 'my beloved son' and as one who brings great pleasure to the Father (3.17).

Chapter 4.1–11 provides Matthew with an opportunity, not so much to demonstrate the devious nature of the devil, who seeks to distract Jesus from his journey to the cross, as to display the authority of Jesus, who confidently rebuts the temptations with OT verses. In so doing, Matthew twice records the devil referring to Jesus' superior status as 'the son of God' (4.3, 6). Not only does Jesus show that the devil's temptations are subvert-ing God's words in the OT, but also Satan is warned, 'You shall not tempt the Lord your God' (4.7), and that he should rather 'worship the Lord your God' (4.10). At the least, Matthew demonstrates that Jesus functions as God's representative. However, it is possible that Matthew is obliquely indicating that Jesus is more than merely God's representative and that the devil is being reprimanded for tempting God in the person of Jesus.

---

[36] Isa. 44.3; Ezek. 36.27; 39.29; Joel 2.28.
[37] Isa. 34.8; 66.6, 15–16, 24.

Thereafter, as a further demonstration of his authority, Matthew describes Jesus preaching, calling people to 'Repent, for the kingdom of heaven is at hand' (4.17), in fulfilment of OT prophecy (4.15, 23). This is followed by Jesus demonstrating his authority in choosing four disciples, who follow him immediately (4.18–22). In contrast to the normal pattern of would-be disciples asking to be followers of rabbis, Jesus decides who are to follow him. Finally, although Matthew follows this information with the statement that Jesus healed and restored demonized people (4.23b–24), his priority is to emphasize the teaching mission of Jesus. This motif is affirmed in the following three chapters (5.1—7.27), Matthew concluding that Jesus' teaching astonished his hearers, 'for he was teaching them as one who had authority' (7.28). The authority of Jesus will later also be demonstrated through his miracles, but it has already been revealed in many ways before the first miracle has been narrated.

Matthew uniquely sets the healing of the leper in the context of large crowds following Jesus, probably referring to the crowds mentioned immediately prior to this narrative who were astonished at his teaching authority (7.28); now they will have another reason to be astonished at Jesus. Matthew also uniquely describes Jesus coming down from the mountain, after teaching, in words that are reminiscent of Moses coming down from the mountain, after receiving the law (Exod. 34.29). Then, Moses taught 'all the people of Israel' who 'came near' but had to hide his face because it shone as a result of his being with God (Exod. 34.29–33). Here, Jesus taught 'great crowds' who 'followed him', but now it will be through wonders as well as words, miracles as well as metaphors, as a result of which he will publicly reveal his glory.

After the leper is healed, Matthew offers a catalogue of miracles, including healings (8.5–17; 9.1–8, 18–31), again seen as fulfilments of OT prophecy (8.17), nature miracles (8.23–27), exorcisms (8.28–34; 9.32–34) and a summary statement (9.35). The superlative authority of Jesus is thus comprehensively affirmed. The healing of leprosy is but the first of many remarkable miracles that manifest such authority.

Messages from Mark

Mark precedes this healing with a number of narratives that lay foundational elements in his presentation of Jesus (see Table 4.1). Mark commences his Gospel by introducing it as 'the gospel of Jesus Christ, Son of God' (1.1). Thereafter, Mark, as Matthew, narrates the mission of John the Baptist (1.2–8), presenting him as the fulfilment of Isaianic prophecy and in the pedigree of Elijah. More startling is the fact that John is described as fulfilling a prophecy that in the OT (Isa. 40.3) referred to a messenger pre-ceding God, whereas John preceded Jesus. This is followed by the affirmation of the Father and the descent of the Spirit on Jesus (1.8–11). A short reference to the temptations of Jesus includes a presentation of Jesus fulfilling the agenda of the Spirit and being with the wild beasts, in what may be presumed to be a recreated Eden (as prophesied in Isa. 11.6–9; 65.25), while the angels 'served' him.[38] Jesus is then defined in his mission of calling followers, teaching and preaching (1.12–15). Although Matthew emphasizes Jesus' authority by adding significant blocs of Jesus' teaching at this point in his Gospel, the authority motif is also clearly located in Mark. However, Mark demonstrates it, not only through the teaching of Jesus, but also and specifically through his miracles.

Thus, following the establishment of the importance of teaching to Jesus, Mark records a miracle, which the onlookers equate with 'a new teaching' (1.27). This is immediately followed by Jesus healing Peter's mother-in-law, resulting in many requesting and receiving healing (1.29–34). Thereafter, Mark reminds the readers of the mission of Jesus that centrally involves preaching (1.38–39).

The status of Jesus demands a positive response

It is to be expected that those with whom Jesus interacts should respond to him appropriately. Thus, Mark sets the readers up for an examination of the response of the leper to his being restored to full health, a response that only he provides in painful detail (1.45).

Jesus' initial response to the leper is worthy of our consideration. Although many NT translations of 1.41 uniquely record Mark stating that Jesus was 'moved with pity' for the man, strong arguments have been offered for this being the less appropriate reading of the original.[39] Many

---

[38] Although some translations offer 'the angels ministered to him' (RSV), the translation of *diakonein* is best understood as 'to serve'. Jesus did not need comfort or support but deserved 'service'. France (*Mark*. pp. 86–7) argues that the presence of wild beasts indicates a place of danger, the angels being there to protect him; he adds that to see a fulfilment of Isa. 11.6–9 is inappropriate because the eschatological era is not being envisaged here in Mark. However, that may precisely be the point of the author – to offer the hope that such an era is being introduced by one who is in control of the wild beasts.

[39] However, Metzger (B. M., *A Textual Commentary on the Greek New Testament*. Deutsches Bibelgesells-chaft, Stuttgart, 1994, p. 65), providing the conclusions of the editorial committee of the UBS Greek New Testament, notes that the external evidence in support of '*orgistheis*' is less impressive than the diversity and character of evidence that supports '*splagchnistheis*'; he also asserts that Mark 3.5, where Jesus is described as angry and 10.14, where he is referred to as indignant, 'have not prompted over-scrupulous copyists to make corrections'. Haenchen (E., *Der Weg Jesu: Eine Erklarung des Markus-Evangeliums und der kanonischen Parallelen*. 2nd ed. de Gruyter, Berlin, 1968, pp. 94–6) and Stein (R. H., *Mark*. Baker Academic, Grand Rapids, 2008, p. 106) support the reading of *splagchnistheis*.

manuscripts have *splagchnistheis* ('he was compassionate') in 1.41, though a minority have *orgistheis* ('he was angry'). If 'he was compassionate' was the original reading, it is difficult to understand why it would have been amended to read 'he was angry'; however, if 'he was angry' was the original reading, it would be quite understandable why a later scribe should amend the text, perhaps fearful of readers misunderstanding Jesus' anger. Furthermore, given the strong verbal similarities between the synoptic accounts, if 'he was compassionate' had been the original reading of Mark, it is not clear why Matthew and, especially Luke, with his strong emphasis on the caring nature of Jesus, should have omitted it, though it is understandable why they may have chosen not to insert that Jesus had been angry.

On the assumption that the more difficult reading (that indicates that he was angry) may be the correct one, a number of suggestions have been offered as to why Jesus may have been angry. It is possible that Jesus was angry with the evil nature of the disease,[40] and in particular 'with Satan at his disfigurement of God's creature',[41] but also due to its being a social barrier.[42] Gundry[43] suggests it is anger against sin. Guelich[44] indicates that Jesus may be expressing anger at the man for approaching him despite being ceremonially unclean; however, Jesus voluntarily touches the man, and thus breaks the same law, and also elsewhere is not troubled about breaking ceremonial laws (Mark 2.15–16, eating with disreputable people; 3.1–6, working on the Sabbath; 5.25–34, being touched by a ceremonially unclean woman).

Bruner,[45] with insufficient evidence, suggests that Jesus was angry because the leper doubted his willingness to heal, while Mussner[46] views it as anger at the injustice done to the lepers in Israel, Theissen indicating that the anger may have resulted from the ineffective actions of miracle workers of the time.[47] It is also possible that anger may have been expressed because of the potential interruption to Jesus' ministry if the leper should disobey his commands.[48]

---

[40] France, *Mark.* pp. 117–18.

[41] See also Hooker, M. D., *A Commentary on the Gospel According to St. Mark.* Black, London, 1991, p. 80; Lane, *Mark.* p. 86.

[42] Pilch, J. J., 'The Health Care System in Matthew: A Social Science Analysis', *BTB.* 16.3, 1986, p. 102; Malina, B. J., Rohrbaugh, R. L., *Social-science Commentary on the Synoptic Gospels.* Fortress Press, Minneapolis, 1992, p. 71.

[43] Gundry, R. H., *Mark: A Commentary on His Apology for the Cross.* Eerdmans, Grand Rapids, 1993, p. 96.

[44] Guelich, R. A., *Mark 1–8.26.* Word, Dallas, 1989, p. 74.

[45] Bruner, *Matthew.* p. 300.

[46] Mussner, *The Miracles.* p. 35; Guelich, *Mark 1–8.26.* pp. 72–4.

[47] Theissen, *Miracle Stories of the Early Christian Tradition.* T. & T. Clark, Edinburgh, 1983, pp. 57–8.

[48] Contra Hooker, *Mark.* p. 80; Telford, G. B., 'Mark 1.40–45', *Interpretation.* 36.1, 1982, pp. 54–8; also France, *Mark.* p. 117.

Supporting the latter option is the fact that Mark uniquely records that Jesus 'sternly charged' (*embrimēsamenos*)[49] the man to obey him, making his disobedience more obvious and telling. The word is used elsewhere in Mark (14.5) where the disciples reproach the woman who poured expensive ointment over Jesus' head.[50] Here, the context indicates that the leper is not being rebuked but strictly charged to obey Jesus, the sternness of the warning either relating to the importance of his obedience or possibly because Jesus is aware that the man may well disobey him.

Thereafter, Jesus 'sent him away'. Although the term is used elsewhere in Mark with reference to demonic expulsion,[51] it is not always used in exorcistic contexts, Mark elsewhere using it to refer to the Holy Spirit 'sending out' Jesus into the wilderness.[52]

The result of the leper's disobedience

Mark uniquely reveals that the leper disobeys Jesus, as a result of which, 'Jesus could no longer openly enter a town, but was out in desolate places' (1.45), meaning that to go to Jesus would be more difficult for people, especially the young, old and infirm. Mark refers to the intensity of the leper's request, uniquely recording that he kneels before Jesus before he is healed (1.40); also, only Mark records his request (in which he incorporates the word *parakalōn* ('imploring') to indicate his desperation for Jesus' help. However, any respect for Jesus appears to be forgotten after the leprosy has been cleansed. The following narrative, by contrast, records a paralytic who, when commanded by Jesus to go home, did so immediately (2.11–12). The verbal pictures painted by Mark, thus far, reveal Jesus who functioned in superlative authority and who is therefore worthy of immediate obedience from would-be disciples (1.16–20), demons (1.26) and people who were healed (1.31; 2.12). In this story, Jesus offers one word, resulting in the leprosy being dismissed, but the 22 words to the leper are disobeyed. The leper failed the obedience test, a test that even demons passed (1.25); Mark desires that his readers fare better.

---

[49] The word may also be translated as 'to speak harshly to' or 'to rebuke'; see Lake, K., 'EMBRIMESA-MENOS and ORGISTHEIS, Mk. 1. 40–45', *HTR*. 16, 1923, pp. 197–8; Cave ('The Leper', p. 247) creates the wrong impression in his translation, 'he roared at them'.

[50] See also esp. Matt. 9.30; John 11.33, 38; Dan. 11.30 uses the term to translate *ka'ah* (to be sad, grieved or timid) and also in association with anger (*orgisthesetai*).

[51] 3.22; 7.26; 9.18.

[52] 1.12; see also 5.40 and 11.15 which refer to people being sent out.

Messages from Luke

The authority of Jesus

The order of Luke's previous narratives (see Table 4.1) also provides him with the opportunity to demonstrate the authority of Jesus. Thus, in his presentation of Jesus, he establishes, more fully than Matthew and Mark, the significance of the one who was to precede him, John the Baptist,[53] and affirms Jesus through the words of righteous people (Elizabeth (1.6, 7, 42–45), Zechariah (1.6, 7, 76), Simeon (2.25)) and God (3.22). He reveals Jesus' unique birth (1.31), which is announced by a multitude of angels (2.9–14). He notes that as well as being called 'Jesus' (2.21), he is also 'the Son of the Most High' (1.32), the recipient of an eternal kingdom (1.32–33), 'the Son of God' (1.35, 38; 4.41), 'the Lord' (1.76), 'the beloved son' (3.22), and 'the holy one of God' (4.34), who refers to the Temple as his 'Father's house' (2.49). He is foretold as being 'a light for revelation to the Gentiles' (2.32) as well as a catalyst for the Jews with consequent personal gain or loss (2.32, 35), and especially associated with 'favour' or grace (*charis*) (1.30; 2.52). Most importantly, Jesus has been referred to in association with the Holy Spirit,[54] who controls events leading to his birth (1.5–25). Luke also identifies his mission mandate (4.18–19) as that which applied to God in the words of Isaiah (61.1–2). Finally, his authority is revealed in his wisdom (2.46–47), in baptizing others with 'the Holy Spirit and fire' (3.16), in judging people (3.17), over the devil (4.1–13), demons (4.31–37) and sickness (4.38–41), and in calling disciples (5.1–11). Immediately prior to the leper being healed, Luke records Peter falling on his knees before Jesus, calling him 'Lord' and requesting that he should depart from him, for he felt so unworthy (5.8). The leper also falls down before Jesus, calling him 'Lord', requesting that he be made clean (5.12). As Peter was accepted and commissioned by Jesus, so also was the leper cleansed and commissioned. All would-be disciples who wish to be commissioned must first be cleansed.

That which may be gleaned from these preceding stories is that Luke develops his portrait of Jesus as one who manifests authority in various ways. In this narrative, Jesus meets one man who, Luke uniquely describes, was 'full of leprosy', 'fell on his face' before him (5.12) and 'begged' Jesus for help (also 8.38). This marginalized, helpless man was healed. Luke concludes by uniquely recording that although many people came to hear

---

[53] 1.8–25, 57–80; 3.2–20.
[54] 1.35, 41, 67; 2.27; 3.16, 22; 4.1, 18.

him and to receive healing, it is not clear that Jesus responded to them, for instead he went to the wilderness in order to pray (5.16). However, he has emphasized his central message – Jesus has time to help the helpless.

Conclusion

Jesus' authority to heal easily and immediately and to restore an outcast is demonstrated, while the commands to the leper after the healing are to be recognized as of particular significance. Healing by Jesus is beneficial, but obedience to Jesus is better.

Jesus heals a centurion's servant
(Matt. 8.5–13//Luke 7.1–10//John 4.46–54)

Table 4.2 Healing a centurion's servant – the literary context

	Matthew	Luke	John
Jesus cleanses a leper	8.1–4	5.12–16	
Jesus heals a paralytic	(9.1–8)	5.17–26	
Jesus calls Levi to follow him	(9.9)	5.27–28	
Jesus eats with sinners	(9.10–13)	5.29–32	
Jesus teaches concerning fasting	(9.14–17)	5.33–39	
Jesus teaches concerning the Sabbath	(12.1–8)	6.1–5	
Jesus heals a withered hand	(12.9–14)	6.6–11	
Jesus chooses the Twelve	(10.1–4)	6.12–16	
Jesus heals and teaches crowds	(5.1–12, 38–48; 7.1–5, 21–27)	6.17–49	
Jesus changes water into wine			2.1–12
Jesus cleanses the Temple			2.13–22
Jesus dialogues with Nicodemus			3.1–21
John witnesses to Jesus			3.25–36
Jesus meets a woman from Samaria			4.1–30
Jesus teaches about his mission			4.31–38
Samaritans believe in Jesus			4.39–42
Galileans welcome Jesus as healer			4.43–45
Healing of a centurion's servant/son	8.5–13	7.1–10	4.46–54
Healing of Simon's mother-in-law	8.14–15	(4.38–39)	
Summary of healings	8.16–17	(4.40–41)	
Jesus resurrects the widow of Nain's son		7.11–17	
Jesus heals a paralysed man on the Sabbath			5.1–18

Main messages from each of the narratives

Although there are differences between this story in John 4.46–54[55] when compared with the record in Matthew 8.5–13//Luke 7.1–10, there are significant similarities, including the location of Capernaum.[56] It is most

---

[55] In Matthew and Luke, the reference is to a centurion (*hekatontarchos*), but to a ruler (*basilikos*) in John; in John, the official refers to the one who is sick as *huios* ('son') (4.47, 50, 53) and *paidion* ('child') (4.49) while Matthew (8.6, 8, 13) describes him as *pais* ('son' or 'servant') and Luke (7.2, 3, 8, 10) as *doulos* ('slave') and *pais* (7.7). The term *pais* is capable of being translated as 'son' or 'servant', but in its 24 NT uses, nearly all are best translated as 'servant'. *Pais* is used in Matthew four times (12.18; 14.2 referring to a servant; 17.18 referring to a boy (17.15, *huios*, son); and 21.15 referring to children).

[56] Luke agrees with John that the person was close to death, while each writer refers to the immediacy of the healing. Matthew agrees with Luke concerning the centurion's assessment of himself (that he is not worthy for Jesus to go to his home), his statement concerning delegated authority, and Jesus marvelling at his faith, some of the wording in Matt. 8.8–10 and Luke 7.6–9 being identical.

probable that the narratives describe the same occasion, though each writer has retold the story in order to focus on different themes.[57]

Messages from Matthew

A Gentile is helped by Jesus

Matthew records this story immediately after the account of the cleansing of the leper, though Luke includes other stories in between, each demonstrating Jesus' authority in word and miracle (see Table 4.2). This time another marginalized person is helped by Jesus, both sufferers believing that Jesus had the authority to heal. On this occasion, the man requesting help from Jesus is not, as the leper, ceremonially unclean because of his sickness but, as a centurion who is probably Gentile,[58] thus uncircumcised, he is outside the law and racially marginalized. As a centurion (in charge of 80 to 100 legionaries), he would have been a Roman; centurions were generally drawn from the ranks of soldiers who, in Roman legions, had to be Roman. As such, he represented a pagan power and an oppressive, intrusive force to the Jews, an object of hate and fear; yet, despite his unsavoury background, Jesus responds to his request for healing. Matthew and Luke refer to the fact that the centurion did not feel worthy for Jesus to enter his house. His humility is an important descriptor of the man, but it is not the reason that motivates Jesus to provide a positive outcome.

A Gentile believes in Jesus

The centurion's faith is demonstrated by his belief that Jesus can heal from a distance, unusual especially because there has been no record hitherto of Jesus healing from a distance in the Gospels. Matthew's wording indicates a stronger belief on the part of the centurion in that he states that if Jesus says 'only' (*monon*) a word, his servant 'will be healed' (*iathēsetai*, future imperative of *iaomai*), whereas Luke inserts the passive imperative verb (*iathētō*) which is translated as 'let [my servant] be healed'.

Helping him come to this conclusion is the fact that, as a centurion, he has the authority, delegated to him by a tribune, to enforce the rule

---

[57] So McHugh, J. F., *John 1–4: A Critical and Exegetical Commentary*. T. & T. Clark, Edinburgh, 2009, p. 316; Davies and Allison, *Matthew 8–18*. pp. 17–18; Hagner, *Matthew 1–13*. p. 203; Luz, *Matthew 8–20*. p. 9; Beasley-Murray, G. R., *John*. Word, Waco, 1991, p. 71; Nolland, *Luke 1–9.20*. p. 314; Marshall, I. H., *The Gospel of Luke: A Commentary on the Greek Text*. Paternoster Press, Exeter, 1978, p. 278. Bock (D. L., *Luke 1.1–9.50*. Baker, Grand Rapids, 1994, pp. 630–3) argues that John records a different healing.

[58] The saying of Jesus that he has not found such faith in Israel further indicates that the centurion is not Jewish.

of Roman law, to control his soldiers and order his slaves. He also can discharge orders to his legionnaires over a distance (through the military chain of command). He concludes that Jesus has the ability to do the same with reference to healing.

It is significant that in this, his first reference to faith in a healing narrative, Matthew ascribes it to a Gentile.[59] The faith referred to is not to be equated with a perception that Jesus is God or that he will certainly heal the servant but is a belief that Jesus has the authority to do that which he wishes. There is no evidence that the centurion follows Jesus thereafter or himself benefits from the ministry of Jesus; this is an example of Jesus offering restoration freely to people in hopeless situations.

It is possible that the statement of Jesus, unique to Matthew, that 'I will come and heal him', may be interpreted as a question, 'Shall I come and heal him?'[60] If so, it is possible that Jesus was testing the man's faith in his ability to heal. However, it is more likely that he is querying the appropriateness of him, a Jew, going to the home of a Gentile and to function beneficently there. If Jesus is asking a question, he is erecting a (temporary) barrier that will test the centurion's faith.[61] However, even so, the centurion metaphorically leaps any such barriers and declares his belief that Jesus is able to bring transformation, and Jesus is impressed (as he is on another occasion with a Canaanite woman).

However, it is much more likely grammatically that Jesus is actually asserting his desire to go and heal the servant,[62] which leads to a dilemma for the centurion, for he is reluctant to have Jesus come to his home because he is a Gentile.[63] This predicament is highlighted by the emphatic use of 'I' (Matt. 8.7 – in effect, 'I, yes I, will come and heal him'). Thus, Jesus draws attention to the fact that, despite the injunction of normal Jewish practice, he is going to attend to this Gentile's servant in his house.

It was not that the faith of the man was the necessary catalyst for the healing; on other occasions, Jesus healed people who were not even expecting to be healed. As Derrett accurately states, the boy was 'cured as a free

---

[59] Luke has previously identified the faith of a paralytic, followed by a reference to Jesus forgiving his sins and healing him (5.20).

[60] Davies and Allison, *Matthew 8–18*. p. 21; Beasley-Murray, *John*. p. 71.

[61] Jesus also does this with the Canaanite woman (Matt. 15.24–27//Mark 7.27–28).

[62] So RSV, NEB, ESV; Gundry, R. H., *Matthew: A Commentary on His Handbook for a Mixed Church under Persecution*. Eerdmans, Grand Rapids, 1982, 1994, pp. 142–3; Hagner, *Matthew 1–13*. p. 204.

[63] Acts 10.28; Jos., *Wars* 2.150; b. *Ohal.*, 18.7 states that Jews would become ceremonially unclean if they entered a Gentile's home; it is not recorded that Jesus ever entered a Gentile's home in order to heal. Indeed, there is no reference to Jesus entering a Gentile home, for any reason, and this is the only recorded healing of a Gentile occurring at a distance.

gift'.[64] Jesus' commendation related to the fact that the centurion realized that Jesus was the right person to ask when no one else could help. Matthew uniquely concludes the narrative with a command that the centurion should 'go', repeated in John 4.50, providing an opportunity for obedience, as with the leper (8.1–4).

Jesus has the authority to welcome Gentiles into the kingdom of God

Not only does Jesus respond positively to the centurion's request, but he also uses it as a springboard to explore membership of the kingdom. Matthew uniquely adds that people will recline at a table with Abraham, Isaac and Jacob, the alternative to being cast into outer darkness.[65] Although he refers to people coming 'from the east and west', which could refer to Diaspora Jews, as it does elsewhere,[66] the presence of a Gentile centurion implies that others, as well as Jews, are also being welcomed. Jesus is here referring to an eschatological banquet to which the people of God were invited,[67] the implication being that a Gentile centurion, representing paganism and oppression, who is not a recipient of divinely initiated covenant promises, would be one of those so welcomed. The implication is that the original prophecy, which was to Jews, there being no OT suggestion that other nations would be able to participate in any eschatological feast, is now being applied also to Gentiles, a shocking revelation.

The three patriarchal heroes, Abraham, Isaac and Jacob, are mentioned elsewhere as being those who will welcome the righteous at the end of time (4 Macc. 13.17).[68] The message is that not only will the attendees recline, but also they will do so with the heroes of the Jewish nation, next to whom it would be expected that fellow Jews would sit.[69] In this, Jesus is reflecting the Isaianic prophecy (56.3–8) which describes an era when Gentiles are welcomed to participate in a relationship with God in 'a house of prayer for all peoples' (56.7).

At the same time, it is the 'sons of the kingdom',[70] a clear reference to those who are to inherit the kingdom, assumed by the Jews to be themselves,

---

[64] Derrett, J. D. M., 'Law in the New Testament: The Syrophoenician woman and the Centurion of Capernaum', *NovT.* 15.3, 1973, p. 183.

[65] See also Luke 13.28–29.

[66] Ps. 107.3; Isa. 43.5; 49.12; Ezek. 37.21; Zech. 8.7; Baruch 4.37; 5.5.

[67] Isa. 25.6; Rev. 19.9; b. *Pes.* 119b.

[68] Luke adds 'the prophets' to this list (13.28).

[69] *1 Enoch* 70.4; *Test. Ben.* 10.6–9.

[70] The audience in Luke is undefined (13.28); the only other reference to this term is in Matt. 13.38, where it refers to those who will benefit from Jesus' teaching concerning the kingdom of God.

who will be 'thrown into the outer darkness.'[71] In that place, there will be weeping and gnashing of teeth',[72] Matthew recording a more severe punishment than Luke, who omits the reference to outer darkness. In the OT, it is God who undertakes the role of determining who are to be members of his kingdom (Exod. 19.6), identifying them as 'the people of Israel',[73] determining the rules for maintaining that membership (Exod. 24.3); it is God who is the judge who determines the destiny of those who are excluded from the kingdom (Isa. 2.4). Here, these authoritative roles are ascribed to Jesus.

Although the OT prophesied of a time when people from all nations would go to 'the house of the Lord' (Isa. 2.2; Mic. 4.2) in order to be taught by God, it is not stated that they would be welcomed as equal partners with Israel. This mission to the Gentiles, only obliquely hinted at in the OT, is, however, clearly stated by Jesus.[74] Jesus is thus identified as setting an eschatological agenda that will include Gentiles as members of God's kingdom. Matthew presents the Gentile centurion as an example of many Gentiles who will enter the kingdom, profiting from its eschatological benefits.

To emphasize the point that the Jews should also trust in Jesus, Matthew and Luke contrast the faith of the centurion with the faith present in the people of Israel, where it would have been more expected. Uniquely, Matthew precedes the statement of Jesus, 'I tell you', with the word *amēn* ('truly'), the assertion demanding the inclusion of a forceful affirmation.[75] Indeed, Matthew and Luke describe Jesus as being struck by wonder at the perception of the centurion; although on other occasions people marvel at Jesus, this is the only record of Jesus being so impressed by a person,

---

[71] This term is only used in Matthew (22.13; 25.30). Darkness (*skotos*) is often used to refer to spiritual darkness (4.16; 6.23; 27.45; Luke 1.79; 11.35; 22.53; 23.44) while the prefix 'outer' (*exōteron*) indicates a spiritual darkness with eschatological overtones (*1 Enoch* 62.11; 63.6, 11; *2 Enoch* 25.4–5; 26.3). Elsewhere, 2 Pet. 2.17 and Jude 13 describe the punishment of false teachers as being destined to 'utter darkness'.

[72] Also 13.42; 22.13; 24.51; 25.30, the verbs being elsewhere used (only in Matthew, except Luke 13.28) and associated with the destiny of hypocrites and evildoers (Matt. 13.41, 50), those not prepared for the marriage feast (Matt. 22.3, 12), infidelity and unpreparedness (Matt. 24.48–50) and laziness (25.26); as such, they represent actions associated with sorrow, regret and anger (Ps. 112.10; Acts 7.54). Such a destiny was intended for Azazel (*1 Enoch* 10.4), nations (Judith 16.17) and kings who opposed God (*1 Enoch* 63.6), and was experienced by Adam and Eve after they sinned in the Garden (*2 Enoch* 26.3).

[73] Exod. 19.3; 1 Chron. 28.5; Ps. 114.2; *1 Enoch* 62.13; 70.4, 'the righteous and the elect'.

[74] Matt. 28.19; Mark 13.1; 14.9. The restrictive commissions only to Israel and not to the Gentiles in Matt. 10.5, 6, 23, appear to be only intended for the lifetime of Jesus.

[75] The term is used 31 times in Matthew by Jesus to confirm an important assertion to be made by him (5.18, 26; 6.2, 5, 16).

who also happens to be a Gentile. Given the uniqueness of that fact, it should be considered as potentially having an even more important part to play in the story than the remarkable healing, which is not unique in the mission of Jesus.[76] It is a Gentile who accepts the authority of Jesus to achieve healing, irrespective of potential obstacles, of which distance is but one. The healing itself is briefly mentioned at the end of the narrative. What brought pleasure to Jesus was the belief of a centurion that Jesus could easily transform the life situation of his servant; other centurions will walk in his footsteps (Mark 15.39; Acts 10.1–48).

Messages from Luke

Luke makes the connection explicit between this story and the previous teaching of Jesus (6.17–49) (see Table 4.2) in which the emphasis has been on lifestyle characteristics to determine appropriate discipleship of Jesus and, in particular, ownership of the kingdom of God (6.20) and the identification of true sons of God (6.35). The healing narrative provides an opportunity for Luke to demonstrate how a Gentile portrays faith and humility that potentially enable him to achieve such objectives. Luke is still teaching, previously in a discourse, but now in a healing story.

In Luke, the request of the centurion that Jesus heal his servant is made explicit (also John 4.47), on the basis of his having 'heard about Jesus'; it is not clear how much he knew of Jesus, and Luke implies that his knowledge may have been quite limited, thus elevating the quality of his faith in Jesus. Luke does not even record that the centurion meets Jesus and yet he still believes that Jesus can heal his servant. Luke provides more evidence of his sense of unworthiness, resulting in a conversation taking place between Jesus and the centurion's intermediaries, Luke writing that his lack of worth resulted in him sending them rather than coming himself. In direct contrast to his perception of his limited worth, the Jewish elders (possibly of the synagogue or, more likely, of the town) conclude that he is most worthy of Jesus' attention, due to his love for his servant and the Jewish nation, having built a synagogue for them.[77]

The centurion refers to Jesus as *kurios* ('lord'), probably a term of respect and not indicative of his belief that Jesus is divine. However, given that he recognizes that Jesus has the ability to heal supernaturally, he may invest

---

[76] Jesus healed (John 9.1–7) and cast out demons (Matt. 15.21–28//Mark 7.24–30) from people at a distance on other occasions.

[77] Bock (*Luke 1.1–9.50*. p. 635) records that whereas a soldier would be paid around 75 denarii per year, a centurion could earn between 3,750 and 7,500 denarii.

more in the term than merely 'sir'. Jesus returns with them towards his home, though some of his friends stop them in order to inform them of the man's unwillingness that Jesus should enter his house. Thereafter, as with Matthew, he asserts his belief that Jesus can achieve a healing miracle by a word and from a distance, drawing a parallel with his authority over his own soldiers and slaves, followed by Jesus' commendation of his faith. The extra data has provided Luke with the opportunity to emphasize that Jesus welcomes people who may feel marginalized and therefore unable to participate in the mission of a Jewish Messiah,[78] but who nevertheless can express faith in Jesus, sufficient to receive his affirmation.

The one who has taught with authority (6.17–49) now functions with authority (7.11–17); after this, Luke records the story of Jesus authorizing a dead man to rise, a watching crowd acknowledging that, in Jesus, 'God has visited his people' (7.16).

Messages from John

Signs can help people to believe in Jesus

John orders his material carefully, first introducing Jesus as God (1.1–18). Nicodemus is the first person (a worthy, respected Jewish leader) who is provided with the opportunity to place his faith in Jesus (3.1–21), followed by an unworthy, hated Samaritan woman who is given a similar opportunity (4.1–38). The data that John records immediately before the healing under consideration refers to Jesus providing Galileans with the opportunity of trusting him (4.43–45) (see Table 4.2).

John records that the man's request is initially met with an apparently negative response by Jesus. This is to be contrasted with Jesus' immediate and positive response to the man in Matthew and Luke. Some have suggested that Jesus is reprimanding the man for only being prepared to believe in Jesus if he sees signs and wonders, indicating that he disapproves of signs.[79] Lindars[80] suggests that Jesus is testing the faith of the man, though, again, the text does not clearly support this view and if this was Jesus' motivation, the man appears to ignore it. Some have therefore concluded that Jesus may be reprimanding the wider audience of potentially

---

[78] In 13.28–29, Luke widens the geographical expanse for would-be guests of the kingdom of God to include 'north and south' as well as 'east and west'.

[79] So McHugh, *John*. p. 319; Beasley-Murray, *John*. p. 71; Davies and Allison, *Matthew 8–18*. p. 22. The term (*semeion*) is used often in the OT to refer to the miracles that occurred mainly prior to the Hebrew release from Egypt (Exod. 7.3; Deut. 4.34; 6.22; 7.19); it is only used here in this Gospel.

[80] Lindars, B., *The Gospel of John*. Oliphants, London, 1972, p. 203; Jones, L. P., *The Symbol of Water in the Gospel of John*. Sheffield Academic Press, Sheffield, 1997, p. 118.

unbelieving observers[81] or stating a fact concerning people in general,[82] especially given the fact that the verb 'see' (*idēte*) is in the second person plural. However, other than the plural nature of the verb, there is nothing else in the narrative that suggests that Jesus is referring to others, and John clearly identifies the man as the one to whom Jesus spoke; there is no mention of anyone else even being present, his servants meeting him later (4.51).

Rather, this story is to be understood as a reference to Jesus' willingness to use signs (in this case, a healing) as stepping stones to enable people to come to faith in him. In this regard, Jesus prefaces the healing with the recognition that signs can be valuable in developing people's perception of Jesus. Thus, he travels about 25 miles from Cana to Capernaum (4.46) where this Gentile lives. The first sign to Jews in Cana (2.11) is now followed by a second sign to Gentiles (4.54).[83]

In response to Jesus, the official simply asks Jesus to come before his son dies, followed by Jesus' promise that he will live. The man is not affirmed for his willingness to believe, as in Matthew and Luke. Instead, John identifies his developing faith. First, John records that the official believes that Jesus can heal, demonstrated by his request in the first place; second, he affirms this by demonstrating the man's readiness to obey Jesus' command to return home, believing Jesus' promise that his son would be healed. Finally, John includes the information that when the man realized that the healing occurred at the precise moment when Jesus had pronounced it on the previous day, he (and his household) again believed in Jesus. Rather than this re-emphasizing the same belief in the ability of Jesus to heal, John is more probably revealing the fact that the man's perspective of Jesus has now developed through the healing.

Initially, he believed that Jesus *could* heal. That belief was then developed to a belief that Jesus *would* heal, on the basis of Jesus offering a verbal promise to that effect. The final description of his believing, with his household, cannot refer to a belief in the healing power of Jesus, for he believed that before meeting Jesus. Rather, when the healing is actually witnessed, another level of perception is experienced by the man, the sign offering the basis for an increased level of faith in Jesus, a more mature perception of his status. A similar progression is evident previously in the

[81] Brown, R., *The Gospel According to John, Vol. 1*. Geoffrey Chapman, London, 1971, p. 191.
[82] Michaels, J. R., *The Gospel of John*. Eerdmans, Grand Rapids, 2010, pp. 277–8; Beasley-Murray, *John*. p. 71.
[83] Note John's use of 'therefore' (4.46) to refer to Jesus' return to Cana.

Samaritans who believed in Jesus because of the word of the woman (4.39) and then believed because of his word (4.41), the latter occasion resulting in their concluding that he was 'the Saviour of the world' (4.42). The healing has proved to the official and his household that Jesus is deserving of a superior trust than was initially anticipated. Jesus' earlier assessment is proven true, that signs do have the potential of effecting a greater appreciation of his status and mission.

Conclusion

A Gentile's request on behalf of someone else, who does not appear in the story, is positively answered by Jesus. The lessons to be learnt from the narrative relate to the quality of the man's faith in Jesus, believing that he can heal from a distance and that he is prepared to respond to someone who is an outsider. Also highlighted is the readiness of Jesus to use supernatural signs to help a marginalized character gain a clearer perception of his status with significant physical and eternal consequences.

Jesus heals Peter's mother-in-law (Matt. 8.14–15// Mark 1.29–31//Luke 4.38–39)

Table 4.3 Healing Peter's mother-in-law – the literary context

	Matthew	Mark	Luke
Cleansing of the leper	8.1–4	(1.40–45)	(5.12–16)
Healing of the centurion's servant	8.5–13		(7.1–10)
Exorcism of the synagogue demon		1.21–28	4.31–37
Healing of Peter's mother-in-law	**8.14–15**	**1.29–31**	**4.38–39**
Summary of healings	8.16–17	1.32–34	4.40–41
Instructions to would-be disciples	8.18–22		(9.57–60)
Jesus preaches elsewhere		1.35–39	4.42–44
Jesus calls his first four disciples	(4.18–22)	(1.16–20)	5.1–11

Main messages from all the narratives

In Simon's house (Matthew refers to 'Peter'), Jesus heals his mother-in-law of a fever, authoritatively and immediately, resulting in it leaving, demonstrated by her being able to serve.[84]

The fever

Not only does the presence of a fever indicate that the woman was indisposed as well as in discomfort,[85] but also it was often viewed by the Jews as a divine punishment[86] and also sometimes as demonically caused.[87]

Peter's mother-in-law

As a woman, she occupied an inferior position in the patriarchal system of the time,[88] although there were exceptions. Much of the evidence supportive

---

[84] b. *Shab.* 66b–7a offers cures for fevers, though they are more related to magical therapies than the simply presented power of Jesus, who provides restoration without prayer, therapeutic aids, words or any set methodology; b. *Ned.* 41a refers to the ability to heal fever as being greater than protecting those who were in the fiery furnace recorded in Dan. 3.6–27. The sudden and inexplicable change in temperature in a person experiencing a fever resulted in many fearing it greatly.

[85] John 4.53 refers to a fever (*puretos*) that resulted in the sufferer being close to death; in Acts 28.8, *puretos* is associated with dysentery.

[86] b. *Ber.* 34b; Philo, *On Rewards and Punishments* 143.

[87] b. *Ned.* 41a; *Git.* 70a.

[88] Thus, Jewish daughters could only inherit from their father (Num. 27.1–11) where there were no brothers who would otherwise take precedence. Similarly, although the OT does not restrict the initiation of divorce only to men (Deut. 24.1–4), the Mishnah (edited around AD 200) made this a male prerogative (m. *Git.* 9.3). Tests for determining adultery were only applied to women but not to men (Num. 5.11–30; m. *Sotah* 3.4; 5.1). Similarly, laws concerning menstruation (Lev. 15.19–30)

of such distinctions is included in rabbinic literature that post-dates the NT era. Nevertheless, it reflected, to a great degree, the ambience of that time in which women were viewed as being of an inferior status compared to Jewish men.[89] It is in this context that it is to be noted that Jesus healed her.[90]

Messages from Matthew

The first three healings in Matthew's Gospel (see Table 4.3) relate to marginalized people (a leper, a Gentile and, here, a woman) but, unlike the previous healings, here Jesus goes to the woman whereas the former two go to him.

The authority of Jesus

Matthew records Jesus taking the initiative in the healing, with no information provided about the woman's fever or any request from the disciples (compare Mark 1.30 and Luke 4.38). Also, except for the final clause, where Jesus is the object, Matthew presents Jesus as the subject of the other clauses; in this way, the attention of the reader is focused on the person and authority of Jesus. Matthew uniquely describes her position as 'having been thrown' (*beblēmenēn*, perfect passive participle from *ballō*, 'I throw'), a particularly strong way of describing her location, used also of the condition of the paralytic who was brought to Jesus (9.2). In amending Mark's wording (*katekeito* (from *katakeimai*, 'I lie down')), Matthew provides a more graphic description of the woman having been 'cast to one side' by her condition, perhaps indicative of its seriousness or the rapidity of its occurrence. Furthermore, both Matthew and Luke record the woman rising on her own with no help from Jesus, thus demonstrating that her

---

were expanded (b. *Nidd.* 13), making it much more difficult for women than men to be involved in Temple worship; the fact that there was a Women's Court, beyond which they were not normally allowed, indicates their secondary status (Jos., *Wars* 5.198–9). Women were also, in time, exempted and then barred from the process of scholarly activity, including learning (b. *Kidd.* 30a, 80b) and from even reading the law 'because of the dignity of the community' (b. *Meg.* 23a); indeed, one rabbi asserted, 'Let the words of the Law be burned rather than taught to a woman' (b. *Sotah* 19a). At the worst, because of their gender, women were portrayed by some rabbis as being involved in magic (b. *Sanh.* 67a; *Pes.* 110a, 111a; m. *Sanh.* 6.4). It was appropriate for some Jews to thank God for not making them pagans or women (b. *Ket.* 11b), or 'a Gentile, a woman or a slave' (b. *Men.* 43b–44a), and to assert that 'Happy is he whose children are sons and woe to him whose children are daughters' (b. *Baba Bathra* 16b). Furthermore, it was even stated by some that 'Four qualities are ascribed to women. They are gluttonous, eavesdroppers, lazy and jealous' (*Gen. Rab.* 58.2) and that when 'Ten measures of speech descended to the world, women took nine and men one' (b. *Kidd.* 47b).

[89] Baskin, J. R., *Midrashic Women: Formations of the Feminine in Rabbinic Literature*. Brandeis University Press, Brandeis, 2002.

[90] It is of interest to note that the Gospels indicate the elevated role of women in the life and ministry of Jesus, supporting him (Matt. 27.55; Luke 8.2, 3), visiting his tomb and witnessing his resurrection (Matt. 28.5; Luke 23.55; 24.10).

healing is complete. Matthew emphasizes the authority of Jesus by immediately recording a summary account of healings and exorcisms, which
he uniquely asserts were evidence that, in his healing ministry, Jesus was
fulfilling an Isaianic prophecy (Isa. 53.4).

The importance of touch

Matthew refers to Jesus' touching of the woman's hand, while Mark refers
only to his taking her hand, and Luke does not mention any such action.
Matthew nowhere identifies the act of touching another person as a
magical feature and only rarely identifies it as a manifestation of compassion (20.29), though it does signify a gentle action. This feature is most
valuable for Matthew's mainly Jewish audience;[91] for a Jew, touching a sick
person would result in ceremonial uncleanness. Hagner provides a chiasm
that underscores the importance of touch to Matthew's narrative:[92]

> A. He saw his mother-in-law
> > B. Lying sick
> > > C. Having a fever
> > > > D. He touched her hand
> > > C1. The fever left her
> > B1. And she rose
> A1. and she served him

It is the authority of Jesus that is being highlighted by the touch rather
than it being a compassionate gesture. Indeed, none of the writers mentions
a motif of compassion on the part of Jesus in this narrative; this of course,
does not exclude the fact that compassion was foundational to his restorative ministry. However, the writers more clearly emphasize the authority
of Jesus in that he touched a woman who was ill, remarkable especially to
Matthew's Jewish readers.

Whereas Mark refers to Jesus taking the woman's hand to help her to
rise,[93] Matthew asserts that Jesus simply touched (*hēpsato*, aorist tense from
haptō, 'I touch') her hand. Elsewhere, Matthew uses this verb in contexts
of healing where Jesus touches people[94] or they touch him (9.21).[95]

---

[91] For discussion of the characteristic of touch in the healing ministry of Jesus, see earlier.
[92] Hagner, *Matthew 1–13*. p. 209.
[93] Matthew records Jesus doing the same on other occasions, but it is after a healing has occurred in
which he touched the person concerned (9.25).
[94] 8.3; 9.29; 14.36; 20.34.
[95] The place of touch in healing contexts is also present in Mark (1.41; 5.27; 6.56; 7.33) and Luke
(5.13; 6.19; 7.14, 39; 8.44–46; 22.51) but not John, and only Matthew records this aspect in
this story. It is not surprising that the Apostles adopted this procedure in their healings of people
(Acts 2.43; 6.7, 8; 9.12–19; 36–42; 14.3; 19.11; 20.10; 28.4, 8).

The appropriate response to Jesus is service

Finally, Matthew restricts the woman to serving (*diēkonei*[96]) only Jesus. Mark and Luke state that she served others ('them', *autois*), thus demonstrating that her healing was complete, but Matthew identifies her serving Jesus only ('him', *autō*); she is presented as the ideal follower of Jesus by responding to her transformation by serving him.

Messages from Mark

Both Mark and Luke record this as the second miracle performed by Jesus, listing it after the exorcism of a demoniac in the synagogue in Capernaum (see Table 4.3), and, with Matthew, before a general statement concerning Jesus' healings and exorcisms. Mark notes the names of four of the disciples, who inform Jesus about the woman's situation. Mark then records the healing briefly, as resulting simply from Jesus taking her by the hand and lifting her up, an action that Jesus undertakes elsewhere.[97] For Mark, the taking of her hand is a practical means of helping her to rise. This is a dramatic change of setting from a demonic intrusion and convulsive expulsion in a synagogue to a domestic scene in a home where a fever that has obstructed a woman in engaging in her duties is quietly and gently removed; Jesus functions authoritatively in both settings.

Messages from Luke

Luke records this healing uniquely before Jesus' calling his first four disciples (5.1–11). Before they are called to follow Jesus, lessons for would-be disciples highlighted in this narrative and the exorcism that precedes it include the importance of Jesus' authority, the service (of the woman) and the obedience (of the demon).

Luke uniquely describes the fever as 'high' (*megalō* from *megas*, 'great, high'). It is a term used elsewhere in Luke to heighten the intensity or greatness of a situation or person.[98] Whatever the severity of the fever, Jesus has the authority to deal with it. It is possible that Luke may intend to further emphasize the authority of Jesus by (only here) describing Jesus, in a posture of supremacy, standing over (*epistas*, from *ephistēmi*, 'I stand

---

[96] The verb *diakoneō* is used elsewhere in Matthew on two occasions (4.11 where the angels serve Jesus; 25.44 with reference to serving those in need); the concept of service is referred to prior to this account in the context of the devil (4.10, *latreuō*) and people (6.24, *douleuō*) being reminded that God is to be served; here, it is Jesus who is identified as the appropriate recipient of service.

[97] Mark 5.41; 9.27.

[98] A great feast (14.16); a large room (22.12); great fear (2.9); a loud voice (19.37); a great prophet (7.16).

above or over') the woman.[99] This is all the more likely when it is recognized that Luke alone refers to Jesus rebuking the fever,[100] the narrative providing a confrontational setting where Jesus confrontationally and successfully overcomes the fever.

It is possible that the fever is demonically inspired as elsewhere demons manifest in sickness (Luke 11.14), and the verb (*epitimaō*) is used in the preceding narrative which results in the expulsion of a demon (4.35) and immediately after in the record of Jesus expelling many demons after rebuking them (4.41; 9.42, 55). Furthermore, as with demonic expulsions, here Jesus is not recorded as touching the woman, though he often touches sick people before healing them.[101] In addition, Luke uniquely uses *sunekomenē* (from *sunekō*, 'I hold fast, oppress') to describe the fever, used elsewhere in Luke to describe people crushing each other and a claustrophobic sense of imprisonment.[102] Finally, whereas Matthew and Mark reveal Jesus attending to the woman, touching her hand and/or taking her hand to lift her up, Luke omits this and identifies Jesus specifically speaking to the fever, and only obliquely to the woman.

Thus, although it may simply be a graphic presentation on the part of Luke to demonstrate the superior authority of Jesus over sickness, the significant changes by Luke to the Markan account indicate that he may be describing the occasion as more representative of a cosmic confrontation between Jesus and demonic forces that manifest in sickness.[103] While Matthew and Mark use the common word *egeirō* to refer to the woman rising, Luke uses *anistēmi*, a favourite word for him.[104] It was used earlier in 4.29 to describe people who rose up to expel Jesus from their city and kill him, resulting in him leaving; here, it is used of a woman who rises in order to serve Jesus, resulting in him staying.

---

[99] Derrett, J. D. M., 'Getting on Top of a Demon (Luke 4.39)', *EvQ*. 65.2, 1993, pp. 99–109.

[100] The term *epitimaō* ('I rebuke, censure') is used elsewhere in Luke of people rebuking others (9.55; 17.3; 18.15, 39; 19.39; 23.40), and of Jesus rebuking a demon (4.35; 9.42; 9.55b) and a storm (8.24). In the OT, the term is used to indicate God's judgement on his enemies (Deut. 28.20; Pss. 9.6; 66.15; 68.31; 76.6; 80.16; 119.21; Isa. 33.17; 51.20; 54.9; Mal. 2.3).

[101] 4.40; 5.13; 7.14; 8.54.

[102] 8.45; 19.43; 22.63; Acts 7.57.

[103] Nolland (*Luke 1–9.20*. pp. 211–12) prefers to believe that it is not a description of demonic possession and expulsion but 'Satanic oppression comparable to demon possession but not to be identified with it'; Marshall (*Luke*. p. 195) views it as 'nothing more than personification of the malady'; Bock (*Luke 1.1–9.50*. p. 437), concludes, 'if this is an exorcism, Luke has not pointed it out by the form'. However, Luke has provided many markers to it being an exorcism, short of using the words 'demon' or 'unclean spirit'.

[104] 5.25, 28; 6.8; 11.7, 8; 15.18, 20; 17.19; 22.45; 24.12; he also inserts it when the other Synoptists use *egeirō* (Matt. 9.7//Mark 2.12//Luke 5.25).

Jesus demonstrates his mandate to the marginalized

This healing provides an opportunity for Luke to develop his agenda to demonstrate that Jesus is concerned to minister to the marginalized, a feature that is common to his Gospel. He uniquely presents people beseeching Jesus on the woman's behalf. In a society that was used to the notion of patronage where someone took responsibility for another person, others took that role upon themselves. Jesus demonstrates that he is in agreement with their stance as he takes control of the situation, removes the fever, and restores her to health and also, more importantly, to her place in society. As elsewhere, Luke is keen to indicate that all may legitimately benefit from the ministry of Jesus, even marginalized women.

This feature may be supported by the following chiasm that Luke may have devised, which results in the woman being central to the setting. As contrasted with Mark and especially Matthew, where Jesus is the subject of the narrative, Luke, in agreement with his wider agenda, demonstrates that Jesus has time for the marginalized:

A. he arose
  B. and he left
    C. the woman was ill with a fever
      D. they asked for *her*
      D1. Jesus stood over *her*
    C1. Jesus rebuked the fever
  B1. the fever left
A1. she arose

Conclusion

Each of the writers, in different ways, reveals the authority of Jesus to restore a woman to health and service, with ease and immediacy, by overcoming all potential obstacles to ensure that her life-setting is transformed.

Jesus heals a paralytic (Matt. 9.1–8//Mark 2.1–12//Luke 5.17–26)

Table 4.4 Healing a paralytic – the literary context

	Matthew	Mark	Luke
Jesus preaches elsewhere		1.35–39	4.42–44
Jesus calls his first four disciples	(4.18–22)	(1.16–20)	5.1–11
Jesus calms a storm	8.23–27	(4.35–41)	(8.22–25)
Exorcism of demons	8.28–34	(5.1–20)	(8.26–39)
Cleansing of the leper	(8.1–4)	1.40–45	5.12–16
Healing of a paralytic	**9.1–8**	**2.1–12**	**5.17–26**
Jesus calls Matthew to be a disciple	9.9	2.13–14	5.27–28
Jesus eats with tax-collectors and sinners	9.10–13	2.15–17	5.29–32
Jesus teaches concerning fasting	9.14–17	2.18–22	5.33–39
Jesus heals a ruler's daughter and a woman with a haemorrhage	9.18–26	(5.21–43)	(8.40–56)
Jesus teaches about eating on the Sabbath	(12.1–8)	2.23–28	6.1–5
Jesus heals a man's withered hand	(12.9–14)	3.1–6	6.6–11

Main messages from all the narratives

Although this is a story in which a paralytic,[105] brought by others,[106] is healed by Jesus, it is his claim as the Son of Man to have the authority to forgive sins on earth that is central to the narrative, and the concept of authority per se that undergirds the narratives, the term 'authority' (*exousia*) being mentioned by each author, Matthew referring to it twice (9.6, 8).

Each Synoptist records that Jesus' initial words to the paralytic were prompted by his perception of 'their faith', implicitly including the paralytic. However, each Synoptist also records that the religious opposition ('scribes') asserted to each other that the act of Jesus in forgiving the man was blasphemous, although the healing resulted in the people glorifying God. This account is the first confrontation with the religious hierarchy recorded by Matthew and Mark, and only the second recorded by Luke. Although his miracles had the potential of revealing life-changing truth about Jesus, not all would take advantage of it.

---

[105] For an exploration of the paralysis, see Cotter (*Christ of the Miracle Stories*. pp. 88–91), who concludes that such bedridden paralysis resulted in death after a short time, no cure being available, quoting Celsus (*De Medicina* 3.27).

[106] Mark alone notes that four men carried him (2.4).

Jesus has authority . . . to forgive sins

Each author describes the healing as being achieved 'in order to' demonstrate Jesus' authority to forgive sins; his ability to heal is not the startling achievement in the minds of the authors but his right to forgive sin. Of significance is the fact that the forgiveness was not granted in response to a confession of sin or repentance. Rabbinic tradition assumed that sin would not be forgiven nor sickness be healed until sin was confessed.[107] However, Jesus unilaterally declares the man's forgiveness.

Not only was the correct procedure not undertaken here, but also, it is Jesus who takes the divine responsibility of forgiving sins. If the man had sinned personally against Jesus, one could understand if Jesus had forgiven him.[108] However, given that the identity of the sins is not mentioned and that there is no evidence that Jesus has even met the man before, it appears that all his sins are being forgiven by Jesus, a divine prerogative, as also indicated by the scribes.[109] However, the writers do not simply assert that Jesus has the authority to announce God's forgiveness. They also reveal that he has the authority to determine when and on what basis that forgiveness should occur. Here, Jesus first declared forgiveness, and only later did he heal the man.

It is possible that the paralysis had been caused by personal sin.[110] A causal connection between sin and suffering was assumed in Jewish and Christian[111] communities, it being believed that once the sin had been confessed and forgiven, physical restoration might ensue. However, none of the writers explicitly relates the paralysis to a specific sin and there is no unambiguous support for a connection made by Jesus that sickness

---

[107] b. *Ned.* 41a; see also Joel 2.12–13 and 1 John 1.9.

[108] It would be bizarre to assume that Jesus is forgiving him for interrupting his sermon or for damaging someone else's property.

[109] Num. 30.5, 8; Pss. 25.18; 32.5; 85.2; 99.8; 103.3; Jer. 31.34.

[110] So Davies and Allison, *Matthew 8–18*. p. 89; Branscomb, H., 'Mark 2.5, "Son, Thy Sins Are Forgiven"', *JBL*. 53, 1934, p. 54; Davids, P., 'A Biblical View of the Fruits of Sin', *The Kingdom and the Power.* (eds) Greig, G. S., Springer, K., Regal, Ventura, 1995, p. 117; Cranfield, C. E. B., *The Gospel According to Mark.* Cambridge University Press, Cambridge, 1959, pp. 97–8; Price (R. M., 'Illness Theodocies in the New Testament', *JRHlth.* 25.4, 1986, p. 310) argues that the paralysis was caused by sin. Caird (G. B., *The Gospel of Luke.* Penguin, Harmondsworth, 1963, p. 94) views it as resulting from sin, but psychosomatically based (contra Fitzmyer, *The Gospel According to Luke I–IX.* Yale, Yale University Press, 1982, p. 580); Marshall (*Luke.* p. 213) notes the possibility that it referred to sickness caused by sin or resulting from the man sharing in universal human sinfulness; Hooker (*Mark.* p. 85) appears to suggest that the paralysis is caused by guilt; also, Dwyer, T., *The Motif of Wonder in the Gospel of Mark.* Continuum, Sheffield, 1996, p. 99; Basset, L., 'La culpabilité, paralysie du coeur: Reinterpretation du récit de la guérison du paralysé (Lc. 5, 17–26)', *ETR.* 71.3, 1996, pp. 331–7; Lane (*Mark.* p. 94) rejects a link with guilt.

[111] John 5.14; 9.2; Acts 5.4–12; 1 Cor. 11. 30; Jas 5.16.

is caused by the sufferer's sin elsewhere in the Gospels.[112] Furthermore, if sin had caused the paralysis and he was forgiven that sin, it is surprising that he remained paralysed after the forgiveness of sins had been pronounced by Jesus.

It is not the apparent linkage between sin and sickness that is of importance here, but rather the recognition that Jesus has come to deal with both, and that he does so with authority and ease.[113] The man's primary need appears to be for physical healing, but Jesus meets his actual primary need, forgiveness for sin, and heals him as well.

By using the present passive tense (*aphientai*, from *aphiēmi*, 'I let go, forgive'), Matthew and Mark may be intending to suggest that the forgiveness of the man has occurred – at that moment,[114] while Luke indicates the certainty of that forgiveness by using the perfect passive tense (*apheōntai*). Either way, Jesus thus fulfils the psalmist's assertions concerning God, 'He forgives all my sins and heals all my diseases' (Ps. 103.3). Even if people had believed that Jesus was Messiah, they would not have expected him to have the authority to forgive sin as that was exclusively God's prerogative. However, where Isaiah 43.25 asserts concerning God, 'I, I am he, who blots out your transgressions', the Synoptists conclude that Jesus shares that authority.

That the scribes (Luke also adding 'and Pharisees') accuse Jesus of blasphemy[115] indicates that they understood Jesus' words to be more than him simply declaring that God had forgiven the man. Instead, they understood Jesus to be taking the place of God in forgiving the man. Furthermore, each writer indicates the demeaning attitude of Jesus' accusers. Some translations include the word 'man' to define Jesus in their accusations. However,

---

[112] Borgen (P., 'Miracles of Healing in the New Testament', *ST*. 35.2, 1981, pp. 91–106) argues that Jesus, to a large extent, broke with the Jewish idea of sickness being a form of divine retaliation.

[113] Cf. Hagner (*Matthew 1–13*. p. 232) states, 'the point of this narrative is that the problem of sin, though not as apparent to the eye as paralysis, is a fundamental . . . problem of humanity that Jesus has come to counteract'.

[114] Davies and Allison (*Matthew 8–18*. p. 89) define it as an 'aoristic present'; cf. Blass, F., Debrunner, A., Funk, R. W., *A Greek Grammar of the New Testament and Other Early Christian Literature*. University of Chicago Press, Chicago, 1961, p. 167; Hiebert, D. E., *Mark: A Portrait of a Servant*. Moody, Chicago, 1974, p. 65; Juel (D. H., *Mark*. Augsburg, Minneapolis, 1990, p. 47) and Luz (*Matthew 8–20*. p. 28) suggest that a divine passive is in mind here, as a result of which Jesus is stating that God has forgiven the man; similarly, Bruner (F. D., *The Christbook: Matthew 1–12*. Grand Rapids, Eerdmans, 2007, p. 412) states, 'Jesus credits God'. Although this is possible, none of the Gospel writers supports this option, explicitly stating that Jesus is the one who has declared forgiveness and this demonstrates his authority so to do as the Son of Man; so Hagner, *Matthew 1–13*. p. 232; France (*Mark*. pp. 125, 129) writes, 'Jesus is not simply stating a fact, but actually forgiving.'

[115] Blasphemy is identified as cursing God or dishonouring him by abusively using (his) 'the name' (Lev. 24.10–17; Num. 15.30), a deed worthy of death (Num. 15.31).

there is no word for 'man' in the Greek. Matthew simply records *houtos blasphēmei* (literally, 'Who is this one who blasphemes?') the term 'fellow' being offered in more translations to indicate the contemptuous or, at least, dismissive or patronizing comments by the religious leaders.[116]

In response to the accusation of the religious leaders, the writers record Jesus asking them some questions. Although they are presented somewhat differently by the respective authors, the main agreement lies in the conundrum that Jesus offers as to whether it is easier to pronounce healing or the forgiveness of sins. At first glance, it might be concluded that it would be easier to offer forgiveness than to pronounce healing, as the former cannot be proven not to have happened.[117] However, the response is not so easy for the religious leaders, for, in their view, they know that each is as difficult as the other and that to achieve the one is to achieve the other, given their belief that sickness is mainly caused by sin. Any declaration of forgiveness would be authenticated if the sickness (that it has apparently caused) is then removed. The writers are also aware that the religious leaders can do neither.

It is significant that each writer refers to Jesus testifying to himself as the Son of Man, the first time that Mark and Luke apply this term to Jesus. Although it could simply be a reference to being a member of humanity,[118] the context indicates otherwise, pointing to the unique authority of Jesus to forgive sins,[119] and more probably relates to Daniel 7.13–14.

There, it describes a supernatural being who receives authority directly from God. The 'son of man' is 'given dominion and glory and a kingdom, that all peoples, nations and languages should serve him; his dominion is an everlasting dominion, which shall not pass away' (7.14). He is anticipated as coming on the clouds of heaven (7.13), an action elsewhere

---

[116] NIV, NASB, ESV.

[117] So also Uth, D. F. 'An Eschatological Interpretation of the Synoptic Miracles in the Mission and Message of Jesus', unpubl. PhD, Southwestern Baptist Theological Seminary, 1991, p. 169; Ross, R., 'Was Jesus Saying Something or Doing Something?', *BibT.* 41.4, 1990, p. 441; Harrington, D. J., *The Gospel of Matthew.* Liturgical Press, Collegeville, 1991, p. 122; Guelich, *Mark 1–8.26.* p. 88; Edwards, J. R., *The Gospel According to Mark.* Eerdmans, Grand Rapids, 2002, p. 79.

[118] See Mark 3.28 (and Eph. 3.5), the only references in the NT where the plural 'sons of men' is used.

[119] So Boobyer, G. H., 'Mark 2.10a and the Interpretation of the Healing of the Paralytic', *HTR.* 47, 1954, p. 120; Murphy-O'Connor, J., 'Péché et communauté dans le Nouveau Testament', *RB.* 74, 1967, p. 182; Hay, L. S., 'The Son of Man in Mark 2:10 and 2:28', *JBL.* 89, 1970, p. 71; Green, J. B., *The Gospel of Luke.* Eerdmans, Grand Rapids, 1997, p. 242; Kingsbury, J. D., *Conflict in Luke: Jesus, Authorities, Disciples.* Fortress Press, Minneapolis, 1991, pp. 73–8; Blackburn (B. L., *Theios Aner and the Markan Miracle Traditions: A Critique of the Theios Aner Concept as an Interpretative Background of the Miracle Traditions.* Mohr Siebeck, Tübingen, 1990, p. 157) understands this term to inevitably identify Jesus as God in the minds of the hearers; he also draws attention to the *Similitudes of Enoch* 48.5; 62.6, 9 where worship is offered to the Son of Man.

associated with God, with an agenda to wrest power away from illegitimate power bases.[120]

The following occasions in which Mark (2.28) and Luke (6.6) use the title are also in the context of Jesus' authority, this time over the divinely instituted Sabbath (also Matt. 12.8), while Matthew's next reference to the title refers to an eschatological figure, an oblique reference to Jesus (10.23).[121] The phrase 'Son of Man' is thus used by the authors in association with sovereign power and authority, and so it serves, as also in this narrative, to accentuate the authority of Jesus, and thereby his status. This was the term favoured by Jesus to refer to himself, being used over 50 times in the Gospels (excluding parallel references) by Jesus.[122] Matthew uses the title most regularly, though Mark and Luke use it on occasions when Matthew does not.[123]

It is no surprise therefore that the Gospels often use the term in eschatological contexts,[124] though mainly in relationship to the authority of Jesus, as the Son of Man, to forgive sins,[125] over the Sabbath,[126] to eat and drink with whomever he wishes (Luke 7.34–35), to be a sign to 'this generation' (Luke 11.30) and 'to seek and to save the lost' (Luke 19.10). However, also, Jesus radically adds the concept of suffering to the role of the Son of Man.[127] As they will do elsewhere, the writers demonstrate that Jesus is greater than Messiah, and the title 'Son of Man' is used in order to elevate the status of Jesus even higher than Messiah. Here, it is used with reference to the authority to forgive sins, and to be able to do so on

---

[120] Exod. 34.5; Num. 10.34; Ps. 104.3.

[121] As well as being used to refer to the Son of Man being betrayed, suffering and dying, the term is mainly used in Matthew to refer to supernatural events associated with supremacy and authority, including the resurrection of Jesus (12.40; 17.9), authority to sow the seed of the good news (13.37), authority over the angels (13.41), sharing glory with the Father (16.27), owning the kingdom (16.28), the commission to seek and save the lost (18.11), sitting on a throne of glory (19.28; 25.31), returning to the earth (24.27, 37, 39; 24.44) with power and great glory (24.30), and sitting on the right hand of power and coming in the clouds of heaven (26.64).

[122] Matt. 8.20//Luke 9.58; Matt. 10.23; 11.19; 12.40; 13.37; 16.13; Luke 12.8; Matt. 17.9, 12//Mark 9.9, 12; Matt. 17.22//Mark 9.30//Luke 9.43; Matt. 20.18//Mark 10.33//Luke 18.31; Matt. 20.28//Mark 10.45; Matt. 25.37, 39//Luke 17.26, 28; Matt. 26.24//Mark 14.21//Luke 22.22; Matt. 26.45//Mark 14.41.

[123] Mark 8.31//Luke 9.22; Luke 17.25; 18.31–33; 22.22; 24.7.

[124] Matt. 16.27//Mark 8.38//Luke 9.26; Matt. 24.30//Mark 13.26//Luke 21.27; Matt. 26.64//Mark 14.62//Luke 22.60; Matt. 24.44//Luke 12.40; Matt. 24.27//Luke 17.24; Matt. 24.37//Luke 17.26; Matt. 13.41; 19.28; 24.30; 25.31; Luke 12.8; 17.22, 30; 18.8; 21.36.

[125] Matt. 9.6//Mark 2.10//Luke 5.24.

[126] Matt. 12.8//Mark 2.28//Luke 6.5.

[127] Matt. 8.18//Luke 9.58; Mark 8.31//Luke 9.22; Matt. 17.12//Mark 9.12; Matt. 17.22//Mark 9.31//Luke 9.44; Matt. 20.18//Mark 10.33//Luke 18.31; Matt. 20.28//Mark 10.45//Matt. 26.45//Mark 14.41; Matt. 12.40//Luke 11.30; Luke 6.22.

earth, a prerogative of God, not Messiah. Until now, only God's prophetic mediators could operate on his behalf and pray that God would forgive[128] or announce his forgiveness of people, but only when he authorized them so to do (Isa. 33.24). Now, that divine authority is discharged by Jesus on earth. Although forgiveness was anticipated in the future as an eschatological blessing, Jesus grants it in the present.

By claiming to forgive the sins of a sick person who had apparently done nothing to deserve forgiveness, the writers place the person and ministry of Jesus in the centre of focus. Thus, Jesus declares himself to be the initiator of the kingdom of God with the authority to forgive sins on earth.

... to have supernatural insight

Each Synoptist records that Jesus supernaturally,[129] 'in his spirit' (*tō pneumati*, Mark 2.8), knew (*idōn*, literally, 'seeing', from *horaō*, I see) what his accusers were thinking 'in their hearts'. Of significance is the fact that such prescience is elsewhere identified with God;[130] now, it is exhibited by Jesus.

... to heal

Each writer records that the healing was seen by all, and occurred immediately, the man rising and leaving them (Mark and Luke also noting that he carried his mat with him).

... to be worthy of people's trust

The story illustrates that Jesus is worthy of the faith of people and, indeed, is worthier than they initially realized. The identity of the faith affirmed by Jesus and referred to by each of the writers appears again to be linked to the confidence of those concerned to present an insurmountable problem to Jesus, in order that he might solve it. Of interest is the fact that the writers describe Jesus 'seeing' their faith, the same word (*idōn*, aorist participle from *horaō*, 'I see', the aorist indicating a decisive glance) being used of the ability of Jesus to see the hearts of his accusers;[131] the word is again used of the witnesses of the healing, the people

---

[128] Deut. 21.8; 1 Kings 8.30, 34, 39, 50.

[129] It is possible that this is a prophetic insight (Marshall, *Luke*. p. 214) or an awareness based on an observation of the body language of the scribes (so Fitzmyer, *Luke*. p. 581) but the implication of the narratives indicates more than both of these.

[130] 1 Sam. 16.7; 2 Chron. 6.30; Ps. 7.9; Jer. 11.20; *1 Enoch* 84.3; *Pss. Sol.* 9.3; Luke 2.35.

[131] For other examples of similar divine insights by Jesus, see Matt. 27.18; Luke 6.8; 11.17; John 2.24, 25; 6.64; 13.11; 16.19.

concluding that Jesus was worthy of their commendation, resulting in their glorifying God.

Matthew's previous reference to faith (8.10) refers to the confidence of the centurion to trust that Jesus could heal from a distance, while Mark's previous reference to faith (1.15) refers to belief in the gospel; this is Luke's first reference to faith, though earlier references to the act of believing (1.20, 45) are located in the context of trusting God.[132] Faith for the writers refers to a readiness to believe that the one in whom they trust can do that which he says he can do because of his superior status.

Jesus does not forgive the paralytic's sins because of the man's faith. Rather, it is because Jesus recognizes that this was the man's greatest need. Even though the claim that Jesus could forgive sins was shocking, most of the people were prepared to accept the authenticity of such a claim, for each account records the fact that the people 'glorified God',[133] Luke uniquely adding that the man himself also glorified God. This narrative is followed by three narratives in each of the Gospels that call more attention to the authority of Jesus in that he calls a tax-collector to follow him, and eats with tax-collectors, followed by his views concerning fasting.[134] His unusual actions and assertions are to be contextualized in that he functions with complete and unique authority. As such, even though he upsets the status quo, it is to be concluded that he has the right to do so.

Messages from Matthew

Matthew places this story after the exorcism of the Gadarene demoniac (see Table 4.4), the sixth miracle in a group of nine. Jesus has come back, specifically 'to his own city', a phrase only used here in Matthew, earlier identified as Capernaum[135] where he had already achieved many miracles (8.1–17).

Matthew's account is characteristically shorter than those of Mark and Luke. Thus, he omits Markan details, including the fact that there were many present and, unusually, that Jesus was preaching when the healing occurred. He also omits the fact that four men brought the paralytic and

---

[132] See later for faith that Jesus can heal (7.9; 8.48; 17.19; 18.42), and faith that Jesus is worthy of service (7.50) and trust (8.25; 17.5–6; 18.8; 22.32).
[133] Mead (R. T., 'The Healing of the Paralytic: A Unit?', *JBL*. 80, 1961, pp. 353–4) assumes this was due to the healing and the forgiveness of the man.
[134] Matt. 9.14–17; Mark 2.18–22; Luke 5.33–39.
[135] 4.13; 8.5; see also Mark 2.1.

does not mention the disruptive nature of lowering him through the roof. However, he does refer to the fact that the faith of the men is commented on by Jesus.

Matthew more clearly identifies that their faith was exhibited by them coming to Jesus, not by any extra effort involved. His readers are thus presented with Jesus, who willingly responds to people who simply come to him, not (just) those who have overcome arduous obstacles to do so. The authority of Jesus over paralysis is affirmed by Matthew uniquely recording that the man was lying on his bed, providing a graphic description of the man's long-standing condition.

Matthew concentrates on the words spoken or thought, Jesus' words to the paralytic, the conclusion of the religious leaders and the summaries of the astonished crowds. Thus, Matthew records Jesus referring to the paralysed man with the friendly word 'son'[136] (*teknon*, as does Mark). Also, and uniquely, Matthew encourages him to 'take heart' (*tharsei*, from *tharsein*, 'to be courageous, brave'), a term only used by Jesus in Matthew (9.22; 14.27). Matthew reveals Jesus putting the man at ease before he informs him of the sensational news that he is forgiven.

Matthew alone heightens the tension of the confrontation by recording Jesus' assertion that the thoughts of the scribes were evil (9.4). It is not that they were merely mulling over or questioning Jesus' words as one might consider a conundrum; they were functioning with evil intent. Later, Matthew will record Jesus referring to his opponents as being evil.[137]

Matthew concludes his account by referring to the responses of the crowds. He records that the people were struck with fear (*ephobēthēsan*, aorist passive verb from *phobeō*, 'I fear')[138] as a result of what they had witnessed, and concludes with the amazement of the crowd being due to the fact that God 'had given such authority to men'.[139] Given that they have already seen the miraculous authority of Jesus to heal, they must be referring to his authority to forgive sins. Matthew has already recorded

---

[136] Only used elsewhere of Jesus in this form of address in Matthew (23.37) referring to the people of Jerusalem and in Mark (10.24) when addressing his disciples.

[137] 12.34, 39, 45; 16.4.

[138] Some later copyists substituted *ethaumasen* ('they marvelled'). The earlier, more difficult (and therefore more likely to be original) reading, and that more widely attested, is *ephobēthēsan*.

[139] Given that the plural for 'man' is used, Twelftree (G. H., *Jesus the Miracle Worker*. InterVarsity Press, Downers Grove, 1999, p. 117) suggests that it may have a wider application to the disciples and beyond them, to function as a 'paradigm for Matthew's readers in their ministry of healing and forgiveness'. This, however, reads too much into the plural aspect of the term used, for it is more likely that they are astonished that such a divine prerogative should be manifested so completely in a person.

Jesus initiating the kingdom of God (4.23), teaching (4.23; 5.1—7.28), healing (4.23–24; 8.1–16), fulfilling OT prophecy (8.17), identifying himself with the Son of Man (8.18–20), calming a storm (4.23–27) and exorcizing demons (8.28–34). In particular, the people of Capernaum have already witnessed him healing (8.1–17). However, now, the assessment of the people is that Jesus is functioning with a new level of divine authority in that he forgives sins.

Messages from Mark

Despite Jesus having exorcized a demon previously in Capernaum (1.21–28),[140] and healing Simon's mother-in-law (1.30–31) and countless others (1.33–34), it is in this narrative, which also occurred in Capernaum, that Mark records the people saying, 'We never saw anything like this.' Given that they have already witnessed Jesus' miraculous authority, it is probable that Mark also is desirous of indicating the authority of Jesus by his claim to be able to forgive sins.

Mark uniquely places the healing in the context of Jesus preaching, noting that many were listening, so many that some had to listen from outside the house. Mark and Luke record that the paralytic was let down through the roof, Mark more clearly identifying this as an interruption of the preaching of Jesus. Mark captures the force of the occasion by narrating it in the historic present tense,[141] and heightens the intrusive nature of the event by uniquely revealing that there were four others involved and that they 'removed the roof' (*apestegasan tēn stegēn*), indicating a comprehensive achievement, the aorist tense of the verb indicating the rapidity of the action, by making 'an opening' (*exoruksantes*, from *exorussō*, 'I dig'). Such an undertaking may well have been quite challenging as roofs were often substantial, including wooden beams, branches and clay to bind them together and to make it rainproof; on occasion, people ate and slept on the roof. On top of that, they would have had to manhandle the man up the stairs that led to the roof. As with Luke, Mark notes that this action was undertaken out of desperation because they could not otherwise place the man before Jesus. Such determination meant that they were even prepared to disturb Jesus as he preached to a large audience.

Both Mark and Luke emphasize the incongruity of Jesus declaring forgiveness by informing their readers that the scribes qualified their

---

[140] Mark alone mentions Jesus returning to Capernaum where his authority was previously shown.

[141] Each of the verbs in 2.3 is in the present tense, though this is amended in Matthew's rendition to imperfect and perfect tenses, Luke preferring aorist and perfect tenses.

accusation of blasphemy by stating, 'Who can forgive sins but God alone?'[142] In contrast to the antagonism of the scribes, Mark records that 'all the people were amazed'.

Messages from Luke

Luke records this narrative after a record of Jesus preaching (4.42–44), calling his first disciples (5.1–11) and cleansing the leper (5.12–16) (see Table 4.4). Now a fresh opportunity is offered to those who witness the authority of Jesus. This present miracle is then followed (as also in Matthew and Mark) by the call of Levi, characterized by his immediate response, Luke uniquely recording that he left all in order to follow Jesus.[143] The healing of the paralytic is in the context of Jesus teaching (*didaskōn*, from *didaskō*, 'I teach'), as contrasted with Mark's use of *laleō* ('I speak'). Jesus received a large audience, described as having 'come from every village of Galilee and Judaea and from Jerusalem', including 'Pharisees and teachers of the law' who 'were sitting there', Luke clearly, and uniquely, identifying them as intentionally listening to Jesus.

Luke includes the statement that 'the power of the Lord was with him to heal' (5.17). The relationship of power with the Lord is very common in the Bible[144] and there are similar phrases in Numbers 14.17 where Moses requests that 'the power of my Lord be great' and Micah 3.8 where Micah refers to himself as being 'filled with power, with the Spirit of the Lord'; the phrase 'the power of the Lord' is unique in the NT as also is the relationship between the phrase and healing. It is reminiscent of Jesus' earlier reference to the Spirit of the Lord being on him (Luke 4.14, 18), and the centrally important Lucan motif of power associated with Jesus.[145] It is possible that Luke is describing a feature of Jesus' ministry, indicating that he functioned supernaturally, and only intermittently, when he received a special anointing of divine power. However, it is more likely that Luke wishes to indicate that Jesus functions with *divine* power, rather than to imply that this power was not always available to him.

---

[142] The underlying Greek is slightly different in that Mark offers '*tis dunatai aphienai hamartias ei mē eis ho theos*', while Luke reads '*tis dunatai hamartias apheinai ei mē monos ho theos*'. Luke replaces *aphienai* (present infinitive active, suggestive of a forgiveness that has ongoing consequences) with *apheinai* (aorist infinitive active, suggestive of the ability to certainly, at that moment, forgive people). Also Luke replaces *eis ho theos* (literally, 'one God') with *monos ho theos* (literally, 'God alone').

[143] Talbert (C. H., *Reading Luke*. SPCK, London, 1982, p. 63) believes that Luke's purpose in recording the healing of the paralytic followed by the call of Levi is to show Jesus as one who restores social outcasts (cf. 5.12–14, 31–32).

[144] Nahum 1.3, 14; 1 Cor. 5.4, 8; Eph. 6.10; 2 Thess. 1.9; 2 Tim. 1.8; 2 Pet. 1.16.

[145] Luke 1.35; 4.14, 36; 6.19; 8.46; 9.1; 10.19; 21.27; 22.69; 24.49.

Luke, as with Mark, reveals the industriousness of those who brought the paralytic, though he inserts a reference to them removing the 'tiles' (*keramōn*) on the roof to enable the man to be lowered to Jesus, more understandable to Hellenistic readers, though the term may simply refer to the clay tiles sometimes used in Palestine. Luke also notes that the man[146] was placed 'into the midst of Jesus';[147] his companions are determined to ensure that Jesus sees him.

Luke graphically reports that 'amazement seized them all' and also that they were 'filled with awe' (*eplēsthēsan phobou*, from *phobos*, 'fear, awe') though it could be as easily translated as 'filled with fear'. Furthermore, Luke notes that the conclusion of the crowd was that they had seen 'unusual' (*paradoxa*, from *paradoxos*, 'strange, remarkable, wonderful', a word used only here in the NT) events.

Conclusion

The authority of Jesus is of paramount importance in these narratives, in particular as the one who forgives sins, as well as being able to heal, as a result of which people can safely trust him for this life and the next. Although each writer records the presence of faith, faith is not viewed as the catalyst for the healing of the paralytic; neither does Jesus commend his friends for their faith nor, initially, meet their obvious desire for the healing of their companion. The writers identify the authority of Jesus by having him indicate the greater need of the paralytic, for forgiveness, and meeting that first. The healing is granted, second, to prove that Jesus truly has the authority to resolve the more difficult and more important dilemma, the need for forgiveness.

---

[146] This is a term used elsewhere, in the vocative case, in Luke, simply to refer to an anonymous person (12.14; 22.58, 60); it is not a discourteous way of referring to someone. It may be Luke's way of defining the paralytic as a man whereas *teknon* (Matthew/Mark) could suggest a child.

[147] This is the only use of this phrase in the NT with reference to people being presented to Jesus.

Jesus heals a ruler's daughter (Matt. 9.18–19, 23–26// Mark 5.21–24, 35–43//Luke 8.40–42, 49–56)

Table 4.5 Healing a ruler's daughter – the literary context

	Matthew	*Mark*	*Luke*
Jesus calms a storm	8.23–27	4.35–41	8.22–25
Exorcism of a Gadarene/Gerasene demoniac	8.28–34	5.1–20	8.26–39
Healing of a paralytic	9.1–8	(2.1–12)	(5.17–26)
Jesus calls Matthew to be a disciple	9.9	(2.13–14)	(5.27–28)
Jesus eats with tax-collectors and sinners	9.10–13	(2.15–17)	(5.29–32)
Jesus speaks about fasting	9.14–17	(2.18–22)	(5.33–39)
Jesus heals the ruler's daughter	9.18–19, 23–26	5.21–24, 35–43	8.40–42, 49–56
Jesus heals a haemorrhaging woman	9.20–22	5.25–34	8.43–48
Jesus heals two blind men	9.27–31		
Jesus is rejected at Nazareth	(13.53–58)	6.1–6a	(4.16–30)
Jesus restores a dumb demoniac	9.32–34		(11.14–15)
Jesus heals and teaches everywhere	9.35	6.6b	(8.1)
Jesus' compassion on the crowds	9.36	(6.34)	
Too few labourers for the harvest	9.37–38		(10.2)
Jesus commissions the Twelve	10.1, 7–16	6.7–13	9.1–6

Main messages from all the narratives

Jesus' authority over death

Each Synoptist demonstrates a new aspect of the authority of Jesus, here relating to his power over death. Jesus' description of the daughter of a ruler[148] as being asleep should not be taken literally.[149] The authors are clear that she had died, Matthew asserting that she had died before the ruler first met Jesus.[150] However, her death is also indicated by the report of the messengers, the presence of the mourners at the ruler's house, their mocking laughter at Jesus' assertion that she was not dead, and her resurrection by Jesus. The words of Jesus, recorded by each author, indicate his

---

[148] Mark identifies him as 'one of the rulers'.

[149] See its euphemistic use (Matt. 27.52; John 11.11–3; Acts 7.60). Weissenrieder (*Images of Illness*, pp. 259–67) offers extensive comment to support the notion that the girl was suffering from a form of hysteria that was sometimes associated in ancient medical texts with a condition that was exhibited by girls of this age on the cusp of puberty. However, although the attendees assume that Jesus thinks the daughter is asleep, it is unlikely that this is the case, given the other data in the narrative that indicate that a death has occurred.

[150] Mark and Luke refer to her being close to death when the ruler first met Jesus.

authority over death, as easy for him to achieve as it would be to wake someone from sleep.

The fact that Jesus removed the crowd is not made explicit in Luke, though it is in Matthew and Mark. It is unlikely that the people's mocking of Jesus would have restricted Jesus in his achieving of the miracle. There is no record anywhere else in the Gospels of someone restricting Jesus in restoring another; rather, he is presented as being in charge of his own divinely inspired agenda. The exclusion of the public is often recorded in healing accounts,[151] though here no reason is offered. It is probable that Jesus' instruction is based on the size of the crowd and the room in which the girl was laid, the noise of the flutes at funerals, referred to by Matthew (also 11.17), and the loud weeping and wailing (Mark, Luke); already with Jesus, his three disciples and the parents, the room would have been congested.

Not only is Jesus portrayed as having authority over death, but it is in the context of no one else being able to function thus. Although a few people may have claimed healing and exorcistic powers, raising people from the dead was of a different order.[152] In this context, it is valuable to note that each author records that, as an element of the resurrection, Jesus takes the girl's hand, though this is not to raise her to her feet, each stating that she rose of her own accord. The use of Jesus' hands may again therefore be taken to imply a transfer of supernatural healing power and an affirmation of his authority. Earlier, Matthew and Mark note the ruler's request that Jesus lay his hand on the daughter, indicating that already in the ministry of Jesus this aspect was increasingly common. However, touching a corpse meant that Jesus would have been ceremonially defiled for seven days and obliged to be ritually cleansed (Num. 19.11–22). That Jesus deliberately touched the corpse must be intended to demonstrate an aspect of his personal authority that indicates that he is not bound by God's laws, but also that he had come to establish a new order where neither ceremonial defilement nor death could obstruct him.

The importance of faith

The faith of the man is first revealed by his willingness to ask Jesus for help even though his daughter was close to death (Mark 5.23; Luke 8.42), as a result of which Jesus went towards his house. His faith in Jesus is further defined by the fact that he still trusted that Jesus could restore his daughter

---

[151] 1 Kings 17.19; 2 Kings 4.4, 33; Matt. 7.33; 8.23; Acts 9.40.
[152] b. *Meg.* 7b refers to a resurrection apparently achieved by a rabbi.

even though she subsequently died,[153] against the advice of people who encouraged him to give up his hope in Jesus. His belief that Jesus had the authority to resolve his dilemma still held firm. This is a story that demonstrates the authority of Jesus over death and focuses on a man who believed that Jesus could achieve the impossible, an act achieved rarely in the OT, but nowhere with the ease of achievement as demonstrated by Jesus.

Messages from Matthew
Jesus' authority over death
Matthew precedes this story uniquely with accounts which demonstrate various examples of the power of Jesus, comprising his authority to cast out demons (8.28–34), to heal, to forgive sins (9.1–8), to choose disciples (9.9), to eat with whomever he wishes (9.10–13), and to determine whether to fast or not (9.14–17). Now, he reveals another level of the authority of Jesus, over death.

Matthew provides the shortest of the three accounts of this miracle, omitting the age of the girl, the reference to the crowds present, the name of the ruler, that he was a ruler of the synagogue, the message to the ruler informing him of his daughter's death, the words of Jesus to the ruler to believe, the fact that Jesus takes Peter, James and John with him, that these disciples and the father and mother went into the dead girl's room, the fact that Jesus spoke in association with the restoration, and the command not to tell anyone about the miracle.

Instead, he truncates the story and starts from the point where the child has already died. Then, he concentrates on the respectful request of the ruler, and his belief that Jesus can restore life to his daughter. Instead of the crowds following Jesus (Mark), Matthew informs his readers that Jesus followed the ruler, the only time this occurs in his Gospel.[154] Previously, Matthew followed Jesus (9.9), and afterwards the blind men followed Jesus (9.27), but on this occasion Jesus leaves his 'unfinished' teaching of the disciples of John the Baptist (9.14–17) and follows the one who needs his touch, ready to respond to his request.

Matthew records that the ruler knelt (*prosekunei*, imperfect tense from *proskuneō*, 'I kneel, worship')[155] before Jesus, so demonstrating his respect

---

[153] Matt. 9.18; Mark 5.35; Luke 8.49.

[154] Matthew often refers to people following Jesus (4.20, 25; 8.1, 23; 9.9, 27; 12.15; 14.3; 19.2, 27; 20.29, 34; 21.9; 26.58; 27.55).

[155] Although the word could be translated 'worship' (so KJV), the context does not indicate that the ruler assumed that Jesus was worthy of worship at this stage (see also 8.2; 15.25), whereas the context indicates such a translation elsewhere (2.2, 8; 4.9, 10).

for him but also a recognition of his authority. This authority of Jesus then becomes the focus of the narrative, for despite the mocking unbelief of the people, Jesus easily raises the girl from the dead, with no words spoken and no disciples to help, and simply by his touch of her hand.

Instead of a potential development in the faith of the ruler being mentioned (as in Mark and Luke), from a belief that Jesus can heal to a belief that he can raise from the dead, the ruler is simply identified as believing that Jesus can do the latter. Surprisingly, there is no commendation from Jesus, despite the man's trust in Jesus. Matthew maintains his focus on Jesus, not the girl (who is passive), the disciples (who are not present), the mourners (who were worthy of reprimand) or even the ruler. Instead, Jesus is central to the narrative, being the subject of nearly every sentence. The message relating to Jesus' authority is further developed by Matthew in the stories that follow in which Jesus heals two blind men and exorcizes a dumb demoniac (see Table 4.5). Thereafter, Matthew alone records Jesus teaching, preaching and healing 'every disease and every affliction' (9.35).

Messages from Mark and Luke

There are many similarities between Mark and Luke, supportive of their being explored together. Both place this account after the stories of Jesus calming the storm and casting out demons from the Gadarene/Gerasene demoniac (see Table 4.5). The authority of Jesus is now further enhanced by his ability to overcome death. With such a history, it is not surprising that they both record that a crowd had gathered, Mark noting twice that it was a great crowd (5.21, 24), Luke recording that not only did the crowd welcome him but also the people were waiting for him (8.40). Mark records that the event took place by the sea[156] (of Galilee) after Jesus had crossed it by boat.

The faith of the man

Both identify the man who requested that Jesus restore his 12-year-old daughter[157] as Jairus, Stein[158] drawing attention to the possibility that the name may be a transliteration of the Aramaic for 'he enlightens', speaking

---

[156] Mark uses the feature of the sea as a literary device and associates it with key events in Jesus' mission (to call disciples, 1.16; to teach, 2.13; 4.1; to restore people, 5.1; 7.31).

[157] The reference to 12 helps to further associate this with the narrative of the haemorrhaging woman who had suffered for 12 years, a fact that each of the Synoptists includes; b. *Ket.* 39a indicates that aged up to 11 years and one day, a female child was deemed a girl, but from thereon until she reached 12 years and one day, she was identified as a virgin and thereafter could marry (b. *Sanh.* 66b).

[158] Stein, *Mark.* p. 266; he concludes, however, that this is too subtle a suggestion, noting that if the writers had wanted the readers to benefit from this feature, they would have made it clear for the non-Aramaic speakers among them.

of Jehovah.[159] Both also record that he was a ruler of the synagogue[160] who, on seeing Jesus, fell at his feet,[161] begging Jesus to come with him. His situation is thus graphically presented as one who owns a position of prestige but who, despite his status, faces a trauma affecting his young, dying daughter, Luke characteristically identifying her as his only daughter.[162]

While Jesus was speaking to the woman who had suffered with a haemorrhage, the man was informed of the death of the daughter, with the recommendation that he should give up on his quest to get help from Jesus. While Mark records that the daughter had died (*apethanen*, aorist tense from *apothnēskō*, 'I die'), indicating that she had definitely died, Luke records the perfect tense (*tethnēken*, from *thnēskō*, 'I die'), indicating the finality of death, that she had died and remained dead.[163] In the first of three statements by Jesus recorded by Mark and Luke, Jesus says to the ruler, 'Do not fear (*mē phobou*, present continuous imperative from *phobeomai*, 'I fear'), only believe' (Mark offers *pisteue*, imperative present continuous active; Luke offers *pisteuson*, imperative aorist active from *pisteuō*, 'I believe'), Luke adding, 'and she will be well' (*sōthēsetai*, future tense of *sōzō*, 'I save').

Jesus encourages the ruler not to fear, though one might have expected Jesus to have exhorted him not to doubt, doubt being the opposite of belief. However, the fear relates to the man's apprehension that he probably felt due to an assumption that the death of his daughter indicated that it was now too late for Jesus to help. Instead, he is encouraged not to have more faith but to have no fear. He has already expressed faith by coming to Jesus and requesting help; Jesus is not encouraging him to exert a deeper or stronger faith. Rather, Jesus encourages him to simply maintain his faith that he can help, even in the face of death.

Jesus' authority over death

Jesus is described as taking Peter, James and John,[164] and the parents, into the child's room, where he speaks to her. Although the writers do not explain this feature, it is possible that it is intended to enable them to

---

[159] Num. 32.41; Josh. 13.30.
[160] To marry the daughter of such a person was considered an honour, b. *Pes.* 49b.
[161] It is impossible to determine whether references to falling down before Jesus (Mark 1.40; 5.6–7, 33–34; 7.25, 28; 10.7; 15.9–10) reflected an attitude of worship and, since it is not explicitly presented as such, it is more appropriate to view it as showing respect.
[162] 7.12; 9.38.
[163] Note also that Luke revises the order by placing *tethnēken* before the subject 'your daughter' for emphasis.
[164] Elsewhere, these three are with Jesus on special occasions (9.2; 14.33).

witness the miracle at first hand, of importance to his disciples who will be granted similar authority later. The Aramaic words of Jesus (*talitha cumi*[165]) that Mark includes are omitted by Matthew and Luke, Luke simply offering a truncated translation, followed by her immediate restoration to life. Luke records that the restoration occurs as a result of her spirit returning, in response to Jesus' words. Although this could refer to her (disembodied) spirit returning to her body, it is more likely to be simply descriptive of the fact that life returned to her when Jesus 'called it back'.[166] Although each Synoptist confirms the resurrection, Mark adds that the girl walked, while both Mark and Luke note that she arose immediately, and that the parents were amazed at the transformation that had occurred simply at the words of Jesus.[167]

Both then record Jesus instructing that the girl be given something to eat (mentioned first in Luke who typically reveals Jesus caring for the vulnerable) and that no one should speak of the miracle; as mentioned before, this was probably due to the concern of Jesus that such miracles would begin to dominate people's expectations of his mission rather than his other aspirations. Both Mark and Luke soon follow this narrative with the commissioning of the Twelve when the authority demonstrated by Jesus here is delegated to his followers, though Mark separates the two sections with Jesus' rejection by his own people in Nazareth, in which the privilege of the Twelve is contrasted with the missed opportunity by those who had known him the longest (see Table 4.5).

Conclusion

The story demonstrates again the authority of Jesus, this time over death, and the importance of faith, identified as the action of the ruler in coming to Jesus for help.

---

[165] The incorporation of translated Aramaic is a characteristic of Mark (3.17; 7.11, 34; 10.46; 14.36; 15.22, 34).

[166] Van der Loos, *Miracles of Jesus*. p. 571.

[167] Mark presents their amazement as *exestēsan ekstasei megalē*, literally, 'they were amazed with great amazement'.

Jesus heals a woman with a haemorrhage
(Matt. 9.20–22//Mark 5.25–34//Luke 8.43–48)

Table 4.6 Healing a woman with a haemorrhage – the literary context

	Matthew	Mark	Luke
Jesus calms a storm	8.23–27	4.35–41	8.22–25
Exorcism of a Gadarene/Gerasene demoniac	8.28–34	5.1–20	8.26–39
Healing of a paralytic	9.1–8	(2.1–12)	(5.17–26)
Jesus calls Matthew to be a disciple	9.9	(2.13–14)	(5.27–28)
Jesus eats with tax-collectors and sinners	9.10–13	(2.15–17)	(5.29–32)
Jesus speaks about fasting	9.14–17	(2.18–22)	(5.33–39)
Jesus heals the ruler's daughter	9.18–19, 23–26	5.21–24, 35–43	8.40–42, 49–56
Jesus heals a haemorrhaging woman	**9.20–22**	**5.25–34**	**8.43–48**
Jesus heals two blind men	9.27–31		
Jesus is rejected at Nazareth	(13.53–58)	6.1–6a	(4.16–30)
Jesus restores a dumb demoniac	9.32–34		(11.14–15)
Jesus heals and teaches everywhere	9.35	6.6b	(8.1)
Jesus' compassion on the crowds	9.36	(6.34)	
Too few labourers for the harvest	9.37–38		(10.2)
Jesus commissions the Twelve	10.1, 7–16	6.7–13	9.1–6

Main messages from all the narratives

The combination of this healing with the restoration of the ruler's daughter

Each of the Synoptists combines the story of the restoration of the ruler's daughter with the healing of an unnamed woman who had experienced a blood disorder for 12 years (see Table 4.6). A number of reasons may be adduced for this, the most basic one being that Matthew and Luke had simply copied what was in Mark's account.[168] Thus, the reason for the combination may be best identified in determining Mark's rationale. Powers argues that the combination of the two accounts suggests that Jesus may be drawing attention to the changed status of women in his new order.[169] Thus, for example, in contrast to the leper (Matt. 8.4) who is instructed to show himself to the priest, the woman is not given any such command, despite the Levitical instructions so to do (15.28–30).

---

[168] Emphases, including salvation (Mark 5.23, 28, 34) and faith (Mark 5.34, 36), are present in both; Dwyer (*Motif of Wonder*. p. 116) notes that both women were unclean (by blood and death respectively); each was helpless (vv. 23, 26), and each is described as 'daughter' (vv. 23, 34–35).

[169] Powers, J. E., '"Your Daughters Shall Prophesy": Pentecostal Hermeneutics and the Empowerment of Women', in *The Globalization of Pentecostalism*. (eds) Dempster, M. W., Klaus, B. D., Petersen, D., Regnum, Oxford, 1999, pp. 326–8.

A central element of both stories is the motif of touch. Each author records that the ruler requested that Jesus touch his daughter, or that Jesus touched her, and that the haemorrhaging woman touched Jesus, both actions indicating faith on the part of those who desired a response from Jesus and both preceding the restorations. Matthew and Mark record the woman's words concerning her determination to touch Jesus, while Mark and Luke record that the crowd pressed upon him. Each Synoptist refers to Jesus' question as to who touched him (twice in Luke), followed by the disciples repeating his question, Luke concluding that the woman confessed that she had touched Jesus. Touch was the catalyst that resulted in the women being restored to life and health, the termination of their ritually unclean designations, and the removal of obstacles that hindered integration in their communities.

The authority of Jesus to heal and incorporate the outcast

The physical condition[170] from which the woman had suffered made her maritally ineligible (since the condition precluded intercourse (Lev. 15.24)) and ceremonially unclean and thus in danger of defiling those who came into contact with her.[171] Indeed, her social predicament was more distressing than her physical condition, which was not life-threatening. The fact that each of the writers reports that she had suffered for 12 years further indicates the incurable nature of the illness, affirmed by Luke's comment that no one could heal her, Mark mentioning that her condition had worsened despite her spending all her money on many doctors.[172]

In the adjoining story, Jesus' mission to a ruler's daughter is interrupted by the touch of a marginalized woman. A ruler of a synagogue, who comes

---

[170] Probably vaginal bleeding.

[171] Lev. 12.1–8; 15.7, 11–30; 20.18; Levine (A.-J., 'Discharging Responsibility: Matthean Jesus, Biblical Law, and Hemorrhaging Woman', in *Treasures Old and New: Contributions to Matthean Studies.* (eds) Bauer, D. R., Powell, M. A., Scholars Press, Atlanta, 1996, pp. 379–98) contends that the evidence to suggest that menstruants were ostracized in Jewish society is exaggerated, basing her evidence on Lev. 15.19–33 and b. *Ket.* 61a which states that a menstruating woman may attend to all the needs of her husband except filling his cup with wine, washing him and making his bed. However, the evidence is not so clear. Lev. 18.19; 20.18 promises divine judgement for partners who participate in intercourse when the woman is menstruating, and other texts identify many restrictions placed on menstruating women (Ezek. 36.17; Jos., *Wars* 5.227; Selvidge, M. L., *Woman, Cult and Miracle Recital: A Redactional Critical Investigation of Mark 5.24–34.* Bucknell University Press, Lewisburg, 1990, p. 83; Selvidge, M. L., 'Mark 5.24–34 and Leviticus 15.19–20: A Reaction to Restrictive Purity Regulations', *JBL.* 103, 1984, pp. 619–23).

[172] Although only a minority of translations (KJV, ESV) include the words, 'and though she had spent all her living on physicians', on the basis of the manuscript evidence the majority of Metzger's committee (*A Textual Commentary.* p. 145) decided to retain the words in the text, though to enclose them in a box to indicate the uncertainty surrounding their presence.

to Jesus publicly, with an urgent need due to the terminal nature of his daughter's condition, and falls before him, has to wait while Jesus ministers to a physically, socially and financially disadvantaged woman who, hidden in a crowd, skirts behind Jesus and bends to touch his garment.[173] Then, Jesus focuses publicly and first on the woman and frees her from her disability, thus providing a message of hope to all who are burdened,[174] while the ruler's daughter dies in the process.

In this and the surrounding story, Mark and Luke identify the haemorrhaging woman as the only one who trembles before Jesus. However, Jesus does not condemn her for her presence among the crowd, which may suggest his readiness to overlook the seriousness of the law which forbade her from being there; more importantly, it indicates his readiness to include the excluded. The crowd fills the space around him, but she becomes central to the story and, for a moment, it is as if the world stands still while Jesus focuses on her and her need.

Each Synoptist, in his reponse to his question, 'Who touched me?', records Jesus offering further truth of positive benefit to the woman, namely her status as 'daughter'. It is significant that each of the authors specifies that a daughter of a ruler was the object of Jesus' care; the same term is now used to refer to an impoverished woman who is healed of her haemorrhage.

The significance of the woman's faith

Each of the Synoptists records the words of Jesus to the woman, 'your faith has made you well' (*sesōken*, perfect active tense from *sōzō*, 'I save'), the perfect tense indicating a permanent restoration.[175] Given that this represents the only clause identically reported by all three Synoptists, it is clear that all three wanted to emphasize that faith has the capacity to heal and save.

---

[173] The record in Mark and Luke that the dying girl was 12 years old while the woman's illness had lasted for 12 years suggests that there is a deliberate contrast, contrasting the 12 years of privilege enjoyed by the ruler's daughter with the destitution suffered by the woman over a similar period; Borg (M., *Jesus in Contemporary Scholarship*. Trinity International Press, Valley Forge, 1994, p. 26) concludes that Jesus substitutes a system of purity with one of compassion.

[174] Cf. Wahlberg, R. C., *Jesus Freed the Woman*. Paulist Press, New York, 1978, pp. 19–21; Mkole (J. C. L., 'A Liberating Women's Profile in Mk. 5.25–34', *ACS*. 13.2, 1997, pp. 36–47) views the passage as the basis for a paradigm for women's liberation in an African Christian context.

[175] The Synoptists elsewhere use the term *sōzō* to refer to non-physical salvation (Matt. 1.21; 10.22; 16.25; 18.11; 19.25), though also to physical healing (Matt. 8.25; 14.30; 27.40, 42, 49). The context must decide, and here it, at least, appears that the reference is to her physical healing and consequent re-admittance into normal society.

Each of the writers also notes that the woman came from behind in order to touch Jesus. This should not be viewed as a sign of her lack of faith (in that she did not present herself to him for his help); rather, it is to be understood as due to her recognition that she should not even have been there, ritually contaminating others in the crowd as well as Jesus (Lev. 15.19–27). Thus, she touched Jesus in a way that would avoid public attention.[176] Such faith is proven to be well placed, for it resulted in her healing and commendation, and is affirmed as such by Jesus.

Mark records that the woman touched Jesus' garment, but Matthew and Luke state that she touched only the fringe (*kraspedou*),[177] possibly to dispel any suggestion that she had grasped Jesus' clothes or, more presumptuously, had touched him; instead, they emphasize that she touched the lowest part of his garments, the part that drifted through the dust. It is also possible that the woman sought to touch the tassels that were added to the hem of garments to remind Jews of their obligation to obey God who brought them out of bondage in Egypt (Num. 15.38–41). Thus, Matthew and Luke may be reminding their readers of her desire to be freed from her physical bondage. Such was her faith in Jesus' power that she believed she would be cured simply by touching his clothes, viewed as an extension of himself. Matthew emphasizes the accuracy of her understanding, recording her belief that 'only' (*monon*) a touch was needed.

The fact that she touched his clothes does not inevitably confirm a magical or superstitious belief on her part, any more than the use of touch by Jesus suggests a belief in magic on his part.[178] Rather, all the Gospel authors not only record that Jesus commended her action and identified it as faith, but also, they do not indicate that he corrected her action or encouraged her to have faith or more faith. The affirmation of Jesus did

---

[176] Tipei (J. F., *The Laying On of Hands in the New Testament: Its Significance, Techniques, and Effects*. University Press of America, Lanham, 2008, p. 123) refers to her 'stealing her healing', coming from behind Jesus, though this, incorrectly, assumes an unwillingness on the part of Jesus to heal her.

[177] Reflective of Saul who grasped (and tore) the edge of Samuel's robe (1 Sam. 15.27). Vermes (G., *The Religion of Jesus the Jew*. Fortress Press, Minneapolis, 1993, p. 16) draws attention to the account of Honi the circle-drawer (b. *Ta'an*. 23b); the fringe of his cloak is grasped by children who ask him to send rain.

[178] Some (e.g. Morris, L., *The Gospel According to Matthew*. Eerdmans, Grand Rapids, 1992, p. 229; cf. France, R. T., *Matthew*. IVP, Leicester, 1985, p. 171) question the quality of her faith while others (Bruner, *Christbook*. p. 429; Patte, D., *The Gospel According to Matthew*. Fortress Press, Philadelphia, 1987, p. 132; Lane, *Mark*. p. 192; Hull, J. M., *Hellenistic Magic and the Synoptic Tradition*. SCM, London, 1974. p. 136; Aune, D., 'Magic in Early Christianity', in *Aufstieg und Niedergang der römischen Welt*. De Gruyter, Berlin, 1980. pp. 550–70) conclude that she engaged in a quasi-magical act that demonstrates the deficiency of her faith.

not confer faith on her action; albeit tentative on her part, her action received the highest approval of Jesus who identified it as an act of faith.

It was not her action of touching Jesus that resulted in the healing but the belief in Jesus that motivated it. Resulting from that belief, each writer records Jesus attributing her healing to her faith. Although, on other occasions, Jesus heals with no faith being identified by the sufferer, when people expressed faith that he could help them he often affirmed their trust, as it indicated that they had recognized the ease of receiving from Jesus that which would do them good. Her action was prompted by the same quality of faith recorded of others, including the ruler in the associated story, who came to Jesus, believing that he could resolve an impossible situation. While Mark and Luke include Jesus' words to her, 'go in peace', Matthew precedes Jesus' words with the exhortation that she should 'take heart'.

Messages from Matthew

Matthew precedes this story uniquely with accounts which demonstrate various examples of the authority of Jesus, comprising his ability to cast out demons (8.28–34), to heal, and most importantly, to forgive sins (9.1–8), to choose disciples (9.9), to eat with whomever he wishes (9.10–13), and to determine whether to fast or not (9.14–17).[179] Before he reveals Jesus' authority over death, he now first reveals his authority to heal and restore a woman who has been bound by a condition that has affected her physically, emotionally and religiously, privately and publicly.

Again, it is what Matthew omits that is often as valuable as what he includes. Thus, it is interesting to note that he excludes data concerning the crowd who followed Jesus, the incurability and worsening nature of the woman's condition, that she had spent all her money on therapies, that she had heard reports about Jesus, the recognition of Jesus that 'power had gone out of him', Jesus' question as to who touched him, the response of the disciples, his looking around to see who had touched him, and the fearful, voluntary confession of the woman that she had touched him.

Instead, he briefly explains her physical need, describing it as 'a discharge of blood' (*haimorrousa*, from *haimorroēō*, 'I bleed, haemorrhage') as contrasted with Mark and Luke (*en rhusei haimatos*, literally, 'in a flow of blood'). Then, he concentrates exclusively on her statement and the healing words of Jesus. The fact that Matthew alone records that her words were 'to

---

[179] Twelftree (*Jesus the Miracle Worker*. p. 118) draws attention to the probability that the author is linking the story with what has preceded it, where Jesus (vv. 14–17) indicates that Judaism cannot contain the ministry of Jesus.

herself' means that the only words spoken aloud are those of Jesus. Also, Matthew (in contrast to Mark and Luke) precedes the healing with the words of Jesus, probably to demonstrate that although the touch of the woman was significant, it was the words of Jesus that were of central importance. In Matthew's record, Jesus is presented as being in charge of the restorative process, the healing only occurring after Jesus had spoken. By contrast, Mark and Luke record that the healing occurred as a result of the woman touching Jesus and before he spoke to her. For Matthew, it was the power of Jesus, manifested in his words, that effected the healing.

The central message relating to Jesus' authority is further developed by Matthew in the stories that follow in which Jesus heals two blind men and exorcizes a dumb demoniac (9.27–34) (see Table 4.6). Thereafter, Matthew alone records Jesus teaching, preaching and healing 'every disease and every affliction' (9.35).

Messages from Mark and Luke

Because of the significant similarities between Mark and Luke, they will be considered together. Both place this narrative immediately after the stories of Jesus calming the storm and casting out demons from a demoniac (see Table 4.6), demonstrating his ability to overcome nature and demons. Before they reveal the authority of Jesus over humanity's greatest enemy, death, they, with Matthew, include a story of a marginalized woman who perceives that Jesus' authority can be actively accessed.

More than Matthew, they graphically highlight the woman's helplessness. Jesus is her last resort and, despite the injunctions relating to her ceremonial uncleanness, she feels she has no choice but to touch Jesus' clothes; Mark uniquely records that 'she had heard reports about Jesus' which had fuelled her motivation to act thus. Her faith acts as a searchlight to illuminate his authority.

Although Matthew records that the healing occurred immediately after Jesus identifies her action as evidence of faith, Mark and Luke assert that she was healed immediately after she touched Jesus, Mark recording that she knew that she had been healed. As evidence of the healing, Mark and Luke record that Jesus knew that power had gone from him, Luke locating this in a statement by Jesus. At the same time at which she knew she had been healed, Jesus knew that healing power had left him.[180] The association of power with Jesus is often located in Luke,[181] though the notion that

---

[180] Although *ek* generally means 'out of' and *apo* generally means 'from', *ek* often also means 'from'.
[181] Luke 4.14, 36; 5.17; 9.1; 10.19; 21.27; 22.69; 24.49; Acts 1.8; 3.12; 6.8; 10.38.

power came from Jesus and resulted in healing is only present elsewhere in the NT in Luke 6.19. It is possible that this information is omitted by Matthew because it might suggest to his readers that Jesus' power functions as a numinous force over which he has no control.[182] It is preferable to understand Luke desiring to reflect the fact that it was supernatural power that had achieved the miracle, albeit owned by Jesus.

Although it is possible that Jesus was perplexed as to what had happened, asking his disciples to help identify the person who had drained his power from him, this is unlikely for a number of reasons. Primarily, Jesus has already been revealed as someone who has supernatural insight.[183] In association with this, both Mark and Luke refer to Jesus using the singular pronoun in asking who touched him. Mark's reference to the fact that 'he looked around to see who had done it' (5.32)[184] and Luke's comment that the woman realized that she had not escaped the notice of Jesus (8.40) demonstrate that Jesus knew more than his question indicated. Thus, it is probable that his question was intended to give the woman the opportunity to publicly confess her action. More importantly, it provided an opportunity for Jesus to explain its significance as a manifestation of her faith in him, especially given that there is no record of any others who may have touched him, due to their proximity to him, being healed by him on this occasion.[185]

Both Mark and Luke record the woman falling down before Jesus and trembling, Mark also adding that she was afraid. She may have feared that she had defiled him,[186] or was simply afraid because of the power available to the one who had asked her to identify herself. Whatever the cause, Jesus responds by providing peace, as an antidote to fear.

As elsewhere (cf. 17.13–19), Luke uses different words to describe the healing process. In referring to the fact that no one could heal her, Luke (8.43) uses *therapeuō* ('I heal'), followed by *iaomai* (8.47) with reference to her physical healing. However, when he records the words of Jesus, he

---

[182] Gundry (*Mark*. p. 270) argues, 'Mark portrays Jesus as so charged with power that it will go out from him even apart from his will.'

[183] Mark 2.8; 3.5; Luke 5.22; 6.8.

[184] It may be significant to note that Mark, by the use of the feminine '*ten*' (v. 32), implies that Jesus was at least aware that the one who touched him was a woman.

[185] See also Mark 3.9–10 referring to crowds seeking to touch Jesus, though there is no record that they were healed as a result.

[186] Cf. Mann, C. S., *Mark: A New Translation with Introduction and Commentary*. Doubleday, Garden City, 1986, p. 286; Loader (W., 'Challenged at the Boundaries: A Conservative Jesus in Mark's Tradition', *JSNT*. 63, 1966, p. 58), without evidence, suggests Jesus responded angrily because the woman had broken the Torah, despite which he healed her.

(with Matthew and Mark) uses, 'I save' (*sōzō*).[187] This may indicate, for Luke, that another level of restoration has taken place – a physical healing and social restoration for a physically and socially marginalized person but also a spiritual restoration. This, allied with Jesus' recommendation to 'go in peace', may indicate more than the woman's physical healing.[188] Her faith coalesces with Jesus' desire to restore and incorporate an outcast. Even though seven days were needed according to the law (Lev. 15.28) before healing could be officially pronounced, Jesus is presented as identifying that the process has already been completed.

Both Mark and Luke follow this narrative with the resurrection of the ruler's daughter and then the commissioning of the Twelve when the authority demonstrated by Jesus here is delegated to his followers, though Mark separates the two sections with Jesus' rejection by his own people in Nazareth (see Table 4.6). This particular story of the woman who accessed her healing from Jesus contrasts with the people of Nazareth who missed the opportunity to benefit from the authority of Jesus; she demonstrates a readiness to recognize his status as being higher than it was in the estimation of those who should have known him best.

Conclusion

The healing of the woman demonstrates Jesus' readiness to heal and redeem marginalized people, even when their expressions of faith seem to fall short of what would be expected.

---

[187] Matthew (9.21, 22) and Mark (5.28, 34) use *sōzō* with reference to her healing, Mark also using *iaomai* (5.29).

[188] Guelich (*Mark*. p. 299) describes the phrase as expressing a common Semitic farewell, as does Robbins (V., 'The Woman Who Touched Jesus' Garments: Socio-rhetorical Analysis of the Synoptic Accounts', *NTS*. 33, 1987, p. 510); however, it is significant to note that the other references to peace in Luke have possible soteriological contexts (1.79; 2.14, 29(30); 7.50; 8.48; 10.5–6); similarly, Hagner (*Matthew 1–13*. p. 249) feels the threefold use of the term *sōzō* in Matthew is to indicate that a deeper salvation is here being offered as well as physical healing.

Jesus heals a withered hand (Matt. 12.9–14//
Mark 3.1–6//Luke 6.6–11)

Table 4.7 Healing a man with a withered hand – the literary context

	Matthew	Mark	Luke
Jesus condemns cities which had rejected him	11.20–24		(10.13–16)
Jesus calls Matthew and eats with tax-collectors	(9.9–13)	2.13–17	5.27–32
Jesus teaches about fasting	(9.14–17)	2.18–22	5.33–39
Jesus calls for people to come to him and rest	11.25–30		
Plucking grain on the Sabbath	12.1–8	2.23–28	6.1–5
The healing of the withered hand	**12.9–14**	**3.1–6**	**6.6–11**
Jesus fulfils Isaianic prophecy	12.15–21		
Jesus restores a blind and dumb demoniac	12.22–23		(11.14)
Jesus is accused of being empowered by Beelzebul	12.24–32	(3.22–27)	(11.15–23)
Jesus speaks about the importance of fruitful lives	12.33–37		(6.43–45)
Jesus denounces the Pharisees' request for signs	12.38–42	(8.11–12)	(11.29–32)
Jesus teaches about a returning unclean spirit	12.43–45		(11.24–26)
Jesus identifies his 'true' family as doing God's will	12.46–50	(3.31–35)	(8.19–21)
Parables of the kingdom	13.1–51	(4.1–25, 30–34)	(8.4–18)
Rejection of Jesus by his countrymen	13.52–58	(6.1–6)	(4.16–30)
Jesus heals many by the sea	(4.24–25)	3.7–12	6.17–19
Jesus commissions the Twelve	(10.7–11, 14)	(6.7–13)	(9.1–6)
Death of John the Baptist	14.1–12	(6.14–29)	(9.7–9)
Jesus chooses the Twelve	(10.1–4)	3.13–19	6.12–16

Main messages from all the narratives

Each Gospel records this healing after the Pharisees question Jesus concerning the legality of his disciples picking grain on the Sabbath (see Table 4.7). Although Jesus had healed on previous occasions, this is the first time that he is recorded as publicly healing on the Sabbath.[189] The healing of the

---

[189] Mark and Luke (Mark 1.21–26//Luke 4.31–36 record Jesus casting out a demon on the Sabbath and Mark 1. 29–31//Luke 4.38–39 record the private healing of Peter's mother-in-law which appears to have taken place on a Sabbath.

withered hand on the Sabbath provides the watchers with another opportunity to determine if they are prepared to accept Jesus' authority to decide what is legitimate activity on the Sabbath.

Each of the three accounts agrees on the physical condition of the man's hand,[190] that the healing took place in a synagogue,[191] the accusatory[192] nature of the Pharisees,[193] that the healing occurred on the Sabbath,[194] the command to the man, 'Stretch out your hand', the rapid ease of Jesus in restoring the man's hand, and the malevolent discussion of the Pharisees concerning Jesus. Not only does Jesus contradict their Sabbath beliefs by healing the man, but he also identifies healing on the Sabbath as doing good.[195] The Talmud later discusses, at great length, permissible activities on the Sabbath, a whole tractate being given to this topic. In particular, such rabbinic traditions forbade offering therapy to sick Jews on the Sabbath unless their life was in danger.[196]

Although the man with the withered hand is healed, he is not the central person in the narrative. Motifs present with reference to others whom Jesus heals elsewhere are missing here, including a request to be healed, Jesus touching the man, a reference to his faith, a recognition concerning the identity of Jesus, appreciation on his part after he is healed, any expression of amazement or wonder by those who witnessed the miracle, and any commissions by Jesus. Little information is given concerning the man

---

[190] Although two different terms are used (Matthew and Luke refer to the hand as *xēran* (from *xeros*, 'dry, withered, paralysed'); Mark uses the term *exērammenēn*, perfect passive participle of *xērainō*, 'I dry up'), both relate to the concept of being dried up or perished; some sort of paralysis is intended. Luke also describes it as the man's right hand. A similar restoration is described in 1 Kings 13.6–7 where a man of God prays for Jeroboam's withered hand to be restored, and *Test. Sim.* 2.11–14 where a withered hand is restored, as a result of Simeon's prayer. Of course, Jesus has no need to pray for this restoration and he simply effects it.

[191] Luke uniquely records that Jesus was teaching in the synagogue, though he does not record that the Pharisees were listening to him, simply that they were watching him to see if he would heal.

[192] The Pharisees have asked questions of Jesus before, concerning his actions, but this is the first time that they do so in order to accuse him; the conflict is becoming clearer.

[193] Luke also refers to the presence of some scribes.

[194] Mark records the word 'Sabbath' twice, Matthew and Luke referring to it three times in the narrative.

[195] Matthew presents Jesus affirming the Sabbath as the appropriate day for doing good, while Mark and Luke imply this in the questions that Jesus offers to the Pharisees.

[196] b. *Yoma* 49a allows for the possibility of medical help on the Sabbath, but only if the person concerned is in danger of losing his or her life (cf. b. *Betzah* 18b). However, there are indications that some rabbis circumvented this basic premise; m. *Yoma* 8.6 allows for medicine to be dropped into a person's mouth if he or she has a throat problem; aiding a pregnant woman to give birth is also allowed (m. *Shab.* 18.3), and it was acceptable to cover a wound with lint, provided that it was not tied on (b. *Shab.* 19.13). Therapeutic remedies were rarely administered, and then only with severe restrictions (b. *Shab.* 21.23–27). The Essenes were even stricter in their determination of legitimate Sabbath activities, picking up a speck of dust being viewed as inappropriate (CD 11.10–14).

other than that he was a person with a withered hand; it is even possible that he may have been part of the plot, being a willing plant to draw the attention of Jesus to himself, though if he was, this is not mentioned by any of the writers.[197] Instead, the focus of attention in each of the Gospels is on the discourse between Jesus and the Pharisees. In particular, each writer demonstrates that the latter have moved from what may have been genuine enquiries or concerns concerning Jesus' ministry to outright opposition. Matthew has already reflected scribal opposition (9.3–4, 34). Each writer records the Pharisees as insidiously provoking a confrontation, Matthew repeating Mark's words exactly: 'so that they might accuse him'.

In this war of words, while the Pharisees offer their thinly veiled accusation in the form of a question, Jesus authoritatively asserts his position which is in direct contrast to theirs. The confrontation is visible, the battle line clearly drawn, and both parties are shown to be as determined as the other; yet, major differences are present in that while the Pharisees have no power to heal the man on the Sabbath or any other day, Jesus does have the power.

The reason for such a malignant decision on their part relates to the identification of the one who has the authority to determine what is appropriate activity on the Sabbath, and especially in a synagogue, the base for teaching by the Pharisees and scribes.[198] Each of the authors demonstrates that they were less concerned that Jesus could heal and more with whether he would do so on the Sabbath and in the synagogue; as such, it is of significance to note that this is the first and only healing that occurs in a synagogue.

From a legal point of view, it might have been difficult for the Pharisees to have made a case against Jesus for healing when he offered no medicinal therapy or even touch, though this does not appear to have restricted them in continuing their plan to eradicate him. At stake is the identity of the one who determines the authentic interpretation of God's law, the raison d'être of the Pharisees.

Jesus affirms what is central to his mission and that is to do good, which, importantly, is also fundamental to God in his dealings with humanity.[199] Thus, Jesus is aligning himself with the will of God and, at the same time, calling into question the protocols and beliefs of the Pharisees as not being supportive of the basic motivation of God to do good to people, an aspect

---

[197] The fact that Jesus does not touch the man may indicate that he is part of the plot to entrap Jesus.
[198] Matt.13.53; Mark 1.21; 6.2; Luke, 4.16, 20; 6.6.
[199] Matt. 7.11; 19.17; Mark 10.18; Luke 1.53; 11.13.

that he expects to be emulated by his followers;[200] after all, the gospel is 'good news'.[201]

Each of the writers records that the hand was completely and immediately restored, with Matthew adding that it was 'healthy like the other'. This is the only narrative to include a reference to Jesus commanding someone to stretch out his or her hand prior to being healed, though elsewhere Jesus stretches out his own hand in order to touch someone whom he subsequently heals.[202] However, the action of the man to obey the command of Jesus is not commended by Jesus or commented on by the authors; to a significant degree, he is passive in the process; he could not actually obey Jesus and stretch out his hand until Jesus had restored it.

Matthew and Mark both record that the religious leaders had decided to 'conspire against him how to destroy him', Mark recording that they did this in consultation with the Herodians.[203] Although the term used for 'destroy' (*apollumi*) is capable of referring to the ruin of a person's character or livelihood, the fact that they talked with the Herodians indicates that a more sinister form of destruction[204] is being explored since the Herodians could influence the king to carry out a sentence of death, capital punishment being outside the reach of the Pharisees.

Luke hints at the passionate vehemence of the Pharisees by recording that 'they were filled with fury (*anoias*, from *anoia*, "folly, madness")',[205] already having hinted at their malicious plan by uniquely recording Jesus asking them if it was lawful to 'destroy' on the Sabbath. Such a response by the Pharisees indicates that they see Jesus' breaking Sabbath traditions as indicative of a much more important stance on his part, akin to blasphemy in that he is claiming the authority of God to determine appropriate Sabbath activity (Exod. 31.14); although the accusation is not placed on the lips of the Pharisees, it has been voiced already[206] and will be later identified as Jesus' major crime.[207] Given the authority regularly

---

[200] Mark 14.7; Luke 6.27, 35.

[201] Matt. 11.5; Mark 1.1; Luke 3.18; 4.18, 43; 7.22.

[202] Matt. 8.3//Mark 1.41//Luke 5.13.

[203] The Herodians were members of a political group who supported King Herod; for the rigidly separatist, religious Pharisees to consort with a political party that aligned itself to a quasi-pagan king demonstrates their determination to achieve their aims.

[204] The term is used elsewhere in Matthew (2.13; 10.28; 21.41; 27.20) and Mark (1.24; 9.21; 11.18; 12.9) to refer to physical death; see also Luke 4.34; 19.47.

[205] The word is only used here and in 2 Tim. 3.9; the NASB suggests 'rage'; the KJV suggests 'madness'.

[206] Matt. 9.3; Mark 2.7; Luke 5.21.

[207] Matt. 26.65; Mark 14.64.

demonstrated by Jesus, their assumption that they had the ability to conclude his ministry and his life prematurely is evidence of their tenacity, their commitment to their perspective, and their complete misunderstanding of his identity.

Messages from Matthew

Matthew precedes this narrative with a stern condemnation of those cities that witnessed the miraculous activity of Jesus but still chose to reject him (11.20–24), a feature to be reflected again in this narrative (see Table 4.7). This is followed by a compassionate message of encouragement to those who were 'heavy laden' to come to Jesus who would give them rest (11.25–30). He then introduces his readers to the pointed question of the opposition concerning whether Jesus was supporting illegal activity by allowing his disciples to eat grain on the Sabbath (12.1–8), concluding with Jesus' teasing response asking for their assessment of a much more serious action undertaken by David who ate of the special 'bread of the Presence' that was intended only for the priests (1 Sam. 21.1–6) and that resulted in the death of Ahimelech, the priest who gave it to him, and 84 of his priestly colleagues, their families and animals (1 Sam. 22.16–19). Matthew then records Jesus stating, with reference to himself, 'the Son of Man is lord of the Sabbath', followed by the opportunity to prove it by healing a man on the Sabbath.

Although it is sensational that Jesus refers to himself as the 'Son of Man', it is much more startling that he identifies himself simultaneously as the 'lord of the Sabbath', each of the Gospels placing the word 'lord' (*kurios*) first in the description.[208] Any Jew would realize that God is the lord of the Sabbath, and here, Jesus is ascribing that role to himself, tantamount to a claim to divinity.

After such narratives affirming Jesus' authority, Matthew links the previous confrontation with this healing by bridging the two episodes with the words, 'He went on from there and entered their synagogue' (12.9) where the Pharisees were waiting. Jesus had unfinished business to attend to with regard to the Pharisees and it was time for him to respond to their sniping accusations, while simultaneously providing them with an opportunity to conclude that their rationale was inadequate and their conclusions concerning him were wrong.

---

[208] Matthew and Luke reverse the order of Mark ('(the) lord is the Son of Man and of the Sabbath') to read almost identically with each other; Mathew adds *gar* (because): '(because) he is lord of the Sabbath and the Son of Man', thus emphasizing Jesus' lordship of the Sabbath (my translation).

Matthew alone records that the Pharisees provocatively asked Jesus, 'Is it lawful to heal on the Sabbath?', Mark and Luke indicating that Jesus responded to their unspoken thoughts. Matthew alone inserts the question concerning the likely response of a person whose sheep needs rescuing on the Sabbath, concluding that a person is more important than a sheep. Also, only Matthew identifies Jesus authoritatively asserting, 'So it is lawful to do good on the Sabbath' (12.12).[209] Mark and Luke, on the other hand, simply record Jesus asking the Pharisees for their perspective: 'Is it lawful on the Sabbath to do good . . . ?'

Matthew truncates Mark's record by omitting the silence of the Pharisees and the anger of Jesus, and only records the restoration of the hand and the consequent rejection by the Pharisees. The focus is on their inability and Jesus' ability to make a difference – and on the Sabbath.

This narrative is not intended to demonstrate Jesus functioning as a rabbi with an alternative opinion as to what determined legitimate Sabbath activity. The stakes are much higher, as demonstrated by the response of the Pharisees. Jesus is bringing not simply an alternative view of the Sabbath but an alternative kingdom, not a new interpretation but a new era.

Matthew follows this narrative (with Mark) with the poignant reflection that Jesus withdrew from there (12.15),[210] having been rejected by some, though 'many followed him', Mark and Luke identifying it as 'a great crowd', though not including any Pharisees. Thereafter, Matthew records Jesus healing everyone who followed him (as do Mark (3.7–12) and Luke (6.17–19)), demonstrating that Jesus has not given up on his mission despite the pain of rejection. Matthew then uniquely refers to Jesus fulfilling Isaiah 42.1–3, the longest quotation from the OT in the Gospel, which refers to the beloved, Spirit-anointed, Servant of God whose compassionate and gentle role is to proclaim justice and hope to Gentiles (12.15–21); thus, Matthew provides God's perspective on the mission and status of Jesus. Where the Pharisees concentrate on casuistry, Jesus fulfils the caring commission of God's Servant who is anticipated as supporting, serving and saving the weak.

Startlingly, this is then followed by the Pharisees accusing Jesus of being empowered by the prince of demons when he exorcizes a demon (12.22–24); while the people wonder if Jesus might be the Son of David (12.23), the

---

[209] In this regard, Matthew records Jesus fulfilling the basic commandment to love one's neighbour (Lev. 19.18; Matt. 19.19).

[210] The term *anaxōreō* ('I depart, withdraw') is used elsewhere in Matthew to refer to people leaving places of danger (Matt. 2.12–14, 22; 4.12; 14.30), in the presence of unbelief (Matt. 9.24) or after confrontations with the religious leaders (15.21); its only reference in Mark is 3.7 and it is absent from Luke's Gospel.

Pharisees denounce him as being demonized, resulting in Jesus intensifying the danger of their stance by asserting that they are in danger of blasphemy against the Spirit who, according to 12.18, is inspiring Jesus to function miraculously (12.24–32). Jesus then identifies one's beliefs and words as indicating the basis of condemnation on the day of judgement, an implicit call to the Pharisees to revisit their conclusions and a hint that he will be present on that day in a judgmental role (12.33–37). After more warnings (12.38–50), Matthew records Jesus spending time with his disciples, teaching them specifically about the kingdom that he had come to initiate (13.1–52), though further confrontations with the Pharisees will soon recur.[211] Tragically, not all who see Jesus functioning authoritatively benefit from the lesson that is being imparted about his status, notably the religious Pharisees.

Messages from Mark and Luke

Mark and Luke agree on much. As well as affirming central elements with Matthew, they offer insights that Matthew has chosen to omit or rephrase. The extra data serves the purpose of again presenting the superlative authority of Jesus to the readers. Both writers present this narrative after a collection of other stories where Jesus provides people, and particularly religious leaders, with the opportunity to decide if they will accept his authority even when it supports unexpected actions or statements, or contradicts their own beliefs and praxis. Thus, they each record Jesus choosing disciples (Mark 1.16–20; Luke 5.1–11), an unusual action given that most rabbis did not choose followers, would-be disciples instead requesting if they could follow them; furthermore, the disciples chosen are not the most likely candidates, given that they are fishermen, with no evidence of any spiritual ambitions. Thereafter, Jesus cleanses a leper (Mark 1.40–5; Luke 5.12–6), followed much more startlingly with Jesus forgiving the sins of a paralytic who shows no prior sign of repentance (Mark 2.1–12; Luke 5.17–26). Unexpectedly, then Jesus is described as not only choosing a despised tax-collector to follow Jesus, but also eating with him and others who were like him, or even more dubious (Mark 2.13–7; Luke 5.27–32), Luke defining it as 'a great feast'. The following narrative relates to Jesus determining the appropriateness of fasting (Mark 2.18–23; Luke 5.33–39).

However, it is in the next narrative that the tide begins to turn against Jesus; until now, questions put to Jesus may have been offered by genuine enquirers who were intrigued by him because he reflected some of their aspirations with reference to the coming Messiah. However, the issue of

---

[211] 15.1–20; 16.1–12; 23.1–39.

healing on the Sabbath is very different and poses a much more difficult problem for some.

Both Mark and Luke do not record the provocative question to Jesus concerning the legitimacy of healing on the Sabbath, but instead they present the scribes and Pharisees[212] watching (*paretēroun*, imperfect active tense from *paratēreō*, 'I watch closely, observe scrupulously') him; the tense of the verb indicates an ongoing perusal of Jesus, making sure that they did not miss the opportunity to accuse him, the verb itself only used in hostile settings in Mark and Luke.[213]

Luke alone records that Jesus 'knew their thoughts',[214] and this appears to be the catalyst for Jesus' request, recorded by Mark and Luke, to the man with the withered hand to rise and come into the middle of the company. This is the only occasion in the Gospels when Jesus requests that someone comes 'into the middle' and this therefore demands enquiry. Although on several occasions Jesus took someone, whom he would heal, away from the crowd (Mark 7.33; 8.23) or removed people from the scene where he would restore a person,[215] generally, Jesus healed people where they were and without centralizing them.

As has been mentioned, it is possible that the man was part of the plot and Jesus may have desired to demonstrate his complete authority in that not only does he see through his opponents' scheme but he even knows who is the bait intended to trap him. One can only imagine the sense of discomfort felt by the man if this was the case, knowing that he has been found out by someone who has significant power available to him; although it has only been used with positive effects, who knows what he might do? However, it is possible that the man is not part of a dastardly plot and is simply an innocent victim, in which case it may be presumed that Jesus deliberately brings him to the fore because he intends to demonstrate clearly to all that he is determined to do good, despite the consequences, and he wishes everyone to have a good view to see this single-minded aspiration. In effect, Jesus provides those who are already staring at him with an opportunity to observe him in action. Rather than the opposition destabilizing Jesus, he reveals his supreme confidence, ability and authority

---

[212] Mark does not specifically identify these as the ones watching Jesus, though the reference to the Pharisees at the end of the narrative is indicative of their being the watchers.

[213] This is the only time Mark uses this word, though it is recorded elsewhere by Luke (in 14.1, it is used to describe the Pharisees who again watch to see if Jesus will heal a man on the Sabbath; in 20.20, Luke refers to 'the Scribes and chief priests' watching to see when they might arrest Jesus; in Acts 9.24, Luke refers to people who watched to see when they could kill Saul).

[214] Luke records this supernatural ability of Jesus elsewhere (5.22; 9.47; 11.17; 22.34).

[215] Matt. 9.25//Mark 5.40//Luke 8.51.

by deliberately, and very publicly, healing the man, whether he wished to be healed or not. Jesus, not they, determine his agenda.

However, before the healing occurs and while the man is still standing with Jesus in the centre, Mark and Luke record Jesus asking the Pharisees, 'Is it lawful on the Sabbath to do good or to do harm, to save life or to kill?'[216] Although it is clear why Jesus asked the former option 'to do good or harm', it is not so obvious why he follows it with a much more sober choice relating to saving life or facilitating death. It is probable that the writers wish the readers to recognize the ability of Jesus to read the thoughts and intentions of his opponents, not just their desire to accuse him but also their preference to rid themselves of him. On the same day that he was planning to do good, they were planning not just to obstruct that but also to do harm, and in particular to kill. The incongruity of their action being considered on the Sabbath is left to the reader to contemplate. Their preference was that Jesus should do nothing; however, given his ability and agenda to do good, this absence of transformation would have been, for him, tantamount to doing harm.

Both Mark and Luke refer to Jesus looking around at them (*periblepsamenos*[217]); the aorist tense of the verb may indicate a sudden, decisive glance in their direction. However, Mark alone notes that they were silent, choosing not to respond to Jesus' question; rather than answer his straightforward questions and thus endanger their stance, they maintain an obstinate silence. Although they may be deliberating patronizing Jesus, ignoring his question in a demeaning fashion, as an irrelevancy, it is more likely that they realize that if they answer affirmatively, they will be undermining their own position by crediting such acts on the Sabbath; if they answer negatively, they will manifest an unloving attitude. They would prefer acts of love to be determined by the law, while Jesus subordinates the law to love; they build a fence around the law with rules, whereas he dismantles any fence that results in the law not manifesting love.

Mark also records two emotions experienced by Jesus on this occasion. The first is anger, while the second is deep grief; given the present passive tense of the verb, 'to be grieved', it is possible that the quick angry look is to be contrasted with an ongoing sadness felt by Jesus, Mark offering that both are due to the hardness/deadness of their hearts. In objecting to the healing of a man whose hand is 'dead', they reveal a more dangerous deadness that relates to their assessment of Jesus.

---

[216] Mark has *apokteinai* (to kill) while Luke has *apolesai* (to destroy).

[217] Of the seven uses in the NT, six are in Mark and all refer to Jesus (Mark 3.5 (Luke 6.10), 34; 5.32; 9.8; 10.23; 11.11).

After the narrative, Mark records Jesus withdrawing to the sea (a place earlier associated with discipleship (1.16) and teaching (2.13; 4.1)), this time explicitly with his disciples, both he and Luke recording that Jesus healed many and cast out demons. However, here Mark reveals the misunderstanding, this time, of the people concerning the status of Jesus; they are so desperate to touch Jesus, in order to receive a supernatural impartation, that they are in danger of crushing him (3.9–10). In a less obvious way to the Pharisees' overt decision to kill Jesus, these people are determined to get something from Jesus and, if that results in injury to him or worse, that appears to be of limited concern to them. The result is that Jesus had to request a boat to protect him from their ardent, but fundamentally selfish, aspirations. Despite his being the Lord, he is viewed as simply someone who can provide them with what they need. The Pharisees and the people, each in their own way, are prepared to harm Jesus.

Thereafter, the trend to misunderstand or oppose Jesus grows. Mark records that Jesus' family appear to have concluded that he has gone 'out of his mind' (3.21), while scribes accuse him of being empowered by Beelzebul (3.22) and having 'an unclean spirit' (3.30). From the healing of the man with the withered hand, Jesus' journey will become increasingly painful and lonely. Despite the presence of the Twelve who had been commissioned to walk with him, Mark has already informed his readers that even one of them will betray Jesus (3.19).

Luke concludes the narrative by recording Jesus going to a mountain where he prayed (6.12), followed by his calling the Twelve, after which they are met by a crowd who had travelled from many places to benefit from his power (6.19). For Luke, the healing of the man with the withered hand has been a catalyst that has resulted in Jesus uniquely spending a night in prayer, followed by his mission being more deliberately articulated in a team enterprise that includes teaching his followers about discipleship (6.20–49). It is poignant to read Jesus in his final instruction to the disciples (6.49) where he speaks of the danger of ruin awaiting those who hear his words but reject them, exemplified in the attitude of the Pharisees in the previous narrative.

Conclusion

The sense of pathos in this narrative is clear, as is the pain of misunderstanding and rejection which intensifies in the context of Jesus' caring mission of salvation to helpless people who are privileged to have God, in the person of Jesus, in their villages.

Jesus heals the blind (Matt. 20.29–34// Mark 10.46–52//Luke 18.35–43)[218]

Table 4.8 Healing the blind man/men – the literary context

	Matthew	Mark	Luke
The rich young ruler	19.16–30	10.17–31	18.18–30
The parable of the labourers in the vineyard	20.1–16		
Jesus' third prediction of the Passion	20.17–19	10.32–34	18.31–34
The disciples and the request for precedence	20.20–28	10.35–45	(22.24–30)
The healing of the blind man/men	**20.29–34**	**10.46–52**	**18.35–43**
The triumphal entry	21.1–9	11.1–11	(19.28–40)
Jesus cleanses the Temple	21.10–17	(11.15–19)	(19.45–46)
Jesus curses the fig tree	21.18–19	11.12–14	
Jesus and Zacchaeus			19.1–10
The parable of the talents	(25.14–30)		19.11–27

Main messages from all the narratives

The three narratives agree in a number of respects including the locality of the restoration being Jericho, the location of the blind man as sitting by the roadside, the use of the title 'Son of David' for Jesus, the request that Jesus show mercy, the rebuke by the onlookers (defined as 'a great crowd' by Matthew and Mark, Luke simply offering a 'crowd'), the persistence of the blind man in repeating his request to Jesus, the fact that Jesus stopped and called him to him, the question asked of him by Jesus and his response, the immediacy of the healing and that he followed Jesus. In each account, the first half involves an interaction between the crowd and the blind man whereas the latter half is dominated by the encounter between the blind man and Jesus.

This is the final healing of Jesus prior to his arrest; Jerusalem is little more than a day's journey away, a distance of nearly 20 miles. In this narrative, the writers provide a story that relates to the importance of accurate sight and, in particular, an accurate perception of the true status and authority of Jesus. As Jesus makes his way to Jerusalem for the final disclosure of himself and his mission, the Synoptists provide an opportunity for the readers to check their own assessments of Jesus by comparing them with the way the blind man evaluates him. In the chapters to come, many will see Jesus, but few will recognize him as the Saviour he is and will be

---

[218] In the exploration of the narratives, the singular will be used, reflecting Mark and Luke who refer to only one blind man.

blinded by their own messianic perceptions; it takes a blind man to see who he truly is.

Each Synoptist precedes this healing narrative with the account of the ruler who concludes that Jesus is not worthy enough for him to give up his wealth in order to follow him, Matthew uniquely following this with a parable, the theme of which relates to the authority of a master to determine the wages for work completed. Each writer then includes Jesus' third prediction of his Passion. Finally, Matthew, in parallel with Mark, records Jesus' teaching concerning the importance of service for would-be followers of Jesus. The literary context thus relates to people's assessments of Jesus and, in particular, whether his status deems him sufficiently worthy of being followed, served and obeyed.

The blind man

The main differences in the synoptic accounts is that Matthew refers to two blind men while Mark and Luke refer to one, and Matthew and Mark record the restoration as occurring when Jesus left Jericho while Luke refers to Jesus entering Jericho.[219] However, these are insufficient to prove that more than one incident is being described here.

Blindness was viewed as one of the most devastating diseases in the Graeco-Roman and Jewish worlds.[220] For the Jews, it was often understood to be a punishment for sin.[221] It functioned as the first in a divinely deter- mined list of physical ailments that precluded a priest from offering the shewbread in the sanctuary (Lev. 21.18); even blind animals were not to be offered as sacrifices to God.[222] To lose one's sight was not only associ- ated with disobedience to God, but also, it resulted in poverty (Judg. 16.21), the destiny of the blind person often being to live as a beggar (Mark 10.46; John 9.8). There was something deeply marginalizing about being blind in the Jewish world; it appeared to the Jews that even God was

---

[219] Morris (*Gospel According to Matthew*. p. 513) suggests, 'there were 2 Jerichos, the site of the OT Jericho . . . and the site nearby of the rebuilt Herodian Jericho. It is not impossible that the miracle was performed as Jesus was leaving one Jericho and approaching the other.' The truncation of Jesus' entrance to and exit from Jericho by Mark may lend weight to this suggestion. See Bock (D. L., *Luke 9.51–24.53*. Baker, Grand Rapids, 1996, pp. 1502–4) for a variety of explanations.

[220] Schrage, W., 'tuphlos', in *The Dictionary of the New Testament, Vol. 8*. (eds) Kittel, G., Friedrich, G.; (tr.) Bromiley, G. W., Eerdmans, Grand Rapids, 1967, pp. 270–94; Wells (L., *The Greek Language of Healing from Homer to New Testament Times*. De Gruyter, Berlin, 1998, pp. 23, 42) notes that at the temples to Asklepios in Epidauros and Athens, blindness was the most common complaint.

[221] Gen. 19.11; Exod. 4.11; Deut. 28.28–29; 2 Kings 6.18; Lam. 4.13–14; Zeph. 1.17; John 9.2; Acts 13.11.

[222] Lev. 22.22; Deut. 15.21; Mal. 1.8; 11QTemple records God forbidding blind people from entering Jerusalem 'lest they defile the city in whose midst I dwell'.

uncomfortable about their presence.[223] Blindness left the person helpless, dependent on others, marginalized and miserable. The rabbis viewed it as one of the four conditions to be equated with death, along with being poor, leprous and childless.[224] It is thus understandable that this man cried for mercy as there had been no precedent for healing of blindness in the OT.[225] Apart from the restoration of sight to Saul (Acts 9.17–18), the healing of blindness is recorded only in the Gospels, where blindness is identified as the most common condition healed by Jesus.[226] To heal blindness would thus have been viewed as an extraordinary act, John 11.37 recording, 'Could not he who opened the eyes of the blind man also have kept this man from dying?', such a feat indicating that since Jesus could restore blindness, it was anticipated that he could even withhold death.

The life-setting of the blind man is briefly recorded, each author referring to the fact that he was sitting by the roadside, Mark and Luke clarifying that this was for the purpose of begging. The fact that he was sitting and not part of the travelling crowd indicates that he was not on his way to the Passover festival; he was an outsider, sitting on that particular road, despite its danger from robbers, in order to beg from the festival attendees, Jericho being a wealthy city with three palaces for Herod and a hippodrome. Thus, the desperate situation of the blind man is graphically presented,[227] in that, unlike the blind man referred to in Mark 8.22 who had friends to bring him to Jesus, no one represents this man to Jesus. Indeed, in the stories in Mark and Luke, the man does not even have a blind colleague – he is on his own.

This is a unique occurrence of a sufferer having to work hard to get an audience with Jesus. Indeed, most of the narrative is taken up with this attempt to reach Jesus. Not only was he in danger of Jesus passing him by, but he also had to overcome the resistance of the multitude. None of the Synoptists records the crowd acclaiming Jesus as the Son of David,[228]

---

[223] Though see Lev. 19.14; Deut. 27.18.

[224] b. *Ned.* 64b.

[225] b. *Git.* 69a and *Meg.* 85b offer some popular therapeutic remedies based on folk medicine; Tobit 11.7–15; 14.12 describes Tobit healing his father's blindness by anointing his eyes with the gall of a fish. Tacitus (*Hist.* 4.81) records the success of Vespasian in this regard.

[226] See Matt. 9.27–31; 12.22; Mark 8.22; John 9.1–7. The blind are also regularly given prominence in the lists of complaints healed by Jesus (Matt. 11.5; 15.30–31; Luke 4.18; 7.21–22; John 5.3; 10.21; 11.37).

[227] See earlier for a discussion of blindness in the ancient Jewish world.

[228] The term became a synonym for Messiah, based on the belief that God had promised to King David that he would have a son who would own an everlasting kingdom and who would enjoy the undiminished and complete love of God (2 Sam. 7.13, 15; 1 Chron. 17.12–13); the term is used in the Triumphal Entry narrative that follows, though probably with militaristic assumptions (Matt. 21.9; Mark 11.10).

but the blind man does, persistently; he who has no ability to see is presented as having a better perception of Jesus than do those with physical sight, the latter inappropriately rebuking him and commanding that he be quiet.[229]

Although, on occasion, Jesus asks people not to broadcast his identity, here it is possible that he wishes to be identified as the one who has come to open the eyes of the blind. This narrative occurs towards the end of Jesus' mission; he will soon be in Jerusalem. The time of secrecy is past; the great unveiling will soon take place. The question remains to be answered as to whether people will merely acclaim Jesus as the bringer of David's kingdom when they see him, and fade away when he does not dance to their tune, or whether they will follow him in the way that the blind man did.

The appeal to mercy

Each author records the persistent appeals to the mercy of Jesus; the issue was whether Jesus would, not could, help. As such, the blind man has a superior perception of the mission of Jesus than do the crowds, who assume that Jesus has no time for him; after all, Matthew and Luke record that he was 'passing by'.[230]

However, as with the previously recorded healing of blind men (Matt. 9.27–31) who also appeal to Jesus' mercy, Jesus does not immediately respond to the man's request; neither does he commend him for his accurate assessment or for his persistence, or affirm that either are evidence of his faith. That is only affirmed (by Mark and Luke) after he acknowledges that Jesus has the authority and ability to heal him. Before the healing occurs, Jesus requests that he come to him, asks him what he requires of him, and only after he specifically requests his sight does the healing occur.

As before, the writers are not emphasizing the role of Jesus' mercy or the importance of persistence in the process of healing; rather, it is the authority of Jesus that is highlighted, and the blind man's affirmation that he can grant him sight becomes the catalyst for the healing.

---

[229] The combination of these words is only recorded elsewhere in Mark 4.39 where Jesus rebukes and commands the storm to be silent, and Luke (4.35) where Jesus rebukes and commands silence from a demon.

[230] This is the only reference in Matthew to Jesus 'passing by anyone', though interestingly, and by contrast to the blind men, he later refers to people 'who passed by [and] derided him [Jesus]' (27.39).

The importance of an accurate perception of Jesus as a catalyst for following him

Each Synoptist presents an unlikely scenario where a blind beggar meets Jesus. Furthermore, that he becomes his follower would not have been anticipated by many. Although a healing occurs, this is not the main emphasis of the writers in recording this narrative. The healing itself occurs in a few words towards the end of the story, although the actual conclusion relates to the motif of 'following', which is itself based on the importance of an accurate perception of the one who is to be followed. Similarly, although the appeal of the man is recorded twice in each Gospel, it is the rebuke of the people that he be silent which is also of particular significance, for it is Jesus who undermines this reprimand and replaces it with an opportunity to make his case even more clearly. Not only are the people who called for silence themselves silenced, but also they are shown to be wrong, in that their assertion is contradicted by the words and action of Jesus.

This is the only time that Jesus is described as 'stopping' in the Gospels. The writers draw attention to the fact that Jesus stops in order to call the man and gives him time to come to where he is and to 'see' exactly who he is. The start of that journey with Jesus will begin when Jesus calls him to be with him, the later decision to follow him being the consequence of this first call to him. Thereafter, Jesus provides him with the opportunity to publicly affirm that he can authoritatively operate with supernatural power. Bruner refers to it as 'a search for a conversation',[231] though it might be more accurate to refer to it as a search for a relationship, in which Jesus provides an opportunity for a sufferer to recognize that Jesus has the power to transform his situation. On the basis of that transformation, a greater choice to change is offered by Jesus to the man.

The request of Jesus that the blind man specifically identify what he wanted from him is not to be categorized as a pedantic insistence on his part that he requests the obvious, or to test the sincerity of the request or the quality of his faith.[232] The man has already expressed faith. No improvement in his faith is needed, no clarification of his request is necessary and no clearer perception of Jesus is required. Rather, Jesus

---

[231] Bruner, *The Christbook*. p. 351.

[232] Bailey (K. E., *Jesus through Middle Eastern Eyes*. SPCK, London, 2008, pp. 173–4) speculatively suggests that Jesus is offering the blind man the opportunity to consider if he is prepared for a life devoid of begging when he will have to undertake work to gain an income, though this is not indicated in the text.

provides an opportunity for the blind man to publicly express his belief in his authority.

It is no surprise that the narrative ends with each author recording that the man followed Jesus; while Matthew inserts *ēkolouthēsan* (aorist indicative of *akoloutheō*) possibly indicating an immediate response, Luke follows Mark and uses the imperfect tense (*ēkolouthei*) with a sense of continuous following. The challenge will be whether he will continue to follow him, not just to Jerusalem for the 'triumphal entry' but also to the cross.

It is in this respect that Matthew and Luke may have deliberately amended Mark's final reference to Jesus, *rhabbouni* ('rabbi') (10.51) to *kurios* ('lord'). The evidence as to who has offered the most accurate perception of Jesus is provided by the authors in that Jesus stops to talk to the blind man, not the crowd; it is to the blind man, not the crowd, that his offer of help is granted, and it is the blind man, not the crowd, who chooses to follow Jesus.

Aftermath

After the healing, Matthew and Mark record the triumphal entry (see Table 4.8). The so-called 'triumphal entry', more than most of the disappointing experiences of Jesus, illustrates the contrast between the Jewish messianic dream and the messianic mission of Jesus. Jesus was praised for being the Messiah the people wanted him to be and was rejected for being the Messiah he was. The words that the people used to acclaim Jesus, reflected in the Synoptics, are from Psalm 118.25–26, the most fundamental characteristic of which was its use as a conqueror's psalm. One hundred years earlier, Simon Maccabees returned to Jerusalem after a victorious battle against the Syrians, and these verses were sung by the crowds to him as a military warrior. They also waved palm branches before him as they did before Jesus, as an acknowledgement of his military prowess, a common practice before kings. Surely, Jesus was conscious of their misunderstanding concerning him. To show how much an anti-climax for Jesus was his entrance into Jerusalem, Matthew and Mark immediately record him cleansing the Temple.

In each of the Synoptics, life in the Temple is portrayed as continuing as normal, despite Jesus' entrance into the city; indifference to Jesus and true worship, and the presence of bigotry and self-righteous dealings of the religious folk, have not been amended by the entrance of the Messiah. Unfortunately, his entrance was but a hiccough in the regular events of the day.

Why Matthew tells the story

The preceding narratives in Matthew, which agree with Mark, illustrate the contrast between those who do not see the truth, despite the presence of data that should aid them in their quest, and those who see the truth simply on the basis of their faith.

The fact that Matthew refers to there being two blind men may reflect the reality that there were two, while Mark and Luke only identify or concentrate on the one, and/or because Matthew wishes to take advantage of the value of the Jewish notion of two witnesses being needed to provide authentic evidence of an accurate perception of the truth.[233] Matthew also omits Mark's reference to the blind man being a beggar; it is his blindness, not his poverty, that matters to Matthew, who seeks to call attention to his role as the one who truly *sees* who Jesus is, despite being blind.

Matthew omits the men's actions, as indicated by Mark, and thus again concentrates on the words of Jesus, and in particular his providing them with the opportunity to reveal the quality of their assessment of Jesus. For Matthew, words as well as actions are important in revealing truth.

Matthew is the only Synoptist to include the compassion of Jesus in this narrative. This is also one of the few occasions where Jesus is identified as having compassion in a healing context.[234] It is curious that he omits Mark's reference to faith as it is an important motif for him; it is possible that the men's faith is anticipated by Matthew as being manifested in their verbal perception of Jesus' status. Mathew also uniquely records Jesus touching[235] their eyes (see also 9.29), probably to identify to the blind men that he was about to restore their sight while also providing the observers with a sign of his unique authority. The emphasis for Matthew seems to be placed on their appeal to mercy that is rewarded by Jesus healing them physically but also transforming them from being faltering blind men into disciples who follow him.

It took a blind man to 'see' the true status of Jesus, as contrasted with the 'spiritual' blindness of the sons of Zebedee, in the incident recorded immediately before this pericope by both Mark and Matthew. In Matthew, the similar question to James and John, and the blind man – 'What do you want me to do for you?' – links the stories, while the different responses

---

[233] Deut. 17.6; 19.5; Matt. 18.16; 26.60; 1 Cor. 13.1; 1 Tim. 5.19; Heb. 10.28; Rev. 11.3.

[234] See also Matt. 14.14; (Mark 1.41 is disputed); Luke 7.13 concerning the widow of Nain's dead son; (Mark 9.2 for the father of the demonized son), though he is identified as being compassionate towards people on other occasions (Matt. 9.36//Mark 6.34; 15.32//Mark 8.2; Mark 9.22; Luke 10.33).

[235] For the significance of Jesus touching a sick person, see earlier.

provide the key message to the readers: the ability to see accurately is most important. The fact that Jesus responds positively to the request of the blind man but not to that of his disciples indicates who has provided the most appropriate answer.

Why Mark tells the story

Mark characteristically offers the longest narrative, recording that the disciples were with the great crowd that accompanied Jesus. He also offers more comment on the location and the identity of the blind man, mentioning his name as Bartimaeus, which he then explains means the son of Timaeus, a blind beggar, the latter feature being repeated by Luke. The reference to his name may indicate that he became a well-known follower of Jesus, especially since he is the only named person who is healed in Mark.

Mark (followed by Luke) records the blind man hearing that 'Jesus of Nazareth' was present, a reference to where Jesus had spent most of his life. However, although the blind man was informed of this fact by others, he chose to invest in Jesus a deeper significance than simply a reference to his place of origin and does not use this term in his call to Jesus, choosing instead, 'the Son of David'. Both Mark and Luke thus reveal the developing perception of the man who does not restrict the importance of Jesus to an earthly, geographical location but expands it to a supra-earthly context. The fact that Mark introduces the title 'Son of David' into his narrative here (and only here) indicates the special insight of Bartimaeus.

Mark uniquely inserts the encouraging words of the people, 'Take heart. Get up; he is calling you.' Although Jesus had previously encouraged people with the words 'Take heart', this is the only occasion in the Gospels where someone else uses them to encourage someone to action. Despite the earlier call that he be silent, his cries have won the day. This motif is emphasized in what may be a chiastic structure:

A. The blind man sat by the road
  B. He heard Jesus
    C. The blind man called to Jesus
      D. 'Jesus, Son of David, have mercy on me'
        E. 'Many rebuked him, telling him to be silent'
      D1. 'Son of David, have mercy on me'
    C1. Jesus and the people called the blind man
  B1. He heard Jesus' request to him
A1. The blind man sprang up (went to Jesus, was healed) and followed him on the road

What is of significance in this analysis, as has already been demonstrated, is that the words of the blind man and the crowds are of central importance in the narrative (and the chiasm) because they represent perceptions concerning Jesus which have significant consequences relating to the possibility that, of the great crowd in the presence of Jesus, only one man will be invited to follow Jesus.

Mark and Luke record Jesus saying, 'Your faith has made you well (*sesōken*, perfect active tense from *sōzō*, "I save")',[236] referring to physical healing, the perfect tense of the verb indicating that the restoration is permanent. However, because *sōzō* has a wider range of meanings beyond merely physical healing,[237] it is possible that the writers are indicating that Bartimaeus has benefited from more than physical restoration, affirmed by the fact that he follows Jesus.

Although each Synoptist records that the blind man/men sat by the roadside (*para tēn hodon*, from *hodos*, 'road, way'), only Mark concludes the narrative with a reference to the fact that he 'followed him on the way' (*en tē hodō*, from *hodos*); he who once passively sat, begging 'by the way', has been transformed and encouraged to actively follow 'on the way'.

Why Luke tells the story

Luke precedes the healing narrative with a number of stories with a common theme relating to the importance of accurate perceptions of truth. In 18.1–8, a widow acts as an example of someone who, like the blind man, persistently asks God for help, knowing that he will provide it; in 9–14, a tax-collector perceives the truth concerning his unrighteousness while a Pharisee is ignorant of his; in 15–17, the disciples reveal how little they know of the mission of Jesus to spend time with vulnerable people; in 18–30, the rich young ruler puts his riches before Jesus; finally, the pathos is increased with a unique reference to the disciples, who do not perceive the significance of the graphic description by Jesus of his Passion soon to come (31–34).

Following this catalogue of events where people fail to see the truth (other than a widow and a tax-collector), Luke inserts the story of another marginalized man, who is blind, but who like the widow and the tax-collector has a more accurate perception of Jesus than many others. Luke

---

[236] These exact words are used seven times in the Synoptics, mostly in the context of physical healings (Matt. 9.22//Mark 5.34//Luke 8.48; Mark 10.52//Luke 18.42; Luke 17.19) and in the context of the forgiveness of sins (Luke 7.50).

[237] Matt. 18.11; 24.13; Mark 10.26; Luke 7.50; 7.19; John 12.47; Jas 5.15.

then uniquely follows this narrative with the story of Zacchaeus (see Table 4.8), another tax-collector, but one who is chief in his profession, who, like the blind man, was determined to see Jesus, and climbed a tree to do so (19.3–10). He, like him, had a clearer perception of the identity of Jesus, resulting in his resolve to overcome his personal problem, lack of height, to ensure that he did not miss Jesus as he was 'passing'. For Zacchaeus, as with the blind man, the encounter resulted in the restoration of spiritual sight; not only does Zacchaeus make some life-changing decisions about his finances (in contrast to the rich young ruler, 18.18–30), but also, he is defined by Jesus as being someone who was lost but who has now been found and is the beneficiary of salvation. The theme of each of these stories is that of 'seeing'.[238]

Luke uniquely uses the verb *eboēsen* (from *boaō*, 'I cry aloud'), to describe the first appeal of the blind man to Jesus (instead of *kradzō*, which was used on two occasions each by Mark and Matthew); it is used elsewhere in Luke a few verses earlier (18.7), referring to God's readiness to respond to those who call for his help. In the former it is God who responds, while here it is Jesus who takes on that divine role. As with Mark, this is the only occasion where the title 'Son of David' is used of Jesus, and thus the emphasis on the accurate insight of the blind man, as reflected in Mark, is maintained in Luke.

Luke uniquely records that Jesus commands that the man be brought to him, indicating the care of Jesus in ensuring that a blind man is safely led to him. Finally, Luke informs his readers that the man glorified God while all the people praised God (9.43),[239] revealing that the people recognized that Jesus was authoritatively functioning with God's backing.

After the healing, Luke also records the triumphal entry but only after first introducing two incidents which emphasize that it was a minority who truly understood who Jesus was and why he had come. The story of Zacchaeus highlights the fact that only one, in a multitude, received Jesus into his home and also received salvation, while those who saw it grumbled

---

[238] Pilch (J. J., 'Sickness and Healing in Luke-Acts', *BibT.* 27.1, Jan. 1989. p. 24) notes that in Luke-Acts, sight/blindness is used in a symbolic way to emphasize spiritual understanding or the lack thereof (Luke 4.18; 6.39–42; 7.21; 8.1–15; 10.21–24; 11. 29–36; 12.54–56; 17.22–33; 23.8, 48; Acts 28.23–31), leading him to conclude that 'for Luke, blindness refers especially to refusal to see and understand'.

[239] The reference to people glorifying God occurs regularly after miracles of restoration in Luke (5.25–26; 7.16; 13.13; 17.15) but also on other occasions referring to Jesus, including his birth (2.20), his teaching (4.15) and his death (18.43), though this is the only reference in the NT to people 'giving praise to God'.

that Jesus had gone to such a person's house (19.1–9). The parable recorded thereafter reveals that most of the citizens of a town whose nobleman who had gone 'into a far country to receive for himself a kingdom', a clear reference by Jesus to himself, rejected him and were rejected by him (19.10–27).

Thereafter, Luke inserts the so-called triumphal entry (19.28–40) in which many people welcome Jesus as a miracle worker and king (19.37–38), signifying their misunderstanding of his true ambitions, seeing him as a military and economic wonder-worker. More tellingly, Luke identifies those who do welcome Jesus thus as specifically 'the whole multitude of *his disciples*' (19.37) while the Pharisees request that Jesus 'rebuke' his disciples. Both, in their different ways, have misunderstood central aspects of Jesus' mission and person, resulting in his sorrow, uniquely recorded in Luke (19.41–44). Finally, most of the people merely welcomed Jesus as a wonder worker, a superstar, Luke specifying their acclamation of 'the mighty works that they had seen'.

Conclusion

Both the crowds and the blind man welcome Jesus as a Davidic figure but, whereas the former misunderstood his mission, the latter recognized his true status; the crowd eventually rejects Jesus, with a loss of potential benefits, while the blind man correctly perceives Jesus' identity and is integrated into his entourage.

Jesus heals two blind men (Matt. 9.27–31)

Table 4.9 Healing two blind men – the literary context

	Matthew
Healing of a paralytic	9.1–8
Jesus calls Matthew to be a disciple	9.9
Jesus eats with tax-collectors and sinners	9.10–13
Jesus speaks about fasting	9.14–17
Jesus heals the ruler's daughter	9.18–19, 23–26
Jesus heals a haemorrhaging woman	9.20–22
Jesus heals two blind men	**9.27–31**
Jesus restores a dumb demoniac	9.32–34
Jesus heals and teaches everywhere	9.35
Jesus' compassion on the crowds	9.36
Too few labourers for the harvest	9.37–38
Jesus commissions the Twelve	10.1–42

The authority of Jesus

This healing comes eighth in a list of miracles achieved by Jesus and is unique to Matthew (see Table 4.9); the restoration of sight to the blind serves as a fitting climax to Jesus' miraculous power. As in 20.29–34, these blind men also refer to Jesus as 'the Son of David', a term used in the context of other miracles, especially in Matthew.[240]

Although there is no OT evidence that healing was specifically associated with the Son of David,[241] the association of the title with the Messiah points to a new age where blindness will cease.[242] Possibly due to the potential misunderstanding of the title identifying Jesus with a dynamic warrior like David, the majority of occurrences are in the context of healing the blind and the marginalized to show the integrative aspects of Jesus' mission. It is they who recognize that Jesus is the 'Son of David'. The Davidic Messiah offers himself to all, but while the crowds misunderstand him, and rulers repudiate him (21.15), it is the blind who 'see' him (9.27–28; 20.31), the Canaanite woman who accepts him (15.22) and infants who applaud him (21.15–16). The message is clear: Jesus is more than a healer; he is Messiah. It takes two blind men to draw this conclusion . . . indeed, they are the first to do so in Matthew.

---

[240] See 9.27; 12.23; 15.22; 20.30–31; Matthew uses the term to refer to Jesus nine times, while Mark and Luke record the title only three times each.

[241] Though see Jos., *Ant.* 6.166, 168.

[242] Isa. 29.18; 35.5; 42.7, 16, 18–20; 43.8; 61.1; Jer. 31.8.

The mercy of Jesus

The term 'mercy' is mentioned in another story that records the healing of blindness, though it is not mentioned in any other healing scenario in the Gospels.[243] However, although the two men beg for mercy for their sight, Jesus does not grant them their request immediately. Jesus heals them, in his own time, after he enters a house and after they follow him. Responding out of mercy is not presented as the reason for Jesus working miraculously; if it was, he would have healed everyone in the nation and the connection would have been much more prominent in the miracles.

The fact that Matthew records that Jesus went into a house is unusual in that it may be assumed to be an unnecessary detail by a writer who is careful in his use of words. Such a movement by Jesus is not recorded in any other healing narrative, and its association with an apparent ignoring of the men's request is unusual. Dismissing any suggestions that Jesus was not interested in healing them and only does so because they follow him, one is left with the possibility that Jesus deliberately offers the privacy of a house as an opportunity for him to reveal more of himself than simply that he is a healer, even of blindness.

Before they are healed, Jesus asks them whether they believe he can heal them, an unusual question, since they have already asked for his mercy (see also 20.32). Rather than it be assumed that their initial request was unhelpfully imprecise or lacked faith, the question of Jesus is more likely posed in order to demonstrate that their healing would follow a simple acknowledgement that he had the authority to heal them. In other words, it was their belief in his authority rather than his mercy that Matthew identifies as being significant in the process of healing. On the basis of their belief that Jesus could, he did.

Consequently, Matthew identifies Jesus as stating that their healing was granted 'according to [their] faith'. Their appeal to his mercy has been climaxed by their belief in his authority, the healing occurring simply by him touching their eyes. Most importantly, Jesus demonstrates that he had the ability to function in a way that was associated with God, Exodus 4.11 specifically stating that to heal blindness was a prerogative belonging to God.[244] This feature of Jesus' authority has already been hinted at by

---

[243] Matthew records people appealing to the mercy of Jesus when requesting that he cast out demons (15.22; 17.15), and blind men doing so when requesting the restoration of their sight (20.30, 31//Mark 10.47–48//Luke 18.38–39); such an appeal is absent in John's Gospel.

[244] Also Ps. 146.8.

Matthew in that he records the men as following Jesus (9.27),[245] a feature referred to a few verses earlier (9.9) with reference to Matthew following Jesus, in response to Jesus' call.

Jesus sternly commands the men to tell no one of the healing, again probably due to his concern that people will either assume that healing is his main mission in life or that their association of him with the Son of David will lead them to believe that he is about to set up a messianic kingdom with political, economic and militaristic elements, as was central to much of the first-century Jewish expectations of the messianic era. Given his command that they tell no one, it is possible that this was why Jesus preferred to heal them in private. However, his command is ignored and they spread the news of their healing throughout the area.

Conclusion

The story is followed by a brief telling of an exorcism (9.33a), more time being spent on the aftermath (9.32b–4) that includes the statement that the crowds marvelled, though the Pharisees concluded that Jesus functioned miraculously as a result of demonic authority. The ability to recognize the 'Son of David' acts as a Matthean marker for an accurate perception of the Messiah. Those who succeed in making such an identification prove themselves to be candidates for the kingdom.

---

[245] This is a keyword in the Synoptics but especially in Matthew, where it is used 19 times with reference to people following Jesus (Mark uses the verb 13 times with reference to people following Jesus, while Luke uses it 11 times). Its most proximate reference in Matthew refers to Jesus following the ruler in order to heal his daughter; here, those needing to be healed demonstrate their faith in Jesus by following him, even when he walks away from them.

Jesus heals in the Temple (Matt. 21.14–17)

Table 4.10 Healings in the Temple – the literary context

	Matthew	Mark	Luke
The disciples' request for precedence	20.20–28	10.35–45	Similar to 22.24–27
The healing of the blind man/men	20.29–34	10.46–52	18.35–43
The triumphal entry	21.1–9	11.1–10	19.28–40
Jesus cleanses the Temple	21.10–13	11.11–17	19.45–46
Jesus heals in the Temple	**21.14–17**		
Jesus curses the fig tree	21.18–19	11.12–14	

Matthew's last healing account (see Table 4.10) forms a climax to Jesus' healing mission. Matthew alone records the fact that 'the blind (*tuphlos*)[246] and the lame (*chōlos*)[247] came to him in the temple'; this is the only record in Matthew of Jesus healing in Jerusalem. However, such supernatural activity in the religious and commercial heart of the nation did not result in the affirmation of Jesus by the religious establishment. Instead, despite Matthew's description of the healings as being *thaumasia* ('wonders'),[248] which he notes the chief priests and scribes actually saw, Jesus was still rejected by them, their indignation being further motivated when they heard children praising him as being the 'Son of David'. At the same time, Matthew notes that afterwards, Jesus removed himself from them, the Temple and Jerusalem, and lodged in Bethany.

The healing of these two marginalized people groups in the Temple is the final catalyst that signals the depth of the rift between Jesus and those who apparently represent God to the Jewish people. Insofar as this is the only occasion noted by any of the Gospels in which Jesus is recorded as healing in the Temple, it signals the commencement of a new era, established by him welcoming and healing those (blind and lame) who were previously often excluded from the Temple.[249] At the same time, in healing

---

[246] Matthew refers to blind people being healed elsewhere (9.27–28; 11.5; 12.22; 15.30–31; 20.30) whereas Mark only refers to the healing of the blind in 8.22–23 and 10.46–49, Luke in 7.21–22 and 18.35, and John only in 9.1–7.

[247] Again Matthew refers to the lame being healed on three other occasions (11.5; 15.30–31), whereas John does not specifically refer to this complaint being healed by Jesus, Mark only once (2.3–12) and Luke twice (5.18–26; 7.22).

[248] Although this word is only used on its own here in the NT, it is used 47 times in the OT (plus 13 times in the Apocryphal books) and each occurrence relates to wonders achieved by God (Exod. 3.20; 1 Chron. 16.19; Pss. 9.2; 25.7).

[249] Lev. 21.17–19; 2 Sam. 5.8; m. *Hag.* 1.1. The Qumranic *Rule of the Congregation* (1QSa 2.4–9; 1QM 7.4–6; 12.7–9) forbade the lame, blind, deaf and dumb from joining the community and the messianic banquet, in particular.

those who God ordained were not welcome in the sanctuary, Jesus elevates his authority to the highest level, but only the blind and the lame benefit from it.

On previous occasions in Matthew, when the lame and blind came to Jesus, he did not immediately heal them; the paralysed man was first forgiven his sins (9.1–7) and blind men were first asked questions by Jesus (9.27–31; 20.29–34). However, on this occasion, both are immediately healed, possibly to quickly demonstrate his healing authority in the Temple. It is also possible that Jesus is supporting his claim to be the Son of David by contrasting himself with David. In 2 Samuel 5.6, 8a, the blind and the lame in Jerusalem are (metaphorically) referred to as those whom David hates and will kill when he conquers the city. Jesus, however, welcomes 'the blind and the lame'. If David is thus described as becoming 'greater and greater, for the LORD, the God of Hosts, was with him' (2 Sam. 5.10), how much greater is Jesus, the Son of David, to be viewed.

It is also possible that a more practical, and ultimately more significant, reason is available for the rapid healing of the blind and lame. The significance of the Temple is that it functioned not as a therapeutic locus but as a place for thanksgiving (2 Kings 20.5; Isa. 38.20) and prayer (1 Kings 8.38). These centrally important religious activities had been denied to the blind and the lame because of their physical condition; Jesus, in dealing with the latter, enabled them to function as legitimate worshippers of God.

Those who recognized their need, the blind and the lame, came to Jesus and were healed by him; those who neither saw their need nor recognized his ability to help them missed their chance to benefit from his power; Jesus contrasts the religious leaders unfavourably, despite their apparent prestige, with children, who had little status in Jewish society (21.16). The religious leaders assumed that the children had drawn the wrong conclusion about the identity of Jesus and were shocked that Jesus did not correct their apparent error, especially insofar as it has been stated in public, and in the Temple, the location of other divine revelations.[250] Instead Jesus identifies their acclamation and assessment of himself as 'perfect praise' (21.16), uniquely quoting Psalm 8.2.

Even though the children may not have appreciated the accuracy of their affirmation of Jesus, Jesus makes it clear that their sentiment was supported by the psalmist who identifies this action by children as being motivated by none other than God himself (Ps. 8.1). Jesus is not merely

---

[250] Matt. 12.6; 21.12–13, 23–27; 26.55; 26.61; 27.51 (also Luke 1.8–21; 2.22–38, 46–49; 19.45–48; 24.45, 53).

acknowledging the potentially precocious words of children, but is couching them in the context of God's affirmation of himself, through children. As elsewhere, Matthew records children in a positive light, God revealing truth to them (11.25), and they themselves being models of the greatest in the kingdom (18.1–4), worthy of entrance to the kingdom (19.14) and of the prayers of Jesus (19.25). Now, they are presented most positively as those who present Jesus in his true identity when religiously trained adults are blind to the truth.[251]

The judgement of the fig tree (21.18–19), which immediately follows this occasion (see Table 4.10), provides Matthew with the opportunity to affirm the judgement that is to come, at least to the religious leaders. Hosea 9.10 describes Israel as a 'fig tree' that God is to judge.[252] The rejection of Jesus is further identified when his authority is questioned by the religious leaders (21.23—22.14). This is followed by further disputes (22.15–46), resulting in his final denunciation of them (23.1–39).

---

[251] In Jewish tradition, the accuracy of the insights of children is associated with their praising God at the time of the Red Sea miracle (b. *Ber.* 56b; *Sotah* 30b).

[252] See also Jer. 8.13; Joel 1.7, 12; Hab. 3.17.

Jesus heals a deaf man who also has a speech defect
(Mark 7.31–37)

Table 4.11 Healing a deaf man with a speech impediment – the literary context

	Mark
John the Baptist is killed	6.14–29
Feeding of 5,000	6.30–44
Jesus walks on water	6.45–52
Jesus heals at Gennesaret	6.53–56
Jesus denounces the Pharisees	7.1–23
Jesus exorcizes a Syrophoenician woman's daughter	7.24–30
Jesus heals a deaf man with a speech impediment	7.31–37
Jesus feeds 4,000	8.1–10
Jesus is confronted by and warns against the Pharisees	8.11–15
Jesus teaches the disciples	8.16–21

Mark alone includes this healing miracle and gives a detailed description. Matthew follows the Markan order extensively both before (from the record of John's death) and after this incident (until Mark's record of another healing (8.22–26). However, he chooses to omit both healing narratives, instead providing a summary account of Jesus' comprehensive healing ministry (15.29–31).[253]

Mark records the story after the restoration of the daughter of another Gentile, a Syrophoenician woman (7.24–30). Then, after the healing of the deaf man, Mark records the feeding of the, probably Gentile, 4,000 (8.1–10) (see Table 4.11). It is probable that the motif that binds these accounts together relates to the supportive care that Jesus offers those who need help, irrespective of their country of origin or external merit. In telling the stories, Mark provides evidence that Jesus' care is more explicit and personal than may have been expected, an especially valuable lesson for Mark's readers who are experiencing persecution in Rome.

First, Mark provides a detailed account of Jesus' journey prior to this event. He travels from Tyre north to Sidon (a journey of at least 30 miles), then south-east to Galilee (a journey of at least 50 miles) before travelling further east, across the Jordan, to the region of the Decapolis, the exact location of the miracle not being recorded. In so doing, Mark has

---

[253] These are the two main omissions of Mark's Gospel in Matthew and Luke.

identified that Jesus has travelled from Gentile cities on the Mediterranean coast, choosing not to stop in Jewish settlements in Galilee, preferring to travel to mainly Gentile territory across the Jordan. Although he is travelling from Galilee to Jerusalem where he is to reach his final destiny, Jesus makes a time-consuming detour to meet one marginalized Gentile. This is important to Mark's readers, many of whom were not Jews. He reminds them that Jesus has a comprehensive mission that includes people from all countries, no journey being too long to meet someone in need, even a Gentile. Indeed, this is not the first time that Mark records Jesus travelling to Gentile territory where he ministers to Gentiles (5.1–20; 7.24–30), and he has already recorded that Gentiles have come to Jesus and been restored to health by him (3.8).[254]

The desire of Jesus to take his time to heal personally and intimately

The unusually comprehensive description of the way that Jesus ministers to the man is probably intended to convey important information to him concerning the healing that is about to occur, as well as informing the readers that although healing is important to the man (and Jesus), there are more important issues at stake here than physical restoration. Mark identifies this person as being deaf and having a speech impediment (*mogilalon*), both of which are rectified by Jesus, the man being enabled to hear and speak unimpeded.

Those who have brought the man request that Jesus lay his hand upon him,[255] which indicates their hope that Jesus will heal him, the action of laying on of hands being associated with healing.[256] However, Jesus does not immediately heal him, but, on this occasion, takes him aside from the others.[257] He may have done this in order to put the man at ease, instead of leaving him to be the centre of the crowd's attention, a welcome initiative for a deaf person who also struggles to speak. There is no indication that Jesus does this because the people manifest a lack of faith in Jesus (indeed, they are the ones who bring the man to Jesus for help), or to keep the miracle a secret (especially since everyone present was aware of it), or to have the quiet necessary to achieve a difficult healing. What is of significance is that Jesus takes time out of his busy schedule to heal

---

[254] Caesarea Philippi is a pagan city (8.27).

[255] The use of the hand indicates a difference with the deaf and dumb demoniac (9.17–25), upon whom Jesus did not lay his hand.

[256] 1.31, 41; 5.23, 41; 6.5.

[257] The only other occasion that Jesus does this is in another unique Markan miracle (Mark 8.22–26).

the man in a gentle, unhurried fashion, which will ultimately reveal that Jesus is not just a healer of crowds but is also committed to individuals, providing restoration in a most personal way.

Jesus first puts his fingers in 'his' (probably the man's) ears.[258] On this occasion, the reference is to Jesus touching not merely the man, as he has done with others in the past (2.41; 5.23, 41), but, in particular, his ears. The fact that the finger is mentioned may be of significance, because, in the OT, it is presented as a metaphor for power.[259] However, it may simply be that Jesus is identifying to a man who is deaf that he is aware of his problem without having to be told.

Then Jesus spits, probably on his own fingers, transferring his spittle to the man's tongue. The use of spittle would have made sense to the man, more than it might to a modern reader. Although the use of spittle in healing is unusual, it is referred to elsewhere in contexts of healing and sickness.[260] Most importantly, it was an accepted feature of the worldviews of many ancient cultures that spittle owned natural curative properties.[261] Although it may be viewed as an element of magical technique,[262] it is more likely that Jesus intended to indicate to the deaf man, who could not hear what Jesus may have wanted to say to him and could not ask questions because of his speech impediment, that something therapeutic was going to happen to him; a symbolic context is thus most likely. The message symbolized in this act is that the spittle, which has come from Jesus' perfectly functioning tongue, is now being transferred to the man's imperfectly working tongue, offering the unspoken message (to a deaf man) that he too will be able to speak perfectly.

---

[258] It is not certain if Mark is referring to the ears of Jesus or those of the man, but the context indicates that it is the latter.

[259] Exod. 8.19; Ps. 8.3; cf. Luke 11.20.

[260] Mark 8.23; John 9.6; Gal. 4.14.

[261] b. *Baba Bathra* 126b indicates that the spittle of the firstborn has healing properties. Some rabbis asserted that the spittle of a fasting man possessed anti-demonic and anti-magical powers, especially if he had been fasting for 40 days (b. *Shab.* 108b; *Sanh.* 49b; *Zeb.* 95b). Pliny (*Nat. Hist.* 27.75; 28.5, 48, 61, 77; 29.12, 32) records that the spittle of a fasting man had power over snake poison, leprosy, epilepsy; Tacitus (*Hist.*, 4.81–2; 6.18) records that Vespasian healed a blind man by placing his spittle on his eyes; see also Blackburn (*Theios Aner.* pp. 218–19) for other examples in Hellenistic and Jewish literature.

[262] So Hull, *Hellenistic Magic*, p. 76. However, other evidence demonstrates that a therapeutic association is more likely. Also, Mark does not explicitly assert that the spittle has magical power and there is limited evidence that spittle was used in magical contexts during Hellenistic or early Roman periods; see also Yamauchi, E., 'Magic or Miracle? Diseases, Demons and Exorcisms', in *Gospel Perspectives 6.* (eds) Wenham, D., Blomberg, C. L., JSOT Press, Sheffield, 1986, pp. 137–9.

Next, Jesus looks up to heaven, an act suggestive of prayer (see 6.41), indicating to the man the source of his power. Then, Jesus sighs[263] (*stenadzō*, 'I groan, sigh'), a word that is only used here in the Gospels, perhaps indicative of his compassion or prayer. Finally, Jesus says to the man, in Aramaic, *Ephphatha*, which Mark translates as 'be opened', the aorist verb signifying a complete and immediate restoration. By providing the translation, Mark undermines any suggestion that this is a magical incantation. The result is that the man is able to hear and speak clearly. Although Jesus exhorts the witnesses not to tell anyone about this miracle,[264] they enthusiastically disobey (also 1.44–45), because they are exceedingly astonished (*huperperissōs exeplēssonto* – a double superlative) at his ability to restore such conditions.

As before, this command to silence is probably because Jesus was keen to ensure that people did not broadcast his healing authority, concerned that it would feed inappropriate aspirations that excluded an appreciation of his spiritual mission and which instead concentrated on physical, restorative aspirations. Even though the healed man is not recorded as speaking, the message of the miracle is clear and the corporate voice of the people sums up the event: 'he has done all things well' (7.37).

Although Jesus could have healed the man immediately, as he did on other occasions,[265] this time Jesus led the man to his healing, purposefully and personally. The reason may be deduced if one remembers the readers of this Gospel. Given the probability that they were Christians based in Rome, they were being (or were soon to be) persecuted and they needed to know that, as well as being a healer, Jesus was aware of their situation. As with the man, he would also function as their personal guide, offering individual attention to them in their unsettling circumstances.

Jesus is soon to reveal that he is to suffer and die[266] and to indicate that the path of suffering will be one that his disciples will also walk.[267] This healing thus provides an important lesson for all would-be disciples. Even though each will follow a different path of suffering, they will all be following Jesus, who will treat them as individuals, taking time to bring them through their suffering to a resolution determined by him.

---

[263] Exod. 2.24, 6.5; Tobit 3.1; Rom. 8.22; this may be understood as indicating deep distress; Cunningham (S., 'The Healing of the Deaf and Dumb Man (Mark 7.31–37)', *AJET.* 9.2, 1990, p. 19) relates it to compassionate prayer; Cranfield (*Gospel According to Mark.* p. 252) identifies it with strong emotion against the power of Satan.

[264] See also 1.44–45; 3.12; 5.43; 8.30; 9.9.

[265] 1.26, 42; 2.12; 5.29, 42; 7.30.

[266] 8.31; 9.12, 31; 10.33–34.

[267] 8.34–35; 10.21, 29–30, 39, 45.

However, there is another lesson to be gleaned from this healing and it relates to the term used to describe the man's speech problem (*mogilalon*). This is the only occurrence of this term in the Bible except for Isaiah 35.6 and it is probable that Mark is recollecting this prophecy. There, the term is used to refer to God restoring the deaf and enabling the tongue that is imperfectly functioning to sing joyfully. It describes God returning in an era dominated by metaphors of wilderness which is to be transformed by him as will be the people who dwell there; they will be ransomed, restored and provided with a life that will be enjoyed in a reconstituted creation (Isa. 35.1–10). The startling message that Mark presents is that it is Jesus who fulfils this OT prophecy; it is Jesus who is coming to end the bondage of people, and this message is most clearly identified in his mission to people in need, including Gentiles.

Jesus heals a blind man (Mark 8.22–26)

Table 4.12 Healing a blind man – the literary context

	Mark
Jesus heals a deaf man with a speech impediment	7.31–37
Jesus feeds 4,000	8.1–10
Jesus is confronted by and warns against the Pharisees	8.11–15
Jesus teaches the disciples	8.16–21
Jesus heals a blind man	**8.22–26**
Peter's declaration concerning Jesus at Caesarea Philippi	8.27–30
Jesus foretells his Passion	8.31
Peter rebukes Jesus and is rebuked by Jesus	8.32–33
Jesus teaches the disciples about discipleship	8.34–38

This miracle, a restoration from blindness, is recorded only in Mark. The healing is prefaced by people bringing the blind man to Jesus in the hope that he will touch him. In response, Jesus leads him away from the people, on this occasion out of the village. Although there is no explicit reference to faith, it is implied in the readiness of the man to go with Jesus, wherever he may lead him. As in 7.31–37, there is no indication in the narrative that Jesus took the man out of the village because of any unbelief on the part of the people.

Jesus is initially recorded as spitting on the eyes of the man. Although this seems a bizarre element in the healing process, it is important to remember the therapeutic properties associated with spittle in the ancient world.[268] The gentle spray of spittle from Jesus on the man's eyes would have offered to him the notion that healing was to be anticipated.

This action was followed by Jesus' question as to the quality of the man's sight, the only time Jesus questions the outcome of his healing ministry. Unusually, the healing is not immediate, and only partial, for the man can only see indistinctly, resulting in Jesus, uniquely, again laying his hands on him, whereupon sight is completely restored. It would be inappropriate to assume that this gradual healing is a paradigm for modern divine healings, which may occur over a period of time, because, except for this one occasion, all the recorded healings of Jesus were immediate. Also unlikely is the suggestion that this was a particularly serious form of blindness that resulted in Jesus' inability to heal the man immediately, given that there is no suggestion anywhere in the Gospels that illness,

---

[268] See the narrative in Mark 7.31–37.

demons or even death could obstruct Jesus in fulfilling his aspirations. Similarly, there is no suggestion in the narrative that the man lacked sufficient faith for the healing to occur or that he needed to be patient.

Mark emphasizes the eventual complete restoration by not only stating that the man's sight was restored (*apekatestē*, aorist tense), but also that he (continually) saw (*eneblepsen* (imperfect active from *blepō*, 'I see') everything (*apanta*) clearly (*tēlaugōs*). After the healing has occurred, the man is told to go home and not to enter the village. It is possible that he did not live there, and therefore he was instructed to go to his home without going through the village. Thus, unusually, the narrative ends with the man not being described as following Jesus or speaking about Jesus.

Insofar as the author does not expand on the significance of the two-part healing, there is value in considering the literary context (see Table 4.12).

Prior to this narrative, Mark records a misunderstanding among the disciples concerning a statement by Jesus, relating to the Pharisees and Sadducees.[269] Jesus responds by asking them, 'Having eyes do you not *see* . . . Do you not yet understand?' (8.14–21).[270] After the healing of the blind man, Mark then records another conversation between Jesus and his disciples concerning his identity. In response to his question, 'Who do men say that I am?', they provide answers. When he asks them for a personal opinion, Peter replies 'You are the Christ.' However, although Peter provides an accurate response, it is soon clear that he, as well as the other disciples, does not understand the sober and painful implications of Jesus' Messiahship. Although Peter's initial identification of Jesus is correct, the following verses reveal Jesus strongly rebuking him for acting as an instrument of Satan because he disagreed with Jesus' prophecy concerning his sufferings to come (8.33). Peter's perception of Jesus was at best partial; he and the other disciples did not perceive the true mission of Jesus and, as such, they were (and remained for some time) partially sighted (9.10, 32, 38).

Mark's unusual record of the gradual healing of the blind man describes a parallel development to that of the perception of the disciples

---

[269] A similar misunderstanding concerning Jesus by the disciples is recorded on the previous occasion when they visited Bethsaida (6.51–52); other references to the disciples misunderstanding Jesus are reflected elsewhere in Mark (4.41; 7.18; 9.32, 34, 38; 10.24, 35–39).

[270] Parallel words and concepts in the passage under consideration and those preceding and following it may be of value in establishing a link, including the words, 'ask' (vv. 23, 27, 29), 'see' (vv. 18, 23, 24), 'eyes' (vv. 18, 25) and 'people' (vv. 24, 27).

concerning Jesus, particularly of Peter, who will come to a full realization of the person of Jesus only after receiving further ministry from him. As with the blind man, full restoration will occur, but it will not be immediate and not at Caesarea Philippi. All would-be disciples, and in particular Mark's readers, can take comfort from this: even the Twelve failed to see Jesus' status immediately and fully. The promise to them, and to future believers, is that such immature perceptions will be perfected, Jesus taking the responsibility to facilitate such progress in sight.

Like the blind man, the readers also find themselves in a period of uncertainty, perplexity, confusion and limited insight concerning their present circumstances. Mark's message to them is that although they may not see clearly, Jesus is still in charge of their lives and he may be trusted to bring them into fullness of sight. The fact that the healing takes place with no witnesses, but that it is recorded by Mark in full, indicates that the beneficiaries of any message associated with the healing are the readers of the Gospel rather than those who brought the blind man to Jesus.

1 Jesus heals the man of his blindness, reminiscent of prophecies in which God is forecast as undertaking this role;[271] what was God's sovereign responsibility is now seen also to be attributed to Jesus.

2 This is the final healing recorded in Mark, except for the healing of another blind man (10.45–52). It may be appropriate to enquire whether Mark is thus hinting to his readers that a new era is commencing for Jesus and his disciples, in which clarity of sight for the future is less certain and the reality of suffering is more definite. There is, hereon, for Mark, a greater emphasis on the topic of discipleship which now includes the notion of suffering.[272]

3 The fact that the healing takes place in Bethsaida[273] is also significant in that it was located on the north-east coast of the Sea of Galilee in predominantly Gentile territory. As with the deaf man with a speech impediment, Jesus has traversed in the opposite direction to his intended destination, Jerusalem, for a purpose – to bring sight to a blind man who cannot even see Jesus, let alone go to where he is. The Markan

---

[271] Ps. 146.8; Isa. 29.18; 35.5.

[272] 8.31–38; 9.17–31; 10.33–44.

[273] It is uncertain if this is a Bethsaida that is located in Jewish (west of the Jordan) or Gentile (east of the Jordan) territory. Iverson (K. R., *Gentiles in the Gospel of Mark*. T. & T. Clark, London, 2007, pp. 86–8), among others, argues for the latter; this being the case, the relevance for non-Jewish readers is significant. Most commentators ignore the geographical uncertainty.

readers are similarly in danger of being unable to 'see' Jesus because their sight has been obstructed by the painful ordeals they are experiencing as a result of following Jesus. The danger awaiting the people of Bethsaida was that, although they had seen Jesus, they had chosen to close their eyes to his truth (Matt. 11.21//Luke 10.13).

The readers of the narrative are thus given the opportunity to gain hope or remain in darkness. The healing of the blind man provides them with a narrative that affirms that Jesus takes the responsibility in leading the blind man to complete healing, demonstrating that he is in charge during those times in his life of darkness, of gloom and also of completely restored sight. They are encouraged to believe the same with regard to Jesus' presence in their lives.

Jesus raises from the dead the son of a widow (Luke 7.11–17)

Table 4.13 Raising a widow's son from the dead – the literary context

	Luke
Jesus heals many by the sea	6.17–19
Jesus teaches	6.20–49
Jesus heals a centurion's servant	7.1–10
Jesus raises a widow's son from the dead	**7.11–17**
John the Baptist wonders about Jesus	7.18–20
Jesus responds to John's questions	7.21–35
Jesus is anointed by a woman	7.36–50

Luke alone records this incident, one of four resurrections narrated by him.[274] It is placed after the healing of a centurion's servant (see Table 4.13), thus drawing attention to the fact that Jesus ministered to both socially significant and marginalized people, the latter represented by a widow. The unfortunate position of a widow in Jewish society was sometimes associated with shame and reproach (Isa. 54.4). The fact that tithes were to be given to widows (Deut. 26.12), and that they were not to be mistreated (Exod. 22.21–23; Jer. 7.5–6) but defended (Isa. 1.17), indicates their vulnerability.[275] Generally, a widow was not eligible to inherit her husband's estate, and any future remarriage was not always looked on kindly; indeed, the high priest was forbidden to marry a widow.[276] In view of her helpless position, it is of interest to note that Jesus helps this widow and miraculously transforms her weak status to one of stability and hope.

The account is followed by the record of John the Baptist's disciples, who are sent by him to request Jesus' confirmation that he is the Messiah. Jesus' reply includes quotations from Isaiah 8.14–15; 29.18 and 35.5–6 which act as evidence that Jesus has fulfilled OT prophecy in his ministry of healing and preaching good news to the poor. The resurrection of the son of the widow of Nain, a small village[277] 6 miles south-east of Nazareth, in particular demonstrates Jesus' mission to the poor.

In the context of a large crowd following Jesus, including his disciples, and a large crowd from the city accompanying the widow, the focus is

---

[274] Luke 8.49–55; Acts 9.36–43; 20.7–12.

[275] A childless widow was obliged to marry her brother-in-law (Gen. 38.8), having to wait for him to be eligible if he was too young at the time.

[276] Lev. 21.14; see also b. *Pes.* 111a–b.

[277] Despite it being referred to as a *polis* (city), it was a village.

nevertheless placed on one person whose isolation, albeit in a crowd, is identified graphically. Her tragedy is rehearsed carefully by Luke in that he mentions that the funeral was of her only son, who had died young (7.14), and that she was a widow. She had already lost her husband; now she has lost her son, her only son;[278] her vulnerability is clear for all to see. Her grief is further emphasized in that, following normal procedure, it is probable that the son has died that day and the body is being taken to burial before nightfall, to be followed by 30 days of mourning. Furthermore, the location of the meeting of Jesus, the giver of life, and death, personified in the corpse, is significant in that it is at the gates of the settlement. Insofar as bodies were to be buried outside the village, the meeting occurs at the threshold of that final journey away from the village community which represented home. However, before they get too far from that haven of hope, Jesus changes the direction of the group and transforms the hopeless journey out of the village into a hope-filled journey back home. The widow may have wondered what she had done to deserve such a calamity and why God had allowed it to happen; she would soon find out that, in the person of Jesus, God had come to resolve the situation.

Not only does Luke reveal to the readers Jesus' emotions but also his words; before any restoration occurs, Jesus encourages the widow to stop weeping; one can only imagine her consternation when a stranger suggested that she should not weep at the death of her only son with all the implications of that loss. But Luke precedes this request with the fact that Jesus went out of his way (*proserchomai*, 'I approach') to meet her; although the verb is used in Luke to refer to people coming to Jesus,[279] this is the only time that it is used of Jesus going to a person. At the same time, he touched the open bier (not a closed coffin but, more likely, a few planks on which the covered body was laid),[280] probably to stop the procession rather than to draw attention to touch as a feature of the miracle. Jesus is not recorded as touching the dead person or raising him to a sitting position. However, insofar as that action would have made Jesus ceremonially unclean (Num. 19.11–12, 16), it is appropriate for Luke to include this information in order to emphasize the supremacy of Jesus, who is not contaminated by death, but is the victor over it; he is, after all, referred to as 'the Lord' (7.13).

---

[278] See also 8.42; 9.38.

[279] 8.24, 44; 9.12, 42; 13.31; 20.27; 23.36, 52.

[280] The word used, *soros*, may refer to a coffin, a receptacle in which the remains of the body are kept, or the bier on which was carried the coffin or corpse.

The fact that Jesus spoke to the widow again identifies her as the focus of his attention. The emphasis on her is further developed in that Luke refers to her seven times in the brief pericope, specifically mentioning that Jesus gave her son to her.[281] In the narrative, the woman is not presented as speaking, only weeping. It is Jesus who functions centre stage, whose words are recorded, who takes control of the situation and who resolves the trauma.

The reference to Jesus' compassion is only used here in a Lukan healing narrative. No specific reason is given, though it may be conceived that she is particularly unfortunate in that not only is she a widow, but now also her only child has died, the trauma being extended in that, as a son, he would have provided for her in her old age. In the previous narrative, Luke presents Jesus as being impressed by a centurion who trusted him to restore his servant; now, Jesus is presented with a woman whose situation is the cause of even greater distress. There is no mention of faith on the part of any present, no request to Jesus that he may intervene, and no hope that he might. Although healings have been recorded thus far in Luke, this is the first reference to death in the Gospel and there is little that would have encouraged the widow to anticipate the possibility that her son would or could be resurrected. However, Jesus does not function as the healer of broken hearts and bodies only when he is asked to intervene, and here he takes the initiative and provides what no one in the crowd would have even thought possible – the restoration to life of one who had died – and he does it with a word, 'arise', followed by the man sitting up[282] and speaking – clear evidence that a remarkable event had occurred; Jesus speaks to a dead man, commanding him to arise, and he does.

After the miracle had occurred, the people referred to Jesus as a great prophet, reminiscent of the words in Deuteronomy 18.15; there are also similarities with the resurrection performed by Elisha (1 Kings 17.10–23).[283] More significantly, they perceived that God had 'visited his people', the same word *epeskepsato* ('visited') being only used elsewhere in Luke in 1.68 with reference to God visiting his people in order to redeem them. Here, Jesus takes on that divine role.

---

[281] The previous reference to *didōmi* ('I give') in Luke is 6.38 in which extravagant giving is described (see also 1 Kings 17.23).

[282] The only other time this word (*anekathisen*) is used in the NT is with reference to the resurrection of Dorcas (Acts 9.40).

[283] The city gate (Luke 7.12; 1 Kings 17.10); a widow and only son (Luke 7.12; 1 Kings 17.12); the concept of his being given to his mother (Luke 7.15; 1 Kings 17.23).

Thus, Jesus is identified as the Lord (7.13), an increasingly popular term used of Jesus in the Gospel. Although Jesus is addressed previously as 'lord' (*kurios*), probably meaning 'master' (6.5), he is much more often described as *the* Lord in Luke,[284] this occasion being the first of many to come in Luke (other than the ascription of the angel to Jesus (2.11)). Of particular significance is that earlier in Luke, the term is used to refer to God;[285] now it refers to Jesus. Little wonder that fear or awe was experienced by all who witnessed the restoration, resulting in them glorifying God. Thereafter, the report was transmitted throughout Judaea.

As before, the healing is of less significance than what it portrays about the person and mission of Jesus. He has come to re-establish togetherness, demonstrating his supremacy by a victory over death, achieved with ease. As the widow re-enters the village with her friends again, her future beckons with hope, and it is Jesus who has made it possible.

---

[284] 7.13; 10.1; 11.39; 13.15; 17.6; 18.6; 19.31, 34; 22.31, 61; 24.34.

[285] 1.25, 28, 58, 68; 2.15; 20.42. The word *kurios* is used of an earthly master (12.37, 42, 43, 45, 46; 14.23; 16.3, 8; 20.13, 15.

Jesus heals a paralysed woman (Luke 13.10–17)

Table 4.14 Healing a paralysed woman – the literary context

	Luke	Matthew
Jesus teaches the crowds	12.1–59	5.25–26; 6.19–34; 10.26–36; 16.2–3; 24.42–51
Jesus requires repentance	13.1–5	
The parable of the barren fig tree	13.6–9	
Jesus heals a paralysed woman	**13.10–17**	
The parable of the mustard seed	13.18–19	13.31–32
The parable of the leaven	13.20–21	13.33
Jesus teaches about the narrow door	13.22–30	7.13–14; 19.30
Jesus weeps over Jerusalem	13.31–35	23.37–39

Luke carefully places this healing, unique to his Gospel, in a context that helps to identify the message undergirding his wider narrative (see Table 4.14). It is set in the context of Jesus teaching in a synagogue on the Sabbath and, with the preceding and following narratives, provides the message of the wider pericope (13.1–30) which relates to the identity of those who are welcomed by God into his kingdom.

Prior to the healing, Luke records Jesus encouraging the Jews to repent and protect themselves from judgement and possible destruction (13.1–5), concluding with a parable of the fig tree (13.6–9). In the latter narrative, the vine grower looks for fruit and, due to its absence, destroys the tree. The force of this uncomfortable message to self-satisfied Jews is apparent: if the fruit of repentance is absent in those listening to Jesus, they will similarly suffer.

However, after the healing narrative, another tree is referred to, the connection between it and the healing made clear by Luke's use of *oun* ('therefore', 13.18). In contrast to the fig tree, this (mustard seed) tree is flourishing, despite starting as a very small seed. More importantly, this tree is associated, by Jesus, with the development of the kingdom of God. Its potential, given its small size, may have been assumed to have been limited but, in reality, it achieved greatness. The message of the parable is that the kingdom of God has the capacity to make a substantial difference in the lives of people despite small beginnings.

The unfruitful fig tree reflects the synagogue ruler in the healing narrative.[286] In his role as leader of a Jewish community, he had so much

---

[286] Jeremiah refers to bad figs (24.2–10) as indicative of the evil deeds of God's people, as a result of which they were judged; the lack of fruit on a fig tree is associated with God's judgement (Jer. 8.13); Mic. 7.1–4 indicates that an absence of fruit on a fig tree is to be equated with the presence of evil. Hos. 9.10 might indicate that the fig tree is a symbol of Israel.

potential to reflect God and his values, but he is destined for judgement because he failed to recognize the true identity of Jesus. However, and by contrast, the flourishing mustard tree represents the new kingdom and is reflected in the once-small woman who functions as a representative of this kingdom. From small and inauspicious beginnings, as reflected in the limited height of the woman due to her being bent over by her illness, the growth of the kingdom is demonstrated in that her remarkable trans-formation benefits many, including those who rejoiced at her healing.

The woman and her disability

The woman is described as having had 'a spirit of infirmity' (*pneuma exousa astheneias*, literally, 'having a spirit of weakness') for 18 years,[287] which resulted in a very severe curvature of the spine. Luke graphically specifies that 'she was bent over and could not fully straighten herself'.[288]

The authority of Jesus

... *to include the excluded*

The woman would have been particularly marginalized because of her disability, exacerbated by the fact that, as a woman, she was already viewed by many men as being an inferior member in a patriarchal society. It is therefore significant to note that in the telling of the story, as in the resurrection of the widow of Nain's son, Luke emphasizes her. Thus, rather than, as elsewhere, commenting on the contents of Jesus' teaching in a synagogue (4.17–21, 43–44) or its authoritative style (4.32), Luke focuses on the one who needs his help; indeed, he refers to her emphatic-ally ('Jesus saw her . . . called to her . . . said (to her) . . . laid his hands upon her' (13.12–13)), also making her the subject of six verbs (she had a spirit of infirmity, she was bent over, she could not straighten herself, she was freed, she was made straight, she praised God (13.11–13)).

Furthermore, Luke records Jesus describing her not simply as a woman, but as 'a daughter of Abraham', a title that has no parallel in the NT.[289] Its

---

[287] This numeral may have symbolic significance; it is mentioned in 13.4. In the OT, 'eighteen' is often used in contexts of subjugation and oppression of the Israelites (Judg. 3.13–14; 10.8; 20.25) and of others (Judg. 20.44; 2 Sam. 8.13; 1 Chron. 18.12).

[288] Wilkinson (J., 'The Case of the Bent Woman', *EvQ*. 49, 1977, pp. 195–205), after analysing the evidence, suggests spondylitis ankylopoietica, which is a fusion of the spinal bones.

[289] The term 'son of Abraham' is used twice in Luke; the one refers to Isaac (3.34), the other meta-phorically to Zacchaeus (19.9) to whom salvation has been granted; Acts 3.25 refers to the children of Abraham as benefiting from God's covenant with him, while Gal. 3.7 states that 'it is those who are of faith who are sons of Abraham'.

significance is not in defining her racial identity, but in affirming her as a person who stands in the line of salvific promises from God.[290] The notion of being a child of Abraham is used elsewhere by Luke to define someone eligible to benefit from God's mercy.[291] That 'a daughter of Abraham' should be refused the opportunity to be healed was, to Jesus at least, unacceptable. Thus, as elsewhere, he laid his hands on her, followed by her complete restoration. Although 4.40 reveals that Jesus laid his hands on many, this is the first and only reference in Luke's Gospel to a woman being touched by Jesus who, because of her status and disability, would not have expected an affectionate touch but more likely a gesture of disregard.

. . . over the Sabbath

A major purpose of the narrative is again to indicate the authority of Jesus to heal on the Sabbath, this being the third of four healings (and one exorcism) achieved by Jesus on the Sabbath, recorded by Luke.[292] Elsewhere, when Jesus initiated a healing without a prior request, it was, as here, to introduce a discussion concerning his authority to function on the Sabbath that led to possible faith in or rejection of him.[293] In particular, Luke uses the incident to identify the true purpose of the Sabbath and to confirm the authority of Jesus as the one who, in establishing justice, has come to liberate the oppressed (4.19), and does so on the Sabbath.[294] This authority is affirmed by the use of the divine title, 'the Lord', for Jesus (13.15).

---

[290] See also 1.72–75; Heb. 11.11–12, 17–19.

[291] 1.54–55; 3.7–9; 13.28–29; 16.22–32; 19.8–10.

[292] This aspect is mentioned elsewhere in each of the Gospels (Matt. 12.10; Mark 1.21–22; 3.4; Luke 4.31–41; 6.6–11; 14.1–6; John 5.1–18; 7.23; 9.14).

[293] See Matt. 12.9–14//s; John 5.2–8; 9.1–12.

[294] Hamm provides a possible chiasm, viewing the narrative as expressing the importance of taking advantage of recognizing the visitation of God through an encounter with the healing Jesus (Hamm, M. D., 'This Sign of Healing, Acts 3.1–10: A Study in Lucan Theology', PhD, St Louis University, 1975, p. 70):

A. 12.49–53. Words of Jesus on the completion of his painful mission
    (In one *oikos* (house), there will be divisions)
  B. 12.54–13.5. Judgement sayings and parables (incl. urgent effort (12.58))
    C. 13.6–9. Growth parable . . . fig tree
      D. 13.10–17. The healing
    C1. 13.18–21. Growth parable . . . mustard tree
  B1. 13.22–30. Judgement sayings and parables (incl. urgent effort (13.24))
A1. 13.31–35. Words of Jesus concerning the completion of his painful mission
    (Your *oikos* (house) will be forsaken)

The synagogue ruler denounces the healing on the Sabbath as being illegitimate.[295] However, Jesus supports the appropriateness of his action while, at the same time, undermining the ruler's interpretation of Sabbath law.[296] Jesus views the ruler as a hypocrite, for he would deny healing for the woman though would willingly work by untying and leading an ox or donkey to provide it with water;[297] he would 'loose' (*luō*) an animal but was unwilling to allow a woman to be 'loosed' (*luthēnai*, aorist tense, from *luō*) from her illness.

It is no coincidence that both the ruler (13.14) and Jesus (13.16) use the same word *dei* ('it is necessary')[298] with reference to their assertions; thus, while the ruler deemed it necessary to work on only six days, Jesus deemed it necessary to heal the woman on the Sabbath. The pedanticism of the ruler concerning the keeping of laws is contrasted with the purpose of Jesus who is concerned to demonstrate love, so fulfilling his agenda identified in 4.18.

... to heal immediately and completely

What is central to the healing is the status of Jesus, who unilaterally heals the woman, associated with his placing his hands upon her. The laying on of hands may be intended to identify the transfer of power from him to her, but it also demonstrates yet again that he does not fear any ceremonial uncleanness associated with illness; at the same time, it indicates that a mere touch is all that is needed to transform a long-standing predicament. However, the healing actually occurs as a result of the command of Jesus, 'you are freed . . .', the perfect tense used suggesting permanence.

As a result, an immediate (*parachrēma*)[299] healing occurs in the woman, consisting of her back being 'made straight', the aorist tense indicating

---

[295] Exod. 20.9 and Deut. 5.13 would be the undergirding verses to support this assumption, on the basis that healing is to be equated with work; b. *'Abod. Zar.* 28b records the view that one should not anoint an eye on the Sabbath; j. *Shab.* 14d, 17f. states that the spittle of a fasting man should not be applied to the eyes on the Sabbath.

[296] See earlier for discussion on the Sabbath.

[297] Sabbath legislation was diverse and complex, as reflected in the Talmud, with a variety of sometimes widely differing interpretations as to what was appropriate activity on the Sabbath (even tying animals up on the Sabbath was questioned but it was allowed in order to stop them from straying (b. *Shab.* 15.2)). However, rather than appeal to this diversity of opinions, Jesus addresses the Jews' hypocrisy.

[298] The word *dei* is used in Luke to refer to priorities of Jesus. Thus, he needs to be in his Father's house (2.49), to preach the gospel (4.43), to suffer . . . and be raised on the third day (9.22; 17.25; 24.7, 26).

[299] A popular word in Luke: ten uses in Luke (8 relating to immediate healings, 1.64; 4.35; 5.25; 8.44, 47, 55; 13.13; 18.43), six in Acts (5 relating to miracles, 3.7; 5.10; 12.23; 13.11; 16.26 (and 16.33)) and only two elsewhere in the NT, both in Matthew (21.19, 20), relating to the immediacy of the death of the fig tree at the word of Jesus.

that it occurred straight away. It is significant to note that the motif of faith is absent; neither is there a request for healing nor a belief on the part of any present that healing was available. Luke records Jesus initiating the healing and thus demonstrates his authority to heal whenever he chooses, including on the Sabbath.

It may be of value to note that the ruler assumes that the issue relates to physical healing, as reflected in his use of the term (*therapeuō*, 'I heal') twice (13.14), a term always used in Luke to refer to physical healing.[300] However, Jesus uses the word *luō* ('I loose') to describe the woman's transformation, with the implication that she has not only been physically healed but also has been more widely loosed – from the physical, diabolic, social, psychological and limiting bondage caused by her illness. This is the only occasion in Luke where *luō* (13.16) and *apoluō* (13.12) are used to describe healing. Jesus brings complete wholeness.

... to overcome any evil influence

Jesus' authority is further affirmed in that he releases the woman from a 'spirit of infirmity'. The identity of the 'spirit' is uncertain. It could refer to the woman being demonized. However, whenever Luke uses *pneuma* in a demonic context, he clarifies its meaning. Thus, although *pneuma* is used of a demon in 4.33, it is included in the phrase, 'having a spirit (*pneuma*) of an unclean demon (*daimoniou akathartou*)'.[301] Also, although he uses *pneuma* in 8.2 to refer to a demon, he clarifies it as being an equivalent term to *daimonion* in the same verse; similarly, *pneuma* clearly refers to a demon in 8.27, 29, 33, 35, 36, for he joins the word with the defining adjective of 'unclean' (*akatharton*); likewise, in 9.39, *pneuma* is used of a demon, affirmed as being a correct interpretation because of the extra qualifications offered (9.42), where the demon is referred to as 'unclean' and specifically as a demon.

More generally, Luke uses *daimonion* when referring to a demon[302] and prefers to use *pneuma* to refer to the Holy Spirit.[303] Finally, the term used for the suffering concerned (*astheneia*) is never used by Luke with reference to demoniacs, and in 8.2 it is used to describe illness rather than demonization.

---

[300] 4.23, 40; 5.15; 6.7, 18; 7.21; 8.2, 43; 9.1, 6; 10.9; 14.3.
[301] 4.33; see also 4.36; 9.42; 11.24.
[302] 4.35; see also 4.41; 9.1; 10.17; 11.15, 18, 19, 20; 13.32.
[303] 1.35; 2.25; 3.22; 4.18; 11.13; 12.10, 12; and 24 occasions in Acts.

It appears unlikely therefore that Luke is indicating a demonic presence. Other evidence may be offered in that nowhere does Jesus touch a demonized person but he touches the woman here, and nowhere does Jesus speak to the demonized person but rather to the demon, but here, he addresses the woman. There is also no description of a demon being cast out. The use of the term *Satan* (13.16) may indicate a malevolent and diabolic context, but it need not demand the strategic activity of Satan, especially since he is never associated with demonized people in the Gospels.[304]

It is probable that the illness is being described by Luke as the result of an evil influence but not resulting in an exorcism. As such, this incident may parallel the healing of Peter's mother-in-law (Luke 4.38–39) where the fever is rebuked. It is thus preferable to view the miracle in terms of a healing from a physical disability, an incident in which a malign, satanic influence has affected this woman.[305]

Jesus provides an opportunity to believe in him

Although the healing is sensational, it is not the healing that is the focus of this pericope; attention is again focused on the attitudes of those present (13.14–17). The religious leader and his colleagues are embarrassingly blind to their loveless reliance on dogma. Instead of rejoicing that one who has been bound by Satan has been released, and that on the most appropriate day, the Sabbath, they are outraged because Jesus has broken the rules that, they perceive, determine correct behaviour for a Sabbath. While recognizing his capacity to heal, for they recommend that people should return the following day in order to be healed (13.14), they fail to see a connection between Jesus' healing authority and his authority over the Sabbath.

Luke identifies the critics of Jesus as being shamed (*katēskunonto*, imperfect tense of *kataiskunō*, 'I am dishonoured, ashamed'). This is the only occasion when this word is used in Luke (and Acts). It does not mean that they realized their error and were ashamed of their mistake, but rather indicates that they had been dishonoured by the stinging and accurate rebuke of Jesus, which had highlighted their egocentric, hypocritical, chauvinistic and unloving attitudes. In an era where honour was valued

---

[304] Though see Luke 22.3; John 13.27; Acts 5.3.
[305] The term 'bond' (*desmos*) is used in Mark 7.35, which describes the miraculous restoration of speech by Jesus in a non-exorcistic miracle, and elsewhere in Luke only in 8.29 to describe a man who was bound in order to protect himself from self-harm.

and dishonour was viewed as a humiliating feature of life, the response of Jesus was serious, affecting the status of the synagogue ruler in the eyes of others. He who had the potential to bestow honour (on Jesus) is dishonoured by his stance to the woman and Jesus; such dishonour places him in the same category as the opponents of God referred to in Isaiah 45.16, 17, who are also shamed.

As often, the miracles of Jesus provide opportunities for the witnesses to place their trust in Jesus, though this does not always happen. On this occasion, *all* the adversaries of Jesus are shamed while the people rejoice at '*all* the glorious things that were done' by him. However, it is only the woman who clearly expresses praise to God, acknowledging that God has worked through Jesus, while the synagogue ruler competes with Jesus and publicly challenges his authority. The woman is excited but the religious leader is exasperated; the former literally stands upright while the latter, and those who agree with him, metaphorically bow low in shame; her back, once bent, is now straight, but the ruler is 'bent' in dishonour.

The parable of the narrow door that follows (13.22–30) (see Table 4.14) is crucial to the wider context (13.1–30) in that it establishes the importance of prompt action, based on an accurate understanding of the authority of the Lord who offers guidance (13.25). Failure to follow Jesus will lead to rejection (13.35). Poignantly, the next healing narrative is also recorded by Luke as occurring on a Sabbath (14.1–6), and other religious leaders question the legitimacy of his healing on the Sabbath, Jesus providing a similar answer to the one he gave to this synagogue ruler. The fact that this is the last recorded visit by Jesus to a synagogue, according to Luke, implies that the presence of Jesus is no longer welcomed by the synagogue authorities.

Conclusion

The significance of this narrative is that it demonstrates the authority of Jesus, both in his ability to heal and in his choice to do so on the Sabbath. It also provides Jesus with an opportunity to mark the Sabbath as the appropriate day for bringing healing, hope and freedom, removing the stultifying effects of bondage and legalism. The authoritative stance that Jesus takes is such that it calls for a decision to follow or to reject him. The catalyst caused by the healing has activated a response but it is varied. The religious leader assumes Jesus has made a mistake, but the woman praises God; the readers must make up their own minds based on the evidence before them as to how they will respond to Jesus.

Jesus heals a man with dropsy (Luke 14.1–6)

Table 4.15 Healing a man with dropsy – the literary context

	Luke	Matthew
Jesus heals a paralysed woman	13.10–17	
The parable of the mustard seed	13.18–19	13.31–32
The parable of the leaven	13.20–21	13.33
Jesus teaches about the narrow door	13.22–30	
Jesus weeps over Jerusalem	13.31–35	13.34–35
Jesus heals a man with dropsy	**14.1–6**	
The parable that focuses on humility	14.7–14	
The parable of the great banquet	14.15–24	some similarities with 22.1–10
Jesus teaches concerning true discipleship	14.25–35	some similarities with 10.37–38

The context is helpful in establishing the importance of this miracle unique to Luke (see Table 4.15). Prior to the healing, Luke records another unique Sabbath healing (13.10–17). That healing is followed by two parables (13.18–21) and Jesus' teaching about the danger of painful judgement and rejection (13.22–30), such a prospect awaiting Jerusalem because the people fail to recognize the status of Jesus (13.31–35).

In the healing of the man with dropsy, a similar theme is being developed by Luke. Again, this healing is criticized by rulers, on this occasion Pharisees. As in 13.10–17, Luke follows the healing with two parables, both of which relate to the healing of the man, both identifying the superiority of compassion over legalism. Finally, paralleling 13.22–30, Luke records Jesus' teaching about true discipleship in 14.25–35.

The man and his disability

The healing takes place in the context of a meal at the home of a Pharisee who was also a ruler. A man is there who is suffering from dropsy,[306] a frustrating, embarrassing and potentially life-threatening condition, made all the worse by the common assumption that it may have been caused by gluttony, sin[307] or an unhygienic lifestyle.[308]

---

[306] Dropsy is a severe condition that involves an internal accumulation of fluids (Lev. 15.1–12) and also, paradoxically, a craving to drink.

[307] b. *Shab.* 33a speculates that it may have been caused by inappropriate sexual activities; *Lev. Rab.* 15.2, commenting on Job 28.25, specifically ascribes it to sin.

[308] b. *Ber.* 25a later suggests that it may have been caused by refusing to defecate.

The healing

The man is not identified in any detail; it is not even mentioned if he requests to be healed, and no faith is expressed by him before or after the healing; indeed, the healing is barely mentioned. Luke refers to the three actions of Jesus – taking the man, healing (*iasato*, from *iaomai*, 'I heal') him,[309] and letting him go – the aorist tense used in each verb indicating the immediacy of the actions.

The miracle provides the opportunity for Luke to demonstrate that Jesus is doing the work of God, healing and setting a person free, and on the Sabbath. The religious leaders are forced to shelter behind Sabbath legislation and silence, for they are not equipped to provide such healing.

The opposition

Before Luke records the healing or even mentions that the man needed restoration, he informs the readers that despite them dining together, the Pharisees were watching Jesus (*paratēreō*), the term being used on three occasions in Luke[310] and once in Acts (9.24),[311] each relating to a malicious action leading to the possibility of accusation, arrest or death; the present tense of the plural participle used by Luke indicates a careful and continuous observation by the Pharisees. Even though Luke uses a very common and apparently casual phrase (*kai egeneto en tō*, loosely translated as, 'and it came about that as . . .'),[312] he is actually introducing an occasion charged with menace, as it appears that a trap is being set for Jesus.

Before the healing occurs, Jesus asks a question concerning the appropriateness (*exestin*, 'is it permissible?') of healing on the Sabbath. Luke reveals the prescience of Jesus in that he writes, 'Jesus answered [the Pharisees]', even though they are not recorded as having asked him a question. The word *exestin* is used on five occasions in Luke and each of them is in the context of Jesus being accused of breaking Sabbath laws (6.2, 4; 20.22) and healing on the Sabbath in particular (6.9; 14.3). Rather than ask them if they thought that he had the power to heal on the Sabbath, Jesus asks whether they would permit a person to heal someone, the irony being that they themselves did not have the power so to do.

---

[309] A popular verb used by Luke to refer to supernatural healings (5.17; 6.18, 19; 7.7; 8.47; 9.2, 11, 42; 14.4; 17.15; 22.51) and four times in Acts (9.34; 10.38; 28.8, 27); Matthew uses it four times, Mark once, and John three times. Of the 26 occasions that *iaomai* is used in the NT, 15 are in Luke-Acts.

[310] 6.7; 14.1; 20.20.

[311] Only elsewhere in Mark 3.2 and Gal. 4.10.

[312] Matthew uses this phrase, or one very similar, once, Mark twice, John once, but Luke uses it 22 times. Only here and in 20.1 does the phrase precede the questioning of Jesus' authority; all the other occurrences are introducing favourable events.

Their silence is not commented on by Luke, though it may indicate that they wished Jesus to implicate himself further (by healing the man). It is also possible that the question offered them a conundrum; if they were to respond that it was not permissible, they might be accused of being uncompassionate, while if they acknowledged that it was permissible in some situations, they might have found themselves perilously close to authorizing the healing of the man by Jesus.

After healing the man, Jesus calls into question the Pharisees' unspoken hypocrisy and selfishness by comparing his healing of this person with the humane rescue of a son or an ox that has fallen into a well on the Sabbath. The illustration Jesus offers in the narrative is particularly apposite since it reflects the willingness of his opponents to rescue an animal from drowning in a well,[313] while they refused to allow him to rescue a man suffering from an accumulation of fluid in his body.

After the healing narrative concludes, Luke records Jesus telling two parables to the guests. In the first, he addresses selfish tendencies (14.7–11), identifying the importance of determining right priorities, concluding with a recommendation that the poor and sick be given prominence in special social gatherings (14.12–14).

The second parable (14.15–24) provides the reader with a comparison between the meal that Jesus attended at the Pharisee's home and the 'great banquet' that is clearly related to the anticipated Jewish messianic banquet, participation in which was anticipated as being a blessed experience. However, Jesus destabilizes the audience of religious leaders by exploring the identity of such participants, questioning whether those who think they are going to be present at that banquet will actually be there.

The challenge to the readers, as well as those present at the time of Jesus' teaching, is that not all those originally invited[314] will accept the invitation; as a result of this rejection, they will be replaced by others who have been searched for, despite their being socially unacceptable. Even though Jesus stayed with the Pharisees, later eating with them (14.7, 15), it does not appear that they chose to follow him, as further accusations followed (15.1–2). In view of their unwillingness to adopt his teaching (15.2), thereafter Jesus turns and speaks to the crowds (14.25), graphically offering them (not the religious leaders) guidelines for discipleship (14.26–33).

---

[313] b. *Shab.* 128b states that it is permissible to rescue an animal if it has fallen into a pit, although some rabbis preferred to provide it with food until the next day when it might be rescued.

[314] *kaleō* ('I call'), 14.7, 8, 9, 10, 12, 13, 16, 17, 24.

Jesus heals ten lepers (Luke 17.11–19)

Table 4.16 Healing ten lepers – the literary context

	Luke
The parable of the dishonest steward	16.1–9
Jesus teaches concerning money	16.10–15
Jesus teaches about the law and divorce	16.16–18
The rich man and Lazarus	16.19–31
Jesus teaches about temptation and forgiveness	17.1–4
Jesus teaches about faith and service	17.5–10
Jesus heals ten lepers	**17.11–19**
Jesus teaches about the coming kingdom of God	17.20–37
The parable of the widow and the judge	18.1–8
The parable of the Pharisee and the tax-collector	18.9–14

This unique record of a healing by Jesus follows a selection of various teachings offered by Jesus to his disciples (16.1–13; 17.1–10) and the Pharisees (16.14–31), loosely related to the lifestyle of a disciple. It is followed by further teaching to the Pharisees (17.20–21; 18.9–14) and the disciples (17.22—18.8) that, significantly, deals with being prepared for the coming kingdom of God (see Table 4.16). In this narrative, although healing may be the obvious priority of the lepers, Jesus anticipates a more pressing priority that only one of them identifies. It relates to the provision of salvation, leading to the possibility of personal discipleship and benefiting from the presence of the kingdom of God. However, only one will realize that potential.

Ten lepers stand some way from Jesus (and probably outside the village), as required by the law,[315] and thus when they address Jesus they do so by raising their voices, specifically referring to him as 'Jesus' and 'master' (*epistatēs*).[316] They appeal to his mercy,[317] being the first people recorded as doing this in Luke.[318] Interestingly, Luke has regularly referred to the fact that mercy is a central element in the character of God;[319] now Jesus will grant it.

---

[315] Lev. 13.46; Num. 5.2–4; various Jewish conclusions have been offered as to the appropriate distance to be maintained by a leper from a non-leprous person (*Lev. Rab.* 16 (116c); 11QTemple).

[316] Only Luke uses this term in the NT and, other than this reference, each is used of Jesus by one of the Twelve (5.5; 8.24, 45; 9.33, 49).

[317] A concept referred to ten times in Luke (nine in Matthew, two in Mark and none in John).

[318] The only other person who appealed to the mercy of Jesus in Luke was a blind man (18.38–39).

[319] 1.50, 54, 58, 72, 78.

Jesus apparently initially ignores the lepers' problem and does not heal them but instead instructs them to show themselves to the local priests. Of course, ancient readers would have understood the significance of this command in that it was the priest who had the sole authority to determine if leprosy had been cleansed, as a result of which a leper would have been eligible to rejoin society, ceremonially clean (Lev. 13, 14). Without any specific reference to the faith of the lepers, and with an absence of touch, Luke records that they were healed while on the way to the priest.

However, although the healing is sensational, it is not the healing authority of Jesus that is the focus of the narrative but, again, the response to Jesus by those who have been healed. One of the healed lepers returns to thank Jesus. However, this narrative does not provide a lesson in gratitude. Rather, it highlights the importance of an accurate perception of the person of Jesus; thus, the presentation by Luke of the man's response is carefully delineated.

As soon as this man recognized that he was healed, rather than continue to the priest, he returns to Jesus. His going to the priest so that he may acknowledge that he has been cleansed is superseded by the more important task of returning to Jesus to honour the one who has cleansed him. Although going to the priest may be valuable, going to Jesus is vital.

Luke records that the man 'turned back', using a word (*hupestrepsen*, aorist tense from *hupostrephō*, 'I return, turn back') which is common in Luke-Acts but only used in three other references in the NT.[320] Thereafter, the man glorifies God, a response offered by others in Luke who had been healed[321] or who were impressed by Jesus,[322] and he does this loudly.[323] Although he could have glorified God where he was or in the synagogue,[324] after he had fulfilled Jesus' command, it is of interest that Luke is keen to inform the readers that the man first returned to Jesus in order to glorify God in his presence. Although it is unlikely that he assumes that Jesus is God and thus worthy of being glorified as such by him,[325] it is probable that Luke desires the connection to be established that Jesus' ministry is sanctioned by God, and thus it is appropriate to glorify God for an action

---

[320] Gal. 1.17; Heb. 7.1; 2 Pet. 2.21. The Gospel of Luke uses it 21 times and Acts uses it 11 times.

[321] 5.25; 13.13; 18.43 .

[322] 4.15; 5.26; 7.16; 23.47.

[323] See also 1.42; 23.46.

[324] Jewish law allowed the presence of lepers in synagogues, albeit behind a screen (b. *Pes.* 67a).

[325] Though the other references to thanks giving in Luke-Acts are all indicative of thanks to God (18.11; 22.17, 19; Acts 27.35; 28.15); Gaiser (F. J., '"Your Faith Has Made You Well": Healing and Salvation in Luke 17.12–19', *Word World*. 16.3, 1996, p. 296) argues that giving thanks to God and thanking Jesus are equivalent actions.

that Jesus has achieved. It is also of significance that in Luke's presentation of a developing appreciation of who Jesus is, the man falls on his face[326] at Jesus' feet and thanks him.

Luke provides an unusually detailed process which prepares the readers to be impressed with the response of the healed man, especially since he was the only one to return and he was a Samaritan. This one person, uniquely described in the NT as 'a foreigner',[327] behaves as a true disciple of Jesus. The previous reference in Luke to Samaritans is in 9.52–53 where they refuse hospitality to Jesus.[328] Now, a Samaritan recognizes his high status. Whereas the other nine lepers presumed Jesus to be a miracle worker and his passing through their village a propitious coincidence, the Samaritan invests much more importance in Jesus. Although the ten lepers were cured, it was the Samaritan who, when he 'saw that he was healed', perceived that the healer was someone sensationally special. In this, he demonstrates his faith in Jesus, a feature which concludes the narrative (17.19).[329]

Luke uses three different verbs to refer to the man's health, which provides further evidence as to the significance of the story and the importance of the man's response. While all are cleansed (*katharizō*, 'I cleanse', 17.14, 17), only the one who recognizes that he has been physically healed (*iaomai*, 'I heal', 17.15), is made whole (*sōzō*, 'I save, heal', 17.19). It is possible that, in using *sōzō*, Jesus is simply using another word that identifies the man's physical healing. However, the variation in words is unlikely to be accidental or merely descriptive of the same condition. It is more likely that Luke desires the readers to recognize that the final words of Jesus refer to the man being cleansed of more than leprosy. Although *sōzō*,

---

[326] The only other times this occurs is by another leper, requesting his healing (5.12), and Jairus, who requests that Jesus heal his daughter (8.41). However, in 17.16, the cleansed leper falls at Jesus' feet after the healing. Such an action indicates an awareness of authority in Luke (5.12; 8.35, 41; 10.39) and is suggestive of worship (Acts 10.26; see also Rev. 22.8–9).

[327] The term used by Jesus to refer to the Samaritan (*allogenes*) is only used here in the NT; it is the term used on the balustrade around the Jerusalem Temple to mark out the Court of the Gentiles and the area dedicated to the Jews. If a foreigner entered the latter, he was liable to receive the death penalty. Ironically, the Samaritan is centrally placed as worshipping at the feet of Jesus. Weissenrieder (*Images of Illness*. pp. 195–209) undertakes a linguistic study of the word in Jewish literature and concludes that it is often used in the context of someone who was ritually impure, asserting that in the context of Luke 17.11–19 the definition of purity is now being recodified. The once ritually impure leper is redefined as 'a pure person who sees the kingdom of God and turns back'.

[328] The hatred between the Jews and the Samaritans had existed for centuries and, by this time, had plummeted to the depths of animosity; just a few years earlier, the Samaritans had desecrated the Jerusalem Temple.

[329] Talbert (*Reading Luke*. p. 165) draws a parallel with the healing of Naaman, the leper (2 Kings 5) who is healed and who returns to Elisha confessing his faith in the God of Israel.

'I save/heal', is used by Luke (8.48) to refer to physical healing, on this occasion it more probably refers to a spiritual transformation,[330] and thus forms a fitting climax to the passage.[331]

This account is recorded immediately after instructions by Jesus to the disciples regarding discipleship, specifically the importance of faith (17.5–6) and obedience (17.7–10). The leper, in his response, fulfils these and shows that he has already begun the life of a disciple. The narrative that follows this incident is also significant. It records Jesus informing the Pharisees that rather than look for the kingdom, they should recognize that it is 'in the midst of you' (17.21), a reference to himself. The parallel is obvious. Although ten lepers were recipients of the ministry of Jesus, only one, who as a Samaritan was not part of the accepted Jewish community, recognized Jesus' significance and benefited from that revelation. By refusing to place their faith in the one who is in their midst, the Pharisees demonstrated that they were less perceptive than this Samaritan. He is the first one of many people on the fringe of society who is recorded by Luke as accurately responding to Jesus. Others will include a widow (18.1–8), a tax-collector (18.9–14), children (18.15–17) and the tax-collector Zacchaeus (19.1–10).

---

[330] See 19.9–10; Acts 4.12; see also Rom. 5.9; 1 Cor. 1.18.

[331] In the earlier passages concerning the cleansing of the leper recorded in each of the Synoptics, *katharizō* is the only word used to describe the curative process.

Jesus heals Malchus' ear (Luke 22.50–51)

Table 4.17 Healing Malchus' ear – the literary context

	Luke
The plot to kill Jesus	22.1–6
The disciples prepare for the Passover	22.7–13
Jesus shares a last supper with the disciples	22.14–23
The dispute as to the greatest of the disciples	22.24–30
Jesus foretells Peter's denial of him	22.31–34
The misunderstanding over the sword	22.35–38
Jesus prays on the Mount of Olives	22.39–46
Jesus is betrayed	22.47–49
Jesus heals Malchus' ear	**22.50–51**
Jesus is arrested	22.52–53
Peter denies Jesus	22.54–62
Jesus is beaten and tried before the Sanhedrin	22.63–71

Although each Gospel records the action of Peter in cutting off this man's ear, only Luke mentions the healing by Jesus.[332] The healing occurs in the context of the tension of the events leading up to the cross (see Table 4.17). Not only have people plotted to kill Jesus, but even his disciples have misunderstood his mission; while Jesus prepares to die for the world, they argue about who is the most important of them. This is then followed by the prophecy of Peter's denial, the misunderstanding of the disciples over Jesus' recommendation that if they do not have a sword they should buy one, and the painful time of prayer in Gethsemane (in which, uniquely, Luke records data that clarifies the trauma of that occasion), which leads to the betrayal by Judas. Even the question from the disciples, only recorded by Luke (22.49), as to whether they should use their swords to protect Jesus from being arrested, demonstrates their false assumption that Jesus needed their help.

It is in the heightened drama of that distressing setting that Luke records that the right ear of the high priest's slave[333] is cut off by a sword.[334] The identities of the person who wields the sword and the slave are not identified by Luke, John (18.10) recording that they were Simon Peter and

---

[332] Matt. 26.51; Mark 14.47; John 18.10.

[333] Rather than indicating an individual of limited prestige, the term more probably refers to the high priest's representative who is leading the arresting party; so also Nolland, J., *Luke 18.35–24.53*. Word, Dallas, 1993, p. 1088.

[334] The *machaira* was a large knife, dagger or small sword used to kill and butcher animals.

Malchus. Luke appears to be more interested in the person and action of Jesus. Matthew portrays a similar emphasis by recording Jesus' words revealing his authority to call 12 legions of angels to help him if he wished and stating that his reason not to do so was in order to fulfil 'the scriptures' (26.53–54). Luke records the authority of Jesus by noting that he heals the man.

This is the only time in the Gospels that Jesus is identified as restoring a part of the body that has been removed. Luke records that Jesus touched the man's ear, which probably means that Jesus picked up the severed ear from where it fell and replaced it, thus restoring him; the aorist tense indicates a quick response and immediate healing.

It is significant to note that no faith is manifested and no request is made for healing; the healing is unilaterally undertaken by Jesus. However, tragically, although Jesus heals the servant of the high priest who, with chief priests, elders and Temple guards, has come to arrest him (22.52), the healing does not even cause them to pause in their determination to kill Jesus (22.54).

A clear and poignant message to be derived from the narrative is that while Jesus does not permit others to defend him from suffering, his mission includes a readiness to remove the suffering of others. While Jesus' suffering will continue in his savage arrest, Peter's denial, his being beaten, mocked, rejected by the crowds and crucified, the only action of Jesus is to heal someone who had been part of the entourage which had come to do him harm.[335] At the same time, and more importantly, the narrative demonstrates that as well as being a healer, Jesus is in control of the events. Even though it appears that his world is crumbling around him and his enemies are determining his destiny, he is actually in charge and will not allow any action to obstruct his path to the cross, the culmination of his mission when the greatest act of healing will be achieved.

---

[335] Josephus (*Ant.* 14.366) refers to such injuries as resulting in the victim being ineligible to serve in a priestly context.

5

The Synoptics: exorcisms

Jesus restores the Gadarene demoniac(s)
(Matt. 8.28–34//Mark 5.1–20//Luke 8.26–39)

Table 5.1 Restoring the Gadarene demoniac(s) – the literary context

	Matthew	Mark	Luke
Jesus heals and exorcizes demons	8.16–17	(1.32–34)	(4.40–41)
Jesus teaches would-be disciples	8.18–22		(9.57–60)
The parable of the sower	(13.1–9)	4.1–9	8.4–8
The purpose of parables	(13.10–13)	4.10–13	8.9–10
The explanation of the parable of the sower	(13.18–23)	4.13–20	8.11–15
Putting a light under a vessel	(10.26–27)	4.21–25	8.16–19
Jesus identifies his 'mother and brothers'	(12.46–50)	(3.31–35)	8.19–21
Parables about seeds		4.26–34	
Jesus calms a storm	8.23–27	4.35–41	8.22–25
Exorcism of the demoniac	**8.28–34**	**5.1–20**	**8.26–39**
Healing of a paralytic	9.1–8	(2.1–12)	(5.17–26)
Jesus calls Matthew to be a disciple	9.9	(2.13–14)	(5.27–28)
Jesus eats with tax-collectors and sinners	9.10–13	(2.15–17)	(5.29–32)
Jesus teaches concerning fasting	9.14–17	(2.18–22)	(5.33–39)
Jesus heals Jairus' daughter	9.18–19, 23–26	5.21–24, 35–43	8.40–42, 49–56
Jesus heals the woman with a haemorrhage	9.20–22	5.25–34	8.43–48

This is the first detailed exorcism recorded by Matthew and Luke, and the second one by Mark. Each of the synoptic writers records this incident after the rebuking of the storm by Jesus,[1] after which the disciples query the identity of Jesus, whose authority is such that even the wind and sea

---

[1] Matthew records that Jesus delivers two demoniacs, though both Mark and Luke refer to only one (see also 9.27–31; 20.29–34); he (21.2) also refers to two animals in the so-called triumphal entry into Jerusalem by Jesus, while Mark and Luke only have one, and two blind men (20.29) in contrast to one blind man in Mark and Luke. This may reflect the Jewish insistence on two witnesses in occasions of testimony in court. The similarities between the accounts suggest strongly that they are reflecting the same event, the difference in numbers being no hindrance to an understanding of the narratives.

obey him (see Table 5.1). The exorcism provides more evidence of that authority by revealing him as one whom demons obey.

The facts, which appear in all the accounts, are that the demoniac(s), who lived among the tombs, came to Jesus, Mark characteristically stating 'immediately' (omitted, as often elsewhere, by Matthew and Luke). Furthermore, the demons[2] identify Jesus as the Son of God, conclusions that will not be drawn by the majority of people when they observe Jesus. The demons also manifest a perception that Jesus had come to torment them and they beg him to allow them to enter pigs, a request to which Jesus accedes. Thereafter, the pigs rush down a steep bank into the sea and drown. Because of the miracle, the people from the city come to see Jesus, witness the man restored, and request[3] that Jesus leaves their neighbourhood. Following the exorcism, the writers offer different narratives, though each of them records healing miracles that further demonstrate the authority of Jesus.

The location

The location of the exorcism is uncertain, Gadara or Gerasa (the latter situated on the north-east shore of Galilee, where a steep cliff overlooks the lake) being the most likely options, cities in the Decapolis. The fact that Jesus had come here, more clearly identified by Mark as the 'other side of the sea' (5.1), indicates that Jesus had moved into pagan territory, providing an opportunity for each of the writers to demonstrate Jesus' readiness to minister to Gentiles.

The demoniac(s)

Each Synoptist records that the demoniac(s) dwelt among tombs, probably located in caves. According to Jewish belief, tombs were ritually impure places, being closely associated with death and demons.[4] Matthew records that the demons were exceptionally fierce and malevolent; Mark describes the demoniac's constant self-abuse; Mark (twice) and Luke refer to the demoniac's physical strength (his ability to wrench apart binding chains and break them). Such behaviour and attributes were clearly antisocial, personally degrading, psychologically and spiritually damaging, and physically destructive.

---

[2] Matthew refers to demons conversing with Jesus while Mark and Luke identify one demon. For ease of presentation, give that the vocal demon is representative of them all, the plural form will generally be used through this exploration of the narrative.

[3] Matthew and Mark use *parakaleō*, the same word used by the demons to beg Jesus to send them into the pigs.

[4] *Jub.* 22.17; b. *Nid.* 17a; *Ber.* 18b.

The personality of the demoniac(s) appears to be indistinguishable from that of the demons; although the latter appear to speak through the human vocal cords, the content and aspirations of the speech are clearly related to the demonic presence and do not reflect any human aspirations. The confrontation is between Jesus and the demons, without the active cooperation of the demoniac(s), who acted only at the instigation of the demons. Indeed, each of the writers indicates that Jesus addressed the demons, not the demoniac(s). It is only after the exorcism is completed that the words of Jesus can be said with certainty to be addressed to the man/men. Similarly, although each of the writers describes the demoniac(s) meeting Jesus, it is not clear whether this has been due to human or demonic volition; given the passivity of the man/men in the narrative, it appears that the demons have a stranglehold on him/them in personality, mind and body – a tragic and pitiful condition.

The identity of the demons

Each of the Synoptics refers to the demoniac(s) as being *daimonizomenoi* (present passive participle of *daimonizomai*, 'I am demonized or demon-possessed'[5]), the present tense indicating that this was an ongoing pervasive influence. Similarly, Luke (8.27) records the concept of the man *exōn daimonia* ('having demons'). The demon is also defined as being *pneuma akathartos*, an 'unclean/dirty spirit' (Mark 5.2, 8, 13; Luke 8.29), while Matthew (8.31) and Luke (8.27, 30, 33, 35, 38) refer to a *daimon* ('demon').

Why the demons are described as 'unclean/dirty' in Matthew and Luke is worthy of exploration. It may be partly due to the importance of cultic purity in the ancient Jewish world, the demons being identified as the antithesis of purity. Also, the term 'unclean spirit' is used in Zechariah 13.2 in association with idolatry and God's judgement. It is appropriate to describe demons thus in order to better explain their polluted nature and the fact that they taint those whom they touch. As such, the presence of the tombs and pigs, other terms reminiscent of impurity, emphasize the pollution of the place in which they choose to exist. They are as far

---

[5] It is a popular term in Matthew (4.24; 8.16, 28, 33; 9.32; 12.22; 15.22) though only used three times in Mark (1.32; 5.15–16, 18), once in both Luke (8.36) and John (10.21). It is preferable to retain the broader meaning of the word 'demonized' as the concept of 'demon-possession' may too easily be assumed to indicate that the demon is inside a person (which may or may not be the truth). The central point is that the demonic force is powerfully controlling the person concerned, so much so that it may be difficult to separate the personality of the person from that of the demon; it is an influential rather than a spatial concept, indicating intrusive, overwhelming and malevolent control rather than an anatomical definition. However, there is evidence in Jewish literature for the notion of a demon inhabiting the body of an evil person (*Test. Naph.* 8.6; b. *Hull.* 105b).

removed as can be imagined from a pure, holy and internally authentic God and thus are best designated as polluted, harmful and internally corrupt.

In the era under consideration, the Jews believed a great deal about demons, although very little is recorded in the OT; much of it was gleaned from other Jewish literature and expanded by the speculations of some rabbis. One of the dangerous conclusions of these conjectures was that demons need not be greatly feared, being viewed as akin to mischievous imps or goblins that could be controlled by certain behaviour, and by water, light or magic; indeed, sometimes it was assumed that they could even be helpful. It was important that the Gospel writers educate their readers to realize that demons were malevolent, desirous of harming not just the body but also the mind, of causing disharmonious relationships not only between people, but also between people and God. Theirs was an agenda with eternal consequences, not merely one restricted to the physical aspects of a person's life.

According to Mark and Luke, the self-identification of the demon is by way of a number, not a name – 'legion' (a Roman[6] term for a group of 4,000 to 6,000 soldiers); it is most probably offered by a representative demon speaking on behalf of others.[7] Their frightening malevolence and, assuming the demon is telling the truth, significant numbers set the scene for the confrontation with Jesus.[8] What is important in all three accounts is that the power of Jesus is seen to be easily superior to the most malevolent of demonic foes, despite their superior numbers.

The declaratory words of the demons

The demons, as elsewhere, manifest a much more accurate awareness of the identity of Jesus than do people. Each Synoptist records the demons preceding their confession of Jesus with the words *ti hēmin kai soi* (Matthew) or *ti emoi kai soi* (Mark, Luke), 'What to us and to you', and more colloquially, 'Why are you here?' This phrase is used in the OT[9] and elsewhere in the Gospels (Mark 1.24; Luke 4.34) and refers to an inappropriate intrusion. The phrase, as used by the demons, possibly indicates a declaration of

---

[6] It is speculative to suggest that Mark is indicating the power of Rome as the 'demonic' force that Jesus has come to conquer.

[7] Cases of possession by multiple demons are recorded elsewhere (Matt. 12.45; Luke 8.2).

[8] That there were 2,000 pigs does not mean that there were 2,000 demons present; it is not clear whether the demon was asserting the truth or seeking to present his power base as more significant than it was.

[9] Josh. 22.24; Judg. 11.12; 2 Sam. 16.10, 19.22; 1 Kings 17.18; 2 Kings 3.13; 2 Chron. 35.21; Jer. 2.18; Hos. 14.9.

malevolent intent on their part, somewhat akin to 'Mind your own business' or 'Why are you interfering in our affairs?' It is thus possible that there is an implied threat in these words, and that the demons are seeking to destabilize Jesus by such forceful and apparently confident antagonism. However, it is more likely that these words reflect the surprise of the demons that Jesus has come to earth and at this time, and more particularly, in order to intervene on behalf of hurting and helpless humanity.[10] Although it is possible that they have sought to demonstrate their self-assurance, it is as likely that the demons are fearfully struggling to come to terms with the fact that Jesus is there. His presence has caused them to panic, their powerlessness being brought into sharp focus by his prestige.

The content of the demonic questions is prefaced by the fact that they 'cry out' and, according to Mark and Luke, do so loudly. Although this also may indicate apparent self-confidence, their shrieks may simply be a cover for or indicative of their fear. While Matthew notes that they refer to Jesus as 'Son of God',[11] Mark and Luke record the demons addressing Jesus as 'Jesus, Son of the Most High God', the addition being used of God in the OT.[12] The titles indicate that they recognize the divine nature of Jesus; he is not merely a Jewish exorcist or prophet and is more elevated than Messiah. They are in the presence of one who has all power available to him; their terror is real, not the least because they know that Jesus has the power to torment them. The clearest references to eschatological judgement and the condemnation of demons identify these actions as being achieved by God;[13] the demons recognize that Jesus has this divine authority.

Matthew also records the demons asking if Jesus has come to torment them 'before the time' (8.29), implying a foreknowledge on their part that such judgement is to be their destiny; their surprise is not that Jesus has such authority but that it is to be manifested sooner than they had expected. Mark and Luke record the demon asking Jesus not to torment them, Mark noting that the request is presented with an oath, 'by God', and using the verb '*horkidzō* ('I adjure, implore'), possibly identifying the last vestiges of demonic desperation. Similarly, Luke refers to the demon begging Jesus

---

[10] This may be all the more concerning to demons since there was a popular belief that the initiation of the kingdom of God would result in the demise of the devil (*Test. Mos.* 10.1).

[11] The demons mimic the twofold reference to Jesus as 'Son of God', which was also used by Satan in Matt. 4.3, 6, but the recorded conversation is considerably shorter on this occasion. The term has already been used of Jesus by the Father (3.17; see also 17.5); in 14.33 and 16.16, it is accurately used to affirm Jesus' identity by his disciples and others (27.54).

[12] Gen. 14.18–22; Num. 24.16; Deut. 32.38; 2 Sam. 22.14.

[13] *1 Enoch* 10.4; 55.4; see also 1QH 7.12.

not to torment it, while Matthew simply reduces the words of the demons, indicating that they knew that they were already defeated and were merely waiting for their punishment at his hands.

The fact that each Synoptist records that the demons identify Jesus in his speech by name has resulted in some suggesting that this may indicate a belief in the pseudo-magical properties of the name whereby the demon hopes to control Jesus.[14] This form of 'name magic' was popular in some ancient religions, including some aspects of Judaism,[15] the assumption being that to know the name of the god meant that one had control of the power possessed by that god. However, it is not clear that the demons hope to take advantage of any such apparent coercive power and, more pertinently, both Mark and Luke follow these demonic declarations with a plea for leniency that Jesus not torment them. Thereafter, each of the Synoptists records the demon begging Jesus to be merciful (Matthew once (8.3) and Mark (5.11, 12) and Luke (8.31–32) twice). It is thus probable that the demons recognize that they are in the presence of one who deserves their obeisance, thus resulting in their prostration before him.[16] The confrontation is one-sided, the authority of Jesus being stressed from the start.

The exorcism

Although Matthew records the exorcism being undertaken immediately by Jesus, Mark and Luke record a conversation between Jesus and the demon in which the name of the demon is requested. Surprisingly, this implies that Jesus had commanded the demon to leave the person beforehand (Mark 5.8; Luke 8.29). Gundry argues that the delay in the demonic expulsion indicates the difficulty of the case, claiming that Jesus did not command the demon to be silent yet, for he needed 'to find out the spirit's name since a command to come out has not worked'.[17] Similarly, Twelftree[18]

---

[14] Iverson, K. R., *Gentiles in the Gospel of Mark*. T. & T. Clark, London, 2007, p. 28; see the much later PGM 8.6–7, 13 for similar occasions where exorcists are reputed to have identified the name of a god in whose power they can exorcize demons. Stein (R. H., *Mark*. Baker Academic, Grand Rapids, 2008, p. 254) states, 'the demons plead; they do not negotiate'.

[15] Deut. 18.5, 22; 1 Sam. 17.45; 1 Chron. 21.19; *1 Enoch* 69.13–25; *T. Sol.* 5.2–9; Matt. 21.9; Luke 13.35; Acts 3.6; 4.7; Col. 3.17.

[16] Blackburn (B. L., *Theios Aner and the Markan Miracle Traditions: A Critique of the Theios Aner Concept as an Interpretative Background of the Miracle Traditions*. Mohr Siebeck, Tübingen, 1990, p. 204) concludes that there is no parallel to the concept of 'this proskynesis of the demon before the exorcist' in Hellenistic and Jewish literature that describes exorcisms in the first-century world.

[17] Gundry, R. H., *Mark: A Commentary on His Apology for the Cross*. Eerdmans, Grand Rapids, 1993, p. 250.

[18] Twelftree, G. H., 'EI/DE ... EGO EKBALLO TA DAIMONIA', in *Gospel Perspectives, Vol. 6: The Miracles of Jesus.* (eds) Wenham, D., Blomberg, C. L., JSOT Press, Sheffield, 1986, p. 379.

views this account as a description of a spiritual battle in which Jesus responds to a binding spell with a request for the identity of the name of the demon 'in order to gain the upper hand' and 'the necessary power to carry out the exorcism'.[19] However, if the name was of importance to Jesus, one wonders why it was not incorporated in his earlier words of expulsion. Also, it would suggest that Jesus needed such data before he could exorcize a demon, which is inconceivable, given his authority as God's Son, as already noted in the narrative.

Jesus does not request information about any demon in other exorcisms, and it is not necessary to see in Jesus' action on this occasion an example of an exorcistic device on his part. Nowhere does the NT advocate the usefulness of or need for identifying demons for the purpose of expulsion. If this was the case, Jesus would be inferior to the demons, who knew his name. Finally, if Jesus needed to know the demon's name in order to consolidate power over the demon, one wonders why the demon gave his name so readily.

Although a confrontation is described here, it is not one between equals; neither is it likely that the writers wish to indicate that Jesus had to discover which weapons were most appropriate for disarming the opposition; as yet, the presentation of Jesus in both Gospels has been that Jesus owns supreme and comprehensive authority over demons (Mark 1.25), sickness,[20] sin,[21] death (Luke 7.15) and creation (Mark 4.39; Luke 8.24). Although the demon may assume differently, victory is assured on the basis of Jesus' authority.

It is most likely that the request is actually made by Jesus to reveal to the observers the intensity of the demonic control on this particular occasion, in that the man was gripped by a multiplicity of demons. Not only does this demonstrate the malevolence of the infestation of the demonic activity, but it also reveals the authority of Jesus who can as easily deal with a large number of demons as he can with one. The implication that the initial request of Jesus was disobeyed by the demon need not result in an assessment that Jesus' power is limited and can be easily thwarted by a demon; elsewhere demons obeyed him,[22] and so will these.

---

[19] See also Twelftree, G. H., *Jesus the Miracle Worker*. InterVarsity Press, Downers Grove, 1999, p. 288.
[20] Mark 1.32–34; 2.10; 3.5; Luke 5.13, 25; 6.10; 7.10.
[21] Mark 1.5; Luke 5.20; 7.47.
[22] Mark 1.34; 3.12; Luke 4.41.

The request of the demons and the response of Jesus

The demons' request that they be permitted to enter the pigs follows a request that Jesus should not command them to go out of the country (Mark). Mark uses *chōra* to refer to a region[23] and it appears that the demons preferred to remain in that area; given that it was dominated by tombs, such a place of death and decay was an appropriate habitation.

Luke's perspective, however, reveals an eschatological destiny in that he refers to their preference not to be sent to the 'abyss', a word that is only used here in the Gospels. Although the OT use of the term metaphorically refers to the opposite of 'high' (Deut. 33.13; Ps. 36.6), the place of the dead (Ps. 107.26; Rom. 10.7) and the depth of the sea (Gen. 8.2; Ps. 32.7), elsewhere and in the NT it takes on a more sobering, malignant and apocalyptic perspective, referring to the eschatological destiny of demons.[24] It is also used to refer to a bottomless pit (Rev. 9.1–2; 17.8), the home and eventual prison of the beast who fights against God's people, which is ruled over by an angel named Apollyon.[25]

Matthew's use of 'if/since' (*ei*) may be to reveal that the demons knew that they would be cast out ('since you are going to cast us out . . .') or an attempt to test the resolve of Jesus or a veiled plea for clemency ('if you are to cast us out . . .').[26] On both counts, the supremacy of Jesus remains certain. For Mark and Luke, the plea of the demons is simply to be dispatched into the pigs. That the demons ask to be sent into pigs may indicate a desire to inhabit bodies; that they belong to pigs makes them suitably unclean homes for dirty demons.[27]

That Jesus accedes to the request has received much comment, though in giving permission Jesus is still in control. If the demons assume that they can trick Jesus and, in entering the swine, postpone the curtailment of their activity by later leaving them to enter other people, they are mistaken; although the demons may be able to control mere men, Jesus is different.

In Matthew, Jesus authoritatively, with one word, 'go',[28] sends the demons into the pigs. Mark and Luke record that he allowed them to go. The demon has not tricked Jesus; on the contrary, Jesus uses their request

---

[23] 1.5; 5.1; 6.55.

[24] *Jub.* 5.6–7; *1 Enoch* 10.4–6, 19; 18.11–16; 2 Pet. 2.4; Jude 6; Rev. 9.1, 3, 11.

[25] Rev. 9.11; 11.7; 20.1–3.

[26] See *Jub.* 10 where the leader of the demons, Mastema, pleads for mercy, which is granted.

[27] Pigs were identified as unclean animals for the Jews (Lev. 11.7; Deut. 14.8); unlike among the Jews, pigs were sacrificed in many ancient religions (Jos., *Ant.* 13.243).

[28] Also used in Matthew by Jesus against the devil (4.10; 16.23).

for a pedagogical purpose.[29] Page,[30] on the basis of the parable of the restless demon (Matt. 12.43–45//Luke 11.24–26), believes that 'they were free to possess others'. However, in that narrative, there is no indication that an exorcism has taken place, Jesus referring to a time when a demon may choose voluntarily to leave one person and thereafter to return if it wishes, but with others. Blue,[31] assuming the Gadarene demons are still potentially being encountered today, comments that 'Jesus did not put an end to Satan's power, rather he bound it so that we may have authority over it'.

However, it begs the question as to what authority is being envisaged if it only results in a demon being removed from one person whereupon it can enter another; such an endless cat-and-mouse exercise hardly signifies authority on the part of Jesus. It is also inconceivable that Jesus should have acceded to the demonic request if it meant that they were able to continue their malevolent occupation after the death of the pigs. To allow them to inhabit other human bodies after the destruction of the pigs would have undermined Jesus' superiority and allowed their evil work to continue. The demons were not sent by Jesus for a short break in the pigs. They have not had the last laugh; they have received their last rites. Rather, the action of Jesus acted as proof to the demonized man that he was truly free of demons; they had left for good. Earlier attempts to control his problem had failed, but now, the problem had been permanently solved, and the dramatic change in behaviour by the pigs was public proof of that remarkable fact.[32]

The fact that the pigs run into the water is instructive as it would have indicated the destruction of both pigs and demons, since the Jews believed that water had the ability to destroy demons.[33] The habitation of the pigs is but a temporary respite for the demons; their final destiny is determined, and the destruction of the pigs in the water states loud and clear to the observers that the demons must have also been destroyed. Although the

---

[29] For example, Hagner (D. A., *Matthew 1–13*. Word, Waco, 1993, p. 228) writes, 'it makes the point that not even the unclean swine were prepared to contain the demons, and the demons end up destroying the swine'; Harper (M., *The Healings of Jesus*. Hodder & Stoughton, London, 1986, p. 40) suggests that it might be to punish the potentially Jewish owners, though no evidence is available for this.

[30] Page, S. H. T., *Powers of Evil*. Baker, Grand Rapids, 1995, p. 156; contra Marshall, I. H., *The Gospel of Luke: A Commentary on the Greek Text*. Paternoster Press, Exeter, 1978, p. 340.

[31] Blue, K., *Authority to Heal*. InterVarsity Press, Downers Grove, 1987, pp. 92–3.

[32] Josephus (*Ant.* 8.2.5) records that Eleazer proves that an exorcism has occurred by commanding the exiting demons to tip up a cup or basin of water.

[33] Matt. 12.43 informs the reader that demons prefer waterless places; in *Test. Sol.* 5.11, the demon Asmodeus begs not to be sent into water (cf. 11. 6); see *Jub.* 5.6; *1 Enoch* 10.18.

incident demonstrates the significant power and destructive nature of the demons, making 2,000 (Mark 5.12) pigs uncontrollable, it is the power of Jesus over the demons which is central to the story.[34]

The aftermath

Those in charge of the pigs fled[35] and reported the incident to the nearby inhabitants, whereupon the people came, and saw the demoniac(s) restored and the demons gone. Matthew, however, records that they specifically came to meet Jesus, choosing not to describe the transformed man or record that he was seen by the crowds (as do Mark and Luke); the rejection of Jesus by the crowds is most personal in Matthew.[36] Each of the Synoptists refers to the fact that they requested that Jesus leave them. Jesus is not invited into their towns and the potential for more transformations is lost. Mark and Luke ascribe the people's request to their being afraid, Luke describing it as 'great' fear.[37] It appears that the people were more concerned about the loss of income and the death of their pigs than they were about the presence of Jesus and the restoration of a devastated person. The unclean demons and pigs have been removed from the presence of people by Jesus but, incongruously, he, the Son of God, has himself been removed by people from their presence,[38] while the restored man begs to stay with him.

While Matthew records few details about the transformed man, Mark and Luke note that he was completely mentally restored (*sōphronounta*, present continuous participle from *sōphroneō*, 'I am in my right mind'), sitting (Luke adds 'at the feet of Jesus') and clothed (perhaps reminiscent of the prophecy of Isa. 58.7 which refers to the naked being clothed). They also record Jesus telling the man, who had no home but lived among the tombs, to 'go home' and tell of his miraculous transformation, which he does. He has been provided with the opportunity to be restored mentally and physically, but also domestically. The one who was homeless and

---

[34] As to whether it was ethical for Jesus to destroy 2,000 pigs and thus probably ruin the livelihood of some of the people, the writers do not offer a comment. Such questioning indicates that the point of the story, which is to demonstrate the value of a person above all else, has been missed.

[35] The only other people who fled from Jesus were the disciples at the crucifixion (Matt. 26.56; Mark 14.50).

[36] It is interesting that Matthew replaces the *aperchomai* of Mark (and Luke) with *metabainō*, perhaps to more graphically identify the nature of their request. Matthew records that they did not wish Jesus merely to leave but to exit from their territory.

[37] By contrast, see Mark 4.40; Luke 8.25, where the disciples are afraid but stay in the presence of Jesus.

[38] This is the only occasion when people asked Jesus to leave them; a similar reference is where Judas left Jesus (Mark 14.10; Luke 22.4).

incapable of functioning among people has now been encouraged to live, taking advantage of a personality that, though once destructive, has been transformed, resulting in his being able to live in harmony with himself and others. In casting out the demons, Jesus also provides him with an opportunity to be a believable witness, requesting that he speak of the miracle that has happened to him. As this was not a Jewish area, the messianic expectations that if raised would elsewhere have impeded the ministry of Jesus, were not so prominent here, and so his testimony is encouraged by Jesus.

What is particularly significant is that although Mark states that Jesus requires that the man should relate 'how much the Lord has done for you', and Luke states that Jesus encourages him to relate 'how much God has done for you', they both reveal that the man told people 'how much *Jesus* had done for him'. The work of Jesus is identified as being synonymous with the work of God.

Why does Matthew tell the story?

Matthew's account is much the shortest (seven compared to Mark's 20 verses) and it concentrates on the authority and ease with which Jesus deals with two fierce demoniacs. The conversation, as recorded by Matthew, is also the shortest of the three accounts, being restricted to a question by the demons and a prompt dismissal by Jesus. There is no dialogue with the demons, no request for information about their identity, no suggestion of a prior command to leave, and limited descriptors of the demons. The demons are given the same amount of space in the narrative as the pigs; Jesus is centre stage. Matthew records this as Jesus' first exorcism and records it after Jesus calms the storm. He who can calm a fierce storm by removing it here calms fierce demons by removing them.

Why does Mark tell the story?

Exorcisms are important to the Markan portrait of Jesus, and four of the 13 healing stories recorded by Mark are exorcisms. It is no surprise, therefore, that it is Mark who provides the fullest description of the demoniac, the exorcism and the aftermath.

After presenting Jesus teaching about the kingdom of God in parables (4.1–34), Mark precedes this, the second of his exorcisms, with Jesus calming the storm, as do Matthew and Luke. He follows the exorcism with the healing of Jairus' daughter and of the woman with a haemorrhage (5.21–34), as does Luke. In this regard, Jesus' authority is demonstrated by achieving miracles that manifest his authority, including the casting out of unclean spirits, the healing of diseases, and even the resurrection of the dead. It is possible that a chiastic structure underlies this emphasis on Jesus' authority:

> A. The disciples wonder about Jesus' authority (4.41)
>> B. Jesus crosses to the other side to where the demonized man is (5.1)
>>> C. The demonized man approaches Jesus, questioning him (2–5)
>>>> D. The demonized man 'worships' Jesus, uniquely naming him as 'Son of the Most High God' (6, 7)
>>>>> E. The unclean spirit requests not to be tormented (7c)
>>>>>> F. Jesus' exorcistic authority over Legion is established (8, 9)
>>>>> E1. The unclean spirit requests not to be sent away (10)
>>>> D1. The unclean spirits obey Jesus (13); the people reject Jesus (14–17)
>>> C1. The restored man approaches Jesus, begging to be with him (18)
>> B1. Jesus sends the man from where he is (19, 20)
> A1. The people wonder about Jesus' authority (20)
>> B2. Jesus crosses back to the other side (21)

Mark concentrates on the misfortune of the victim, noting that he continuously, night and day, called out and cut himself with stones. He also emphasizes the bleak, deathly impurity of his location, mentioning three times that he lived among the tombs (contrasted with Matthew and Luke who record it once each).

Mark is also the only author who indicates that the demoniac knelt before Jesus, suggestive of obeisance or reverence, Luke recording that the man 'fell down before him'.[39] It is not clear whether they are referring to the unclean spirit or the demonized man who is manifesting this action; it probably refers to the demon's awareness of the prestige of Jesus, whereas the man is unlikely to have seen Jesus before and such an act of obeisance would be thus unexpected. Given that the speech is that of the demon, it does not follow that any attitude of worship comes from a positive attitude towards Jesus; it does so because it has to – after all, it has already acknowledged that Jesus is 'the Son of the Most High God'.

Mark and Luke reveal Jesus getting out of a boat to meet the demoniac and, after the transformation had occurred, returning to it. This detour, which relates the only occasion when Jesus got out of a boat, had been intentional, resulting in the transformation of one man, who may not even be a Jew. Whatever his racial identity, he was a tragic case, bound, homeless, physically mistreated by the unclean spirits which had control

---

[39] The verb *proskuneō* used by Mark is only used once elsewhere in his Gospel (15.19) where those who mocked, beat and spat on Jesus knelt and 'worshipped' him.

over him and lonely – in need of someone who could rescue him and sit with him. The readers of Mark's Gospel themselves knew what it was to experience the horrors associated with living in a city where their lives were often determined by malignant forces who controlled them, resulting in them being imprisoned, maltreated and lonely. Mark offers a message of hope that Jesus is still available to be with them as he was with the demoniac. The unclean spirits who traumatized the man are judged by Jesus; the message is clear that all those who malevolently oppress the weak and vulnerable will have to answer for their deeds.

Why does Luke tell the story?

As identified earlier, Luke portrays the pathetic nature of the man's condition more graphically than Matthew and Mark, his hopelessness and loneliness being prominently presented. Thus, he notes that the demoniac, who used to live in the city, now lived without a home, and had been naked for a long time, and under the dominating force of a demon that 'seized him' and drove him into the desert, an inappropriate place for a person to dwell. As frequently elsewhere, Luke here also presents Jesus as caring for the marginalized, valuable to Luke's largely non-Jewish readers to help them appreciate that racial heritage is of limited interest to Jesus who desires to transform people who need his intervention, whatever their cultural or racial identities. Although Luke largely follows the order of Mark before and after this narrative, the exorcism being the second in a group of four miracles, he concludes the section with Jesus delegating his power to his disciples (9.1–6), so establishing the link between the activity of Jesus and his followers who are charged to continue his work, an emphasis that will permeate his second volume, Acts.

Conclusion

Jesus is presented as the one who has dominion over demonic forces. Both demons and transformed people obey him. However, seeds of rejection are to be identified in this story and it will not be long before many reject Jesus, while only a few will request to stay with him. The road to Calvary is coming into focus. Though one demonic skirmish has been won, victory in the battle for human hearts will not be so easy.

Jesus restores a dumb (and blind) demoniac
(Matt. 12.22 (23–45))//(Mark 3.22–27)//Luke 11.14 (15–26))

Table 5.2 Restoring a dumb (and blind) demoniac – the literary context

	Matthew	Mark	Luke
Jesus calls for people to come to him and rest	11.28–30		
Plucking grain on the Sabbath	12.1–8	2.23–28	(6.1–5)
The healing of the withered hand	12.9–14	3.1–6	(6.6–11)
Jesus fulfils Isaianic prophecy	12.15–21		
Jesus heals crowds by the sea	12.15	3.7–12	(6.17–19)
Jesus fulfils Isaianic prophecy	12.16–21		
Jesus chooses the Twelve	(10.1–4)	3.13–19	(6.14–16)
Jesus' family try to 'protect' Jesus		3.20–21	
The Lord's Prayer	(6.9–13)		11.1–4
The parable of the friend at midnight			11.5–8
Jesus teaches about asking and receiving	(7.7–11)		11.9–13
Jesus restores a dumb (and blind) demoniac	**12.22–23**		**11.14**
Jesus is accused of being empowered by Beelzebul and responds to it	**12.24–32**	**3.22–30**	**11.15–23**
Jesus speaks about the importance of fruitful lives	12.33–37		(6.43–45)
Jesus denounces the Pharisees' request for signs	12.38–42	(8.11–12)	(11.29–32)
Jesus teaches about a returning unclean spirit	**12.43–45**		**11.24–26**
Jesus identifies his 'true' family as doing God's will	12.46–50	3.31–35	(8.19–21)
Parables of the kingdom	13.1–51	4.1–25, 30–34	(8.4–18)
Rejection of Jesus by his countrymen	13.52–58	(6.1–6)	(4.16–30)
Death of John the Baptist	14.1–12	(6.14–29)	(9.7–9)
A woman blesses Jesus			11.27–28
Jesus teaches about light and darkness	(5.15; 6.22–23)	4.21	11.33–36
Jesus denounces the Pharisees	(15.1–9; 23.4–7, 13, 23–39)	(7.1–9)	11.37–54

Main messages from all the narratives

This exorcism is again a catalyst determining one's response to Jesus. The responses of the majority appear to be initially positively inclined to Jesus, though the religious leaders are aggressively antagonistic. It is to be determined if the readers will do any better in their assessment of Jesus. Matthew and Luke record these accounts in very different contexts, Matthew largely following Mark who omits the description of the exorcism. However, each of the Synoptics associates the exorcism with the accusation that Jesus is empowered by Beelzebul (see Table 5.2). Both Matthew and Luke identify the man as being dumb[40] as a result of a demon, presenting the expulsion of the demon as the cause of the man's ability to speak, though Matthew also refers to Jesus healing him.[41]

The accusation

The exorcism and healing are recorded very briefly; the aftermath is more important to the writers as it records the differing opinions of the witnesses to Jesus, as well as Jesus' own definition of his authority and the implications associated with it. Although Luke does not identify the accusers, Matthew refers to them as Pharisees; their view of Jesus is contemptuous, Matthew indicating this by their use of *houtos* ('this one', 12.24), a rather demeaning way of referring to Jesus. The Synoptists each record the accusation against Jesus that 'he casts out demons' by the power of Beelzebul, 'the prince/ruler of the demons',[42] Mark (3.30) adding that Jesus was accused of 'having an unclean spirit', the present tense of the verb indicating a continuous presence of the demonic force in association with Jesus.

More importantly, Beelzebul is later associated with Satan by each of the writers, indicating the malevolent nature of the indictment against Jesus; he is accused of being empowered by the arch-enemy of God, not a mere ruler of the upper echelons of the demonic kingdom. Their accusation is a serious one, given that such activity was forbidden by God.[43]

The term 'Satan' is best translated as 'adversary', the term being used in the OT with reference to opposition of God and his people (1 Chron. 21.1;

---

[40] Matthew adds that the man is also blind.

[41] The aorist tenses used indicate the immediacy of the removal of the demon and the subsequent restoration of speech.

[42] The name is not used of a demon in any earlier literature. *Test. Sol.* (3.1–6; 4.2; 6.1–11) refers to Beelzebub as the ruler of demons, but since this text is assumed to have Christian influences, it probably postdated the NT; 2 Kings 1.3, 6 refer to Baal-zebub as 'the god of Ekron', a Philistine city. Not only can the word refer to 'Lord of habitation/home' (Baal-zebul) and thus refer to the authority of Beelzebub over families, but also, on the lips of the religious authorities, it is associated with the malignant historical enemy of the Jews and also with refuse, a potential alternative meaning being 'the Lord of flies/dung' (Baal-zibul). The notion of a demonic prince is referred to elsewhere, although not as Beelzebul (*Jub.* 48.15; *Test. Dan.* 5.6; Eph. 2.2 (see also John 14.30; 16.11)).

[43] Lev. 19.26; Deut. 18.10–12; Ezek. 13.18, 20.

Zech. 3.1) and descriptive of evil people (Ps. 109.6). Although viewed in the OT as completely under God's control,[44] in the NT Satan is presented as having a malevolent,[45] earth-related (Luke 10.18) agenda, encouraging sin,[46] and opposing Jesus,[47] and God,[48] though operating under God's sovereignty.[49]

Jesus operates with God's authority

Matthew and Luke reveal that Jesus requested that his accusers identify the power involved when their 'sons'[50] cast out demons.[51] This appears to indicate that Jesus may have acknowledged that Jewish exorcists had power to cast out demons, on the basis of which he asks by what authority they so function. If they assume that their exorcists expel demons by the power of God, their rejection of Jesus should be reconsidered. However, although Jesus may be teaching that a similar divine authority is manifested in his exorcisms and in those achieved by Jewish exorcists,[52] nevertheless he still regards his exorcisms as owning a unique character. Both Matthew and Luke offer '*egō ekballō*' ('I, I cast out'), the emphatic use of the personal pronoun indicating that his exorcisms are special.

In particular, Matthew describes the fact that Jesus exorcizes demons by the Spirit of God, while Luke attributes them to 'the finger of God'. This is a rare reference identifying the Spirit as the source of exorcistic authority; it may be an allusion to Isaiah 11.2 in which the Spirit of the Lord is prophesied as resting on Messiah, thus revealing that the exorcisms are evidence of his messianic status. Elsewhere in his Gospel, Luke does not associate the Spirit with Jesus' miracles and this may have been the reason for the different wording. It is also possible that Luke offers his alternative rendering in order to more clearly highlight the divine role of Jesus, since the term is only used elsewhere with reference to God[53] and, in particular, his creative acts, including creation, the sending of the plagues

---

[44] Job 1.6–12; 2.1–7; Zech. 3.2.

[45] Luke 22.31; 1 Thess. 2.18.

[46] Acts 5.3; 1 Cor. 7.5; 2 Cor. 2.11; 12.7.

[47] Matt. 4.10//Mark 1.13//Luke 4.8; Matt. 16.23//Mark 8.33; Luke 22.3; John 13.27.

[48] Acts 26.18; 2 Thess. 2.9.

[49] Rom. 16.20; Rev. 12.8; 20.2, 7.

[50] This is probably a reference to people associated with the Pharisees, rather than a literal reference to their sons (8.12; 9.15).

[51] Matt. 12.27–28 is almost identical to Luke 11.19–20. Jewish exorcism is referred to in 1 Sam. 16.14–23; Tobit 1—3; Mark 9.38; Acts 19.13–14; Jos., *Ant.* 8.45–9; *Wars* 7.185; Justin, *Dial.* 85; Iren., *Haer.* 2.6.2.

[52] He affirms another exorcist in Mark 9.38–40.

[53] Exod. 8.19; 31.18; Deut. 9.10; Ps. 8.3; Isa. 2.8; 17.8.

of Egypt and the giving of the Ten Commandments.[54] As God provided for his people, so also does Jesus, the same authoritative 'divine finger' functioning in both settings. Thus, the authors elevate his ministry to an unsurpassed level of divine authority, while demonstrating that it is most definitely not satanic.

Jesus' healings are linked to the presence of the kingdom of God

Matthew and Luke record Jesus introducing the concept of the kingdom of God in association with his exorcisms, the words 'If/Since . . . I cast out demons, then the kingdom of God has come upon you' being identical in the original Greek. Jesus' exorcisms uniquely demonstrate that the kingdom of God has been initiated, not that it is soon to come; it is an announcement not only that God's kingdom has come, but also that Jesus is the one who has brought it. Although Matthew prefers the term 'the kingdom of heaven', here he uses 'the kingdom of God', possibly to demonstrate that the satanic kingdom that Jesus is opposing is to be replaced by the supreme kingdom of none other than God.

Previously, in 11.2, Luke records Jesus teaching his followers to pray to the Father, 'Thy Kingdom come'; here, Jesus answers that prayer and brings the kingdom himself. Although elsewhere Luke clearly identifies the kingdom as being given by God (12.32; 22.29–30), the lines are here blurred as Jesus also manifestly initiates it. Although the exorcism is important, it is Jesus, the exorcist, who is central to the narrative, and in particular, the source of his power.

The exorcisms indicate that Satan has been defeated – by Jesus

Each of the Synoptists identifies Jesus as focusing on the folly of the accusation of the opposition, noting that any divided kingdom would be doomed, with the implication that this would also be the case with Satan's kingdom (a concept only occurring here in the NT); if Jesus was assumed to be casting out demons by Satan's authority, he would be undermining Satan's reign.

Each of the writers identifies Jesus as having authority over a 'strong man'[55] (presumably referring to Satan) and plundering his property. Matthew

---

[54] The term 'hand' in the OT and NT is often used with reference to God (Exod. 9.3; 1 Kings 8.15, 46; 2 Chron. 6.4; Ps. 10.12; Isa. 1.25; Ezek. 33.22; Matt. 3.12). Woods (E. J., *The 'Finger of God' and Pneumatology in Luke-Acts.* Sheffield Academic Press, Sheffield, 2001) demonstrates that there are no convincing parallels in the use of this expression 'finger of God' in Greek or Roman literature (pp. 71–87, 98), though it is used in later Jewish literature (pp. 64–71, 96–7).

[55] The term used in Isa. 49.24–25 is *gigas*, 'giant', also used of the residents of Canaan (Num. 13.33).

and Mark express this authority by means of the metaphor of binding,[56] while Luke prefers 'conquering'. The one who binds/conquers the strong man is, by definition, the stronger of the two. There are a number of biblical references to 'strong men' who needed to be 'bound' before their property could be taken, including the inhabitants of Canaan,[57] and Cyrus (Isa. 49.24–25). As God overpowered 'strong men' in the past, now Jesus also overpowers a strong demon. He is able to function in this regard because he has already bound the strong man and is now demonstrating that previously won triumph in his exorcistic ministry.

The actual occasion of that earlier victory is not made explicit, though attention has been drawn to Luke 10.18 (with an implied pre-creation expulsion of Satan from heaven, though no clarification is offered by Luke); it is also possible that the victory was achieved during the confrontation between the devil and Jesus in the wilderness. However, since Luke 10.18 is set in the context of exorcisms performed by the Seventy-Two, it is perhaps better to see each exorcism as evidence of the previously determined victory. Whenever the initial 'binding' occurred and whatever was involved in it, these details are less important to the writers than the fact that it has occurred. Satan is identified as a defeated foe; although not without power, he is unable to deflect, let alone, defeat Jesus. This divine role of Jesus becomes clearer in that Jesus, elsewhere, instructs his followers to expel demons, not in God's name but in his name.[58]

Jesus fulfils prophecies concerning the activity of God in the present

Although the miracle is sensational, it is possible that Matthew and Luke may also be drawing attention to the supreme person and status of Jesus by the possible allusion to Isaiah, who prophesies that this highly unusual miracle of the healing of the blind and dumb/deaf will occur when God returns.[59] Jesus is portrayed as the one who fulfils that prophecy. Perhaps more poignantly, the context of those prophecies is that God is defined as functioning miraculously to demonstrate his love for his people (43.4) and to remove their fear (43.5). Indeed, such miracles

---

[56] This concept of 'binding' graphically portrays the outcome of an exorcism, as do the parallel terms 'loosing/releasing' (Mark 7.34–35; Luke 13.16), also associated with the expulsion of the devil or demons. The verb 'binding' with 'loosing' is also reflected in a non-exorcistic setting in Matt. 16.19; 18.18, best understood as quasi-technical terms used in rabbinic circles, akin to 'forbidding' and 'allowing', describing the authority to provide or restrict permission to a Jew in a given setting (e.g. to teach, to be released from a vow or to be excommunicated).

[57] Num. 13.18, 31; 20.20; Deut. 7.1; 9.1.

[58] Matt. 10.1; Mark 6.7; Luke 9.1; Acts 16.18.

[59] 29.5, 13, 18, 19; 35.2, 4, 5; 43.1, 3, 8, 10.

were intended to demonstrate that God was their unique Lord and Saviour (43.10–11), the cause of their redemption and joy.[60] By attributing these miracles to a diabolic source, the Pharisees are excluding this event from being an opportunity for the people to identify it as a divinely inspired exorcism and, even more significantly, they are removing it as a testimony to the fact that God has fulfilled his prophecy through Jesus in their lifetime and village.

To assume that Jesus' power is diabolic is dangerous

Matthew and Luke record that Jesus knew what his accusers were thinking, itself a sign of his supernatural authority, but the narrative reveals the increasing chasm between Jesus and religious Judaism. In response, Matthew (12.30) and Luke (11.23) identically record Jesus' conclusion that those who choose not to be 'with' him are therefore 'against' him,[61] 'scattering' while he 'gathers'. Finally, Matthew (12.31–32) and Mark (3.28–30; cf. Luke 12.10) refer to the accusation of the Pharisees as being directed not just at Jesus, but more insidiously and dangerously (for the accusers) at the Holy Spirit, for which forgiveness is excluded (Matthew adds 'in this age or the age to come'), Mark identifying it as 'an eternal sin' (see Exod. 20.7). In particular, it is identified by each Synoptist as blasphemy. Mark identifies Jesus as introducing his assertion with the words, 'Truly (*Amēn*), I say to you', indicating the seriousness of the charge against the Pharisees.

Luke records the narrative of the returning demon[62] immediately after this restoration of the dumb demoniac. Matthew also includes this narrative, but he appears to indicate more clearly that Jesus is referring to the Pharisees, because he strongly denounces them in the intervening verses (12.33–43). He then concludes the account with a reference to the danger awaiting 'this evil generation', a term used six verses earlier in response to

---

[60] 29.19, 23; 35.10.

[61] These are the only references in the Gospels to people being 'against' Jesus.

[62] Although Jesus may be specifically referring to those from whom a demon has been removed, warning them to fill their lives with a positive replacement, it is probable that he is more broadly warning those who have witnessed Jesus' actions and especially those who have benefited from his ministry to take advantage of this introduction to the new kingdom and enter it, allowing it to transform them. Gundry (R. H., *Matthew: A Commentary on His Handbook for a Mixed Church under Persecution*. Eerdmans, Grand Rapids, 1982, 1994, p. 246) identifies the evil spirits with the Pharisees, while Luz (U., *Matthew 8–20*. Fortress Press, Minneapolis, 2001, p. 221; contra Bock (D. L., *Luke 9.51–24.53*. Baker, Grand Rapids, 1996, p. 1092) more broadly specifies Israel as that which is in danger, and Keener (C. S., *A Commentary on the Gospel of Matthew*. Eerdmans, Grand Rapids, 1999, p. 369) associates it with 'this evil generation'.

a request by the Pharisees (12.39). For Matthew, the narrative concerning the dangerous demonization, due to the additional demonic dwellers, is especially directed at the Pharisees.

The significance of the pericope concerning the returning unclean spirit is to demonstrate that although exorcism liberates a demoniac, to ensure continuing freedom, submission to the one who has proven to be authoritative is needed. The writers do not explore whether demons that are cast out are free to roam and return, whether they favour waterless territories, can only enter 'empty' bodies, or prefer to wander in groups of seven. To attempt to glean data that relates to demonic activity is to be resisted. The message is a pastoral one – to fail to take advantage of an exorcism is dangerous. However, the Pharisees go further and reject the one who facilitates such exorcisms.

Why does Matthew tell the story?

Matthew precedes the narrative by detailing the confrontation between Jesus and the Pharisees, concerning Jesus breaking their Sabbath laws (12.2, 10). While they decide how to destroy him, Jesus withdraws from them (12.14–15) and announces his mission (12.18–21) by quoting Isaiah 42.1–4. After the exorcism, Matthew (as also Luke) inserts statements by Jesus against the Pharisees, condemning those who blaspheme against the Spirit (12.31–32). Matthew thus sets the narrative in the context of a developing antagonism on the part of the Pharisees against Jesus, and his rejection of them and their views. At the same time, it is Matthew who inserts the statement that some perceived that Jesus might be the Son of David, his emphasis on the messianic nature of Jesus being maintained. On other occasions, a mother of a demonized child recognizes Jesus as the Son of David (15.22), as do blind men (9.27; 20.31), crowds (21.9) and children (21.15). However, there is no evidence that the reaction of the crowd here goes beyond these verbal assertions and enquiries.[63] The potential of benefiting from the kingdom which 'has come upon you [plural]' (Matt. 12.28; Luke 11.20) has not been taken advantage of by many.

Why does Mark tell the story?

Mark does not record the exorcism or any details about the demoniac. However, like Matthew, he places the confrontation between Jesus and the

---

[63] The presence of *mēti* in the question (12.23) anticipates the answer 'yes' to the question; thus, 'might not this be the Son of Man?'

Pharisees, whom he uniquely reveals have come from Jerusalem, presumably with the intention of, at least, verbally attacking Jesus.[64] He also follows it with the reference to blasphemy against the Spirit (3.28–30). However, prior to the passage under examination, Mark inserts two narratives in which Jesus heals many and casts out many demons and then chooses the Twelve (3.7–19).

The fact that Matthew and Luke insert the exorcism while Mark does not is interesting, especially given the fact that Mark refers to exorcisms more often than Matthew or Luke. It is possible that for Mark, the reference to an exorcism may distract from his message which relates to identifying those who accurately affirm Jesus and those who do not (3.31–35). Thus, the Pharisees increasingly oppose Jesus (2.1—3.6) and accuse him of being inspired by Beelzebul (3.22), the crowds are prepared to crush him in order to receive some benefit from him (3.7–10), one of his newly chosen disciples is prophesied as going to betray him (3.19), and even his family (*hoi par' autou exēlthon*, literally, 'the ones who have come out with him', probably describing his family or friends) try to grasp (*krateō*,[65] 'I take, seize, arrest') him, possibly to protect him (from himself or others or both) or remove him, so as to protect themselves from trouble from the religious authorities (3.20).

Inserted in the narrative is a solitary reference to demons who affirm him as the Son of God (3.11), offering the most accurate definition of Jesus' identity. Neither the religious leaders, nor the crowds, nor those he chooses to follow him appreciate his true status; not even his family understand who he is, resulting in Jesus' startling statement that it is those who obey God who are best defined as members of his family (3.33–35).

Why does Luke tell the story?

Luke does not place this exorcism in the context of a confrontation with the Pharisees; they are not even referred to. However, after also recording Jesus' response to the accusation of some that Jesus functions with Beelzebul's power, he follows it immediately with Jesus' description of the return of an unclean spirit to an unprotected person. He then criticizes those who persistently ask for signs.[66]

---

[64] France (R. T., *The Gospel of Mark*. Grand Rapids, Eerdmans, 2002, p. 169) notes 'they have come looking for a fight'.

[65] When used to describe an action of Jesus, it is always positive, describing the action of Jesus in administering healing (1.31; 5.41; 9.27). However, when used of others about Jesus, it is always used in a malevolent context (6.17 (of John the Baptist); 12.12; 14.1, 44, 46, 49).

[66] 11.24–32, 46–52; 12.1–3.

Before the exorcism, Jesus teaches his followers to pray for the Holy Spirit from heaven (11.13); after the exorcism, he is confronted by foes who seek a sign from heaven (11.16). Although the former will be granted to his disciples, his enemies will not receive the latter (11.29–36). Finally, Luke refers to a solitary, anonymous 'woman in the crowd' who identifies Jesus positively (11.27), while the conclusion of the crowd (11.29), the Pharisees (11.40–44, 53–54) and the lawyers (11.45) is negative.

Conclusion

Ostensibly, this is an exorcism narrative in which Jesus' authority over a repugnant and harmful demon is again demonstrated. However, more significantly, the exorcism is presented as a catalyst for appreciating the person and mission of Jesus. On this occasion, the silent demon obeys Jesus, who removes it, while the religious leaders ominously castigate Jesus, and as a result they are identified as in league with Satan himself.

Jesus restores the demonized daughter of a Syrophoenician woman (Matt. 15.21–28//Mark 7.24–30)

Table 5.3 Restoring a Syrophoenician woman's demonized daughter – the literary context

	Matthew	Mark
Jesus is rejected at Nazareth	13.53–58	6.1–6
Jesus commissions the Twelve	(10.1, 5, 7–11)	6.7–13
John the Baptist is killed	14.1–12	6.14–29
Feeding of 5,000	14.13–21	6.30–44
Jesus walks on water	14.22–33	6.45–52
Jesus heals at Gennesaret	14.34–36	6.53–56
Jesus denounces the Pharisees	15.1–20	7.1–23
Jesus restores a Syrophoenician woman's daughter	**15.21–28**	**7.24–30**
Jesus heals many	15.29–31	
Jesus heals a deaf man with a speech impediment		7.31–37
Jesus feeds 4,000	15.32–39	8.1–10
Jesus is confronted by the Pharisees	16.1–4	8.11–13
Jesus warns the disciples about the Pharisees	16.5–12	8.14–21

Main messages from all the narratives

Matthew and Mark precede this narrative with a lengthy discussion, between Jesus and the Pharisees (see Table 5.3), concerning that which defiles a person, a discussion in which Jesus stresses the danger of an immoral lifestyle that reflects internal deficiencies. Prior to this, the narratives in both Gospels stress the importance of faith in Jesus as a basis for receiving his commendation and support. The exorcism recorded in this narrative is less important than the related discussion,[67] despite this being the only exorcism achieved from a distance recorded in the NT, the exorcism being recorded with few details and no exorcistic command.

Matthew and Mark both indicate that this narrative contains important data concerning the breadth of the mission of Jesus, but Matthew more skilfully intermingles the conversations between Jesus and the disciples, and Jesus and the woman, in order to present the main motifs of this narrative.[68]

---

[67] The only information recorded about the demoniac is that she is the woman's young daughter.

[68] Davies and Allison (W. D. and D. C., *Matthew 8–18*. T. & T. Clark, London, 1991, p. 541) note the four requests (three of the woman and one of the disciples) followed by the four responses of Jesus. Furthermore, they identify the fact that Matthew introduces *apokrinomai* ('I answer') on the first three occasions with *ho de* ('but he'), but the final time, it is prefaced by *tote* ('then'), so as to draw attention to the fact that the question-and-answer routine has now reached its climactic conclusion.

Although Mark presents this as another of Jesus' exorcisms, Matthew also emphasizes certain truths concerning the person of Jesus. Both identify the woman as being prepared to bring her problem to Jesus, thus indicating faith in him, but Matthew introduces aspects into the narrative to elevate the quality of her faith and the accuracy of her perception concerning Jesus' person and mission.

The Syrophoenician's perception of Jesus

The woman believed that Jesus would respond positively to her desperate need. Her belief that Jesus could help her is indicated in that Mark records that she sought him, even though he had preferred to be alone (7.24). Indeed, this is the only occasion when a woman verbally requests the healing intervention of Jesus.[69] Jesus did not go to her; she went to him. Only Matthew records her calling to Jesus, 'Lord, help[70] me', this request demonstrating her readiness to trust him. Earlier, he uniquely records her asking for mercy from Jesus, a term used elsewhere by him with reference to people's requests to Jesus for healing.[71] Both authors highlight the desperate nature of the woman's request, Mark recording that she fell down at his feet,[72] begging[73] Jesus to cast the demon out of her daughter. Matthew, however, refers to her bowing or kneeling (*proskuneō*,[74] 'I worship, kneel, offer obeisance or reverence') before Jesus.

She believed that Jesus could cast out a demon from a distance

The woman does not request that Jesus go with her to her daughter, but believes that he could transform her daughter from a distance; such a perception was commended by Jesus earlier of a Gentile centurion who believed that Jesus could heal his son without going to him (Matt. 8.10).

She recognized that Jesus was the Messiah

Matthew records that she appealed to Jesus as '*kurie*[75] *huios David*' ('lord, son of David'); a Gentile woman is presented using this messianic term

---

[69] John 4.27 provides an example of the surprise felt by the disciples when they heard Jesus was talking with a woman.

[70] The word (*boētheō*) is only used here in Matthew and twice in Mark (9.22, 24), also with reference to a demonized person.

[71] 9.27; 17.15; 20.30, 31.

[72] Only Jairus is elsewhere identified as falling at Jesus' feet (5.22) and he was a named, Jewish, male, synagogue ruler, as far removed as possible, socially and culturally, from this woman.

[73] The imperfect tense is used, suggesting a persistent request.

[74] The term is used more by Matthew in the context of Jesus (11 times) than Mark (twice), Luke (three times) and John (once).

[75] Matthew records her using this term of Jesus twice more, Mark once in total.

for Jesus when the previous verses describe Jewish religious leaders failing to recognize him, instead choosing to oppose him. Although the term 'lord', used of Jesus by the woman three times, may be simply indicating respect, the title 'Son of David', especially when spoken by a Gentile, is best understood as a term of exaltation.

She perceived the universal mission of Jesus

The mother of the demonized girl is carefully described by the authors. Mark refers to her as a Greek and a Syrophoenician, by birth. Matthew and Mark identify Jesus as going away from (*ekeithen*[76]) Galilee, withdrawing 40–50 miles north-west,[77] to the Gentile cities of Tyre[78] and Sidon. This is in the opposite direction to Jerusalem, his ultimate destination where he will die for Jews and Gentiles. Elsewhere, Mark (3.8) and Luke (6.17) record that people from Tyre and Sidon came to hear Jesus. Here, Jesus goes to them.

Matthew describes her as a Canaanite, a unique use of the term in the NT. Even though the country of Canaan was non-existent at the time, it reminded his readers not only of her non-Jewishness but also that she was a member of a race that was associated with the ancient antagonism between the Jews and the Canaanites,[79] the latter of whom were associated with pagan worship, sacred prostitution and child sacrifice. Matthew thus portrays her as a resented representative of a nation that has a history of animosity towards the Jews and also God.[80] This is a woman who, historically, has no right to receive any benefit from the Jewish God or the Saviour of the Jews. However, she recognized the breadth of Jesus' ministry, in contrast to the Pharisees[81] and even the disciples.[82] Indeed, Matthew records that the disciples repeatedly[83] requested that she should be dismissed because she had been crying after them for some time; too quickly have they forgotten recent times when they also cried to Jesus for help and he responded positively (14.26, 30).

---

[76] When this word is used in Matthew, it is with reference to Jesus engaging in a positive activity (choosing disciples (4.21; 9.9), healing (9.27; 12.15; 15.29) and teaching (11.1; 12.9; 19.15), resulting in people following him (14.13)).

[77] One cannot be certain if this is where Jesus was prior to going to Tyre and Sidon; the most recent reference to his location was Gennesaret (Matt. 14.34//Mark 6.53).

[78] Josephus refers to the people living in Tyre as the greatest enemies of the Jews (*Ag. Ap.* 1.13).

[79] Gen. 15.21; Exod. 13.11; Neh. 9.8.

[80] Exod. 33.2; 34.11; Deut. 20.17; Josh. 3.10; Acts 13.19.

[81] Matt. 15.3–9, 13–14; 16.1–4; Mark 7.6–7; 8.11–13.

[82] Matt. 15.16–20; 16.8–12, 22–23; Mark 6.51–52; 8.17–18, 32.

[83] The present continuous tense of *kradzō* indicates this. This insular, selfish attitude is noted elsewhere (Matt. 14.15; 19.13; Mark 6.36; 10.13; Luke 9.49; 18.15).

Jesus does not accede to the request of his disciples and send her away; he simply ignores it. Jesus' refusal to grant the requests, both of the woman and of the disciples, becomes a springboard for her next move. Although the situation does not appear to be promising, she reveals the extent of her faith in him. Indeed, she comes to him on the basis of her belief that he has come to this world, and to her town, to help people in need, whatever their racial backgrounds.

After the exorcism, Matthew records Jesus continuing his healing ministry to more Gentiles, the people glorifying 'the God of Israel' (15.29–31), while Mark describes the healing of a dumb man living in the Decapolis. Both Matthew and Mark, by recording this miracle, have sought to indicate that the gospel is available to Gentiles as well as Jews.

- *Even though Jesus does not initially respond to her request, she persists . . .* Matthew records that Jesus did not initially respond to her, not even 'a word'. On other occasions, Matthew uses the word *apokrinomai* ('I answer') to refer to Jesus responding to John the Baptist (3.15), his disciples (13.10; 14.28), unbelieving scribes (12.39; 15.3), Sadducees (22.29), his betrayer Judas (26.23) and even Satan (4.4), as well as others who come with needs (8.8; 17.17);[84] but this time, he does not respond to her. Even when he does, on both occasions his words are not encouraging (15.24, 26); however, the final time he answers her (15.28), it is to announce that she has great faith. Her tenacity is clearer in Matthew than Mark in that Matthew records her as leading the conversation, Jesus simply responding to her assertions.
- *Even though Matthew records Jesus stating that his mission is to the house of Israel, she persists . . .* Matthew is the only Gospel writer to record Jesus' mission as being to the 'house of Israel' (10.5–6; 15.24), and he indicates that it is 'only'[85] to the house of Israel.[86] Moreover, he uniquely indicates that this is a God-given mission, Jesus having been 'sent' thus (15.24).[87] However, the woman demonstrates an awareness that others may also benefit from Jesus' mission.
- *She appeals to the justice of Jesus . . .* Matthew and Mark record Jesus stating that it would not be fair (*kalos*, 'good') if the bread, which is provided

---

[84] The only other time that Jesus does not answer people is when he is accused at his trial (Matt. 26.62; 27.12, 14).

[85] The word 'only' is inserted to help the English translation flow more smoothly; the more literal translation would be, 'I was not sent if (it was) not into the house of Israel'.

[86] This is a term used for the Jews 126 times in the OT (Exod. 16.31; 40.38; Ezek. 44.12, 22) and in Matt. 10.6; Acts 2.36; Heb. 8.8, 10.

[87] Only once elsewhere (10.24) does Matthew record that Jesus had been sent; 15.24 is the only occasion where the intended audience is identified.

by right for the children,[88] should be thrown to the dogs.[89] However, she replies that it would be quite acceptable for dogs to eat the unwanted crumbs that fall to the floor. Her faith in Jesus is more apparent in Matthew than Mark in that Matthew omits the encouraging word of Jesus, 'first', recorded by Mark ('Let the children first be fed'), which at least indicates the possibility that the dogs may be fed afterwards. Her words indicate that she recognizes that even the dogs have a right to eat the bread. The presence of the dogs at the table was not illegitimate, both the children and the dogs benefiting from the master. Indeed, although in Mark the crumbs belong to the children, in Matthew they belong to the master; and it is to the Master that she appeals.

The woman is claiming the privilege of receiving the ministry of Jesus, just as the Jews do, and at the same time. She acknowledges the priority of the Jews in benefiting from the ministry of Jesus, but also acknowledges that she, a Gentile, may be legitimately helped by Jesus. Against the background of his previous condemnation of the Jewish leaders, for being 'blind guides' (Matt. 15.14), Jesus' commendation of the faith of this non-Jewish woman is striking.

The use of the word *kunarion* for 'dog', in referring to the woman, seems rude on the part of Jesus,[90] and elsewhere it is used in disparaging contexts.[91] If the term was used as a provocative description of her race, her tenacity and certitude are even more remarkable. However, the word used (*kunaria*) is a diminutive noun that may indicate an affectionate term for a pet dog;[92] this is how the woman viewed the term, referring to dogs

---

[88] That the Jews are called God's children is well supported in Jewish literature (Exod. 4.22; Deut. 14.1; 32.6; Isa. 1.2; 49.15; Jer. 31.9; Hos. 11.1), and in the NT (Acts 3.26; 13.24; Rom. 1.16; 2.9–10; 15.8).

[89] See Exod. 22.31, 'You shall not eat of any flesh that is torn by beasts in the fields; you shall throw it to the dogs.'

[90] So Scott, J. M. C., 'Matthew 15.21–28: A Test Case for Jesus' Manners', *JSNT.* 63, 1996, pp. 36–7; see also Burkill, T. A., 'The Historical Development of the Story of the Syro-phoenician Woman (Mark 7.24–31)', *NovT.* 9, 1967, pp. 172–3; others also assume that Jesus is rejecting the woman, including Rhoads, D., 'Jesus and the Syrophoenician Woman in Mark: A Narrative-Critical Study', *JAAR.* 62, 1994, p. 358; Guelich, R. A., *Mark 1–8.26.* Word, Dallas, 1989, p. 387; Horsley, R. A., *Hearing the Whole Story: The Politics of Plot in Mark's Gospel.* Westminster Press, Louisville, 2001, p. 215.

[91] E.g. Exod. 22.31; 1 Sam. 17.43; 24.14; 2 Sam. 3.8; 9.8; 16.9; 1 Kings 16.4; 20.19; 2 Kings 9.36; Job 3.1; Pss. 22.16; 68.23; Prov. 26.11; Isa. 56.10–11); it is similarly always used in a demeaning way in the NT (Matt. 7.6; Phil. 3.2; Rev. 22.15).

[92] Harrington, D. J., *The Gospel of Matthew.* Liturgical Press, Collegeville, 1991, p. 235; Luz, *Matthew 8–20.* p. 340; Turner, D. L., *Matthew* Baker, Grand Rapids, 2000, p. 388; Davies and Allison, *Matthew 8–18.* p. 554; Mounce, R. H., *Matthew.* Hendrickson, Peabody, 1991, p. 153; Schwartz (J., 'Dogs in Jewish Society in the Second Temple Period and in the Time of the Mishnah and the Talmud', *JJS.* 55.2, 2004, pp. 250–3) provides evidence to indicate a more affectionate (even sentimental) attitude to dogs in Persian, Greek and Roman cultures.

that lived in the children's house. Pertinently, France also notes, 'written words cannot convey a twinkle in the eye'.[93] Jesus is challenging but not chastening her, stimulating not censuring her.

This narrative needs to be set against the rest of Jesus' mission which includes ministry to other Gentiles as reported by Matthew (4.23–25; 8.28–34) and Mark (3.7–12; 5.1–20; 7.31–37). The fact that Jesus restores this woman's daughter indicates that she is an appropriate beneficiary of his supernatural intervention. Indeed, the woman's response delights Jesus, and Matthew explicitly identifies it as indicative of 'great faith', while Mark implicitly relates her responses to her faith. It is significant to note that the only other time that Jesus reckons a person's faith as being 'great' is with reference to another Gentile (Matt. 8.10). The woman had demonstrated faith by coming to Jesus in the first place, and Jesus gave no indication that her faith needed to be developed or corrected; it may benefit from being affirmed, but it needs no improvement.

Having been provided with challenging hurdles, the woman clears them all with ease and no more obstacles are provided. The lesson, for her, the hearers and future readers, is clear. This woman, a Gentile nobody, as far as Jewish leaders were concerned, has presented Jesus with a marvellous example of faith in him. It is thus not necessary to view Jesus as being unwilling to help a Gentile, or claim that he is chauvinistic or that the woman has cleverly and aggressively pressed her case and thus forced Jesus into action or changed Jesus' mind. She is not commended by Jesus because of her erudition or verbal skills but because of her ability to perceive, beyond his words, the universal mission that he has come to fulfil.

The fact that the metaphor used by Jesus is of table fellowship is not only significant in that it symbolizes the close relationship of a family, but also it has eschatological overtones of a messianic banquet, presided over by the Messiah, to whom all will be invited.[94] Indeed, the references to bread in the narrative may not be coincidental since both Matthew and Mark record the feeding of 4,000 Gentiles with bread afterwards (Matt. 15.32–39; Mark 8.1–10) (see Table 5.3). The Syrophoenician woman shines as a radiant example of one who, in contrast to the disciples, the Pharisees and the Jews, reveals real insight into the heart of Jesus and his mission.

---

[93] France, R. T., *Matthew*. IVP, Leicester, 1985, p. 247; see similar suggestions in Mounce, *Matthew*. p. 153; McNeile, A. H., *The Gospel According to St. Matthew*. Baker, Grand Rapids, 1980, p. 231; Schnackenburg, R., *The Gospel of Matthew*. (tr.) Barr, R., Eerdmans, Grand Rapids, 2002, pp. 150–1; Camery-Hoggart, J., *Irony in Mark's Gospel: Text and Subtext*. Cambridge University Press, Cambridge, 1992, p. 151.

[94] Matt. 8.11; Luke 22.30; 1 Cor. 10.21.

Jesus restores an epileptic demoniac
(Matt. 17.14–21//Mark 9.14–29//Luke 9.37–43)

Table 5.4 Restoring an epileptic demoniac – the literary context

	Matthew	Mark	Luke
Peter's confession at Caesarea Philippi	16.13–20	8.27–30	9.18–21
Jesus foretells his Passion	16.21–23	8.31–33	9.22
Jesus teaches about the cost of discipleship	16.24–28	8.34—9.1	9.23–27
The Transfiguration	17.1–9	9.2–10	9.28–36
Jesus teaches about Elijah	17.10–13	9.11–13	
Jesus casts out a destructive demon	**17.14–21**	**9.14–29**	**9.37–43**
Jesus again foretells his Passion	17.22–23	9.30–32	9.43–45
Jesus provides Temple tax from a fish	17.24–27		
Jesus identifies true greatness	18.1–5	9.33–37	9.46–48

Main messages from all the narratives

Each Synoptist records Peter correctly identifying Jesus as Messiah, after which Jesus announces the Passion to come and teaches the disciples about the cost of discipleship. This is followed by the Transfiguration, though Matthew and Mark insert a brief discussion between Jesus and the disciples concerning the coming of Elijah. Each account is then followed by another prophecy of Jesus' coming Passion; the end is drawing near. The accounts of the exorcism vary considerably, and these variations will be explored later, but the central elements relate to the inability of the disciples to restore a demonized person, Jesus responding by rebuking their faithlessness and casting out the demon.

The father of the epileptic demoniac

The father, with a large crowd, comes to Jesus as he descends from the mountain with his disciples, Mark recording that the remaining disciples had been arguing with some scribes before Jesus returned. Matthew presents the man as showing respect to Jesus, recording that he knelt before him, referred to him as 'lord' and requested mercy for his son. Mark and Luke, however, merely record the man referring to Jesus as 'teacher'. Luke notes that the man asks Jesus to 'look upon' his son; Mark does not even record that the father asked Jesus to cast the demon out, simply addressing the inability of the disciples so to do. However, Matthew especially, and to a lesser degree Luke, present the father as one who exhibits faith in Jesus, anticipating that he has the authority to transform his son.

The demoniac

Matthew alone describes the sufferer as an epileptic[95] (17.16), the trans-formation being described as a healing by Matthew; however, each Synoptist records that a malevolent demon was expelled by Jesus. Matthew describes the man previously as falling into the fire and water, suffering terribly. Luke, more extensively, describes him being seized by the spirit, causing him to suddenly cry out, convulsing him until he foams, and leaving him shattered, so that his family members are unwilling to leave him alone. In view of these symptoms, one may sympathize with the disciples who may have been destabilized by such a malignant force that has caused epilepsy, deafness and dumbness.

The conversation between Jesus and the disciples

Although the exorcism of such a malicious demon is sensational, that is not the reason for the inclusion of the narrative; what is most important is the subsequent conversation, which is variously presented in the synoptic accounts. Matthew and Mark note that the disciples privately asked Jesus why they were unable to cast out the demon, which might indicate that they had tried so to do. However, there appears to be little reason to support this since, if they had tried, surely the demon would have been removed, given that Jesus had already granted them authority to so function.[96]

It is not initially clear to whom Jesus' rebuke is addressed. Various options include the father, the crowd, the disciples, the scribes[97] and/or the people of Israel. The use of the plural personal pronoun 'you', and the word 'generation', by each of the authors suggests that the father is not being singled out for condemnation; indeed, he has already demon-strated his faith in that he has come to Jesus' disciples in the first place and, now, to Jesus. It is possible that Jesus refers to the crowd, though this is unlikely as they have not demonstrated any perversity or faithless-ness and no evidence has been offered that would indicate that they

---

[95] The term *seleniazomai* (literally, 'I am moonstruck', also Matt. 4.24) is to be interpreted with reference to an ancient belief held by some that the moon affected people, though since the symptoms described are similar to epilepsy, it is referred to as epilepsy by translators, even though the Greek verb does not specifically refer to epilepsy. A Greek term, *epilēpsis*, not used here, is one of a number of words used to refer to the phenomenon now described as epilepsy, but which in the ancient world was not consistently identified as a single and separate illness. Weissenrieder (A., *Images of Illness in the Gospel of Luke*. Mohr Siebeck, Tübingen, 2003. pp. 269–77) offers a comprehensive exploration of the ancient views concerning the causes of such phenomena.

[96] Matt. 10.8; Mark 6.7; Luke 9.1.

[97] Mark specifically mentions them arguing with the disciples; see also Mark 2.6; 3.22–30; 10.33; 11.18, 27; 12.35, 38; 14.43, 53; 15.1.

deserved rebuke or correction; indeed, Mark records that they welcomed Jesus (9.15).[98]

Given that the disciples had already been granted the authority to deal with demons, it appears that they were the most likely targets for Jesus' rebuke. They were the only ones who had not achieved their potential. It may be questioned whether Jesus would have described the disciples as being faithless, *apistos* ('unbelieving'), recorded by each of the Synoptists and, also, in Matthew and Luke, as 'perverse'. However, the word *apistos*, which is only used twice elsewhere in the Gospels, there refers to the disciples (Luke 12.46; John 20.27).

The rebuke of the disciples relates to the fact that they did not exorcize the demon. Mark indicates that the father assumed they were not strong (*ischuō*, 'I am strong') enough, while Matthew and Luke refer to his perception that they lacked the ability (*dunamai*, 'I can, am able to') to deal with the demon. The terms are somewhat interchangeable but the latter places the focus on the heart of the problem – the assumption that the disciples were not capable of exorcizing the demon, an assumption that appears to have been shared by the disciples as well. Their incapacity, however, is to be interpreted in the light of their not appropriating the authority that had been previously delegated to them by Jesus. In that regard, they demonstrated their unwillingness to believe the validity of their earlier commission by Jesus.

Why does Matthew tell the story?

Matthew omits many details of the Markan account. There is no reference to the argument between the disciples and the scribes, probably in order to focus on the conversation between Jesus and the father. There is no reference to Jesus asking the people for the reason for the argument, or to his request of the father as to how long his son has been thus affected, while even the malevolence of the demon is muted[99] and Jesus' command to the demon is truncated. The emphasis is firmly on the ease of the miracle for Jesus and the subsequent teaching on the importance of faith as the necessary element in fulfilling missions ordered by Jesus.

For each of the Synoptics, this is a narrative that stresses the supernatural ability of Jesus, here in exorcism, but for Matthew (and to a lesser degree

---

[98] The only other use of this word *aspadzomai* is in Mark 15.18 where the welcome offered to Jesus by soldiers at his crucifixion was sarcastic and humiliating; however, this need not determine its meaning here where the context indicates a readiness to greet him.

[99] The facts that the demon convulsed the son on being brought to Jesus and that he was left as a corpse after the exorcism are omitted by Matthew.

also Mark, but unlike Luke), it also reminds the readers that Jesus had delegated the same authority to his followers, Matthew including the promise that 'nothing will be impossible for you' (17.21; 19.26).

The identification and significance of faith

The identity of the faith referred to by Jesus is not clarified by Matthew (Luke does not include the reference to the potential of the faith of a mustard seed until 17.6). However, by noting that Jesus tells the disciples their faith was too small, and adding that only a very small[100] amount of faith was necessary to achieve momentous deeds, Matthew implies that their faith was even less than minute. Indeed if, as is likely, the earlier rebuke is addressed to the disciples, their faith is to be identified as non-existent, for there they are described as 'faithless' (*apistos*).

Hawthorne[101] suggests that the description of their faith as being little may have been 'to soften the severity of Jesus' rebuke, even though its choice tended to create a paradox by the words that follow that teach that faith, even a little faith, can achieve the impossible'.[102]

Clearly, the disciples had demonstrated that they had faith sufficient to follow Jesus and had trusted him in the past and carried out his wishes. On this occasion, however, their faith in his words had deserted them. In this narrative, the disciples evidenced no readiness to believe the promise made by Jesus that they had been given authority to cast out demons. In response, Jesus teaches them that when (minute) faith is present, remarkable exploits are possible, Matthew uniquely referring to the possibility of even a mountain being moved, an exploit previously identified as only being achievable by God.[103] This is the heart of the message – the disciples are promised that they can bring about transformation previously only achievable by God, because his resources, functioning in Jesus, have been made available to them; they simply have to believe it.

When the disciples had obeyed Jesus' instructions in the past, and thus demonstrated their faith in his words, they had achieved miracles.[104] However, on this occasion they fail – not because of inadequate resources but because of their failure to take advantage of the resources provided.

---

[100] The mustard seed is a symbol of smallness, rather than the smallest seed available.

[101] Hawthorne, G. F., 'Faith: The Essential Ingredient of Effective Christian Ministry', in *Worship, Theology and Ministry in the Early Church*. (eds) Wilkins, M. J., Paige, T., JSOT Press, Sheffield, 1992, p. 255.

[102] On four occasions, the phrase 'little faith' is used by Matthew (6.30; 8.26; 14.31; 16.8); 8.26 and 14.31 refer to occasions when the disciples expressed some faith in Jesus.

[103] Isa. 40.4; 49.11; Zech. 14.10.

[104] Mark 6.13; Luke 9.6; 10.17.

Why does Mark tell the story?

Mark provides the longest account. He uniquely introduces the conversation between Jesus and the father, the fact that a crowd ran to Jesus, greeted him and were 'greatly amazed', the latter term being used generally after a miracle had occurred, not before.[105] More significantly, Mark includes considerably more information about the exorcism than the other writers, Jesus calling the demon a 'deaf and dumb spirit'. By speaking to this 'deaf spirit', Jesus indicates that although the demon had afflicted its victim with deafness, it was not itself deaf.

Mark also describes the malevolence of the demon more graphically before, during and after the exorcism. He records that the demon had been present from childhood, seizing the boy and dashing him to the ground, the present tense indicating a regular occurrence. Also, it caused him to roll about, foam at the mouth, grind his teeth and become rigid (*xērainō*, 'I dry up'[106]). Like Matthew, he notes that it had led the boy to being thrown into fire and water, adding that this had been in order to destroy him.[107] Mark specifically notes that the disturbed reaction of the demon was a direct result of its awareness of its proximity to Jesus. Mark also comments on the fact that when the demon left the son, it cried out, greatly convulsing[108] him and leaving him like a corpse, resulting in many there concluding that he had died.

Mark alone (and uniquely here in the Gospels) records Jesus' command that the demon should not re-enter the son, implying thereby that this was a possibility[109] (*mēketi eiselthēs eis*, 'never enter into him again'), the double reference to *eis* (into) indicating the emphatic nature of the command of Jesus. Jesus is presented as being confidently victorious, while the demon is revealed as maliciously malevolent but fundamentally subservient. However, Mark does not record that the demon was immediately cast out. Instead, Jesus first engages the father in conversation. For Mark also, it is the content of a conversation that is particularly important with reference to the overall impact of the story. It is only after the lesson about belief

---

[105] Mark does not record why this occurred and there is no evidence that it was due to Jesus' demeanour after his Transfiguration, especially since he recommended to his disciples that they say nothing about what they had witnessed (Mark 9.9). It is probable therefore that Mark intended to record the expectation of the crowd on simply seeing Jesus.

[106] See also Mark 3.1; 4.6; 5.29; 11.20, 21.

[107] Mark also highlights the active malevolence of the demon in that it *cast* the boy into fire and water whereas Matthew records the boy as *falling* into fire and water.

[108] See also 9.20 (1.26; Luke 9.39).

[109] See also Matt. 12.43–45; Luke 11.24–26.

has been communicated to the father (and the readers) that the exorcism is recorded.

Mark also records the father requesting help from Jesus on the basis of Jesus' compassion (9.22), stating, 'If you can do anything . . . help us', the plural reflecting the fact that the pain of the son is being felt by others. Jesus replies with the words, 'If you can! All things are possible to him who believes.' Jesus responds to his implied doubt concerning Jesus' ability by repeating the man's request as an exclamation.

It is possible to interpret Jesus' exclamation, 'if you can', as a rebuke ('*if* you can . . .'), as if he is surprised that the man could doubt his ability. However, Jesus does not reprimand the father for any doubt, nor for lacking faith or for having insufficient faith; neither does he correct his faith. Even when he requests that Jesus help him to believe, there is no reference to Jesus acceding to his request or affirming that it is an appropriate request. The fact is that the man has already expressed belief by coming first to the disciples and now to Jesus.

The faith of the man is further affirmed by the fact that he realizes that Jesus can help him (9.22, 24). It is even possible that the sentence 'if you can do anything . . .' should be translated as 'since you can do anything . . .', the word *ei* being capable of meaning 'if' or 'since' (Matt. 9.30), thus indicating a high appreciation of Jesus' authority.

It is thus likely that Jesus repeats the man's words in a positive sense, to reveal the potential available to the one who trusts in him. It is not Jesus who refers to the man as lacking in faith; that is the man's perception of himself. He reflects hope in the context of, thus far, unrealized dreams, but it is sufficient for Jesus. He believes that Jesus is worth approaching, and Jesus assures him that this assessment, even though he fears that it is insufficient, is enough.

Thereafter, while Matthew and Luke comment on the importance of faith, Mark also comments on the importance of prayer in accessing divine resources.[110] Prayer is not elsewhere a feature in the exorcisms of Jesus or his followers. The reference to prayer here is not simply articulating the importance of asking God for help in exorcisms or, in particular, because this was a particularly strong demon that necessitated extra prayer for its

---

[110] Some texts include 'and fasting', though this is omitted in other significant manuscripts. The idea that fasting is appropriate in exorcistic praxis (or healing) is nowhere (else) mentioned in the Bible and Jesus does not specifically record that his disciples should fast (though see Matt. 6.16–18). If it is appropriate to include the practice of fasting, that would indicate that exorcisms should not be always anticipated as being immediate since fasting occurs over a period of time. However, it may indicate a life of dependency on Jesus, evidence of which is time spent praying and fasting.

removal. Rather, it more probably describes a lifestyle that reflects an ongoing relationship with God and an eagerness to determine his will.

The focus is not on prayer as the means to achieve power so much as on the necessity of developing a relationship with the one who is the source of power, central to which is prayer. Mark defines a life of obedience to Jesus as one that is dominated by prayer, dependency on God, reflected in both talking to him and, most importantly, listening to what he has to say.

Why does Luke tell the story?

Luke's account is similar in length and content to that of Matthew. As may be imagined, he adds elements that focus on the human tragedy, noting twice that the man begs Jesus and his disciples to help him and identifying horrific consequences of the demonic attacks on the son, specifically recording that when the boy was brought to Jesus, the demon convulsed him. He also notes that a day has passed while Jesus was up the mountain (9.37), indicating the probability that the man's request that the disciples cast out the demon from his son was offered a day earlier. His faith in Jesus is indicated by his willingness to stay until Jesus appears. Furthermore, it is Luke alone who notes that having healed (*iaomai*,[111] 'I heal') the son, Jesus gave him back to his father (see also 7.15).

Luke also notes the aftermath, as far as the crowd is concerned, insofar as they were astonished[112] at the manifestation of the majesty (*megaleiotēs*,[113] 'grandeur') of God, presumably as a result of witnessing the exorcism which, he also records, led them to wonder (*thaumazō*).[114]

Instead of exploring the significance of faith as does Matthew, and the value of prayer as does Mark, Luke emphasizes the healing power of Jesus and its significance in identifying the presence and mission of God through Jesus. Of particular significance to his disciples is the fact that Luke thereafter warns them that he is soon to be arrested, followed by evidence that they did not understand his words because they argued as to who was the greatest and criticized, ironically, a successful exorcist (9.46–55). Again, the readers are provided with the opportunity to determine if they have

---

[111] Luke's favoured term to describe a healing from an illness (5.17; 6.19; 7.7; 8.47; 9.2, 11; 14.14; 17.15; 22.51; Acts 9.34; 10.38; 28.8) and with reference to exorcisms (6.18; 9.42). By contrast, Matthew (8.8, 13; 15.28) uses the word three times to refer to physical healing, Mark just once (5.29) and John twice (4.47; 5.13).

[112] The other two occasions where this word is used in Luke describe people's astonishment at Jesus' wisdom (2.48; 4.32).

[113] The word is only recorded three times in the NT (Luke 9.43; Acts 19.27; 2 Pet. 1.16), the latter specifically referring to Jesus.

[114] Used by Matthew and Mark four times each but 13 times by Luke (five also in Acts).

better understood the personal commissions given to them by Jesus and obeyed them any better than the disciples have obeyed theirs.

Conclusion

Through these narratives, a range of lessons are offered by the writers. While they agree on many details of the story, they also offer clear perspectives of their own and seek to teach their readers different lessons. However, each presentation affirms the necessity of obeying commissions given by Jesus to all would-be disciples.

Jesus delivers a demoniac (Mark 1.21–28//Luke 4.31–37)

Table 5.5 Delivering a demoniac – the literary context

	Mark	Luke
Temptations of Jesus	1.12–13	4.1–13
Start of Jesus' ministry	1.14–15	4.14–15
Jesus' sermon in Nazareth		4.16–30
Jesus calls his first four disciples	1.16–20	(5.1–11)
Exorcism of the synagogue demon	1.21–28	4.31–37
Healing of Simon's mother-in-law	1.29–31	4.38–39
Summary of healings	1.32–34	4.40–41

Main messages from all the narratives

Mark precedes this account with the calling of Simon, Andrew, James and John to be disciples, while Luke precedes it with the rejection and attempted assassination of Jesus after his sermon at Nazareth (see Table 5.5). Both writers record the incident as Jesus' first miraculous act. However, while Luke most probably intended to depict it as evidence of Jesus' mission, as outlined in 4.18–19, Mark links it with establishing the kingdom of God (1.15).

The exorcism happened in a synagogue on the Sabbath, where Jesus was teaching, and it is recorded with only minor differences between the two accounts. No comment is offered with reference to the demonized person being in the synagogue, the presence of Jesus being the reason why the demon identified itself publicly.

Both Mark and Luke introduce this narrative with a comment that many people were astonished at the authority[115] with which Jesus taught, Mark adding that it was different from that of the scribes. Although the content of his teaching had similarities to that of John the Baptist, there is no record of people being astonished at John's teaching. It is possible that the writers are drawing attention to the difference in Jesus' teaching style in that he did not refer to any other teachers in his teaching, as did the rabbis. However, it is unlikely that John the Baptist would have referred to scribal views either, and it is best to conclude that the writers simply wished to emphasize the astonished response of the listeners rather than to specify a reason.

---

[115] This is the first reference to Jesus' authority in Mark and Luke (also Mark 2.10; 3.15; 11.28; Luke 5.24; 9.1).

Both writers conclude the narrative with Mark specifically relating the exorcism to Jesus' teaching, while Luke inserts their question, 'What is this word?' However sensational the exorcism, it is the message that is relayed by it that is most important to the writers. That message relates to the authority of Jesus.

The words of the demon

The 'unclean spirit' (Mark) or 'spirit of an unclean demon' (Luke)[116] is described as crying or shrieking, Mark adding 'with a loud voice'. The introduction by Luke in 4.34 of the Greek term *ea* ('ah') used by the demon may be an expression of surprise, displeasure or precocious interruption. The words of the demon thereafter are similar to those recorded elsewhere, including the question 'what have you to do with us?'[117] However, the terms used of Jesus, on this occasion, are different, the demon identifying Jesus as 'Jesus of Nazareth'[118] and emphasizing that it knows that Jesus is 'the holy one of God'.[119] The latter title is infrequently used of prophets or those functioning in the context of the presence of God.[120] It is unique to this narrative in the Synoptics and, at the very least, indicates knowledge of the person and status of Jesus. The demons are indicating more than that Jesus is a prophet, given their assumption that he has the authority to destroy them, an ability granted to no prophet.[121]

Although the words of a demon may generally be assumed to be untrustworthy, on this occasion they are true. They probably represent a true recognition of Jesus' superiority, resulting in fear on their part. It is less likely that the words are offered in the hope that Jesus may be destabilized by its knowledge of him and his mission; Jesus is not easily startled, especially by such a malevolent minion. Given that in other exorcisms, resistance to expulsion is not uncommon, as here also, despite the inevitable outcome, it is possible that the demon is playing for time.

---

[116] Such a description explicitly contrasts it with the Holy Spirit, who has been referred to a number of times already by Luke. Luke uses the term *daimonion* 23 times in the Gospel and more than the other Synoptists. It is used 12 times by Mark (though Mark uses *daimonizomai* four times as compared to only once by Luke). Mark uses 'unclean spirits' (12) more than Luke (six).

[117] Matt. 8.29//Mark 5.7; Luke 8.28.

[118] The term is used elsewhere in Mark (10.47; 14.67; 16.6) and Luke (18.37; 24.19) on the lips of people.

[119] See comment on Matt. 8.28–35//s.

[120] 2 Kings 4.9; Ps. 106.16; Sir. 45.6; the term 'holy one of Israel' often refers to God (Pss. 71.2; 78.41; Isa. 29.23; 30.15; 43.3; 54.5).

[121] The plural reference here is not representative of multi-possession, for the demon is later identified in the singular; rather, the single demon is understood as speaking on behalf of all demons.

The response of Jesus

This incident and the recorded exorcism of the Gadarene demoniac are the only occasions in which Jesus engages a demon in conversation. On this particular occasion, it involves only a rebuke by him,[122] 'be silent (*phimeō*,[123] 'I muzzle') and come out of him'. Both verbs are in the aorist tense, indicating that a prompt response is anticipated. Such a command to silence may have simply been due to a desire by Jesus to prevent the garrulous demon from talking, or to stop the unhelpful revelation of Jesus to the crowds, either because of the malignant source of that revelation or because of its untimely nature.

Mark alone records that the expulsion occurs after the demon convulses its victim, while Luke maintains the superiority of Jesus more explicitly with the demon leaving immediately and without a struggle, simply harmlessly throwing the victim to the ground. However, the Markan presentation should not be assumed to undermine the authority of Jesus, and such an exit did not undermine the crowd's affirmation of Jesus. It is possible that since, in two of the three Markan exorcisms, the demon is recorded as convulsing its victim, and in the third as destroying its eventual victims, the pigs, non-peaceful exits were expected. The fact that its final activity is evil reveals something of the malevolence of the demon.

The aftermath

The crowd's amazement results in the people discussing what they had witnessed, followed by an ('immediate', Mark) dissemination of the news of the exorcism throughout Galilee. Their amazement was because Jesus overcame 'even' (adverbial use of *kai*) a demon, and also because of the ease of the miracle – achieved simply by speaking a few assertive words. Luke records their question, 'What is this word?' while Mark reports them asking, 'What is this? Is it a new teaching?' Luke refers to the 'authority and power' (Mark only records 'authority') that supports Jesus' commands that are obeyed by demons. Although the terms sometimes overlap in meaning, in this context it is likely that Luke intends the readers to recognize the special authority of Jesus, demonstrated by his superior status over the demons.

---

[122] See comment on Matt. 8.16–17//s. The use of this term (*eptimaō*, 'I rebuke') is not a technical or magical term. It is used in the OT to indicate the powerful sovereign word of God (Pss. 9.5; 67.30); elsewhere, it is used where no demonic expulsion is anticipated (e.g. Mark 4.39//Luke 4.39; Mark 8.30, 32, 33; Luke 9.55; 18.15).

[123] The word is used to refer to people being speechless, silent (Matt. 22.12, 34; 1 Pet. 2.15), a storm being stilled (Mark 4.39), and the muzzling of an ox (1 Tim. 5.18).

No mention is made of the demoniac after the exorcism; indeed, he is passive and silent throughout. Thus, it is not surprising that there is no record of any command or guidance to him by Jesus or any activity undertaken by him.[124] The challenge to the readers is whether they will be as impressed with Jesus as were the onlookers and, more importantly, whether they will be similarly cognizant of the true identity of Jesus and as obedient as the demons were.

Tragically, Mark's relating of Jesus' encounters with the people that follow demonstrates their increasing uncertainty as to whether they would trust him (2.1—3.5), resulting in their determination to kill him (3.6). Luke meanwhile demonstrates that the demons are better at recognizing who Jesus is than are the people of Nazareth where he was brought up, for they also try to kill him, attempting to throw him off a cliff (4.16–30). It is significant that the narratives in which the devil recognizes the status of Jesus and tries to make him deviate from his chosen path (4.1–13) and the one where the demons recognize that he is to be obeyed (4.31–37) are dissected by an account in which the Jews choose to do the opposite.

---

[124] Contrast Mark 5.15–20//Luke 8.35–39.

Jesus restores a dumb demoniac (Matt. 9.32–34)

Table 5.6 Restoring a dumb demoniac – the literary context

	Matthew
Jesus calms a storm	8.23–27
Exorcism of the Gadarene demoniac	8.28–34
Healing of a paralytic	9.1–8
Jesus calls Matthew to be a disciple	9.9
Jesus eats with tax-collectors and sinners	9.10–13
Jesus teaches concerning fasting	9.14–17
Jesus heals Jairus' daughter	9.18–19, 23–26
Jesus heals the woman with a haemorrhage	9.20–22
Jesus heals two blind men	9.27–31
Jesus restores a dumb demoniac	**9.32–34**
Jesus has compassion for the crowds	9.35–38
Jesus commissions the Twelve	10.1–42

Introduction

Because this story is similar to another exorcism in 12.22–24, it is possible that it is a description of the same event. However, given the differences between the two narratives,[125] it is more likely that two similar but separate events are in view.

This miracle concludes a collection of seven healings, one exorcism and the calming of the storm by Jesus, mingled with examples of his authority in choosing his disciples, eating with people he chooses, and determining when it is appropriate for his disciples to fast. Now, he performs another exorcism which, for the first time in the Gospel, simultaneously results in the healing of a physical complaint.

As elsewhere, the man is described as being 'demonized', the present passive tense indicating the ongoing nature of this oppression and that the man is not in control of the situation or the demon; specifically, he has no control over his voice because the demon has made him dumb. Although faith is not mentioned here, the fact that Matthew reveals (for the first time) that people brought the demoniac to Jesus suggests that they recognized that he had power to help.

---

[125] In the first exorcism, the demoniac is dumb, while in the second he is also blind; in the first, Jesus is accused of being empowered by the prince of demons who is identified, in the second, as Beelzebul; in the second, people wonder if Jesus is the Son of David, though this is not present in the first, while the first uniquely refers to the crowd's assessment that nothing like this had been seen in Israel.

The relationship between the demonization and the man's dumbness[126] is not explored by Matthew;[127] instead of referring to the man being healed of his dumbness, Matthew simply records that after the demon was removed, the man spoke, implying that the former act was the cause of the latter consequence. Neither is there any interaction with the demon (8.29–32). The exorcism in which the demon is dismissively cast out is told in passing, demonstrating an effortless authority by Jesus. The demon and the demoniac are silent figures; more importantly, so is Jesus silent – he does not even tell the demon to go. The focus is on what is said afterwards by the witnesses to the event.

Although the exorcism results in the man being able to speak, his words are not identified. However, the speech of the crowds and the Pharisees is revealed, with the crowds marvelling[128] at the uniqueness of this miracle in Israel, and the Pharisees denouncing Jesus as a malignant exorcist, crediting the exorcism to the power of the prince[129] of demons operating through Jesus. The Pharisees have, up to now, been presented as asking questions concerning Jesus' authority (9.11, 14), but now, for the first time, their opposition is clearly identified and soon becomes malevolent (12.14). It is little wonder that Matthew soon records Jesus commissioning the Twelve (10.1–42) (see Table 5.6). The exorcism has resulted in a severe break with the religious leaders, resulting in Jesus preparing for a time when people who need help will receive it from others, in his absence.

---

[126] *Kōphos* is capable of meaning 'deaf' (8.11; Luke 7.22) and 'dumb', its meaning here relating to dumbness because of the reference to the man speaking after the demon has been removed.

[127] Disease and demonization are distinguished from one another in 8.16; see earlier for the connection between demonic activity and physical impairment.

[128] This is the first and only time in Matthew that people are revealed as marvelling as a result of an exorcism by Jesus; elsewhere, they marvel at his authority over the sea and wind (8.27) and over illness (15.31), and at his words (22.22; 27.14). The disciples similarly wonder at Jesus' actions (8.27; 21.20), as do the crowds later (15.31).

[129] The word *archōn* is used in 9.18, 23; 20.25 to refer to a ruler.

6

The Synoptics: nature miracles

Jesus calms a storm (Matt. 8.23–27//Mark 4.35–41//Luke 8.22–25)

Table 6.1 Calming a storm – the literary context

	Matthew	Mark	Luke
Jesus heals and exorcizes demons	8.16–17	(1.32–34)	(4.40–41)
Jesus teaches would-be disciples	8.18–22		(9.57–60)
The parable of the sower	(13.1–9)	4.1–9	8.4–8
The purpose of parables	(13.10–13)	4.10–13	8.9–10
The explanation of the parable of the sower	(13.18–23)	4.13–20	8.11–15
Putting a light under a vessel	(10.26–27)	4.21–25	8.16–19
Jesus identifies his 'mother and brothers'	(12.46–50)	(3.31–35)	8.19–21
Parables about seeds		4.26–34	
Jesus calms a storm	**8.23–27**	**4.35–41**	**8.22–25**
Exorcism of a Gadarene demoniac	8.28–34	5.1–20	8.26–39
Healing of a paralytic	9.1–8	(2.1–12)	(5.17–26)
Jesus calls Matthew to be a disciple	9.9	(2.13–14)	(5.27–28)
Jesus eats with tax-collectors and sinners	9.10–13	(2.15–17)	(5.29–32)
Jesus teaches concerning fasting	9.14–17	(2.18–22)	(5.33–39)
Jesus heals Jairus' daughter	9.18–19, 23–26	5.21–24, 35–43	8.40–42, 49–56
Jesus heals the woman with a haemorrhage	9.20–22	5.25–34	8.43–48

Main messages from all the narratives

Although the narratives preceding the stilling of the storm differ in each of the Synoptics, each of them follows this narrative with the exorcism of a demoniac (see Table 6.1). It is unlikely that both accounts are describing a demonically inspired storm,[1] even though each records Jesus rebuking (*epitimaō*) the storm, the same form of the word (*epetimēsen*, aorist active) being used in the exorcism that follows.[2] It is more likely that the similar

---

[1] Mark only records Jesus using *phimoō* ('I muzzle, silence') elsewhere in 1.25, with reference to Jesus silencing a demon (see also Luke 4.35).

[2] Although the term is used with reference to the devil or demons (Matt. 17.18; Mark 9.25; Luke 9.42), it is also, and more often, used in other contexts, referring to the disciples rebuking children (Matt. 19.13), people rebuking other people (Matt. 20.31; Luke 19.39), people rebuking Jesus (the

themes present in the two narratives are that both the storm and demons obey Jesus. It is probable that the two stories are connected because the exorcism occurred precisely after Jesus had crossed the stormy sea; not even a malevolent storm was going to stop him dealing with a diabolic situation.

Each writer records that this is a journey undertaken by Jesus and the disciples. Given that storms were relatively common on Galilee, this must have been particularly severe to have destabilized even those seasoned sailors present.[3] There may be an allusion to the story of Jonah, which also records a dangerous storm and features fearful sailors where the central character is asleep, the storm being calmed by God. However, contrasts with the story of Jonah abound, especially in that the storm subsided only when he was thrown overboard, while here it is Jesus' presence that calms the gale. Furthermore in Jonah, the storm ceased as a result of prayer, whereas in this narrative no prayer is offered.[4]

However, there are many accounts of storms and sea voyages in ancient literature which have the effect of elevating the respective heroes. The most important of these were the *Odyssey* (traditionally viewed as being authored by Homer) and Virgil's *Aeneid*.[5] Each was used as a textbook to be read, memorized and dramatized by pupils. In particular, the texts identified principles of life and conduct, appropriate to becoming model citizens. These stories recounted the lives of heroes battling against the odds to cross the Greek (Mediterranean) Sea, overcoming the strategies of various gods, storms and natural enemies along the way, resulting in the achievement of their objectives. The supremacy of the gods supporting these heroes is proven by their ability to support their protégés against all the obstacles facing them. Here, Jesus calms the storm and reaches his destination with no external help, his personal power being superlative.

---

thief on the cross, Luke 23.40; Peter, Mark 8.32), leaders rebuking believers (2 Tim. 4.2), and Jesus rebuking his disciples (Mark 8.33; Luke 9.55). Also, Jesus does not 'cast out' any demon from the storm, as he does in exorcisms, and none of the authors explicitly defines it as an exorcism. Indeed, each of the Synoptists records the disciples concluding that Jesus has power over the winds and sea, not over any demonic initiators of the storm. Interestingly, in the exorcism that follows, none of the authors records Jesus rebuking the demon, although *epitimaō* is used in other exorcisms.

[3] Pss. 55.8; 83.15; Isa. 28.2; 29.6.

[4] *Test. Naph.* 6.1–10 recounts a story concerning Jacob and his sons caught in a storm, which is calmed as a result of the prayers of Levi, while j. *Ber.* 9 records a Jewish child asking God to calm a storm that threatened to sink a ship on which he was travelling.

[5] The *Odyssey* is a sequel to Homer's *Iliad* and recounts the adventures of the Greek hero Odysseus (or Ulysses, as he was known in Roman myths) and his long journey home to Ithaca following the fall of Troy. In the *Aeneid*, the prize of the sea voyage undertaken by Aeneas and his Trojan companions was Rome; Robbins, V., 'By Land and Sea: The We-Passages and Ancient Sea Voyages', in *Perspectives on Luke-Acts*. (ed.) Talbert, C. H., ABPR, Danville, 1978, pp. 215–42.

A startling element of the narrative is that it records the humanity of the sleeping Jesus, perhaps tired after a day of teaching, alongside his divinity, in that the wind obeys him. At the same time, the fact that in the middle of seismic activity Jesus is able to sleep indicates his supreme sense of stability.[6] Matthew records Jesus as sleeping continuously (*ekatheuden*, imperfect tense from *katheudō*) as does Mark (*katheudōn*, present participle), while Luke uses *aphupnōsen*, aorist from *aphupnoō*, 'I sleep'). Each of the writers records the disciples waking Jesus. Although they may have wanted him to physically help them, it is possible that they hoped for supernatural aid.

Each author draws attention to the ease and authority of Jesus in dealing with the storm. Also, they record not only that the storm ceases but that it becomes calm, Matthew and Mark contrasting the great (*megas*) storm with a great (*megas*) calm,[7] a feat that had previously only been achieved by God.[8]

It appears that Jesus causes the storm to cease for the benefit of his disciples' peace of mind rather than self-preservation; the story does not indicate that Jesus was roused in the nick of time, just before the boat was terminally swamped by the waves. Neither do the Synoptists commend the disciples for making Jesus aware of the problem. The implication may be drawn that even if the storm had continued, they would have reached their destination safely. Jesus knew that and slept in the certainty that nothing could thwart his mission; the same opportunity for trust was available to the disciples but they failed to take it. The one who had initiated the journey was capable of authoritatively ensuring that it was completed, storm or no storm.[9] In fact, each author indicates this truth. Matthew records that the disciples followed him, implying that he is trustworthy, while Mark and Luke record Jesus stating that the disciples are to 'go across to the other side'; the destination has been determined by Jesus and that objective will be achieved.

The comment by Jesus relating to the disciples' limited faith may indicate that Jesus anticipated that they had the authority to silence the storm themselves, though there is no record of Jesus delegating this authority to his disciples before this event. It is thus probably a reference to their limited

---

[6] Job 11.18–9; Pss. 3.5–6; 4.8.
[7] Matt. 8.24, 26; Mark 4.37, 39.
[8] Job 9.8; Pss. 29.3, 10; 89.8–9; 107.29; Isa. 4.6; 17.12–14; 25.4; 32.2; 43.1–16.
[9] Ps. 46.3 speaks of a time when the waters of the sea roar and foam but the reader needs not fear because 'God is in the midst' (5) and 'with us' (7, 11), help being promised 'when morning dawns' (5).

readiness to trust in him, a limitation that does not preclude his resolving the problem and assuaging their fear. Given that this is recorded speech, it is difficult to anticipate the tone with which the words are spoken. Although he may be reprimanding them, he may as easily be speaking with a smile, encouraging them because he is more committed to them than they realize. His words are not specifically offered because they were frightened, but because they were frightened despite his presence with them. It is not the presence of fear that is the issue, but the absence of faith; fear may be removed when it is replaced by faith in Jesus.

Why does Matthew tell the story?

Prior to the narrative outlining the calming of the storm, Matthew records a conversation between Jesus and a disciple (8.21–22) in which the latter delays a response to Jesus' call, instead of promptly obeying him. The following narrative records a devastating storm that obeys Jesus, followed by a description of demons who also obey Jesus. This is then followed by a paralytic who obeys Jesus and is thus healed (9.6–7) and the prompt obedience of Matthew who becomes a disciple (9.9). All would-be disciples are reminded of the centrally important place of obedience to Jesus, who has all authority.

Matthew alone refers to the disciples following Jesus into a boat, the verb 'to follow' being used elsewhere in association with the concept of discipleship[10] and other followers of Jesus.[11] No words of command are needed (as recorded in Mark and Luke); it is as if wherever Jesus goes, his disciples automatically follow. By contrast, Mark records that 'they took him with them'.

The supremacy of Jesus is also highlighted by Mathew in that he alone records the disciples referring to him as 'Lord', requesting that he 'save' (*sōzō*) them, both terms indicative of the supremacy of Jesus, as is the fact that Jesus rebuked the winds, to be contrasted with the singular 'wind' in Mark and Luke. As contrasted with Mark and Luke, who identify Jesus rebuking the wind after he awoke (*diegeirō*), Matthew notes that it was after he arose (*egeirō*), Jesus more clearly presented in a spatial and controlling position of supremacy.

Furthermore, in contrast to Mark and Luke, Matthew identifies Jesus conversing with the disciples during the storm, only rebuking the storm after the lesson concerning faith had been offered. The storm itself is

---

[10] 4.20, 22; 8.19, 22; 9.9, 19; 10.38; 16.24; 19.27, 28; 20.29, 34; 27.55.
[11] 4.25; 8.1, 10; 9.27; 12.15; 14.13; 19.2.

identified by Matthew as *seismos*, as contrasted with Mark and Luke who have *lailaps*.[12] For Matthew, the explicit message is that it is possible not to fear in a storm but rather to experience faith.[13]

The disciples are defined only by Matthew as having 'little faith'; in other words, they have some faith – after all, they did follow Jesus into the boat. Also, only Matthew records that after the miracle, they marvelled, as contrasted with Mark and Luke, who both speak of them exhibiting fear or awe (*phobeō*). Matthew records their fear (*deilos*[14]) but only before the miracle occurs, after which their fear is dissipated. The lesson to be learnt is that the one who asks would-be followers to promptly obey him also has the authority to ask the wind to obey him. They are safe with him – and therefore they should trust him.

Why does Mark tell the story?

Mark's account is the longest, providing extra details, including the fact that they set sail in the evening. He also refers to the presence of other boats, that they had left a crowd, that Jesus went onboard 'just as he was', and that the waves beat into the boat. He also notes that the disciples call into question Jesus' care for them, ('Don't you care . . . ?'[15]) and that they identify him only as 'Teacher'. Mark records the disciples' fear most explicitly, the concept being referred to three times during and after the storm. Finally, Mark records Jesus asking them if they have any faith, implying that they have none. The words of Jesus to the storm, only in Mark, are

---

[12] The term *seismos* is nowhere else used in the NT but it is present in the OT, where it refers to an earthquake (Isa. 29.6; Ezek. 38.19; Amos 1.1; Zech. 14.15) or noisy commotion (Jer. 10.22; 23.19), but more importantly, for this narrative, in contexts of divine judgement (Jer. 25.32), often in an eschatological setting.

[13] Davies and Allison (W. D. and D. C., *Matthew 8–18*. T. & T. Clark, London, 1991, p. 68) emphasize the importance of Jesus' words of affirmation in this chiasm:

8.23a	Jesus boards		
8.23b	the disciples follow		
8.24a–b	a storm arises		
8.24c	Jesus is sleeping		
8.25	the disciples address Jesus		
8.26a	Jesus addresses the disciples		
8.26b	Jesus arises and rebukes the storm		
8.26c	the storm calms		
8.27	the disciples are amazed		
8.28	Jesus disembarks		

[14] This word is only used three times in the NT (here and Mark 4.40, with reference to this narrative, and Rev. 21.8 describing the fearful and cowardly who are destined for the lake of fire. It appears to be similar to *phobos*, both words being used synonymously.

[15] However, the presence of the particle *ou* anticipates a positive response from Jesus.

appropriate: 'Peace! Be still!' The present and perfect tenses respectively affirm the abiding nature of the anticipated peace and stillness. Mark presents Jesus as supremely in control (uniquely recording that he was asleep in the safest part of the boat, on a cushion) and authoritatively dealing with the storm before he teaches his disciples, whereupon the wind ceases immediately.

Despite asking Jesus for help, the disciples are still identified by Mark as having an absence of faith, possibly in Jesus' power to rescue them, but possibly relating to their inability to be at ease despite their proximity to Jesus. It is uncertain whether they experienced fear or awe after the miracle, as the word used (*phobeō*) can mean both; perhaps it is safer to acknowledge the presence of both, though more probably the emphasis is on their being afraid.[16] If this is the case, it demonstrates that in the presence of a miracle the disciples reflect fear as well as faith. It may be that Mark reflects their growing, but still insubstantial, appreciation of the majesty of Jesus (and therefore their safety) in that they take him 'just as he was', perhaps indicating their limited awareness of his power and status, resulting in their perplexity at the end of the narrative, for they were not prepared for such authority being exercised from the one who got into the boat with them. At the same time, they had been provided with the best seats to witness the miraculous action of Jesus. Although other boats were sailing at the same time, it was only those who had Jesus in their boat who were granted the clearest opportunity of seeing his authority being administered over the storm. The challenge to them was whether they would draw the accurate conclusions as to the significance of this authority of Jesus.

Why does Luke tell the story?

Luke sets the context similarly to Matthew and Mark, though he specifically notes that they were in danger. Luke is interested in sea voyages in which the one commissioned by God achieves his objective and arrives at the chosen destination, despite potential obstacles including storms, thus demonstrating the authenticity of the missions and the authority of the one who commissioned them. As in Acts 28.31, where Luke identifies Paul's mission with the final word 'unhindered', so also Jesus will complete his journey, as will all who follow him, unhindered by any 'storm'.

---

[16] Elsewhere in Mark, the verb is not used positively or in the context of awe; rather, it is used of people fearing Jesus after he had exorcized a demon, resulting in them asking that he leave them (5.15), or of fear of the unknown (5.33, 36; 6.50; 10.32; 16.8) or being scared (6.20; 9.32; 11.18, 32; 12.12); this is the only time that the noun *phobos* is used in Mark.

The disciples are recorded as referring to Jesus as 'Master, Master'. This title is used elsewhere (by the disciples) in Luke with reference to Jesus.[17] Jesus responds to their fear with reduced words, asking them 'Where is your faith?' as if they had mislaid it. As a consequence of the miracle, Luke records their mixed emotions of fear and wonder, as they struggle to come to terms with the revelation of their master, who is increasingly spectacular.

Conclusion

This is a narrative intended to teach lessons relating to discipleship and the status of Jesus. There will be more lessons to learn, and the greater the readers' appreciation of the status of Jesus, the easier it will become to trust him.

---

[17] 5.5; 8.45; 9.33, 49.

Jesus feeds over 5,000 people (Matt. 14.13–21// Mark 6.32–44//Luke 9.10b–17//John 6.1–13)

Table 6.2 Feeding over 5,000 people – the literary context

	Matthew	Mark	Luke	John
Rejection of Jesus by his countrymen	13.52–58			
Jesus commissions the Twelve	(10.7–11, 14)	6.7–13	9.1–6	
Jesus heals at the Sheep Pool				5.1–47
Death of John the Baptist	14.1–12	6.14–29	9.7–9	
The disciples tell Jesus of their deeds and words		6.30–31	9.10a	
Feeding of 5,000	14.13–21	6.32–44	9.10b–17	6.1–13
The people want to make Jesus king				6.14–15
Jesus walks on the water	14.22–27	6.45–52		6.16–21
Peter walks on the water	14.28–32			
Jesus affirmed as Son of God by the disciples	14.33			
Peter's declaration that Jesus is the Christ	(16.13–20)	(8.27–30)	9.18–20	
Jesus foretells his death and resurrection	(16.24–28)	(8.34—9.1)	9.21–27	
The wider significance of the feeding of the 5,000				6.22—7.1

Main messages from all the narratives

Each of the Synoptists records this miracle after describing the death of John the Baptist (though Mark and Luke also insert a brief reference to the disciples telling Jesus of their exploits; see Table 6.2) where a banquet and its gory aftermath are described. The contrast could not be greater with the description of simple food that is to be miraculously multiplied by Jesus. This narrative marks a clear break with the mission of John the Baptist. Although John had an important and God-given commission, his death signals the exclusive presentation of the one who is superior even to him. This is the only miracle narrative located in each of the Gospels, and they contain significant similarities and dissimilarities. The similar data in each of the accounts provides clues as to the central lessons in the minds of the writers; it is only, for example, John who explicitly, and characteristically, identifies this as a sign.

Jesus' preference to be alone

First of all, each writer records that Jesus had been followed by many people. However, the Synoptists indicate that Jesus had preferred privacy, while John similarly notes that Jesus went up a mountain to be with his disciples, away from the crowds.[18] None of the writers records why Jesus wished to do this, John simply recording that when he went up the mountain, he sat down (from *kathēmai*[19]), the imperfect tense indicating a desire for an elongated period of relaxation.

John records that Passover was due, an occasion that required Jesus to travel from Galilee to Jerusalem for a busy time of celebration and religious observances, while the Synoptics reveal that, immediately before the feeding miracle, Jesus was told that John the Baptist had been murdered. It is thus probable that Jesus wished to benefit from a break from his busy life and from any emotional upheaval caused by the macabre death of his cousin and forerunner.[20]

However, despite his emotional and physical needs, Jesus was prepared to help the people who had followed him, their determination to be with him manifested by their travelling on foot (Matthew and Mark), Mark recording that they ran to him and arrived at his destination before he did. The readiness of Jesus to help people is variously affirmed, Matthew and Mark noting that he had compassion on them.

Jesus feeds thousands

Because of the distance from villages, the isolation of the location and the unavailability of food, the Synoptists record the disciples encouraging Jesus to send the crowds away to get food, though there is no evidence that they were in danger of starving. Although this may be viewed as sensible advice, it also indicates their assumption that Jesus would benefit from their guidance, a feature that had never happened before in their relationship with him and did not occur thereafter either. Indeed, Jesus had asserted that he followed only a divinely appointed schedule[21] and they should have learnt this lesson by now. At the same time, this provides an ideal opportunity for Jesus to teach his disciples a lesson about himself.

---

[18] Mountains are identified in the Gospels as being valuable for significant occasions and/or purposes including teaching (Matt. 5–7), the Transfiguration (Matt. 17.1; Mark 9.2; Luke 9.28) and choosing disciples (Mark 3.13). When Jesus goes up a mountain on his own, it is for the purpose of prayer (Matt. 14.23; Mark 6.46; Luke 6.12) or as part of his being tempted by the devil (Matt. 4.8; Luke 4.5).

[19] The only other time this word is used in John is when Jesus sits on the colt when entering Jerusalem (12.15).

[20] Although each of the Synoptists mentions the desire to be apart (*kat' idian*), Mark mentions it twice (6.31, 32).

[21] Mark 1.37–38; 5.36; 8.12; Luke 2.49; 4.42–43.

However, first, each of the Synoptists records Jesus suggesting that the disciples should provide food for the people. John records Jesus deliberately testing Philip by asking how they may buy sufficient bread to feed the people, both he and Andrew concluding that it was impossible. John inserts words that reveal that the question was intended for the potential benefit of Philip as Jesus had already decided what he would do. Given the failure of the disciples to anticipate that Jesus may be considering a miraculous provision, and with the affirmation of their own inabilities to meet the need, the stage is set for Jesus' revelation of his supernatural resources.

However, it is worth pausing to wonder why the Synoptists record Jesus requesting that they feed the crowds. It is possible that Jesus is highlighting the impotence of the disciples or the impossibility of the situation, in order to demonstrate his superior authority. However, earlier, each of the Synoptists record Jesus commissioning the disciples to function supernaturally, while Mark and Luke include the disciples reviewing with Jesus the deeds they had undertaken as his representatives. On this occasion, however, they miss the opportunity to realize their potential when Jesus encourages them to feed the people. Since Jesus had instructed them to feed the people, it may be deduced that he would have ensured that they had the ability to fulfil their commission.

Each writer records that the disciples offered five loaves and two fish to Jesus.[22] It is not clear as to whether this is to demonstrate the sense of hopelessness of the situation felt by the disciples or to teach that Jesus is prepared to use and enhance whatever his followers offer to him. However, although Andrew's offer of five loaves and two fish may have had value, it is clear that Jesus had a better plan which would teach the disciples a lesson about him and them, in partnership with them.

The Synoptics each present Jesus as being in control, his authority affirmed by each writer recording that Jesus took charge of the seating arrangements,[23] Mark and Luke adding that the people sat in groups of 50 and/or 100 people. They each also record that Jesus looked up to heaven,[24] and

---

[22] Much has been made of these numbers, especially since they are recorded in each Gospel narrative, though it is not clear that any suggestion (eg. five = books of the Torah; two = the OT prophetic and historical books) has significant value or meaning.

[23] Luke adds that Jesus asked his disciples to facilitate the seating arrangements.

[24] Although the writers are careful not to record that Jesus needed to pray for a miracle, this action is probably to indicate the source of his power and authority (Matt. 3.16, 17; 7.11); heaven is the habitation of God (Matt. 6.1, 9; 10.32, 33; Luke 8.13; John 11.40; 17.1); it is where God's will is always done (Matt. 6.10) which can also be replicated on earth (Matt. 18.18); signs of significance were derived from heaven (Matt. 16.1; Mark 8.11; Luke 11.16); and elsewhere, Jesus looks to heaven before functioning supernaturally (Mark 7.34).

blessed (*eulogeō*)[25] and broke the bread[26] before giving it to the disciples to give to the people, while John relates that Jesus gave thanks and distributed the bread and fish to those seated. Finally, and again confirming the supernatural authority of Jesus, each Gospel notes that as well as the people being satisfied, there were 12 baskets of bread remaining. This feature is not commented on by the writers and it may be simply intended to indicate the lavish[27] nature of the miracle, the number 12 being symbolic of a completed number.[28] Although a connection with the Last Supper is possible,[29] the differences in the narratives are considerable, and it is more likely reflective of the eschatological messianic banquet anticipated by the Jews.[30]

Thus, the authority of Jesus is established, initially appearing to affirm his prophetic status. In 2 Kings 4.42–44, Elisha the prophet fed 100 men with 20 barley loaves, with some bread left over. The fact that Matthew and Mark record that Jesus withdrew to the *erēmos* (desert, wilderness, lonely place) is reminiscent of its location as the place where prophets lived and ministered.[31] More importantly, this is the place where God is prophesied as coming to rescue his people (Isa. 40.3), where people were expected to meet with and hear from God,[32] and which will be transformed by God.[33] It was also the location for Jesus being tested by the devil (Matt. 4.3–4), where he was encouraged to make bread out of stones. On that occasion, he refused so to do because it would have resulted in him following a diabolic agenda. However, the fact that he created bread for the crowds indicated that this miracle was achieved in accordance with the

---

[25] This word can mean, 'I bless, praise, extol', and thus could be descriptive of Jesus 'blessing' the food. However, the normal practice of Jews would be to praise or extol the heavenly provider (b. *Ber.* 35a, 46a). The fact that each of the Synoptists uses this term also in Jesus' last meal with his disciples cannot be merely coincidental (Matt. 26.26; Mark 14.22). This is all the more likely when it is realized that the OT records only God or people being blessed, never food or other material objects.

[26] Reminiscent of the Last Supper (Matt. 15.36; Mark 14.22; Luke 22.19; 1 Cor. 11.24); see also when he fed 4,000 people (Matt. 15.36; Mark 8.6).

[27] There was more left over than there was at the beginning! Heil (J. P., *The Meal Scenes in Luke-Acts.* SBL, Atlanta, 1999, pp. 61–5) explores the 'overabundant' nature of the miracle that anticipates the eschatological messianic banquet of the kingdom of God.

[28] Twelve tribes of Israel, 12 apostles, the strong association with the new Jerusalem (Rev. 21.12, 14, 16, 21; 22.1), 12 thrones in the afterlife (Matt. 19.28), 12 legions of angels (Matt. 26.53).

[29] Matt. 15.36; Mark 14.22; Luke 22.19; 1 Cor. 11.24.

[30] Hagner, D. A., *Matthew 14–28.* Word, Dallas, 1995, pp. 418–19; France, R. T., *The Gospel of Mark.* Grand Rapids, Eerdmans, 2002, p. 262; Stein, R. H., *Mark.* Baker Academic, Grand Rapids, 2008, p. 316.

[31] Elijah (1 Kings 17.2–6), Elisha (2 Kings 6.1–2), John the Baptist (Matt. 3.1; Mark 1.3).

[32] Exod. 5.3; 7.16; 8.23; Num. 9.1.

[33] Isa. 32.15; 35.6; 41.8; 43.19–20.

divine programme. However, although the identity of Jesus' prophetic status may be ascertained in the miracle, it is more reminiscent of God providing bread miraculously to the Israelites in the wilderness (Exod. 16.4; Neh. 9.15), a point specifically made by John (6.31). The provision of bread is an activity undertaken by God (Matt. 6.11; Luke 11.3); here, Jesus provides it.

However, there is also a lesson here for the benefit of the disciples concerning their potential. The Synoptics note that Jesus gave the food to the disciples and the disciples gave it to the people. They partnered Jesus in his miracle. Furthermore, there is no reference that the disciples came back to Jesus for more food. The implication is that the miracle kept happening – on the basis of their obedience to his command to give the bread to the people.

The Synoptists do not record any response from the crowd, nor does Jesus offer any teaching concerning the miracle; it does not even appear that the crowd realized that a miracle had occurred. The lesson is for the followers of Jesus. Jesus is presented with the creative ability previously only associated with God. However, he chooses to involve his disciples in the miracle and to achieve his objective with their active involvement.

Why does Matthew tell the story?

It is Matthew who most clearly links the withdrawal by Jesus from the area with the news of the death of John the Baptist (14.13), his death explicitly being identified by Jesus as prefiguring his own (17.12). Matthew (unlike Mark and Luke) omits the reference to the disciples revealing to Jesus what they had achieved by word and deed, thus making the narrative concerning the demise of John part of a seamless transition to the feeding miracle.

Matthew replaces the Markan *aperchomai* ('I go away') with *anachōreō*; in every other reference in Matthew, *anachōreō* is used to refer to departures caused by fearful and unwelcome news[34] or unhelpful confrontations (15.21).[35] It is no wonder that Matthew (also Mark) also inserts that he went to an unidentified and 'lonely place' (*erēmon*[36] (desert) *topon* (place)),[37]

---

[34] 2.12–14, 22; 4.12; 12.15; 27.5.

[35] The word is only used once in Mark (3.7), referring to Jesus leaving after the religious leaders plot to destroy him, and once in John (6.15) where Jesus leaves in the face of the inappropriate demands of the people that he be their king. Luke uses the similar word *hupochōreō* ('I withdraw, retreat').

[36] The addition of *topos* (14.13; Mark 6.32) places the focus not, as a noun, on the geographical location, but adjectivally, on the kind of place it represented – it was 'lonely'.

[37] Even though Luke records that Jesus went to Bethsaida, which does not indicate a place away from people, there is no necessary conflict; Luke is probably simply helping his largely non-Jewish readers to be aware of the geographical location of Jesus.

Matthew emphasizing the loneliness by retaining the reference to the journey being by boat,[38] though with no reference to any sailing companions. Indeed, Matthew uniquely makes no mention of the disciples until the evening. This was intended to be a journey for private reflection, not ministry related to the crowds or the disciples; Jesus' focus on the physical needs of the crowds due to his compassion appears to have been in the context of personal pathos, highlighting his readiness to help people despite his personal pain.

Why does Mark tell the story?

In Mark, as with Matthew, the narrative is preceded by an extended description of the death of John the Baptist (6.14–29) and is also followed by the account of Jesus walking on the water (6.45–52), as also in Matthew and John. Mark uniquely prefaces the account with a reference to Jesus' desire that they may rest. The notion of rest was not often present in the ministry of Jesus; the only other reference in Mark (14.41) was when Jesus encouraged his disciples to rest in Gethsemane when he was about to be betrayed. More specifically, Mark uniquely records that they had not even had time to eat because of their meeting so many people (6.31), who had run 'from all of the towns' in order to arrive before him.[39]

With Matthew, Jesus' compassion is seen to be directed to the crowd, though Mark uniquely identifies this as being due to Jesus' perception that the people were like sheep in need of a shepherd, an emotion previously recorded as being felt by God.[40] Mark alone records the response of the disciples to Jesus' request that they should provide food for the people, asking, presumably ironically, whether they should use 200 denarii to buy food for the people, since there is no evidence that they had such funds.[41] Thus, the hopelessness of the situation is clear in Mark, setting the scene for the remarkable miracle.

Why does Luke tell the story?

Luke records this narrative immediately after Jesus' commission of the Twelve (9.1–6) followed by Herod's perplexity over the news of Jesus whom he speculates may be a resurrected John the Baptist (9.7–9). Luke concludes

---

[38] This is not the first time that Jesus has taken advantage of a boat to leave a disappointing situation (8.23; 9.1) or to leave crowds (14.22; 15.39).

[39] Mark often, and uniquely, refers to people running to Jesus for help (5.6; 6.55; 10.17).

[40] Ezek. 34.5–6; Num. 27.17 refers similarly to the Israelites, as a result of which God appointed Joshua to be the leader after Moses; here, Jesus is identified as the leader.

[41] Since a denarius is equivalent to a day's wage for a labourer, this is a substantial amount of money.

with a statement to Jesus by the disciples concerning what they had done, forming a springboard for Luke to reveal what Jesus can do – a new type of miracle. The feeding of the 5,000 is immediately followed, not as in the other Gospels by Jesus walking on the water (which is completely omitted from Luke's narrative), but by Peter's declaration of Jesus being the Messiah (9.18–20), Jesus' prophecy that he will be rejected (9.21–27) and his Transfiguration (9.28–36), the latter coming later in the records of Matthew (17.1–8) and Mark (9.2–8). This unique joining of these narratives (see Table 6.2) appears to be intended to provide the disciples and the readers with an opportunity to reflect on the identity of Jesus. The one who provides a miracle of provision, reminiscent of God's creative act for the Israelites, is the suffering Messiah who also superlatively radiates divinity.

This is a story which identifies the power and person of Jesus who provides food for a famished crowd.[42] He is not just equivalent to John the Baptist, as assumed by Herod; with Peter, he is to be identified as Messiah. However, this narrative provides evidence to indicate that Jesus is not just greater than John the Baptist but also greater than the Messiah. He supernaturally provides food for everyone[43] as did God for Moses and Elijah, who are soon to be introduced as inferior to Jesus (9.28–36). Most importantly, Luke uniquely records that Jesus welcomes ordinary people to him so that he can feed them.[44]

The tragedy, implicit in this story, is that despite the above hints, the answers to Jesus' question, 'Who do the crowds say that I am?' (Luke 9.18), are varied (John the Baptist, Elijah, a resurrected prophet) but incorrect. This failure to correctly identify Jesus is reflected regularly hereon in Luke.[45] Even though Peter's declaration that Jesus is Messiah is correct (Luke 9.20), even this is also inadequate since Jesus is greater than Messiah.

Why does John tell the story?

John records this sign-story (6.14) after an extended discourse following the healing of a man who had been ill for 38 years (see Table 6.2), which revealed Jesus' authority over the Sabbath and, more significantly, demonstrated that he shared authority with God (5.1–47). After the feeding of

---

[42] Luke alone records that the people could have gone to 'the villages . . . to lodge and get provisions', thus indicating that they were not far from civilization.

[43] Luke uniquely places 'all' (*pantes*) emphatically as the final word in the reference to the people being fed (9.17).

[44] This is a word only used by Luke in the NT, but this is the only occasion where it refers to Jesus welcoming anyone (Luke 8.40; Acts 2.41; 8.27; 21.17; 24.3; 28.30).

[45] 9.22, 44, 53; 10.10–16; 11.29–32, 37–54.

the 5,000, John (as with Matthew and Mark) records the narrative of Jesus walking on the water.

Jesus is supremely in charge throughout. He is the one who sails to the other side of Galilee, the people following him, there being no reference to the disciples until he sits down with them on the mountain. However, although the crowds have come expecting more miracles, Jesus chooses to spend time with his disciples, there being no reference to any healings. John reveals that Jesus asks Philip concerning the possibility of purchasing bread in order to test him. He needs no advice from Philip or anyone else. Indeed, Jesus is identified as already having determined what to do and, as with the Synoptics, he instructs the disciples to make the people sit down but, in contrast to the Synoptics, Jesus gives the food directly to the people, not to the disciples in order that they might distribute it to the people; the disciples simply gather up the remnants – Jesus creates the miracle. Jesus is thus portrayed as providing individual miracles to each of the people. The story of the provision of bread thus becomes the basis for a presentation of the provision of eternal life, both being granted by Jesus. Only he can provide these miracles, the question to Philip highlighting this fact.

Because of this emphasis on the supreme authority of Jesus, it is no surprise that there is an absence of the Synoptists' reference to the compassion of Jesus for the crowd or that they were in 'a lonely place' away from any towns or that it was late when the miracle occurred. For John, the miracle is not intended to satisfy the need of people who were isolated, and who had been with Jesus for a long time or who were even hungry. This is a miracle intended to teach about the divine identity of the bread-giver. As part of this portrayal, Jesus is seen to offer extravagant hospitality, generously giving to the people as much as they wanted and more besides (6.11). Similar abundant provision had been offered at Cana in the lavish provision of wine and, as such, it presents an opportunity for Jesus to reflect aspects of his character as one who has come to bless people profusely, with 'much fruit' (15.5, 8), fullness of joy (15.11; 16.24) and even 'much fish' (21.11). Jesus who was 'full of grace and truth' (1.14) has made it possible for all to benefit 'from his fullness . . . grace upon grace' (1.16).

As elsewhere in John, the miracle (6.1–13) is less significant, and related in fewer words, than the subsequent teaching (6.22—7.1) that relates to it. In the extended discourse, Jesus asserts that the people had missed the significance of what the miracle indicated. Although they had deduced that it affirmed Jesus' prophetic credentials (6.14), and had sought Jesus because of it (6.24), Jesus records that they had only contented themselves with having their physical hunger satisfied (6.26). Instead people, incongruously, ask him for a sign similar to Moses feeding the people in the wilderness in order to legitimize his claims (6.30–31); they had benefited from the sufficiency of the provision but failed to consider the status of the provider.[46]

Most importantly, the miracle forms the backdrop for the message that Jesus is not on earth just to provide bread miraculously to satisfy hunger, but much more importantly, it is intended to remind the readers that he does so with a divine precedent. Thus, (i) Jesus provides perishable food supernaturally which is less significant than his ability to provide eternal food (6.27); (ii) Jesus identifies that the bread was not given to the people by Moses but first by God who gave it to Moses who then distributed it to the people; Jesus does not replace Moses as the bread-giver but functions as God; (iii) the bread, given by God, was not able to keep them alive forever (6.58) and is to be contrasted with the heavenly bread of God which comes through Jesus (6.32–33, 58); (iv) Jesus proclaims himself on three occasions (6.35, 48, 51) to be the bread of life which has the capacity to provide eternal life (6.27, 51, 58) for all people (6.51), his concern being that none should be lost (6.39), as reflected in his request to his disciples to ensure that not even the crumbs of bread were lost; (v) Jesus identifies himself as the unique Saviour (6.44–45), who has come down from heaven (6.50, 51, 58) and who alone can raise people 'at the last day' (6.44, 54); (vi) Jesus uses the divine 'I am' three times of himself (6.35, 48, 51). The narrative thus reveals that it is Jesus who, as the bread of life, now takes the place of God in providing sustenance to people.

Even though the people requested more of 'the true bread from heaven' of which Jesus spoke (6.34), they had not realized the spiritual connotations, because when Jesus identified himself as that true bread, they chose to reject it/him. Many were unimpressed by Jesus' claims to be superior to Moses and they doubted that a son of Mary and Joseph could 'come down from heaven' (6.41–43). They (including disciples (6.61)) grumbled (6.41) and disputed among themselves, misunderstanding him when he referred to the 'living bread' as his flesh which they must 'eat' in order to gain eternal life (6.51–58); they chose to interpret materially that which Jesus had intended metaphorically. Symbols of intimate fellowship between Jesus and those who 'feed on him' were interpreted crassly as if Jesus was introducing a cannibalistic process of ingestion. As a result, some of his

---

[46] Note the identity of the Feast of Passover being mentioned prior to the miracle, as if to locate in the minds of the readers God's provision for his people at that time.

disciples chose not to believe in him (6.64), and many left him (6.66), one choosing to betray him (6.64, 70–71) while other Jews sought to kill him (7.1). Although Peter confirms, on behalf of the Twelve, that they would still follow Jesus (6.68–69), this assertion will be starkly and painfully examined at Jesus' betrayal.

Somewhat tragically, John uniquely records that the people, having benefited from the sign of the miraculous feeding, sought to seize him in order to make him king (6.14–15). The next time that people acclaim him as king is similarly the result of a misunderstanding of the purpose of his mission (12.13). Consequently, John records that Jesus left them, returning to the mountain again, in order to spend time on his own (6.15).[47] The sign that Jesus offers has not achieved the intended response as the people merely conclude that he is to be applauded as prophet and king.

A decisive turning point has occurred and it has been a miracle benefiting thousands that has been the catalyst. However, a sign that had the potential to lead many to eternal life has been misread and the death of Jesus is instead the eventual outcome. The people's short-lived desire to acknowledge him as the long-awaited prophet and to make him their king (6.14–15) will result in a more sinister crown waiting for Jesus (19.5).

Conclusion

A remarkable act of provision has been recorded, unusually, by each of the Gospel writers, but there is more here than a miracle of increased supplies of bread. It also brings into focus the status of Jesus who functions as did God in the OT. With such a pedigree, the failure to follow Jesus is identified as even more inappropriate.

---

[47] The next mountain he will climb will be the Mount of Olives (8.1) with connotations of the cross.

Jesus walks on the water (Matt. 14.22–33// Mark 6.45–52//John 6.16–21)

Table 6.3 Walking on the water – the literary context

	Matthew	Mark	John
Jesus commissions the Twelve	(10.7–11, 14)	6.7–13	
Jesus heals at the Sheep Pool			5.1–47
Death of John the Baptist	14.1–12	6.14–29	
Feeding of the 5,000	14.13–21	6.30–44	6.1–13
The people want to make Jesus king			6.14–15
Jesus walks on the water	**14.22–27**	**6.45–52**	**6.16–21**
Peter walks on the water	14.28–32		
Jesus affirmed as Son of God by the disciples	14.33		
Jesus heals at Gennesaret	14.34–36	6.53–56	
Jesus denounces the Pharisees	15.1–20	7.1–23	
The wider significance of the feeding of the 5,000			6.22—7.1

Main messages from all the narratives

This miracle occurs after the feeding of the 5,000 in each of the Gospels that record it, though it is immediately followed by various narratives (see Table 6.3). Matthew and Mark indicate that it was Jesus who suggested that the disciples sail to the other side of the lake before him while he dismissed the crowd whom he had just miraculously fed.[48] Thereafter, Matthew and Mark record that, after he discharged the crowds, he went up a mountain[49] in order that he might pray,[50] the purpose of his prayer not being identified.[51] By the time he left, it was 'evening' (Matt. 14.25; Mark 6.48) and 'dark' (John 6.17).[52]

---

[48] John merely records that the disciples sailed across the lake, there being no reference to their following Jesus' instructions.

[49] It is possible that this is intended to be a symbolic as well as a geographical feature since it was where theophanies occurred in the OT (Exod. 19.3; 24.15) and the NT (Matt. 17.1//Mark 9.2), though none is recorded here.

[50] Other than his teaching his followers how to pray (6.8–15) and 11.25–26, this is the first reference to Jesus praying in Matthew; he is next recorded praying in Gethsemane (26.36, 39, 42, 44; also Mark 14.32, 35, 39). The only other reference to Jesus praying in Mark is in 1.35.

[51] Given that Jesus is infrequently mentioned as praying in Matthew and Mark, one wonders why he prayed on this occasion. Given the traumatic nature of the Gethsemane prayers (recorded by both Matthew and Luke), it is possible that Jesus here also wished to pray because of the circumstances he was currently undergoing (he had been rejected by those who knew him best, lost his friend and forerunner, John the Baptist, and commissioned those who were to follow after him); perhaps the pain of the journey and its conclusion were beginning to be felt more acutely by him, resulting in his desire to spend time with his Father.

[52] The next and final reference to physical darkness is at the empty tomb where Jesus' absence there was even more startling than his presence here.

Each author records that a strong wind was whipping up the waves, which Matthew and Mark describe as 'tormenting' the boat, as a result of which the journey was very difficult; Matthew notes that they had travelled 4 furlongs, John identifying it as 25 stadia.[53] Matthew and Mark specify that it was during the fourth watch[54] when the disciples saw Jesus, indicating that they had struggled against the wind all night. They also record that they did not realize that it was Jesus, but assumed it was a ghost (*phantasma*),[55] the aorist passive tense of the verb signifying that terror had gripped them. Similarly, John refers to their being afraid but does not specify why.

That Jesus walks on the water is reflected only in this narrative and is reminiscent of an action of God;[56] Jesus functions as God did. Furthermore, it is God who has, in the past, rescued people who were in danger at or in the proximity of the sea[57] and who had power over the sea,[58] as a result of which he is to be worshipped (Ps. 107.31–32). Thus, for the writers, Jesus demonstrates similar divine authority which begs the questions, 'Who is he?' and 'Should we worship him?'

Of interest is the fact that each of the accounts records Jesus' words, *egō eimi* ('It is I/I am') *mē phobeisthē* ('do not fear'), Matthew and Mark both prefacing them with *tharseite* ('Be encouraged'). The former two words are used elsewhere to refer to God and although it is possible that they are simply a reference to himself by Jesus ('it's me'), it is also possible that they are drawing an association with God,[59] especially in John where this link is more explicit.[60]

Lessons that may be gleaned from each account relate to the importance of realizing that if Jesus determines the journey (both Matthew and Mark

---

[53] A stadia is about 200 metres; 25 stadia equals about 5 kilometres.

[54] A night (6 p.m.–6 a.m.) was split into four 'watches' of three hours each; thus, the fourth watch is about 3–6 a.m.

[55] The word is only used here and in the Markan parallel (6.49); it is possible that it relates to a perception that spirits roamed the world especially at night, since darkness was associated with antisocial or diabolic behaviour. Many Jews believed that light from torches would protect them from demons, if they were walking in the dark. Night spirits were called *lilin*, evening spirits were called *telane*, and because of their numbers at night, b. *Ber.* 43a and *Yoma* 21a counsel against greeting anyone at night in case they were actually demons; sleeping alone at night was dangerous (b. *Shab.* 151b); the evenings of Wednesdays and the Sabbath were also dangerous as 18 myriad destructive demons would seek to harm people (b. *Pes.* 112b). Drinking water at night was also to be avoided because of the proximity of demons to it (b. *Pes.* 3a), protection being available if Ps. 29.3–9 were recited (it contains the phrase 'the voice of the LORD', seven times).

[56] Job 9.8; Ps. 77.19; Hab. 3.15.

[57] Exod. 14.10—15.21; Ps. 107.28–30; Jonah 1.1–16.

[58] Job 26.11–12; Pss. 89.9–10; 107.25, 29.

[59] Gen. 17.1; 26.24; 31.13; Exod. 3.6, 14.

[60] 6.35, 41, 48, 51; 8.12, 18, 28, 58; 10.7 (see also Matt. 28.20; Mark 14.62).

refer to Jesus making the disciples travel by boat with the intention of their going to the other side of the lake), whatever happens, there is no reason for worry. When Jesus sends his followers on a mission (as here), the fulfilment of that commission is guaranteed, John graphically noting that as soon as Jesus entered the boat, they reached the shore 'immediately'.

Furthermore, the narrative identifies the importance of recognizing Jesus, even when it is dark, and not allowing the darkness (or whatever it may represent) to obscure seeing him. Even though the disciples did not recognize him, he still went to them. Finally, Jesus' authority over the wind and ability to walk on the tormenting waves is expressed in Matthew and Mark in that as soon as he entered the boat, the wind ceased; on this occasion, he did not even need to speak to it. There is no suggestion that Jesus rescues the disciples from the wind; indeed, no danger is apparent – Jesus is in control.

Why does Matthew tell the story?

Unusually, Matthew extends a narrative that he has copied from Mark, by uniquely recording Peter walking on the water to Jesus. Although he does not specify a reason, it is possible that Matthew offers a number of potential lessons for would-be disciples. Peter does not presumptuously attempt to walk on water; he does so only after asking Jesus for permission ('Lord, if it is you, command me to come to you on the water') to which Jesus responds 'Come'. Indeed, it is preferable to translate *ei* (which is sometimes best translated as 'if') as 'since' (thus, 'Lord, since it is you, command me to come to you on the water'). This appears likely since Jesus has already identified himself to the disciples. Peter is not checking if he is real but acknowledging his presence, offering a request based on that fact. It is also noteworthy that he is prepared to obey Jesus even though it means he will leave the safety of the boat and walk into the raging storm. Similar calls will be made to many of Jesus' followers in the days to come and they can draw comfort from Peter's experience in that when their faith wavers, Jesus' arm will not.

The initial obedience of Peter is rewarded by his supernaturally walking on the waves, though later he is afraid and, as a result, begins to sink. Jesus' question, 'O you of little faith, why did you doubt?' is significant,[61] for it reminds Peter (and the readers) that although Peter expressed faith

---

[61] The word *oligopistos* refers to a person who does not trust and is used five times in the NT, all by Jesus, four of which are in Matthew (6.30(//Luke 12.28); 8.26; 14.31; 16.8), all in the contexts of speaking to his disciples.

by obeying Jesus, his doubt[62] undermined that faith. Nevertheless, Peter is to be commended for his initial obedience and by his readiness to call to Jesus to save him, followed by Jesus' immediate[63] response to take his hand and rescue him. The focus is not only on the disciple who functions supernaturally, but also on Jesus who saves immediately. It is not the walk of Peter that is the climax of the narrative but the rescue by Jesus. The incident is reminiscent of Psalm 69.1–3, 14–5 where God saves the drowning psalmist, concluding with worship (69.30–34).

This is followed by the confession of the sailors that Jesus is the Son of God (14.33), the first occasion in Matthew when a person identifies Jesus as 'Son of God'. It is left to the Roman centurion to be the final authentic witness to Jesus being the Son of God (27.54). Finally, Matthew reports that, after reaching the shore, people recognized Jesus and they encouraged others to bring the sick to him; their perception was such that they believed that even a touch of his clothing would result in their restoration (14.34–36). Little wonder also that this perception is accompanied by their obeisance,[64] uniquely noted by Matthew; he alone identifies Jesus (twice) as 'Lord', with its implicit connections with the divine name. Interestingly, the previous situation where the disciples refer to Jesus as 'Lord' is also in a storm (8.25).

Walking on the water is something that only God can do, albeit metaphorically. However, there is another lesson for the followers of Jesus – then and now – and Peter is learning it. God alone is intentionally described as walking on the sea (Job 38.16), but here, Jesus shares that divine authority with one of his disciples. Peter recognizes Jesus and asks for his permission to join Jesus in a divine activity, an activity that only God has done in the past. And Jesus says, 'Come'. Peter was the only one who caught a glimpse of who Jesus truly was, and appears to sense that Jesus would be pleased if he asked him whether he should do what Jesus himself was doing. When Jesus, who is God, commissioned Peter to join him in a divine activity, he obeyed – and Jesus did the rest. On this occasion, Peter was the miracle; this was a miracle just for him, and for any other follower who is prepared to respond positively to Jesus' commission, 'Come'.

---

[62] The word *distazō* ('I doubt') is only used twice in the NT, both in Matthew (14.31; 28.17), the other reference relating to the doubt expressed by some when Jesus appeared to the disciples in his resurrected body.

[63] Uniquely, Matthew inserts 'immediately' with reference to the promptness of the rescue afforded to Peter by Jesus. The use of this word (*eutheōs/euthus*) by Mark is very common and in parallel narratives is often omitted by Matthew, but here he adds it. More significantly, it is the only occasion in Matthew where Jesus is said to act immediately; the message of Jesus' desire to save and to do so immediately is thus advanced by the author.

[64] The word *proskuneō* often refers to an attitude of worship (28.9) as it also does in 28.17.

Why does Mark tell the story?

Mark records that although the disciples did not see Jesus, he saw them, while still on the land, their fear being a sufficient reason for him to go to be with them. However, Mark does not indicate that Jesus went to them having seen them struggling in the gale. On the contrary, Jesus first spent time in prayer and only went to them some hours after they had left him. The message of Mark is that even though far from them, Jesus was still watching them – they were never out of his sight. However, perhaps more importantly, the fact that he did not go to help them indicates that he trusted them to achieve their objective without his active involvement. After all, it was he who had told them to go to the other side of the lake. Such a message would have been of crucial importance to the beleaguered readers in Rome.

Mark records that Jesus meant to pass them by, though offers no explanation for this. France suggests that this reflects an inaccurate assumption of the disciples,[65] though others[66] argue that the verb used, *parerchomai*, is used to indicate that a theophany is intended, similar to God passing by Moses (Exod. 33.19–23).[67] Such interpretations seem better than to believe that Jesus had intended to pass them, given that he had seen them struggling. Nevertheless, that is what Mark writes, and perhaps the uncomfortable nature of these words is the reason why Matthew omits them.

It is therefore quite possible that Jesus actually did anticipate passing them and meeting them on the beach when they eventually arrived. Indeed, the fact that he had instructed them to go by boat before him to the other side indicates that he had anticipated that they would be able to fulfil his commission; there was no need for him to help them. They had already learnt that when he commissioned them to undertake tasks before, they fulfilled them successfully (6.7–13, 30, 39–42); the assumption was that they would succeed again. Indeed, Mark indicates that although the wind was against them, they were making headway and moving steadily towards their destination. He does not refer to any storm that was causing the boat to sink; neither does he describe the disciples as being in danger. The reason that Jesus joins them in the boat is not because they are in peril or even

---

[65] France, *Mark*. p. 272; Cranfield, C. E. B., *The Gospel According to Mark*. Cambridge University Press, Cambridge, 1959, p. 226.

[66] E.g. Guelich, R. A., *Mark 1–8.26*. Word, Dallas, 1989, pp. 350–1.

[67] The verb is also used in Amos 7.8; 8.2 with reference to God no longer passing by Israel, though it is unlikely that Mark's readers would have noted the link; if a theophanic reference is intended, it is likely that Mark would have indicated this, especially in view of the Transfiguration that will be recorded just two chapters later.

need his help; it is because he sees that they were panicked by his presence on the water. Recognizing that he has been the cause of their terror, he immediately speaks to them, calming their fear, and joins them in the boat.

The message to the readers is that all followers of Jesus who are commissioned by him should anticipate the fulfilment of that commission; it may be a struggle – but achievement is certain. However, at the same time, when fear takes over, Jesus is prepared to change his agenda in order to assuage that apprehension. It is conceivable that if the disciples had recognized the figure was Jesus, they would not have needed him to provide peace, for their appreciation of his identity would have carried them through the shock of seeing him walk on the water. On this occasion, they are still learning about the remarkable nature of Jesus, and here, he has to slow his journey down in order to enable them to learn the lesson concerning who he is and his sovereignty, not just over the waves but also with reference to their commissions.

Mark records a mixed response from those in the boat, despite the fact that Jesus got into the boat with them. In 6.51, the writer provides four different words to emphasize the intensity of their astonishment (*lian* ('greatly'), *ekperissou* ('exceedingly'), *en heautois* (in themselves) *existanto* ('they were amazed', imperfect tense from *existēmi*,[68] 'I am amazed'), *kai ethaumazon* ('and they wondered', imperfect tense from *thaumazō*, 'I wonder').

Mark also identifies their hearts as being hardened (*pepōrōmenē*, from *pōroō*, 'I am blind, obtuse'), a feature of the disciples expressed elsewhere (4.13; 8.17–18). He links it to their lack of understanding about the significance of the miracle of the bread previously referred to. Mark may be referring to the fact that they have still not recognized the divine status of Jesus as reflected in Jesus miraculously feeding thousands – as did God in the OT. However, it may also be that Mark may be intending to indicate a misunderstanding of their own status – as followers of Jesus, who had been granted significant authority with consequent potential for success, as reflected in their involvement in the feeding of 5,000 (6.41).

Why does John tell the story?

Uniquely, John records that after Jesus feeds the 5,000, the people asserted that he was the prophet associated with the eschaton and sought to force

---

[68] The term *existēmi* is used on three other occasions in Mark, two of which relate to healings achieved by Jesus (2.12; 5.42) though it is not clear that such amazement resulted in the witnesses following Jesus. The other reference (3.21) is best translated not as 'astonished' but as 'out of his senses' and relates to the people's perception that Jesus was confused about his status or, worse, had gone mad. The miracles that he performed did not always lead to faith.

him to be king. As a result, Jesus withdrew to the mountain; in the absence of any suggestion that it was to pray, the implication is that it was to get away from an unwelcome attempt to distract Jesus from his mission.

There is no invitation to Peter to walk on the water in John's account, Jesus does not calm the sea, nor is the wind described as ceasing. What is present is Jesus' ability to walk on the water, indicative of a divine authority over the sea that was owned by God. John also uniquely notes that it was the evening and also dark and that Jesus 'had not yet come to them' (6.17). Although the disciples were not expecting Jesus, John hints to the readers that Jesus will go to them; he will find them in their darkness. His words 'it is me' (*egō eimi*, 'I, I am') again reflect to the reader his divine status (6.20), resulting in their desire that Jesus 'get into their boat'.

John records that as soon as Jesus entered the boat, they landed on the shore. This is not intended to indicate that Jesus did not walk on water and that he was really in the shallows. It is possible that another miracle occurred in that the rest of the journey across the lake happened instantaneously, but also possible that John is recording the fact that Jesus had walked to them from the side of the lake from where they had come, determined to be with them, joining them in the boat, even though they were already so close to land.

Conclusion

The miracle is presented briefly and straightforwardly, despite its sensational nature. However, this action breathes the innate divinity of Jesus who, when on his own, easily functions as did God (metaphorically) as recorded in the OT. In seeing Jesus function thus, the disciples are privileged with receiving an insight into the private prerogatives of their God, as reflected in Jesus, even participating in his divine authority.

Jesus feeds over 4,000 people (Matt. 15.32–39//Mark 8.1–10)

Table 6.4 Feeding over 4,000 people – the literary context

	Matthew	Mark
Jesus denounces the Pharisees	15.1–20	7.1–23
Jesus exorcizes a Syrophoenician woman's daughter	15.21–28	7.24–30
Jesus heals many	15.29–31	
Jesus heals a deaf man with a speech impediment		7.31–37
Jesus feeds 4,000	**15.32–39**	**8.1–10**
Jesus is confronted by the Pharisees	16.1–4	8.11–13
Jesus warns the disciples about the Pharisees	16.5–12	8.14–21

Main messages from all the narratives

There is little reason to assume that Matthew and Mark are retelling the story concerning the feeding of the 5,000. Not only is it too close to that record in the respective Gospels for a sensible repetition by the authors, but also there is a distinction in the words used and the feeding of the 5,000 more explicitly occurs in Jewish territory.[69]

Both authors record this narrative after a collection of healing and exorcistic miracles that involve non-Jewish people, Mark uniquely offering a prior healing story of someone living in the Decapolis (see Table 6.4). Matthew (uniquely in the NT) refers to them as glorifying the God of Israel (15.31); it appears that God was not their God. One key message of this feeding miracle, therefore, is that Gentiles have the opportunity to benefit from Jesus as much as Jews, both writers recording that Jesus has already spent three days with them.[70] Also, each notes that the disciples refer to being in the desert, as if to remind the readers of the miraculous provision by God of the Israelites in the desert.

Both writers refer to the compassion of Jesus,[71] relating this to the fact that the people were hungry and too far from their homes to gain sustenance. Both authors record Jesus asking the disciples how the crowd can be fed and that they respond with an assessment that they have seven loaves and a few small fish. They have so quickly forgotten that the one who satisfied (*kortadzō*, Matt. 14.20//Mark 6.42) over 5,000 people

---

[69] For example, in the feeding of the 4,000, the word *spuris* (basket) is used (Matt. 15.37; Mark 8.10, 20), but with reference to the feeding of the 5,000, *kophinos* (basket) is used (Matt. 14.20; 16.9; Mark 6.43; 8.19).

[70] Nowhere in the Gospels is Jesus described as spending three days with Jews.

[71] Mark 8.2 is repeated exactly by Matthew (15.32).

can as easily satisfy (*kortadzō*, Matt. 15.33, 37//Mark 8.4, 8) 4,000, Matthew specifying that women and children were to be added to the number of 4,000. The fact that seven loaves are mentioned has caused much speculation, but the explanations are so diverse, and sometimes obscure, that they are unlikely clarifications.

The actions of Jesus are similar here to those in the feeding of the 5,000 narrative in that both narratives record that Jesus gave thanks, broke (the bread), and gave the fish and bread to the disciples in order that they might give them to the people; again, the intention of Jesus that the disciples should participate in the miraculous provision is identified.

The narrative does not conclude with a christological reflection, a word from Jesus to the crowd or a reaction from the crowd. It is as if the lesson has already been demonstrated and shockingly so – Jesus has granted to Gentiles the same caring, practical and miraculous provision as he had done to the Jews. Not only is Jesus in charge, but precisely because he is in charge, it is instructive to note that all are welcome and no one is excluded. Moreover, each is privileged to participate in a miraculous provision. The writers record Jesus healing the sick (Matthew) and teaching about 'many' issues (Mark), and that he continued until the evening.

After the miracle, Jesus sent the people away and left the area by boat, Mark recording that he did so with his disciples, returning to Jewish territory. Both authors follow the feeding of the 4,000 narrative with warnings about the Pharisees and Sadducees who demand heavenly signs as proof of Jesus' authority (see Table 6.4). The incongruity of this request is demonstrated by the writers in that they make these requests after Jesus has fed 4,000. Each writer associates this miracle with later teaching by Jesus about the leaven-like Pharisees (Matt. 16.5–12//Mark 8.14–21). Jesus is the giver of true bread, not the insubstantial and destructive leaven of the Pharisees which will spoil those it contaminates.

Jesus curses the fig tree (Matt. 21.18–19//Mark 11.12–14)

Table 6.5 Cursing the fig tree – the literary context

	Matthew	Mark
The disciples and the request for precedence	20.20–28	10.35–45
The healing of the blind man/men	20.29–34	10.46–52
The triumphal entry	21.1–9	11.1–12
Jesus cleanses the Temple	21.10–13	(11.15–19)
Jesus heals in the Temple	21.14–17	
Jesus curses the fig tree	**21.18–19**	**11.12–14**
Jesus cleanses the Temple	(21.10–13)	11.15–19
The fig tree withers	21.20–22	11.20–26
Jesus disputes with the Temple leaders	21.23–27	11.27–33
The parable of the two sons	21.28–32	
The parable of the vineyard and tenants	21.33–46	12.1–12

Main messages from both narratives

Matthew demonstrates the lordship of Jesus over the Temple by revealing him welcoming people who should not have been there, healing them and receiving the praise of children as the Son of David (21.14–15). Matthew places this account after Jesus cleanses the Temple and thus denounces the current Temple system (21.12–17) while Mark places it before it (11.15–19) (see Table 6.5). Thus, both writers anticipate that the cursing has a symbolic significance[72] to the cleansing of the Temple and associated aspects of condemnation and judgement.

Both Matthew and Mark record that Jesus was hungry, which may imply that his cursing of the tree was due to this and because the tree had no fruit.[73] However, it is not necessary to assume that Jesus punished the tree because it failed to assuage his hunger. This would indicate that Jesus was petulant and unreasonable, especially since Mark reminds the readers that it was not the season for figs.[74]

Mark records that Jesus went to the tree because, from a distance, he could see that it had leaves, which resulted in the possible assumption that it would also have fruit, for the presence of leaves on the tree indicated that some fruit might be present, even unripened fruit.[75] As such, it functioned

---

[72] Hooker (M. D., *A Commentary on the Gospel According to St. Mark*. Black, London, 1991, p. 262) views it as an acted-out parable while Evans (C. A., *Mark 8.27–16.20*. Word, Waco, 2001, p. 208) identifies it as a dramatized prophecy.

[73] Earlier when Jesus was hungry, he refused to provide food for himself (Matt. 4.2–4).

[74] One of the most common trees in Israel, providing two harvests annually, at the end of June and between August and October.

[75] Pliny the Elder (*Nat. Hist.*, 16.49) notes that the fig tree unusually bears fruit before leaves.

as an excellent symbol of the Temple which also had the outward show of fruitfulness, but on closer examination (Mark 11.11) this was seen not to be the case; the fact that not even early undeveloped figs were on the tree accentuates its paucity of potential, indeed its barrenness.

Matthew indicates that the withering of the tree was immediate,[76] Mark noting that it occurred overnight. Indeed, what surprises (*thaumazō*,[77] 'I wonder') the disciples is the fact that the tree withered in response to his command and that it did so quickly and completely, 'to its roots' (Matt. 21.20). The physical destruction of the Temple is hinted at and certain. This is emphasized by Mark in that he records that on the day before he cleansed the Temple, Jesus went into it and looked around (*periblepsamenos*,[78] aorist participle from *periblepō*, 'I look around') at everything before returning the following day to cleanse it, after which he cursed the fig tree. The Temple is to be replaced – an unbelievably momentous event to the Jews – and Jesus is seen to not only prophesy it but also to authorize it. The message is clear – the one whose authority is such that he can curse a fig tree and kill it should be listened to. Not only does he have authority over a fig tree and God's Temple, but he also has power over the created order, even as far as removing mountains (Matt. 21.21; Mark 11.23).

This is the final miracle achieved by Jesus in Mark and, as such, one anticipates a significant reason for its inclusion. It acts as a powerful statement concerning the radical transformation that will result as a consequence of Jesus' death in a few days' time. The fruit of the fig tree was positively associated with Israel (Hos. 9.10), while the fig tree was often associated with judgement on Israel[79] and the nation being cursed by God as a symptom of that judgement;[80] at the same time, figs had the capacity to act as a therapy (Isa. 38.21) and were associated with times of blessing[81] and plentiful provision.[82] The Temple, as the dwelling place of God, had so much potential for good. If it was to be destroyed, it indicated that such potential would no longer be present. Furthermore, if the Temple is to be destroyed, it begs the question as to what might replace it.

---

[76] Matthew only uses this word (*parachrēma*) on two occasions (21.19, 20), both referring to the immediacy of the withering of the fig tree.

[77] This word is used elsewhere in Matthew to refer to the wonder of the onlookers who saw Jesus' miraculous acts (8.27; 9.33; 15.31).

[78] This is a favourite word in Mark (3.5, 34; 10.23; 11.11), it only being used elsewhere in the NT in Luke 6.10.

[79] Isa. 28.4; 34.4; Jer. 5.17; 8.13; 24.1, 5, 8; Hos. 2.12; 9.16; Joel 1.12; Amos 4.9; Mic. 7.1; Hab. 3.17; Rev. 6.13.

[80] Ps. 105.33; Jer. 29.17; esp. Mark 13.28.

[81] 1 Kings 4.25; 2 Kings 18.31; Mic. 4.4; Zech. 3.10.

[82] Deut. 8.8; Song of Sol. 2.13; Isa. 36.16; Joel 2.22.

The coin in the fish (Matt. 17.24–27)

Table 6.6 The coin in the fish – the literary context

	Matthew
The Transfiguration	17.1–9
Jesus teaches about Elijah	17.10–13
Jesus casts out a destructive demon	17.14–21
Jesus again foretells his Passion	17.22–23
Jesus provides Temple tax from a fish	**17.24–27**
Jesus identifies true greatness	18.1–5
Jesus teaches about temptation	18.6–9

This is a story unique to Matthew (see Table 6.6), in which Jesus is identified as a teacher by tax-collectors but revealed as a miracle-worker by Matthew. The fact that he has inserted this story, and thus broken the flow of following the Markan narrative that he has maintained for some time, indicates that it is more important than might be first imagined.

It is possible that Matthew wishes to identify an important aspect of Jesus' mission which is to demonstrate care for others, as also expressed in the next narrative in which Jesus gives time to children (18.5), despite his public announcement that he knows he is soon to die (17.22–23). Thus, here, he pays Peter's Temple tax, as well as his own. Matthew also demonstrates Jesus' readiness to keep the Temple rules, even though he will later forecast its destruction (24.1–2), and specifically records that Jesus is concerned not to offend the tax-collectors. However, the purpose of the miracle more probably relates to a lesson for Peter and other sons of God, not the Temple tax-collectors.

The context of the miracles relates to a discussion concerning the annual payment of half a shekel/two drachmas as Temple tax (loosely related to Exod. 30.13), payable by every adult Jew towards the Temple sacrificial system. The tax was equivalent to two denarii and, since a denarius was equivalent to a daily wage of a labourer (20.2), it was not an insubstantial amount.

It appears that neither Peter nor Jesus had money for the Temple tax. However, not everyone thought that the Temple tax was legitimate, including even some Sadducees (who were closely allied to and supportive of it), and especially Pharisees and Essenes.[83] On previous occasions, Matthew

---

[83] The Qumran community believed that it should be paid as a once-in-a-lifetime charge (4Q159.6–7) while the Sadducees argued that it was intended to be voluntary (m. *Seqal.* 1.4), while the Pharisees simply objected to paying tax to a corrupt Temple.

records Jesus upsetting people by acting and speaking against the pre-
vailing beliefs of the people – he touched the ceremonially unclean (8.2),
he forgave sins without people first saying sorry (9.2), he ate with the
worst of people (9.10), he decided if and when it was appropriate to
fast (9.15), and he broke Sabbath laws by healing on the Sabbath (12.10).
However, here, even though many would have agreed with him if he had
refused to pay, he decided to meekly pay the tax.

The first lesson to be gleaned from the narrative concerns the privilege
of sonship and, in particular, of God's sons. Jesus asks whether sons of
kings should pay temple taxes or whether this should be left to others,
including their subjects. Peter provides the correct response in that sons
of a king are not expected to pay taxes to the king since they are members
of his family.

It is possible that Jesus was speaking of the Jews when he refers to
'sons', as he does elsewhere (8.10–12; 15.26). However, it is more likely
that he is referring to his disciples. The lesson offered is that God has
a superior relationship with his sons as contrasted with his subjects. Thus
Jesus, as God's Son, is not subject to the Temple tax since the Temple
belongs to his Father. The subversive comment questions the legitimacy
of the Temple tax for sons of God; since God, in effect, levies the tax, his
sons are released from having to pay it.[84]

Jesus is not making a statement concerning the validity or morality of
the Temple tax, but drawing attention to the different status of Jews, who
owned the Temple as their own and thus paid taxes for its maintenance,
and Jesus' followers, who although also Jews were more specifically God's
sons (not merely sons of the Temple) and therefore released from such
payment.

A second lesson relates to Peter and all other would-be disciples, for
in paying the tax, surprisingly, Jesus chooses to include Peter in the miraculous process, which begs the question, 'Why?' In this miracle, Jesus is not
demonstrating the importance of paying the Temple tax or obeying rules.
Rather, this is an opportunity to teach through the miracle.

A few verses earlier (17.14–21), Matthew records Jesus casting out a
demon, and a few verses before that (17.1–9), Jesus is transfigured on the
mountain and God announces again, 'This is my beloved son'. The supreme
authority and status of Jesus is clear. Jesus could have easily created a coin
out of nothing and given it to the tax-collectors. But he is more interested

---

[84] For more, see Horbury, W., 'The Temple Tax', in *Jesus and the Politics of His Day*. (eds) Bammel,
E., Moule, C. F. D., Cambridge University Press, Cambridge, 1984, pp. 265–86.

in involving Peter in the miracle than in simply paying a temple tax. Jesus tells him to go fishing and to do so with a hook and line. He does not ask him to go to the sea and wait for a fish to jump into his hand; Peter is asked to catch a fish, an activity that he is skilled in. Although Jesus initiates the miracle, Peter has a central part to play – it is he who catches the fish.[85] Jesus prefers to involve Peter in a miracle that will enable Jesus to achieve his objective (paying the Temple tax) rather than to supernaturally provide it on his own. It appears that Jesus intended his follower to know that if he truly followed him and obeyed him, they would both share in his mission together. The fisherman who has been required to be a fisher of men (4.19) catches a fish and receives more than he anticipated. He may be a junior partner with Jesus, but nevertheless, Peter is reminded by Jesus that his divine plan is to incorporate followers as partners in the process of facilitating his will on earth.

---

[85] Bauckham (R., 'The Coin in the Fish's Mouth', in *Gospel Perspectives, Vol. 6: The Miracles of Jesus.* (eds) Wenham, D., Blomberg, C. L., JSOT Press, Sheffield, 1986, pp. 219–52) identifies stories recorded in rabbinic literature (b. *Git.* 68b; *Shab.* 119a; *Baba Bathra* 133b) that record valuable items being miraculously found in fish (pp. 239–40).

The miraculous catch of fish (Luke 5.1–11)

Table 6.7 The miraculous catch of fish – the literary context

	Luke
Jesus heals many and exorcizes demons	4.40–41
Jesus declares his intention to preach	4.42–44
The miraculous catch of fish	**5.1–11**
Jesus heals a leper	5.12–16
Jesus heals a paralytic	5.17–26
Jesus calls Levi	5.17–26

There are some similarities between this narrative and that in John 21.1–14, mainly related to the remarkable catch of fish under the guidance of Jesus. However, the contents and the settings in their respective Gospels are so different that each will be considered separately. Although this may have been a natural event, in that Jesus may have seen the shoal of fish from where he was, whereas the disciples were not able so to do from the boat, the response by those present, and in particular by Peter, makes this unlikely. Although those with him were astonished at the catch (5.9), it caused Peter to identify himself as someone who was unworthy to be in the presence of Jesus, whom he defines as 'Lord'. Thus, Luke inserts into this miracle narrative Jesus calling his first four disciples, who are defined as leaving everything and following him.

The narrative follows Jesus' intention to preach (4.43) (see Table 6.7) and relates that, since there were so many people present (5.1), he does so from a boat (5.3). Interestingly, the content of or the response to the teaching is not identified by Luke. Instead, he records the narrative of the large catch of fish – a story that one would anticipate might be less valuable than a record of the contents of Jesus' teaching. However, a new lesson is being presented for the specific benefit of a few fishermen, not the nameless crowds. It concerns their new missions as Jesus' disciples. Although the miracle is associated with the obedience of the disciples to the command of Jesus to sail out to deep water and cast their nets, despite their failure to catch any fish during the previous night, it is more clearly associated by Jesus with their commission to 'catch men' (5.10).

Luke records that the catch of fish was so large that the nets began to break, and even with the help of another boat they were both in danger of sinking. This fact is the platform for the emphasis on Peter's perception of Jesus and himself. Thus, Luke focuses on Peter, identifying the boat into which Jesus steps as belonging to Peter, Jesus telling Peter to steer the boat into deep waters, and referring to him by his full name for the first time, Simon Peter; prior to this occasion, he has been identified as Simon (5.4, 5).

Peter demonstrates the ideal development of a disciple in that he (i) obeys Jesus' command to let the nets down into the water; (ii) falls on his knees before Jesus; (iii) confesses his unworthiness and describes himself, in particular, as a sinner;[86] and (iv) although initially addressing Jesus as 'Master',[87] latterly refers to him as 'Lord' (5.8), which, although not necessarily indicating divinity, appears to be more than 'Sir'. Then (v) Peter (along with the others) expresses astonishment (*thambos*, only used elsewhere in the NT in Luke 4.36 and Acts 3.10, to refer to the amazement of people at miracles achieved by Jesus or his followers[88]) at the catch of fish.

Thereafter (vi) Peter receives the encouraging words of Jesus, 'fear not' (uniquely used in Luke and only by angels (1.13; 30) or Jesus (8.50; 12.32), with reference to people who have been granted a promise or a commission that will be fulfilled), and the affirmation that in the future he 'will be catching men'. Finally (vii), as all true disciples should,[89] along with the other fishermen, Peter leaves everything and follows Jesus (5.11). This is the first occasion in Luke when anyone is described as following Jesus, though others will also follow, including Matthew (5.28).

---

[86] The only other occasion this is used in Luke is to refer to the woman who anointed Jesus' feet (9.37, 39).

[87] Luke uses *epistatēs*, often used by the disciples to refer to Jesus (5.5; 8.24, 45; 9.33, 49; 17.13).

[88] While Peter is amazed at the miraculous occurrence here, later, in Acts 3.10, he becomes the channel through whom the risen Christ functions, causing others to be similarly astonished.

[89] 9.23; 18.22; 22.39.

7

John

Healings

Jesus heals at the Sheep Pool (5.2–47)

Table 7.1 The healing at the Sheep Pool – the literary context

	John
Samaritans believe in Jesus	4.39–42
Galileans welcome Jesus	4.43–45
Healing of the centurion's servant	4.46–54
Jesus heals at the Sheep Pool	**5.2–9a**
Jesus states . . .	
his authority over the Sabbath . . .	5.9b–11
that his authority is equivalent to God's authority	5.12–18
that the Son does what the Father does, fulfilling his will	5.19, 30
that the Father loves him, the Son	5.20
that the Son has the same authority as the Father to give life	5.21
that the Father has given his authority to judge to the Son	5.22, 27, 29
that the Son deserves the same honour as does the Father	5.23
that the Son has the authority to give eternal life	5.24
that the Son will speak to the dead	5.25, 28
that the Son shares the same life as the Father	5.26
that the Son is the Son of Man	5.27
that he is affirmed by John the Baptist	5.31–35
that he is affirmed by his works (granted to him by the Father)	5.20, 36
that he is affirmed as having been sent by the Father	5.36
that he is affirmed by the Father	5.37–38
that he is affirmed by the OT	5.39
that he is affirmed by Moses	5.46
Jesus condemns his accusers for rejecting him	5.40–47

As with most of John's signs, he follows them with an extended discourse that identifies the significance of the miracle. This healing immediately follows the healing of someone who was close to death in Galilee (see Table 7.1). Now Jesus heals a paralytic in Jerusalem, and this narrative will be followed by his feeding 5,000, in Galilee again. John provides no details to link the stories, though he carefully provides a strategic line of continuity in the theological themes that he provides in his Gospel; as a result of this thread, he is able to lead the reader through related narratives to an increasing appreciation of his subject, Jesus. He demonstrates this careful development in chapter 1 when, step by step, he presents information concerning the Logos, using repetition, ambiguity and metaphor, to intrigue the readers but, more importantly, to create a literary scaffolding that, if climbed, will lead to truth, in this case, concerning the divinely supreme nature of the Logos and his Incarnation – the miracle of *God* becoming a man.

The narrative relates to one man who is healed, in a context where many are ill. He alone is chosen. However, he expresses no faith in or even recognition of Jesus nor does he request that Jesus heal him.[1] Prior to the healing, Jesus asks the man if he wants to be healed.[2] To such a question, the man responds with the complaint that he cannot get to the water quickly enough to benefit from its apparent therapeutic powers. It is not necessary to assume that Jesus' question was intended to ascertain the man's desire to be healed, nor to rebuke him for an apparent lack of desire. The man's presence there indicates his desire to be healed. Elsewhere, when Jesus seems to be testing someone, it is specifically identified as such by the author (6.5). It may be intended to indicate the hopelessness of the man's situation in that not only has he been there for 38 years, but also he has no one to help him, in contrast to the previous healing in John where an official goes to Jesus on behalf of a sufferer (4.46).

It is possible that John records this interaction specifically to emphasize the lack of expectation of healing, for the man is not recorded as anticipating any restoration by Jesus. He is oblivious to the fact that the answer to his problem is standing before him, his hope being singularly focused on the alleged therapy of the pool.[3]

---

[1] Dickinson (R., *God Does Heal Today*. Paternoster Press, Carlisle, 1995, p. 104) suggests the man was chosen because he had been waiting there the longest, though the text does not indicate this.

[2] Carson (D. A., *The Gospel According to John*. IVP, Leicester, 1991, p. 243), offering 4.10, 6.32–33 as examples, describes this as one of 'the elliptical offers' often made by Jesus; Thomas (J. C., '"Stop Sinning Lest Something Worse Come upon You": The Man at the Pool in John 5', *JSNT*. 59, 1995, p. 10) comments on the use of *hugiēs* which, to him, indicates the idea that Jesus asks the man if he desires to be made whole, rather than to be healed. However, given that the man is unaware of the identity of Jesus and therefore ignorant of any potential within Jesus to grant him spiritual wholeness and insofar as his physical healing is discussed in verses 9, 10, 13, the suggestion is unlikely.

[3] The poor textual attestation of 5.3–4 (relating to an angel who would occasionally trouble the water, whereupon the first person able to enter it thereafter would be healed) is recognized by many scholars; see Metzger, B. M., *A Textual Commentary on the Greek New Testament*. Deutsches Bibelgesellschaft, Stuttgart, 1994, p. 209; Fee, G. D., 'On the Inauthenticity of John 5.3b–4', *EvQ*. 54, 1982, pp. 207–18, for evidence to support this conclusion. For an alternative view, see Hodges, Z. C., 'The Angel at Bethesda – John 5.4', *BibS*. 136, 1979, pp. 25–39.

Although the healing itself of the paralysed man is worthy of consideration, it is the response of some who accuse Jesus of healing on the Sabbath
that functions as a springboard for an extended statement by Jesus that
reveals his authority as being of much greater significance than that of a
healer. As such, it reveals him as having the authority to function uniquely
on the Sabbath, John demonstrating that Jesus is worthy of trust not just as
a healer but as the Son of God.[4] In staccato-like statements, Jesus proclaims
that his authority is best understood in parallel with the authority of God.

The authority of Jesus to heal a long-standing illness instantly

Jesus takes the initiative. He heals a man who has been ill for 38 years,[5]
commanding him to take up his bed and walk, as a result of which he is
immediately healed.[6] John records that the healing happens as a direct result
of Jesus' words of command, as also in each of the three other restorations
recorded in the Gospel of John.[7]

The authority of Jesus over the Sabbath

Only after recording the healing does John record that it occurred on a
Sabbath.[8] The actions of Jesus (in healing and instructing the man to carry
his bed, as did the man in carrying his mat[9]) broke Sabbath legislation,
causing an outrage among the Jews, who now, for the first time in John's
Gospel, are identified as being hostile to Jesus (5.18), resulting in their
pursuing or persecuting him (5.16), the imperfect tense of *diōkō* ('I pursue,
persecute'), indicating a repetition of the act. Even Jesus' earlier cleansing
of the Temple (2.13–22) is not described as resulting in such anger on the
part of the Jews.

The authority of Jesus is shared with the Father

It is the claim by Jesus that he is cooperating with the Father that causes
the severe conflict with the Jews (5.17), for it is an implicit claim to deity.

---

[4] Similarly, the identification of the feast is not clarified; elsewhere, John identifies particular feasts
(7.2; 10.22; 11.55; 13.1; 19.14, 31) and it is possible that it is mentioned simply to indicate that
many people were present.

[5] The mention of the length of time may simply indicate the long-standing nature of the man's suffering, although many have noted a similar length of time in Deut. 2.14 with reference to the journey
of the Israelites.

[6] The Greek aorist tense is used here to indicate instantaneous healing. Thus 'take' (v. 8) is *aron*, first
aorist imperative; 'took up' (v. 9) is *ēren*, first aorist indicative; also note the use of the present
peripatei and imperfect *periepatei* to indicate the continuous nature of his ability thereafter to walk.

[7] 4.50; 9.7; 11.39.

[8] See also 9.14.

[9] See Num. 15.32–35; Jer. 17.21; m. *Shab.* 7.2; 10.5 forbid the carrying of burdens on the Sabbath.

This puts the healing on the Sabbath in the shade, for Jesus implicates God in his Sabbath healing. If Jesus is deemed to be working on the Sabbath with God, this means that God is working on the Sabbath and thus breaking his own Sabbath. Indeed, Jesus refers to God as 'my Father' (5.17), as a result of which the Jews conclude he was making himself equal with God (5.18) which, for them, was 'insane blasphemy',[10] as a result of which they sought to kill him (5.18). However, Jesus is not expressing independence from God but dependence on God, though the Jews assumed that to claim equality with God was to present oneself as a competitor or alternative to God.

The unique relationship enjoyed by Jesus with the Father is further explicated by Jesus in the ensuing verses (5.19–30). Such is their unity that they work together, Jesus knowing what the Father does, and sharing equivalent authority with him (5.19, 20). Furthermore, the Father loves the Son, implicitly referring to Jesus (5.20), and provides him with the ability to raise the dead, a prerogative that normally belongs to God alone (5.21; cf. 2 Kings 5.7). God's authority to judge has also been entrusted to the Son by the Father (5.22), and the same honour (5.23) and quality of life (5.26) is shared by them. The Son is also described as having the authority to grant eternal life (5.24–29), which is received whenever the Son's words are believed. Not only can he give physical life, but now Jesus indicates that he can grant eternal life. This authority is affirmed by multiple witnesses. including the works of Jesus (5.20, 36), John the Baptist (5.31–35), the Father (5.37), the OT Scriptures (5.39), Moses (5.45–46)[11] and this healing. As such, the healing is but the introduction to a more significant characteristic related to Jesus; it is a sign to a higher claim than that he can heal.

The authority of Jesus over the consequences of sin

An important element in the words of Jesus to the man is his exhortation to sin no more, so that nothing worse should happen. This exhortation does not necessarily mean that Jesus supports the view that sickness is always, or even often, caused by sin, though it is possible that on this occasion the illness of the man has been the result of sin, and the admonition not to sin is a personal warning.

However, it has been shown previously that Jesus, though aware of the link between the two in the minds of his contemporaries, never explicitly

---

[10] Cf. Bultmann, R., *The Gospel of John*. Westminster Press, Philadelphia, 1971, p. 244.
[11] As in 1.17, 45; 3.14; 6.32; 7.19, 22, 23; 8.5; 9.28–29, Moses is introduced as having a supportive role with reference to Jesus and his mission, pointing to the latter's superiority.

links personal sickness to sin. On the only occasion when such a link is explicitly discussed, John records Jesus' rejection of the notion (John 9.3). It is unlikely, therefore, that Jesus here is indicating a relationship between a specific sin and a consequential sickness. The absence of the motifs of forgiveness and repentance, and the fact that sin is only mentioned to the man at a later stage, when its potential connection with illness would be lost on the attendant witnesses of the healing, strongly suggest that this prohibition did not relate to a specific sin that had caused the sickness.

The nature of the 'worse fate' is not clarified. Given the extent of the man's suffering for the previous 38 years, it is probable that Jesus has in mind eternal consequences of a life of sin, especially given that average life expectancy in the first century was less than 35 years. Thus, he is concerned that the future destiny of the man should not be prejudiced by sin, the present imperative verb, 'sin no more', indicating a sinful life rather than a sinful act. Jesus advises him to aim for a life that seeks after God; otherwise even the trauma of 38 years as an invalid will be preferable to the worse fate that will befall him. Jesus thus provides him with a fresh start and forgives him his previous sins.

Jesus provides an opportunity to believe in him

The healing acts as the catalyst in the discussion that follows, creating the possibility of the man expressing faith in him, not as a healer only, but also as the Son of God. John records that Jesus later locates the man and affirms him as being well.[12] This narrative demonstrates that the healing was permanent,[13] but also it discloses a soteriological dimension, for the healing has provided him with an opportunity to develop a new life, dictated not by sin but by Jesus. The restoration of this man stands as an object lesson to those who see the miracle. The potential for faith is available for the large number of onlookers but, unlike the situation in the previous story when the onlookers expressed their faith, Jesus is here persecuted (5.16) and threatened (5.18) by those who witnessed the miracle. Only one person accurately identifies Jesus; the others miss the signpost.

Conclusion

Insofar as the healing forms the basis of a wider discussion concerning the person of Jesus, it is important to recognize that the important element

---

[12] The term *hugiēs* is used in verses 6, 9, 11, 14, 15, though only once elsewhere in John (7.23) and five times in the rest of the NT.

[13] The Greek perfect tense used here appears to indicate this.

in this narrative is not the healing by Jesus, remarkable though it is, but the person of Jesus. The issue is not whether or how or why Jesus healed the man, but who Jesus is. Thus the final words of the pericope, contained in the phrase 'Will you believe?', are a crucial marker in the literary presentation of the author. The tragedy is that although some will believe (Jesus' disciples (2.22), Samaritans (4.29, 39, 42) and a royal official (4.50, 53)), others will not. The fact that the miracle takes place near water may be significant because it creates a positive expectation in the minds of the readers, based on the positive nuances of water-related incidents mentioned earlier in the Gospel.[14] The previous narrative, described as the second of Jesus' signs (4.54), resulted in a number of people expressing faith in Christ. The stage is set for a similar event, but this time, only one person is healed. The crowd seems to fade into the background as this one man becomes the centre of attention. The author's hope is that his readers will be more observant than the majority.

---

[14] John 1.25, 26, 31, 33, John's baptism; 2.1–11, the miracle of water into wine; 3.5, birth by water and the Spirit; 3.23 and 4.2, water baptism; 4.9–15, living water.

Jesus heals a blind man (9.1–41)

Table 7.2 Healing a blind man – the literary context

	John
Jesus and the adulterous woman	8.1–11
Jesus proclaims himself to be the light of the world	8.12
Pharisees reject Jesus' testimony	8.13–20
Jesus proclaims his authority and that he is the Son of Man	8.21–29
Some believe in Jesus	8.20–31
Further confrontation between Jesus and Jews	8.32–58
People try to kill Jesus	8.59
Jesus heals a blind man and proclaims himself the light of the world	**9.1–7**
The man three times identifies Jesus as his healer	9.8–15, 25
Pharisees refute that Jesus is from God, accusing him of breaking the Sabbath	9.16 (24)
The man identifies Jesus as a prophet	9.17
The parents are fearful of identifying Jesus as Messiah	9.18–23
Jesus is accused of being a sinner	9.24
The man for the third time asserts that Jesus is his healer	9.25–27
The man is reviled by Pharisees and accused of being a disciple of Jesus	9.28–29
The man witnesses to Jesus, identifying him as someone to whom God listens, and as a unique healer of blindness	9.30–33
The man is reviled by Pharisees and accused of being a sinner	9.34
Jesus finds the man who has been rejected by the Pharisees but who has 'found' Jesus	9.35
The man is willing to believe that Jesus is the Son of Man	9.35–35
The man calls Jesus 'Lord' and worships Jesus	9.37–38
Jesus asserts that sin causes spiritual blindness	9.39
Jesus identifies the Pharisees as being 'blind'	9.40–41

John again functions as a literary craftsman, recording this incident and its aftermath, after an extended discussion between Jesus and the Jews concerning his identity (8.1–59) (see Table 7.2). Previously, John has recorded a story of a woman who has been forgiven and commissioned by Jesus (8.1–11), followed by Jesus identifying himself as the light of the world (8.12). However, although some initially believe in Jesus (8.31), their belief is short-lived[15] as they reject him and his provenance. A similar confrontation will occur after the healing (9.13–34), the healing of the blind man functioning as a bridge between the two occasions. The restora-

---

[15] 8.45, 53, 57.

tion of sight to a blind man indicates that, in contrast to those who can see, it is a blind man who truly understands who Jesus is.

The blindness

The man is not named and is simply characterized as being blind. He has no expectation of any transformation, not even requesting healing from Jesus. However, his testimony to Jesus is of significance to the narrator. The one who identifies himself simply as the man who was blind (9.9) is the one who later more completely acknowledges who Jesus is (9.38).[16]

When his disciples question Jesus as to the cause of the man's blindness, insofar as it is from birth, a fact that the narrative records six times (9.1, 2, 3, 19, 20, 32), Jesus responds that it was neither the man's fault nor his parents'.[17] However, Jesus describes it as an opportunity for the works of God to be made manifest through himself (9.5; see also 3.21; 8.12). It appears that Jesus is, in effect, indicating that the blindness was part of a divine plan to manifest the presence of God in his healing. This sits somewhat awkwardly with our sense of divine fairness. However, this is an accurate rendering of Jesus' words and, at least, indicates that the healing is of significant importance – not only is a man going to be able to see the light (both physically and spiritually), but also, Jesus is going to be revealed as 'the light of the world'.

It is Jesus, not the blind man, who is the focus of the narrative, and the reference to Jesus as 'I am' (9.5) helps to affirm this, especially because this is the name of God in the OT. Not only that, but Jesus is identified with light, a divine characteristic (1.4, 7, 8).[18] Isaiah 10.17 refers to God as 'the light of Israel', while here, Jesus is the light of the world. At the same time, Isaiah 49.6 prophesies that the Servant will be a light to the Gentiles, bringing salvation.

---

[16] Hamm (M. D., 'Sight to the Blind: Vision as Metaphor in Luke', *Biblica.* 67, 1986, pp. 457–71) views this as a picture of the spiritually blind having their eyes opened, an event anticipated in the messianic reign (Isa. 29.28; 35.5; 42.7); Derrett (J. D. M., 'John 9.6 Read with Isaiah 6.10; 20.9', *EvQ.* 66. 3, 1994, pp. 251–4) suggests that John was reflecting Isa. 6.10 to emphasize that the prophecy of Isaiah was being fulfilled in the ministry of Jesus.

[17] For the connection between personal sin and sickness/suffering, see Exod. 20.25; Deut. 5.9; Pss. 51.5; 89.33; Tobit 3.3–4; b. *Ta'an.* 21a; *Ber.*58b; *Shab.* 55a; *Gen. Rab.* 63.6 interprets Gen. 25.22 as revealing how an unborn child can suffer physical deformity through the action of the mother; *Song of Sol. Rab.* 1.41 suggests that a foetus is implicated in the worship of an idol by its mother.

[18] Jehovah creates light (Gen. 1.15, 17), provides light (Exod. 13.21) and is defined by David as 'my light' (Ps. 27.1; see also Isa. 60.20) whose words give light (Ps. 119.130). Similarly, his glory is paralleled with light (Isa. 60.1).

The healing

It is significant to note that the OT records no healings of blindness, whereas Jesus is recorded as healing blindness more times than any other condition. Also, the man is found near the Temple (8.59—9.1), but proximity to such a sacred place does not effect restoration; it is proximity to Jesus that matters.

Jesus does not immediately heal the man but anoints the man's eyes with clay – earth (mentioned three times) that he mixed with spittle. The spittle is probably intended to indicate that a therapeutic act is going to follow, spittle being associated with healing in many ancient (and modern) cultures.[19] The reference to 'earth' may indicate that a creative act is about to be performed by Jesus, though the parallels with God's creation of Adam and Eve are limited.[20] Nevertheless, the identity of God as the potter does provide some interesting allusions.[21] John provides a clue as to why Jesus may have made clay and placed it on the man's eyes in that he did it on the Sabbath (9.14), as a result of which the Pharisees concluded that Jesus 'does not keep the Sabbath' (9.16).[22] It is incongruous that a man who could not see should be provided with an extra obstacle to sight in that the clay now covers his blind eyes; he is, at it were, doubly blind. It may simply be that Jesus provides an encouragement for the man to obey him by covering his eyes with mud that will necessitate his washing it off, whereupon he will see the mud that once covered his blind eyes.

Then, John records Jesus' first words to the man, commanding him to go and wash in the Pool of Siloam,[23] a name which John records as meaning 'sent'. The man obeys and returns, seeing. John informs the readers that it was not due to any curative powers of the pool that the man was healed but because he had obeyed Jesus, the one who had sent him there. As Jesus was sent by God (9.4),[24] so also was John the Baptist (1.6, 33; 3.28). Jesus sent the disciples (4.38), and now this man has the opportunity to follow in this tradition and function as a sent one.

---

[19] See commentary on Mark 7.33 and 8.33.

[20] Frayer-Griggs (D., 'Spittle, Clay, and Creation in John 9.6 and Some Dead Sea Scrolls', *JBL*. 3, 2013, pp. 665–70) defends an association with the creation of man by reference to Dead Sea texts (1QS 11. 21–2; 1QH 20.24–7, 31–2) in which spittle and clay are described as being used by God to create man.

[21] Job 10.9; 33.6; Isa. 29.16; 45.9; Jer. 18.6.

[22] Jesus may be deliberately revealing his readiness to rebut Sabbath law; anointing someone's eyes with spittle was not permitted on the Sabbath (b. *Abod. Zar.* 28b; j. *Shab.* 14d, 17–18).

[23] Carson (*John.* p. 365) accepts the possibility that the author wishes his readers to link this information with the incident recorded in Isa. 8.6 in which the Jews rejected the waters of Shiloah, Siloam being a transliteration of the Hebrew *Siloah*. It is at the pool of Siloam that Jews will reject Jesus.

[24] Also 3.28, 34; 4.34; 5.23, 24, 33, 36, 37, 38 et al.

It is not clear from the narrative that the man expected anything more than the removal of the mud from his eyes; perhaps he viewed the application of clay and spittle as a sincere but failed attempt to bring about his sight. However, his level of expectation is irrelevant to the healing.

The lesson

The willingness of the blind man to obey Jesus, without any guarantee of healing, is in stark contrast to the unwillingness of the onlookers, who can see, to respond positively to Jesus. The healing is described in only seven verses but, as in the previous healing narrative, it acts as a sign to what follows as it sets the scene for a crucial presentation of Jesus (9.8–41).

John includes this healing because, as a sign (9.16), it demonstrates the authority of Jesus, not just as a healer but, more importantly, as 'the light of the world'.[25] Jesus is again identified as functioning, on the Sabbath, together with God (5.17, 19), the healing being identified as one of 'the works of God' (9.3) achieved by Jesus who has been sent by God (9.4), the use of the plural, 'We must work . . .', possibly implicating God in this.[26]

A significant purpose of this miracle is to trace the journey of perception of the identity of Jesus by a man who was once blind. John starts by revealing that not only does the man not request healing, or express faith in Jesus' power to heal, but he has no idea even of the identity of Jesus, neither does Jesus introduce himself to him. However, thereafter, the man demonstrates an increasingly accurate perception as to Jesus' identity. First, he refers to him as a man who is called Jesus (9.11); thereafter, he indicates that he is worthy of obedience (9.11). Subsequently, he identifies Jesus as his healer (9.15, 25), a prophet (9.17), worthy of discipleship (9.27),[27] a unique healer of blindness (9.32), someone to whom God listens (9.31),[28] sent from God with authority (9.33), the Son of Man[29] (9.35–38) and,

---

[25] 8.12; 9.5; see 1.7–9.

[26] Michaels (J. R., *The Gospel of John*. Eerdmans, Grand Rapids, 2010, p. 543) suggests that Jesus is referring to the blind man; others suggest it refers to the disciples (Edwards, M., *John*. Blackwell, Oxford, 2004, p. 99; Barrett, C. K., *The Gospel According to St. John*. SPCK, London, 1978, p. 357) or the readers (Keener, C., *Gospel of John: A Commentary*. Hendrickson, Peabody, 2003, p. 779).

[27] The humour of John is obvious to the readers who, as observers, see the man innocuously questioning whether the Pharisees who have denounced Jesus may be changing their minds.

[28] The OT often asserts that God refuses to listen to sinners (Ps. 66.18; Isa. 1.15; 59.2) and loves to listen to the righteous (Pss. 34.15; 145.19).

[29] The previous occasion this term was used in John (6.53–54) resulted in people abandoning Jesus; here, the blind man worships him. This term is used in John as the preferred self-designation of Jesus (1.51; 3.13–14; 5.27; 6.27, 53, 62; 8.28; 12.34); it functions as a synonym for the Messiah. In 9.22, John notes that to confess that Jesus was the Christ would have resulted in excommunication

finally, the Lord who is worthy of his trust and worship (9.37–38).[30] The man has reached the climax of his perception as to the identity of Jesus and, rather than Jesus commission him to another task, he is left before Jesus in an attitude of worship, the final destination of the story having been reached.

Despite the provocative and bullying interrogation of the Pharisees, the man who was blind functions as a courageous, authentic and worthy witness to Jesus (9.10, 15, 26, 30), while the parents, who can see, are 'weak' witnesses, bound by fear, and the Pharisees, who can also see, are 'blind' witnesses (9.18) whose error is exacerbated by the fact that they strike fear into the hearts of ordinary people (9.22). The Pharisees see Jesus as an ordinary man with no pedigree (9.29), who is not from God (9.16) but is a Sabbath-breaker (9.16) and a sinner (9.24). They, whose role was to teach, accuse the man of presumptuously seeking to teach them; in reality, he does teach them but they are not good students. Unwittingly, the man functions as a disciple while also emulating Jesus, for Jesus also taught the Pharisees[31] and was rejected as one who was perceived to be demonized (7.20; 8.48, 52) and a liar (8.13), whom they sought to arrest (7.30, 32, 45) and kill (8.40, 59).

Jesus later re-enters the narrative and 'finds' the healed man, who had been cast out by the religious establishment (9.35–41). Earlier, Jesus had 'found' Philip (1.43) and requested that he follow him, while Andrew 'found' Simon (1.41) and Philip 'found' Nathanael (1.45), both also following Jesus. Jesus now 'found' the man he had healed of paralysis (5.14), providing him with the opportunity of living a new faith-based and active life. The only other time in the Gospel where Jesus finds someone is with reference to Lazarus (11.17), who receives new life. Here, the healed man is to be offered the opportunity to begin a new life in relationship with the one who has not just healed him but who is worthy of his worship. His healing has been part of the journey that has resulted in his being 'found' by Jesus at a new level.

---

from the synagogue. Jesus is testing the man's readiness to risk that punishment and he passes the test by affirming publically that Jesus is the Son of Man. He trusts Jesus to provide him with the information as to the identity of the Son of Man and, without hesitation, believes Jesus, as contrasted to the Pharisees who hear the same words but come to a different conclusion.

[30] The term used for the act of worship (*proskuneō*) although capable of simply meaning, 'I kneel before') is used in John elsewhere with a deeper devotion than that of mere respect; in 4.20–24 and 12.20 it is used with reference to the worship of God. In kneeling, the man realizes that Jesus is worthy of worship.

[31] 7.14–24, 28–29, 37–39; 8.12–58.

Having found him, Jesus confirms the 'blindness' of those who have rejected the sign that he has provided for them. The gradual development of the man's perception of Jesus is to be contrasted with the growing obduracy of those who refuse to believe. The light that provides brightness for the blind man, who wishes to see, creates a shadow for those who prefer to remain sightless. When his opponents reject the healing as a witness to Jesus' identity and mission, Jesus identifies them as being (spiritually) blind. Their emphatic statement, 'we know that this man is a sinner' (9.24) indicates how set their minds are.[32] However, the consequences of this self-imposed blindness are serious. As a result, when the Pharisees recommend that the healed man should give glory to God (9.24), they fail to see that this is exactly what he does (9.38). Similarly, their dismissive comment that they do not know the provenance of Jesus (9.29) draws from the man an exclamation of wonder and irony that they[33] should be ignorant of such a miracle-worker. The healing which has opened the spiritual eyes of one man has confirmed the blindness of many others.

Tragically, this story is recorded after an occasion when the Jews, including Pharisees, abused Jesus by calling him a Samaritan, accusing him of having a demon (8.48) and attempting to stone him to death (8.59) after his attempt to help them realize his true identity (8.12–58), itself being preceded by his reference to himself as the light of the world (8.12). Consequently, Jesus rejects them (8.43–44), calling them liars (8.55) and children of the devil (8.44), accusing them of dishonouring him (8.49) and not knowing God (8.55). The result is that while Jesus includes the blind man, the religious community excludes him. The challenge to the readers is whether they will follow in the footsteps of the blind man or the Pharisees.

This narrative is followed by the encouraging message, especially to all those who have chosen to follow Jesus and will thereby be excluded by the Jewish community (9.34), that Jesus is the shepherd of all. He is 'the door' (10.7, 9), the 'good shepherd' (10.11, 14) who knows his sheep (10.14), gives them abundant life (10.10) and lays down his life for them (10.15). Many conclude he is demonized (10.20), though others are not certain (10.21). However, while many reject him and try to arrest and kill him (10.21, 39) because of his reference to 'my Father' (10.29) and his claim to be united with him (10.30), others believe in him (10.42). The battle for the hearts of people continues.

---

[32] Note the emphatic use of the personal pronoun.
[33] Note the emphatic use of the personal pronoun, 'you yourselves do not know …'

Jesus raises Lazarus from the dead (11.2–44)

Table 7.3 Raising Lazarus from the dead – the literary context

	John
Many reject Jesus	10.31–39
Some accept Jesus	10.40–42
Jesus hears that Lazarus is ill	11.1–4
Jesus decides to go to raise Lazarus from the dead	11.5–16
Jesus consoles Martha	11.17–24
Jesus proclaims himself to be the resurrection and the life	11.25
Martha identifies Jesus as the Christ and the Son of God	11.26–27
Jesus consoles Mary	11.29–34
Jesus is moved emotionally	11.33–37
Jesus raises Lazarus from the dead	**11.38–44**
Some believe in Jesus while the religious leaders plan how to kill him	11.45–57
Mary anoints Jesus' feet	12.1–7

John 11.2–57 contrasts Lazarus' journey from death to life with Jesus' journey from life to death. The former occurred as a result of Jesus going to Lazarus' tomb,[34] while the latter will be concluded by religious leaders in Jerusalem who arrange for Jesus to be placed in a tomb.[35]

Jesus, having been informed of Lazarus' illness, states that the illness (and subsequent death) was to be a vehicle for the glorification of the Son of God[36] while also providing an opportunity for the disciples to believe (11.15). However, not all will believe or see the glory of God as a result of the miracle. It is not that the signs are flawed because they do not always convince all who witness them of the truth of the person to whom they point; the purpose of signs is to point in the right direction, though the observer may choose to reject what they indicate. Before the resurrection occurred, many rejected Jesus, seeking to arrest and stone him, accusing him of blasphemy (10.31, 33, 39), while many believed in him (10.42). After the resurrection of Lazarus, although many believed in Jesus (11.45),

---

[34] 11.17, 31, 38; 12.7.

[35] 20.1–4, 6, 8, 11. The tombs of Lazarus and Jesus are the only ones referred to in the Gospel.

[36] 11.4, 40; see also 9.3. That Jesus chooses not to go immediately to Lazarus, waiting instead for two days to pass, probably indicates his determination to follow the plan of God rather than the dictates of others; however, verse 15 indicates that he is eventually motivated to go by the opportunity this provides to develop their faith in him. *Gen. Rab.* 100.64a describes the Jewish belief that the spirit of a person permanently leaves the body of the deceased after three days; it is therefore possible that Jesus is waiting a sufficient time to prove that Lazarus was indeed dead, to highlight the supernatural nature of this miracle.

others chose not to (11.46), actively seeking to arrest and destroy him (11.53, 57). Even such a miracle does not guarantee that people will follow Jesus.

John records Jesus stating that although some will reject him and 'stumble' in the process (11.10), he is still prepared to provide opportunities for others to 'see the light of the world' (11.9). As such, he asserts to his disciples, concerning the death of Lazarus, 'I am glad that I was not there, so that you may believe' (11.15). The death of Lazarus was to provide a fresh and unique opportunity for people to increase their belief in Jesus.

The resurrection of Lazarus takes only two verses (11.43–44), occurring as a result of a word by Jesus. However, it is surrounded by details concerning other people, namely the disciples (11.3–16), Martha (11.17–27) and Mary (11.28–37), Jesus (11.38–42) and 'the Jews' (11.45–57). Although the resurrection of Lazarus is at the heart of this catalyst (see Table 7.3), it is its role as a sign that is instrumental in determining if any others will also 'come to life'.

Martha is recorded as believing that Jesus could have healed Lazarus and is also convinced that Lazarus would be resurrected 'at the last day' (11.24). However, she does not expect a resurrection in this life (11.39). Nevertheless, other evidence in the narrative indicates that her faith in Jesus, before the resurrection, is developing. Thus, she is aware that God *will* respond to Jesus and grant his requests (11.22), and she confidently confesses the identity of Jesus as 'the Christ, the Son of God'. Andrew, John the Baptist and the Samaritan woman acknowledge that Jesus is the Messiah (1.41; 3.28; 4.29), John the Baptist identifies him as the Lamb of God (1.36), Nicodemus as 'a teacher come from God' (3.2), Samaritans as the Saviour of the world (4.42), Peter as the 'holy one of God' (6.69), the man who was blind as 'the son of Man' (9.38), John the Baptist as 'Son of God' (1.34) and also Nathanael (1.49). However, it is only Martha who identifies Jesus as both together – 'the Christ, the Son of God' (11.27). She alone functions as the one who has achieved what John had hoped for in writing his Gospel (20.31); the question remains whether others (including the readers) will emulate Martha.

Furthermore, John records that Martha says, 'I believe' (*egō pepisteuka*, 11.27); not only does she stress the fact that *she* believes (note the emphatic personal pronoun), but also that she *believes* (the perfect tense indicating the certainty of her stance). In these words, she acknowledges her belief that God has stepped into this world in the person of Jesus.

Mary, who is then introduced, repeats the words of Martha concerning the difference that Jesus would have made if he had come earlier. However, the positive addition offered by Martha is omitted. Mary expresses little hope and simply weeps; there is not even an acknowledgement that she might see Lazarus in the next life. She is simply distraught and without hope. The Jews are introduced next and they are not just faithless, offering no expectation of a resurrection, but also critical of Jesus, identifying his delay as a lack of compassion. In the light of these eyewitnesses in the narrative, Martha shines brightest.

The intense emotion displayed by Jesus (11.33, 35), resulting in tears, has been the subject of much discussion. It is possible that he is empathizing with the sorrow of those present or, as suggested by some contemporary observers (11.36), it was due to his great love for Lazarus. However, given that Jesus was soon to resurrect Lazarus, neither seems to be a logical reason for his tears. Morris[37] writes of the possibility that it relates to the anger[38] of Jesus against the pain caused by death, while Brown speculates that it is directed against Satan.[39] It is possible that 12.27, 13.21 support the notion that the suffering to come prior to his death may be the cause of Jesus' emotional distress. However, a closer reason for emotional pain is available. Given the potential of the sign to lead people to truth and life, the sorrow expressed by Jesus may specifically relate to the frustrating perversity of those who are determined not to believe, despite the most sensational miracles being presented to them. Though some may take advantage of the sign to lead them to truth, the majority will not.[40] Despite the presence of light, they ignore it, stumbling in the process because they choose to exist as if it is not there (11.9, 10). At the same time, even those who love Jesus intimately and believe in him implicitly are examples of those who misunderstand who he is and the authority that he owns (11.40).

Of the people referred to before the miracle, the disciples demonstrate a resigned readiness to go to their death (along with Jesus), while Mary's perception of Jesus is limited to his healing ability, and the Jews present see the event as a tragic element of life, Jesus being no more than a power-less person in the drama. Martha alone offers a ray of hope, manifesting a higher regard for his status. In this context, John records the intimate

---

[37] Morris, L., *The Gospel According to John*. Marshall, Morgan & Scott, London, 1972, p. 556; so Barrett, *John*. p. 399; Beasley-Murray, G. R., *Word Biblical Themes: John*. Word, Waco, 1989, p. 68.

[38] The word 'moved' (*enebrimēsato*) (11.33) is used elsewhere to describe anger.

[39] Brown, R., *The Gospel According to John, Vol. 1*. Continuum, London, 1971, p. 435; Brodie (T. L., *The Gospel According to John: A Literary and Theological Commentary*. Oxford University Press, Oxford, 1993, p. 395) and Bruce (F. F., *The Gospel of John*. Eerdmans, Grand Rapids, 1996, p. 246) suggest the anger is directed at sin, death and Satan.

[40] 11.37, 46, 53, 57.

moment between Jesus and his Father where he thanks the Father for listening to him (11.41–42);[41] someone believes in Jesus.

Ironically, as Jesus states that Lazarus' death is not the end for Lazarus (11.4), John hints at the fact that death will be the end for Jesus, plotted by those who had heard about the resurrection of Lazarus (11.45–57). The attempt to end the signs of Jesus, and thus the potential of others believing in him, results in the most remarkable sign of his death on the cross that has global consequences in terms of initiating millions into the ranks of his disciples. While Caiaphas concludes, 'it is expedient for you that one man should die for the people', he assumes that this is to ensure that 'the whole nation should not perish' (11.50); in reality, it ensures that the whole world might 'not perish but have eternal life' (3.16).

It is in the following narratives, which commence with the anointing of Jesus by Mary (12.1–7), that a connection with the death and resurrection of Jesus is most explicit. In the latter account, Mary anoints Jesus' feet with very expensive ointment in a lavish display of affection, in the presence of Lazarus, Martha and his disciples. In response to Judas' insensitive, deceitful outburst at the extravagance of Mary, Jesus refers to his burial, concluding that he will not be with them forever. Crowds of Jews are then described as coming to Jesus (12.9) on account of the resurrection of Lazarus, but this is accompanied by the religious leaders planning for his death (12.10). They also have missed the significance of the signs.

In 12.12–5, John records the so-called triumphal entry into Jerusalem by Jesus when 'a great crowd' welcomed him. However, tragically, John records that, although their enthusiasm was exuberant and accompanied by quoting OT promises (12.13), those prophecies related to the coming of a king of Israel (Ps. 118.26; Zech. 9.9). Although they had correctly understood Lazarus' resurrection as a sign that pointed beyond the miracle, as a result of which, they, in great numbers (12.19), welcomed Jesus (12.18), they had misread it and thought it indicated that Jesus was to bring a new world that would be expressed by a life of liberty from oppressive physical and political bondage, and the presence of prosperity and national hope. Although John anticipates that the entrance of Jesus into Jerusalem was the fulfilment of OT promise concerning the establishing of the supernatural kingship of Jesus (12.15), the people viewed it simply in nationalistic terms. It is no coincidence that immediately after the

---

[41] Although Michaels (*The Gospel of John.* p. 643) writes that this 'is in effect his petition to the Father', there is no evidence that Jesus asks the Father to raise Lazarus from the dead; indeed, Jesus provides the reason for the prayer which is that the people would realize his divine provenance and status.

presentation of this narrative, John records Jesus explaining that his hour has come, as a result of which he will die (12.23–24), the anticipation of the event causing him mixed feelings of great sorrow (12.27), despite its being an opportunity to glorify God and draw people to himself (12.28–33).

For John, no further sign will be offered to people; the next will be Jesus' death and resurrection. Indeed, he records that, thereafter, Jesus 'departed and hid himself from them. Though he had done so many signs before them, they still did not believe in him' (12.36–37). John then concludes with Isaianic prophecies, demonstrating that the rejection of Jesus coalesces with the divine plan.[42] In this regard, Jesus reflects God who was also rejected in spite of all the signs that he performed (Num. 14.11). The challenge to the readers of John and the observers of Jesus is whether they will place their faith in Jesus merely as a miracle-worker – even one who can resurrect the dead, or whether they will recognize that the resurrection of Lazarus is a sign that points to a greater truth – that Jesus is God.

---

[42] 12.38–41; Isa. 6.1, 10; 53.1.

Nature miracles

Jesus changes water into wine (2.1–11)

Table 7.4 Turning water into wine – the literary context

	John
The Logos is introduced as divine . . .	1.1–2
. . . as creator and uncreated . . .	1.3
. . . as life and light	1.4–5
John the Baptist affirms him	1.6–8
The Logos enlightens authentically . . .	1.9
. . . but is not received by those to whom he came	1.10–11
Those who believe in him become God's children	1.12–13
The Logos becomes flesh, manifesting glory . . .	1.14
. . . and is affirmed by John the Baptist again	1.15
The Logos dispenses grace . . .	1.16–17
. . . and is identified as the only (Son) of God	1.18
John the Baptist affirms him again . . .	1.19–28
. . . as Jesus and the Lamb of God . . .	1.29–31
. . . on whom the Spirit of God remains . . .	1.32–33
. . . and the Son of God	1.34
Jesus chooses disciples	1.35–51
Jesus turns water into wine	**2.1–11**
Jesus cleanses the Temple	2.13–22

A variety of interpretations have been offered for the narrative, some weakly suggesting a link with the Eucharist because of the presence of wine. Van der Loos[43] views it as demonstrating that Jesus was willing to remedy domestic problems of life, while Armerding[44] identifies Jesus as affirming marriage. It is probable that the unusual nature of this miracle has resulted in such suggestions. It is, at first glance, incongruous that the first of only seven miracles recorded by John should describe Jesus providing wine to a party that has drunk itself dry. It is true that it would have been embarrassing to the groom to have been accused of not providing sufficient wine for his guests and was, potentially, a cause of legal redress. However, although Jesus could have been thanked for resolving a domestic crisis, it appears an odd diversion after such a high Christology has been presented and at such length in the previous chapter. In fact, because of the previous and following data, it is to be anticipated that

---

[43] Van der Loos, H., *The Miracles of Jesus*. Brill, Leiden, 1965, p. 615.
[44] Armerding, C., 'The Marriage in Cana', *BibS*. 118, 1961, pp. 320–6.

John is recording a narrative that holds a supremely important lesson, for it acts as a sign of inordinate significance. That which will be revealed in the miracle is not that Jesus has come to help a beleaguered bridegroom but that he has come to provide a superior relationship with God, even better than that which God himself initiated with the Jews.

It will be demonstrated that the miracle was intended by John to demonstrate that Jesus had come to introduce an initiative that would build on but replace the old covenant, associated with Judaism, with a new covenant. Hints in this direction may be afforded by the fact that it happens on the third day (2.18), reminiscent of the resurrection of Jesus. Indeed, John refers to the fact that this miracle was an opportunity for the glory associated with Jesus to be revealed and for the disciples to believe in Jesus (12.11).

The placing of the narrative after the contents of the previous chapter is very important in establishing the significance of this sign-miracle (see Table 7.4). Not only is Jesus identified as owning divine attributes (1.1–18), but also, multiple affirmations are offered of Jesus by John the Baptist (1.6–8, 19–34), the Spirit (1.32–33), would-be disciples (who identify him as Teacher (1.38), Messiah (1.41), the one who was spoken of by the prophets (1.45), and the king of Israel and Son of God (1.49)), and the angels (1.51). Furthermore, Jesus is defined as existing from the beginning, in relationship with God (*pros ton theon*, literally 'towards God') and as God (1.1), in association with creation (1.3), life (1.4) and the active and authentic light (1.5, 9), and as having the authority to enable people to become the children of God (1.12). To Jesus, John applies the features of being 'full of grace and truth' and 'glory' (1.14, 17), whose relationship with the Father is unique (1.18) and with whom the Spirit chooses to remain (1.33). Thereafter, having already been defined as the Logos (1.1), Jesus is defined as the Messiah (1.41), and more importantly the Son of God and the king of Israel (1.49). This exalted description of Jesus anticipates further disclosures of his divine nature, the following miracle providing an example of that divine status.

It is crucial to recognize that the miracle occurs after this supreme presentation of Jesus, for without it, the changing of water into wine may be misunderstood and its strong, symbolic undergirding framework be missed. This is a miracle that demonstrates much more than that Jesus offers a compassionate act to release people from a trauma; instead, it relates to the authority of Jesus to release people from a familiar religion that has lost its potential for life-giving transformation (1.17).

It becomes the first miracle in John's Gospel that begins to fulfil the prospect that Jesus would bring life and light to the Jews (1.4–11) and

authorizes people to 'become the children of God' (1.12–13). The incongruity of the Son of God attending a wedding makes sense only if he
is going to function in the authority of his being God. The fact that it
is followed by the authoritative and decisive cleansing of the Temple is
also significant (see Table 7.4), John uniquely placing this incident earlier
in the life of Jesus than the Synoptists. Not only has Jesus come to change
water into wine, but he has a much greater transformative role that affects
Jewish religion as a whole.

There is an implicit challenge to the reader in that it appears that only
a minority of the guests appreciated who had provided the wine. The
steward assumes it was the groom, while the groom appears to be ignorant
of the true provider because he does not disclaim his involvement in the
provision. Only the disciples and Mary appear to be aware of the true
miracle-worker;[45] the question is whether the reader will do better than
the majority and not just identify the miracle-worker but understand what
it reveals about him.

The wedding

Little is told about the wedding; no reference is made to the bride or
groom or their relationship with Jesus or Mary. Such information is
not needed for this is a narrative about Jesus and the glory that is related
to him. It is possible that the location of the miracle at a marriage is
significant.[46] Such a theme is used elsewhere with reference to the end
times, and the Church[47] is identified as the bride[48] and 'wife' (Rev. 21.9);
furthermore, the concepts of marriage and the bride are recorded in
Revelation 19.7 while 'the marriage supper of the Lamb' is referred to
in 19.9. The marriage feast was a centrally important element in Jewish
weddings, so much so that some rabbis taught that it was acceptable to
exclude oneself from scholarly pursuits or festal responsibilities on such
occasions;[49] the importance of weddings was affirmed by the assertion
that even God attended the wedding of Adam and Eve.[50] At Cana, Jesus
was present at a wedding.

---

[45] Even the servants are only aware of water being placed in the jars.
[46] God and Israel are identified as united as bride and groom (Isa. 54.5–8; 61.10; Jer. 2.2; Hos. 1.1—2.20).
[47] Associations between the inauguration or establishment of the new kingdom and wedding feasts are drawn elsewhere (Matt. 22.1–10; 25.1–13; Luke 14.7–24).
[48] 2 Cor. 11.2; Eph. 5.25; Rev. 21.9.
[49] b. *Ket.* 17a; *Sukkah* 25b; *Ber.* 2.10.
[50] b. *Baba Bathra* 75a; *Gen. Rab.* 8.13; 18.1.

The conversation between Mary and Jesus

Jesus' response to his mother, who informs him that the wine has run out, has caused much discussion as it appears that his attitude is disrespectful, especially because the clause 'What have you to do with me?' or 'What is this to me and you?' (*ti emoi kai soi*), is used elsewhere by demons to Jesus, accusing him of interfering.[51] It is possible that she was asking for a miracle, perhaps to avoid the social embarrassment faced by the groom, and that he was reticent to follow her advice, though such a request is not explicit and such reticence is not borne out by the fact that he did provide more wine.

Jesus elsewhere tested the readiness of people to trust him (6.6, 53–66). Thus, Jesus may be rhetorically asking his mother why he should get involved in an issue that is none of his concern, though the reader is encouraged to anticipate, as did Mary, that Jesus has already decided the answer to his own question. She does not respond to his rhetorical question but instead anticipates that he is to be trusted to resolve the dilemma and consequently tells the servants to obey whatever he commands them, even though he does not indicate that he will command them to do anything. But Mary knows her son.

The use of the term 'woman' (*gunai*) to refer to his mother sounds harsh, though it is to be remembered that nowhere in the Gospel does John identify her by name. However, this word is used elsewhere in John (4.21; 8.10) in contexts where Jesus had initiated a relationship with the women concerned, as a result of which they had benefited. Also, it is used twice in conversations with his mother (19.26) and Mary Magdalene (20.13, 15) in very caring contexts. It is possible that John here specifically identifies Mary, not by name but as Jesus' mother, and on three occasions, to indicate her relationship with him. As his mother, she knew her son; she may not know what he will do, but she knows that he will do something.

The statement of Jesus, 'My hour has not yet come', is also worthy of consideration. It refers either to the miracle that occurs next or to something else, perhaps his death, in which he will be glorified.[52] However, a reference to his death seems out of place in this context. It is more likely that Jesus was unwilling to appear to respond to the situation as if his mother had offered him with guidance when, in reality, he always followed an agenda set by God. However, she alone was right in recognizing that

---

[51] Mark 1.24; 5.7; 11.24. Although it is used in contexts of hostility elsewhere (2 Sam. 16.10; 19.22; 1 Kings 17.18; 2 Kings 3.13), that does not necessitate its use here; on occasion, hostility is not the setting as demonstrated in Hos. 14.8 where God simply identifies his disengagement with idols.
[52] 12.23, 27–28; 13.1; 16.32; 17.1; 19.14.

Jesus would act. In this regard, he disengages with his mother but not in any hostile way.

Of importance is the fact that on two occasions, John refers to people trying to arrest Jesus but being unable to do so because his 'hour had not come' (7.30. 8.20); their agenda did not coalesce with his, for his destiny had been divinely pre-determined. Jesus also refuses to take the advice of his disciples to go to eat (4.31) and to attend a feast, John recording twice that it was because his 'time has not yet [fully] come' (7.3–8), although he then went to the feast (7.11). It is in this context that the words of Jesus may be best understood. Jesus follows a divine strategy, not one that has been initiated by anyone else (5.21).

The miracle

The large jars, referred to by John, were used to contain water that would have been used for Jewish purification rituals, not for drinking from, as clarified by John. John specifies that the water was placed in stone jars (as contrasted with clay or earthen jars); the former ensured that the water remained uncontaminated from any ceremonial impurity as contrasted with clay jars. Water for ceremonial purposes was important in Judaism and it is this water that is replaced and transformed into wine. Given that Jesus could simply have provided wine, instead of first arranging for 120–180 gallons of water to be brought from a well and poured into the jars, it implies that Jesus was seeking to teach a lesson relating to replacement and improvement.

The fact that there were six jars has regularly been understood as being symbolic, given that they were one short of seven, the perfect number, as understood by Jewish readers. If this is so, and it is not certain, it would help to affirm the suggestion that the miracle is intended to make a more powerful statement than merely to indicate that Jesus can manufacture wine from water; his role is to produce superior wine that does not merely and externally purify ceremonially (as does water), but which offers the best internal cleansing.

One need not pause to consider whether the wine was fermented; this was not an issue relevant to the original setting, neither does the author defend the action of Jesus or indicate that the people were drunk. However, the presence of wine in the narrative is important. Wine was identified as a gift from God that brought joy and pleasure;[53] indeed, Sirach 31.27–28 writes, 'it has been created to make men glad'. The lesson offered by John

---

[53] Judg. 9.13; Eccles. 9.7; Ps. 104.15.

relates to being transformed, not being intoxicated. Wine was associated with prophesied events when God would revisit his people (Hos. 14.7), abundance of wine being indicative of God's restoration of their fortunes in a messianic age,[54] whereas an absence of wine was viewed as evidence that God had abandoned his people (Isa. 16.10; 24.7–11). The references to wine therefore symbolically reflect the joy and blessings associated with God's presence and blessing. The statement of Mary, 'They have no wine', gains new pathos if it may be taken to indicate the spiritual poverty of Judaism.

The lavish quantity and quality of the wine provided by Jesus is also significant. Jesus provides much wine and the best wine. That the servants filled the jars 'to the brim' indicates the amount of wine that Jesus provided. The fact that the jars were filled with water makes the words 'to the brim' redundant. However, John is keen that the readers recognize the lavish nature of the provision of so much wine by Jesus. The testing of the wine by the steward resulted in his astonishment as to its quality. Such extravagance is a feature of Jesus' ministry in John,[55] in his life (12.3) and his death (19.39). The one who gives a large quantity of wine (2.6) is also the one who will give the Spirit without measure (3.34); the one who is full of grace (1.14) and joy (3.29) gives graciously from his resources.

John does not explore the response of the bridegroom, who was apparently oblivious to this incident, nor the impact of the wine on the guests; no further conversation is needed between Mary and Jesus and no clarificatory sermon is needed by Jesus. It is sufficient for John to identify the miracle as the first of Jesus' signs. However, to assume that the sign is merely to point to Jesus as a miracle-worker underestimates the literary craftsmanship of the author whose desire is to point the reader to a much higher status for Jesus, who unilaterally and miraculously provides an excess of the best wine, reminiscent of the action of God.

It is with these issues in mind that it is possible to understand why John chooses to place this particular miracle first. It encapsulated central features of the mission of Jesus that was to replace a divinely initiated mode of relating to God with the provision of a new one. In this miracle, the disciples were provided with an opportunity to encounter the glory of Jesus, resulting in their believing in him to a greater degree than before the wedding.

---

[54] Isa. 25.6; 29.17; Jer. 31.5; Hos. 14.7; Joel 2.22, 24; 3.18; 4.18; Amos 9.13–15; *1 Enoch* 10.19; Baruch 29.5.
[55] 6.13, the excess of leftover food; 7.38, the 'rivers' of living water, referring to the Spirit; 10.10, abundant life; 14.2, the 'many' rooms being prepared for believers; 14.12, the potential of 'greater' works made available to his followers; 14.13, 14 (15.7), the comprehensive availability of resources in response to prayer to Jesus; 15.8, the ability to bear much fruit; 15.11; 16.24; 17.3, full joy; 21.8, 11, the full net of 153 fish caught miraculously.

The miraculous catch of fish (21.1–14)

Table 7.5 A miraculous catch of fish – the literary context

	John
Jesus is resurrected and meets Mary Magdalene	20.1–18
Jesus appears before the disciples and gives the Spirit	20.19–25
Jesus appears to Thomas	20.26–29
Jesus achieved many signs	20.30–31
Jesus provides a miraculous catch of fish	**21.1–14**
Jesus commissions Peter	21.15–23
John's conclusion	21.24–25

This final sign occurs on the third occasion of Jesus meeting the disciples after his resurrection (21.14) (see Table 7.5), John identifying it as an occasion in which he 'revealed himself' (21.1, 14). This is more than simply appearing to them in the flesh, for in it he manifested (*ephanerōsen*) his glory; in 2.11, the same word is used to refer to Jesus revealing himself through the miracle of changing water into wine.

On the first occasion when Jesus revealed himself to his disciples, he gave them peace (20.19); a commission similar to his own from the Father (20.21); the Holy Spirit (20.22) and the authority to forgive sins (20.23). On the second occasion (20.26), he demonstrated the value of a sign to enable belief, when he encouraged doubting Thomas to elevate his perception of Jesus by touching his wounds; as a result, his reticence to believe was exchanged for certainty (20.28).

On this, the third occasion, John provides a final miracle of Jesus, performed exclusively for his disciples, that will validate him yet again in their estimation and affirm his desire to provide lavishly for them. It commences with them not realizing that Jesus was the man advising them. However, the miraculous catch of fish acts as a sign to his identity, resulting in Peter (21.7), and the others (21.12), realizing who Jesus was and determining to be where he was.

Their obedience to his command results in a significant catch of fish (14.15–24; 15.10–11).[56] Whether or not there was symbolic value in the number 153,[57] the plentiful nature of the catch replicates the bountiful nature of Jesus' provision expressed earlier with regard to the wine at Cana

---

[56] *Test. Zeb.* 6.6 refers to an abundant catch of fish which was the sign of the favour of God.

[57] Von Wahlde (U. C., *The Gospel and Letters of John, Vol. 2.* Eerdmans, Grand Rapids, p. 883) provides a list of some of the optional interpretations for the fact that it was 153 fish that were caught, including the speculative suggestion, of Jerome (in his commentary on Ezek. 47.6–12), that it was

and the bread and fish for the thousands, with food left over; they did not even need fish for breakfast as Jesus already had taken care of that, cooking fish for them, giving it to them with bread (21.9, 13).

John recognizes that it is Jesus, and Peter precedes the boat in reaching Jesus. Even more importantly, thereafter, each of them recognizes that 'it was the Lord' (21.12),[58] and Jesus commissions Peter, who appears to be representative of them all (21.15–23). Those who are commissioned by 'the Lord' are expected to follow him (21.22) and to fulfil their commissions wholeheartedly (21.15–17), sacrificially (21.18–19) and single-mindedly (21.21–23).

At the same time, the one who commissions his followers is presented as doing so after he has miraculously provided for them. The implication is obvious – the one who calls people into service is able to facilitate them in their endeavours. The Gospel has come to a fitting conclusion, the emphasis being on the readers being requested to respond to its message that commenced, in 1.1, with a regal presentation of its subject, who has been manifested throughout in an increasing revelation of grandeur. He is worthy of their obedience, service and worship.

---

thought to reflect all the different types of fish in the sea. Augustine noted that it was the sum of the numbers 1–17, presentable in a triangular form (as also 666); Michaels (*The Gospel of John.* pp. 1037–9) offers the notion that it may reflect the truth that as none of the fish were lost, so also Jesus will never lose those who are his (6.39; 10.28–29; 17.12; 18.9). Keener (*Gospel of John, Vol. 2.* p. 1231) speculates that 153 is the numerical value of 'children of God' in Hebrew; other suggestions based on gematria are also offered, the creativity of the proponents seeming to know no bounds.

[58] This is the first occasion in the Gospel that Jesus is referred to as 'Lord' by Peter (hereafter in 21.15, 16, 17; by John, 13.25; 21.20). Here, he acknowledges that Jesus is the Lord, not merely as a respectful term, but probably with an association of divinity (also 20.18, 25; 21.12).

Select bibliography and further reading

Achtemeier, P. J., 'Jesus and the Disciples as Miracle Workers in the Apocryphal New Testament', in *Aspects of Religious Propaganda in Judaism and Early Christianity*. (ed.) Fiorenza, E. S., University of Notre Dame Press, Notre Dame, 1976, pp. 149–86.

Achtemeier, P. J., '"And He Followed Him": Miracles and Discipleship in Mark 10.46–52', *Semeia*. 11, 1978, pp. 115–45.

Achtemeier, P. J., 'The Lucan Perspective on the Miracles of Jesus: A Preliminary Sketch', in *Perspectives on Luke Acts*. (ed.) Talbert, C. H., ABPR, Danville, 1978, pp. 550–65.

Alana, O. E., 'Jesus' Healing Miracles: A Sign of His Loving Compassion for Humanity', *AfricEcclRev*. 42.3–4, 2000, pp. 106–13.

Aleshire, S. B., *Asklepios at Athens: Epigraphic and Prosopographic Essays on the Athenian Cults*. J. C. Gieben, Amsterdam, 1991.

Alison, J. 'The Man Blind from Birth and the Subversions of Sin. Some Questions about Fundamental Morals', *Theology and Sexuality*. 7, 1997, pp. 83–102.

Allen, E. A., 'What is the Church's Healing Ministry? Biblical and Global Perspectives', *IRM*. 90. 356–7, 2001, pp. 46–54.

Anderson, H., *The Gospel of Mark*. Oliphants, London, 1976.

Applebaum, S., 'Psychoanalytic Therapy: A Subset of Healing', *Psychotherapy*. 25.2, 1988, pp. 202–13.

Armerding, C., 'The Marriage in Cana', *BibS*. 118, 1961, pp. 320–6.

Asamoah-Gyadu, J. K., 'Mission to "Set the Captives Fee": Healing, Deliverance, and Generational Curses in Ghanaian Pentecostalism', *IRM*. 93.370–1, 2004, pp. 389–406.

Aubin, M., 'Beobachtungen zur Magie im Neuen Testament', *ZNW*. 4.7, 2001, pp. 16–24.

Aune, D. E., 'Magic in Early Christianity', in *Aufstieg und Niedergang der roemischen Welt*. (ed.) Hasse, W., de Gruyter, Berlin, 1980, pp. 507–57.

Aus, R. D., *Feeding the Five Thousand: Studies in the Judaic Background of Mark 6.30–44 par. and John 6.1–15*. University Press of America, Lanham, 2010.

Avalos, H., *Illness and Health Care in the Ancient Near East*. Harvard Semitic Museum Publications, Atlanta, 1975.

Bailey, K. E., *Jesus through Middle Eastern Eyes*. SPCK, London, 2008.

Bailey, K. M., *Divine Healing: The Children's Bread*. Christian Publs., Camp Hill, 1977.

Baldwin, R., *Healing and Wholeness*. Word, Milton Keynes, 1988.

Bammel, E., 'The Feeding of the Multitude', in *Jesus and the Politics of His Day*. (eds) Bammel, E., Moule, C. F. D., Cambridge University Press, Cambridge, 1984, pp. 211– 40.

Barker, M., 'The Time Is Fulfilled: Jesus and Jubilee', *SJT*. 53.1, 2000, pp. 22–32.

Barnett, P. W., 'The Feeding of the Multitude in Mark/John 6', in *Gospel Perspectives, Vol. 6: The Miracles of Jesus*. (eds) Wenham, D. and Blomberg, C. L., JSOT Press, Sheffield, 1986, pp. 273–93.

Barrett, C. K., *The Gospel According to St John*. SPCK, London, 1978.

Baskin, J. R., *Midrashic Women: Formations of the Feminine in Rabbinic Literature*. Brandeis University Press, Brandeis, 2002.

Basset, L., 'La culpabilité, paralysie du coeur: Reinterpretation du récit de la guérison du paralysé (Lc. 5.17–26)', *ETR*. 71.3, 1996, pp. 331–7.

Bastin, M., 'Jesus Worked Miracles', *LV*. 39.2, 1984, pp. 131–9.

Batto, B. F., 'Curse', in *Dictionary of Deities and Demons in the Bible*. (eds) van der Toorn, K., Becking, B., van der Horst, P. W., Brill, Leiden, 1995, pp. 398–404.

Bauckham, R., 'The Coin in the Fish's Mouth', in *Gospel Perspectives, Vol. 6: The Miracles of Jesus*. (eds) Wenham, D. and Blomberg, C. L., JSOT Press, Sheffield, 1986, pp. 219–252.

Bauckham, R., *Jesus and the Eyewitnesses: The Gospels as Eyewitness Testimony*. Eerdmans, Grand Rapids, 2006.

Baxter, W, 'Healing and the "Son of David": Matthew's Warrant', *NovT*. 98.1, 2006, pp. 36–50.

Beasley-Murray, G. R., *Word Biblical Themes. John*. Word, Waco, 1989.

Beasley-Murray, G. R., *John*. Word, Waco, 1991.

Beernaert, P. M., 'Jesus controverse: Structure et théologie de Mark 2, 1–3, 6', *NRT*. 95, 1973, pp. 129–39.

Beernaert, P. M., 'Jesus Christ and Health', *LV*. 41.4, 1986, pp. 35–48.

Bernadaki-Aldous, E., 'Blindness as Ignorance: Seeing as Light, Truth, Moral Goodness', in *Blindness in a Culture of Light*. Peter Lang, New York, 1990.

Betz, H. D., 'The Cleansing of the Ten Lepers (Luke 17.11–19)', *JBL*. 90, 1971, pp. 314–28.

Betz, H. D., *The Greek Magical Papyri in Translation, Including the Demotic Spells, Vol. 1: Texts*. University of Chicago Press, Chicago, 1986.

Blackburn, B. L., *Theios Aner and the Markan Miracle Traditions: A Critique of the Theios Aner Concept as an Interpretative Background of the Miracle Traditions*. Mohr Siebeck, Tübingen, 1990.

Blackburn, B. L., 'Miracles and Miracle Stories', in *Dictionary of Jesus and the Gospels*. (eds) Green, J. B., McKnight, S., Marshall, I. H., IVP, Leicester, 1992, pp. 549–60.

Blackburn, B. L., 'The Miracles of Jesus', in *Studying the Historical Jesus*. (eds) Chilton, B., Evans, C. A., Brill, Leiden, 1994, pp. 353–94.

Blackburn, B. L., 'The Miracles of Jesus', *The Cambridge Companion to Miracles*. Cambridge University Press, Cambridge, 2011, pp. 113–30.

Blass, F., Debrunner, A., Funk, R. W., *A Greek Grammar of the New Testament and other Early Christian Literature*. University of Chicago Press, Chicago.

Bligh, J., 'Signs and Wonders: Contemplating the Miracles of the Gospels', *The Way.* 11, 1971, pp. 44–53.

Bligh, J., 'Four Stories in St. John: The Man Born Blind', *HeyJ.* 7, 1996, pp. 129–44.

Blomberg, C. L., 'The Miracles as Parables', in *Gospel Perspectives, Vol. 6: The Miracles of Jesus.* (eds) Wenham, D. and Blomberg, C. L., JSOT Press, Sheffield, 1986, pp. 327–59.

Blomberg, C. L., *Matthew.* Broadman, Nashville, 1992.

Blomberg, C. L., 'Your Faith Has Made You Whole', in *Jesus of Nazareth Lord and Christ.* (eds) Green, J. B., Turner, M., Eerdmans, Grand Rapids, 1994, pp. 75–93.

Blomberg, C. L., *The Historical Reliability of John's Gospel.* IVP, Leicester, 2001.

Blue, K., *Authority to Heal.* InterVarsity Press, Downers Grove, 1987.

Blythin, I., 'Magic and Methodology', *Numen.* 17/18, 1969/70, pp. 45–53.

Bock, D. L., *Luke 1.1–9.50.* Baker, Grand Rapids, 1994.

Bock, D. L., *Luke 9.51–24.53.* Baker, Grand Rapids, 1996.

Bock, D. L., *Studying the Historical Jesus: A Guide to Sources and Methods.* Baker Academic, Grand Rapids, 2002.

Bohak, G., *Ancient Jewish Magic. A History.* Cambridge University Press, Cambridge, 2011.

Bokovay, W. K., 'The Relationship of Physical Healing to the Atonement', *Didaskalia.* 3, 1991, pp. 24–39.

Bonneau, N., 'Suspense in Mark 5.21–43', *Theoforum.* 36.2, 2005, pp. 131–54.

Bonner, C., 'Traces of Thaumaturgic Technique in the Miracles', *HTR.* 20, 1927, pp. 171–81.

Boobyer, G. H., 'Mark 2.10a and the Interpretation of the Healing of the Paralytic', *HTR.* 47, 1954, pp. 115–20.

Borg, M., *Jesus in Contemporary Scholarship.* Trinity International Press, Valley Forge, 1994.

Borgen, P., 'Miracles of Healing in the New Testament', *ST.* 35.2, 1981, pp. 91–106.

Borobio, D., 'An Inquiry into Healing Anointing in the Early Church', *Concilium.* April 1991, pp. 37–49.

Botha, J. E., 'The Meaning of *pisteuo* in the Greek New Testament: A Semitic-Lexicographical Study', *Neotestimentica.* 21.2, 1987, pp. 225–40.

Bourguignon, E., *Possession.* Chandler and Sharp, San Francisco, 1976.

Brady, J., 'The Role of Miracle Working as Authentication of Jesus as "The Son of God"', *Churchman.* 103.1, 1989, pp. 32–9.

Branscomb, H., 'Mark 2.5, "Son Thy Sins Are Forgiven"', *JBL.* 53, 1934, pp. 53–60.

Brawley, R. L. *Luke-Acts and the Jews: Conflict, Apology and Conciliation.* Scholars Press, Atlanta, 1987.

Bretherton, L., 'Pneumatology, Healing and Political Power: Sketching a Pentecostal Political Theology', in *The Holy Spirit in the World Today.* (ed.) Williams, J., Alpha, London, 2011, pp. 130–50.

Broadhead, E. K., 'Christology as Polemic and Apologetic: The Priestly Portrait of Jesus in the Gospel of Mark', *JSNT.* 47, 1992, pp. 24–32.

Broadhead, E. K., 'Mark 1,44: The Witness of the Leper', *ZNW*. 83, 1992, pp. 257–65.

Broadhead, E. K., 'Echoes of an Exorcism in the Fourth Gospel?', *ZNW*. 86.1–2, 1995, pp. 111–19.

Brodie, T. L., *The Gospel According to John: A Literary and Theological Commentary*. Oxford University Press, Oxford, 1993.

Brooking, T. A., 'Luke's Use of Mark as Paraphrasis: Its Effects on Characterisation in the "Healing of Blind Bartimaeus" Pericope (Mark 10.46–52//Luke 18.35–43)', *JSNT*. 34.1, 2011, pp. 70–89.

Brown, C., *Miracles and the Critical Mind*. Eerdmans, Grand Rapids, 1984.

Brown, M. L., *Israel's Divine Healer*. Paternoster Press, Carlisle, 1995.

Brown, R., 'The Gospel Miracles', in *The Bible in Current Catholic Thought*. (ed.) McKenzie, J. L., Herder and Herder, New York, 1962, pp. 18–26.

Brown, R., *The Gospel According to John, Vol. 1*. Geoffrey Chapman, London, 1971.

Browne, S. G., *Leprosy in the Bible*. Christian Medical Fellowship, London, 1970.

Bruce, P., 'John 5.1–18: The Healing at the Pool: Some Narrative, Socio-Historical and Ethical Issues', *Neotestamentica*. 39.1, 2005, pp. 39–56.

Bruner, F. D., *Matthew: A Commentary, Vol. 1*. Word, Dallas, 1987.

Bruner, F. D., *The Christbook: Matthew 1–12*. Eerdmans, Grand Rapids, 2007.

Bryan, S. M., 'Power in the Pool: The Healing of the Man at Bethesda and Jesus' Violation of the Sabbath (Jn. 5.1–18)', *TynBul*. 54.2, 2003, pp. 7–22.

Bryce, D., 'Sailors, Seismologists and Missionaries: Matthew 8.23–27', *Lutheran Theological Journal*. 1, 2002, pp. 2–12.

Buck, E., 'Healing in the New Testament', *Consensus*. 17.2, 1991, pp. 63–77.

Bultmann, R., *The History of the Synoptic Tradition*. Harper & Row, New York, 1963.

Bultmann, R., *The Gospel of John*. Westminster Press, Philadelphia, 1971.

Burger, C., 'Jesu Taten nach Matthaeus 8, 9', *ZTK*. 70, 1973, pp. 272–87.

Burkett, D., *The Son of Man in the Gospel of John*. JSOT Press, Sheffield, 1991.

Burkill, T. A., 'The Historical Development of the Story of the Syro-phoenician Woman (Mark 7.24–31)', *NovT*. 9, 1967, pp. 161–77.

Cabannis, A., 'A Fresh Exegesis of Mk. 2.1–12', *Interpretation*. 11, 1957, pp. 324–7.

Caird, G. B., *The Gospel of Luke*. Penguin, Harmondsworth, 1963.

Calestro, K. M., 'Psychotherapy, Faith Healing and Suggestion', *IJP*. 10.2, 1972, pp. 83–113.

Camery-Hoggatt, J., *Irony in Mark's Gospel*. Cambridge University Press, Cambridge, 1992.

Capps, D., *Jesus the Village Psychiatrist*. John Knox Press, London, 2008.

Carlson, P. K., 'A Healing Ministry in the Church Today.' DMin, Fuller Theological Seminary, 1992.

Carroll, J. T., 'Sickness and Healing in the New Testament Gospels', *Interpretation*. 49.2, 1995, pp. 130–42.

Carson, D. A., *The Gospel According to John*. IVP, Leicester, 1991.

Cave, C. H., 'The Obedience of Unclean Spirits', *NTS*. 11, 1965, pp. 93–7.

Cave, C. H., 'The Leper: Mk. 1.40–45', *NTS*. 25, 1978, pp. 245–50.

Chae, Y. S., *Jesus as the Eschatological Davidic Shepherd*. Mohr Siebeck, Tübingen, 2006.

Charlesworth, J. H., 'Solomon and Jesus: The Son of David in Ante-Markan Traditions (Mark 10.47)', in *Biblical and Humane*. (eds) Elder, L. B., Barr, D. L., Malbon, E. S., Scholars Press, Atlanta, 1996, pp. 125–51.

Charlesworth, J. H., 'The Son of David: Solomon and Jesus (Mark 10.47)', in *The New Testament and Hellenistic Judaism*. (eds) Borgen, P., Giversen, S., Hendrickson, Peabody, 1997, pp. 72–87.

Chilton, B., 'Jesus ben David: Reflections on the Davidssohnfrage', *JSNT*. 14, 1982, pp. 88–112.

Chirban, J. T., 'Healing and Spirituality', *PP*. 40.4, 1992, pp. 235–44.

Comber, J. A., 'The Verb 'therapeuo' in Matthew's Gospel', *JBL*. 97, Sept. 1978, pp. 431–4.

Cotter, W. J., *Miracles in Graeco-Roman Antiquity*. Routledge, London, 1999.

Cotter, W. J., *The Christ of the Miracle Stories: Portrait through Encounter*. Baker, Grand Rapids, 2010.

Craffert, P. F., *The Life of a Galilean Shaman: Jesus of Nazareth in Anthropological-Historical Perspective*. Cascade Books, Eugene, 2008.

Craghan, J., 'The Gerasene Demoniac', *CBQ*. 30, 1968, pp. 522–36.

Craig, W. L., 'The Problem of Miracles: A Historical and Philosophical Perspective', in *Gospel Perspectives, Vol. 6: The Miracles of Jesus*. (eds) Wenham, D. and Blomberg, C. L., JSOT Press, Sheffield, 1986, pp. 9–48.

Cranfield, C. E. B., 'St. Mark 9.14–29', *SJT*. 3, 1950, pp. 65–71.

Cranfield, C. E. B., *The Gospel According to Mark*. Cambridge University Press, Cambridge, 1959.

Crossan, J. D., *The Historical Jesus: The Life of a Mediterranean Peasant*. T. & T. Clark, Edinburgh, 1991.

Crowlesmith, J. (ed.), *Religion and Medicine*. Epworth Press, London, 1962.

Cummings, J., 'The Tassel of His Cloak: Mark, Luke, Matthew – and Zechariah', *SB*. 2, 1978, pp. 47–61.

Cunningham, S., 'The Healing of the Deaf and Dumb Man (Mark 7.31–37)', *AJET*. 9.2, 1990, pp. 14–22.

D'Angelo, M. R., 'Gender and Power in the Gospel of Mark: The Daughter of Jairus and the Hemorrhaging Woman', *SBL Papers*. 1994.

Daunton-Fear, A., 'Deliverance and Exorcism in the Early Church', in *Exorcism and Deliverance: Multi-disciplinary Studies*. (eds) Kay, W. K., Parry, R., Paternoster Press, Milton Keynes, 2011, pp. 69–85.

Davey, F. N., 'Healing in the New Testament', in *The Miracles and the Resurrection*. SPCK, London, 1964, pp. 54–61.

Davids, P., 'A Biblical View of the Relationship of Sin and the Fruits of Sin', in *The Kingdom and the Power*. (eds) Greig, G. S. and Springer, K., Regal, Ventura, 1995, pp. 111–32.

Davies, M., *Rhetoric and Reference in the Fourth Gospel*. JSOT Press, Sheffield, 1992.

Davies, M., *Matthew*. JSOT Press, Sheffield, 1993.

Davies, M. L., 'Levitical Leprosy: Uncleanness and the Psyche', *ExpTim*. 99.5, 1988, pp. 136–9.

Davies, S., *Jesus the Healer*. SCM, London, 1995.

Davies, T. W., *Magic, Divination and Demonology*. Ktav, New York, 1969.

Davies, W. D. and Allison, D. C., *Matthew 8–18*. T. & T. Clark, London, 1991.

Davis, E., 'Biblical Inscriptions on Hebrew Medical Amulets', *Koroth*. 8.5–6, 1982, pp. 185–8.

Davis, S. T., 'The Miracle at Cana: A Philosopher's Perspective' in *Gospel Perspectives, Vol. 6: The Miracles of Jesus*. (eds) Wenham, D. and Blomberg, C. L., JSOT Press, Sheffield, 1986, pp. 419–42.

Dawson, A., *Healing, Weakness and Power: Perspectives on Healing in the Writings of Mark, Luke and Paul*. Paternoster Press, Milton Keynes, 2008.

Dawson, G. G., *Healing: Pagan and Christian*. SPCK, London, 1935.

Day, P., *An Adversary in Heaven: Satan in the Hebrew Bible*. Scholars Press, Atlanta, 1988.

Derrett, J. D. M., 'Law in the New Testament: The Syrophoenician Woman and the Centurion of Capernaum', *NovT*. 15.3, 1973, pp. 161–86.

Derrett, J. D. M., 'Contributions to the Study of the Gerasene Demoniac', *JSNT*. 3, 1979, pp. 2–17.

Derrett, J. D. M., 'Mark's Technique: The Haemorrhaging Woman and Jairus', *Biblica*. 63, 1982, pp. 474–505.

Derrett, J. D. M., 'Christ and the Power of Choice (Mark 3.1–6), *Biblica*. 65.2, 1984, pp. 168–88.

Derrett, J. D. M., 'Positive Perspectives on Two Lucan Miracles', *Downside Review*. 104, 1986, pp. 272–87.

Derrett, J. D. M., 'Getting on Top of a Demon (Lk. 4.39)', *EvQ*. 65.2, 1993, pp. 99–109.

Derrett, J. D. M., 'John 9.6 Read with Isaiah 6.10; 20.9', *EvQ*. 66.3, 1994, pp. 251–4.

Derrett, J. D. M., 'Gratitude and the Ten Lepers (Luke 17, 11–19)', *Downside Review*. 113.391, 1995, pp. 79–95.

Dewey, J., 'The Literary Structure of the Controversy Stories in Mark 2.1–3.6', *JBL*. 92, 1973, pp. 394–401.

Di Lella, A. A., 'Health and Healing in Tobit', *BibT*. 37.2, 1999, pp. 69–73.

Dickinson, R., *God Does Heal Today*. Paternoster Press, Carlisle, 1995.

Dore, J., 'La signification des miracles de Jesus', *RevSciRel*. 74.3, 2000, pp. 275–91.

Dormandy, R., 'The Expulsion of Legion: A Political Reading of Mark 5.1–20, *ExpTim*. 111.10, 2000, pp. 335–7.

Doughty, D. J., 'The Authority of the Son of Man', *ZNW*. 74, 1983, pp. 161–81.

Dowd, S. E., *Prayer, Power and the Problem of Suffering*. Scholars Press, Atlanta, 1988.

Dragutinovic, P., 'The First Miracle of the Son of God in the Gospel of Mark (Mark 1.21–28): A Contribution to Mark's Christology', *Sacra Scriptura*. 8.23, 2010, pp. 185–201.

Duling, D. C., 'Solomon, Exorcism and the Son of David', *HTR*. 68, 1975, pp. 235–52.

Duling, D. C., 'The Therapeutic Son of David: An Element in Matthew's Christological Apologetic', *NTS*. 24.3, 1978, pp. 393–9.

Duling, D. C., 'Matthew's Plural Significant "Son of David" in Social Science Perspective: Kinship, Kingship, Magic, and Miracle', *BTB*. 22, 1992, pp. 99–116.

Dunn, J. D. G., *Jesus and the Spirit*. SCM, London, 1975.

Dunn, J. D. G., and Twelftree, G. H., 'Demon-Possession and Exorcism in the New Testament', *Churchman*. 94, 1980, pp. 210–25.

Dupont, J., 'Le paralytique pardonné', *NRT*, 82, 1960, pp. 940–58.

Dupont, J., 'Blind Bartimaeus (Mk. 10.46–52)', *TD*. 33.2, 1986, pp. 223–8.

Dupont-Sommer, A., 'Exorcismes et guérison and les escrits de Qumran', *Congress Volume, Oxford 1959*. (ed.) Anderson, G. W., Brill, Leiden, 1960.

Dwyer, T., 'The Motif of Wonder in the Gospel of Mark', *JSNT*. 57, 1995, pp. 49–59.

Dwyer, T., *The Motif of Wonder in the Gospel of Mark*. Continuum, Sheffield, 1996.

Edelstein, L. and Edelstein, E. J., *Asclepius: A Collection and Interpretation of the Testimonies*. 2 vols, Hopkins, Baltimore, 1945.

Edwards, J. R., *The Gospel According to Mark*. Eerdmans, Grand Rapids, 2002.

Edwards, M., *John*. Blackwell, Oxford, 2004.

Ellenburg, B. D., 'A Review of Selected Narrative-Critical Conventions in Mark's Use of Miracle Material', *JETS*. 38.2, 1995, pp. 171–80.

Elliott, J. K., 'The Conclusion of the Pericope of the Healing of the Leper and Mark 1.45', *JTS*. 22, 1971, pp. 153–7.

Elliott, J. K., 'The Healing of the Leper in the Synoptic Parallels', *TZ*. 34, 1978, pp. 175–84.

Evans, C. A., 'Jesus and Apollonius of Tyana', in *Jesus and His Contemporaries*. (ed.) Evans, C. A., Brill, Leiden, 1995, pp. 245–50.

Evans, C. A., 'Jesus and Jewish Miracle Stories', in *Jesus and His Contemporaries*. (ed.) Evans, C. A., Brill, Leiden, 1995, pp. 213–43.

Evans, C. A., *Mark 8.27–16.20*. Word, Waco, 2001.

Eve, E., *The Jewish Context of Jesus' Miracles*. Sheffield Academic Press, Sheffield, 2002.

Eve, E., *The Healer from Nazareth: Jesus' Miracles in Historical Context*. SPCK, London. 2009.

Fee, G. D., 'On the Inauthenticity of John 5.3b–4', *EvQ*. 54, 1982, pp. 207–18.

Ferguson, E., *Demonology of the Early Christian World*. Edwin Mellen Press, Lampeter, 1984.

Fiorenza, E. S., 'Luke 13.10–17: Interpretation for Liberation and Transformation', *Theology Digest*. 36, 1989, pp. 303–19.

Fitch, W. O., 'The Interpretation of St. John 5.6', *SE.* 4, 1968, pp. 194–7.

Fitzmyer, J. A., *The Gospel According to Luke: I–IX.* Yale University Press, Yale, 1982.

Fossum, J., 'Understanding Jesus' Miracles', *BR.* 10 Feb. 1994, pp. 16–23, 50.

France, R. T., 'The Worship of Jesus', in *Christ the Lord.* (ed.) Rowdon, H. H., IVP, Leicester, 1982, pp. 17–36.

France, R. T., *Matthew.* IVP, Leicester, 1985.

France, R. T., *The Gospel of Mark.* Eerdmans, Grand Rapids, 2002.

Frayer-Griggs, D., 'Spittle, Clay, and Creation in John 9.6 and Some Dead Sea Scrolls', *JBL.* 3, 2013, pp. 659–70.

Freeman, D. L., Abrams, J. Z., *Illness and Health in the Jewish Tradition.* Jewish Publication Society, Philadelphia, 1999.

Fridrichsen, A., *The Problem of Miracle in Primitive Christianity.* Augsburg, Minneapolis, 1972.

Fuller, R. H., *Interpreting the Miracles.* SCM, London, 1963.

Gaiser, F. J., '"Your Faith Has Made You Well": Healing and Salvation in Luke 17.12–19', *Word World.* 16.3, 1996, pp. 291–301.

Gaiser, F. J., *Healing in the Bible: Theological Insight for Christian Ministry.* Baker, Grand Rapids, 2010.

Galipeau, S. A., *Transforming Body and Soul: Therapeutic Wisdom in the Gospel Healing Stories.* Paulist Press, New York, 1990.

Garland, D. E., 'I Am the Lord Your Healer: Mark 1.21–2.12', *RevExp.* 85.2, 1988, pp. 327–43.

Garland, D. E., *Reading Matthew: A Literary and Theological Commentary on the First Gospel.* Crossroad, New York, 1993.

Garland, R., 'Miracle in the Greek and Roman World', *The Cambridge Companion to Miracles.* (ed.) Twelftree, G. H., Cambridge University Press, Cambridge, 2011, pp. 73–94.

Garrett, S. R., *The Demise of the Devil.* Fortress Press, Minneapolis, 1989.

Garrett, S. R., 'Light on a Dark Subject and Vice Versa: Magic and Magicians in the New Testament', in *Religion, Science and Magic: In Conflict and in Concert.* (eds) Neusner, J., Frerichs, E. S., McCracken Flesher, V. P., Oxford University Press, Minneapolis, 1989, pp. 142–65.

Gerharddson, B., *The Mighty Acts of Jesus According to Matthew.* (tr.) R. Dewsnap, CWK Gleerup, Lund, 1975.

Gibbs, J. M., 'Purpose and Pattern in Matthew's Use of the Title "Son of David"', *NTS.* 10, 1963–4, pp. 446–64.

Glasswell, M. E., 'The Use of Miracles in the Markan Gospel', in *Miracles.* (ed.) Moule, C. F. D., Mowbrays, London, 1965, pp. 151–62.

Gnilka, J., *Jesus of Nazareth.* Hendrickson, Peabody, 1997.

Goldingay, J. (ed.), *Signs, Wonders and Healing.* IVP, Leicester, 1989.

Gould, E. P., *The Gospel According to Mark.* T. & T. Clark, Edinburgh, 1897.

Grant, R. M., *Miracle and Natural Law in Graeco-Roman and Early Christian Thought.* North Holland Publ. Co., Amsterdam, 1952.

Green, J. B., 'Jesus and a Daughter of Abraham (Luke 13.10–17): Test Case for a Lucan Perspective on Jesus' Miracles', *CBQ*. 51, 1989, pp. 643–54.

Green, J. B., *The Theology of the Gospel of Luke*. Cambridge University Press, Cambridge, 1995.

Green, J. B., *The Gospel of Luke*. Eerdmans, Grand Rapids, 1997.

Greig, G. S. and Springer, K. (eds), *The Kingdom and the Power*. Regal, Ventura, 1995.

Grindheim, S., 'Everything Is Possible for One Who Believes', *TrinJourn*. 26.1, 2005, pp. 11–17.

Gross, E. N., *Miracles, Demons and Spiritual Warfare*. Baker, Grand Rapids, 1990.

Guelich, R. A., *Mark 1–8.26*. Word, Dallas, 1989.

Guijarro, S., 'Healing Stories and Medical Anthropology: A Reading of Mark 10.46–52', *BTB*. 30.3, 2000, pp. 102–12.

Gundry, R. H., *Matthew: A Commentary on His Handbook for a Mixed Church under Persecution*. Eerdmans, Grand Rapids, 1982, 1994.

Gundry, R. H., *Mark: A Commentary on His Apology for the Cross*. Eerdmans, Grand Rapids, 1993.

Guthrie, G. H. and Duvall, J. S. *Biblical Greek Exegesis*. Zondervan, Grand Rapids, 1998.

Haber, S., 'A Woman's Touch: Feminist Encounters with the Hemorrhaging Woman in Mark 5.24–34', *JSNT*. 26.2, 2003, pp. 171–92.

Haenchen, E., *Der Weg Jesu: Eine Erklarung des Markus-Evangeliums und der kanonischen Parallelen*. 2nd ed. de Gruyter, Berlin, 1968.

Hagner, D. A., *Matthew 1–13*. Word, Waco, 1993.

Hamm, M. D., 'Sight to the Blind: Vision as Metaphor in Luke', *Biblica*. 67, 1986, pp. 457–77.

Hamm, M. D., 'The Freeing of the Bent Woman and the Restoration of Israel: Lk. 13.10–17 as Narrative Theology', *JSNT*. 31, 1987, pp. 23–44.

Hamm, M. D., 'What the Samaritan Leper Sees: The Narrative Christology of Luke 17.11–19', *CBQ*. 56.2, 1994, pp. 273–87.

Han, K. S., 'Theology of Prayer in the Gospel of Luke', *JETS*. 43.4, December 2000, pp. 675–93.

Hankoff, L. D., 'Religious Healing in First-Century Christianity', *JP*. 19.4, Spring 1992, pp. 387–407.

Harper, M., *The Healings of Jesus*. Hodder & Stoughton, London, 1986.

Harrington, D. J., *The Gospel of Matthew*. Liturgical Press, Collegeville, 1991.

Harris, M. J., 'The Dead are Restored to Life: Miracles of Revivification in the Gospels', in *Gospel Perspectives, Vol. 6: The Miracles of Jesus*. (eds) Wenham, D. and Blomberg, C. L., JSOT Press, Sheffield, 1986, pp. 295–326.

Hawthorne, G. F., 'Faith. The Essential Ingredient of Effective Christian Ministry', in *Worship, Theology and Ministry in the Early Church*. (eds) Wilkins, M. J., Paige, T., JSOT Press, Sheffield, 1992.

Hawthorne, G. P., *The Presence and the Power*. Word, Dallas, 1991.

Hay, L. S., 'The Son of Man in Mark 2.10 and 2.28', *JBL*. 89, 1970, pp. 69–75.

Hedrick, C. W., 'Miracle Stories as Literary Compositions: The Case of Jairus' Daughter', *PRS*. 20.3, 1993, pp. 217–33.

Heil, J. P., 'Significant Aspects of the Healing Miracles in Matthew', *CBQ*. 41, 1979, pp. 274–87.

Heiligenthal, R., Wohlers, M., Riesner, R., 'Wunder im frühen Christentum – Wirklichkeit oder Propaganda?', *ZNW*. 4.7, 2001, pp. 46–58.

Held, H. J., 'Matthew as Interpreter of Miracle Stories', in *Tradition and Interpretation in Matthew*. (eds) Bornkamm, G., Barth, G., Held. H. J., T. & T. Clark, Edinburgh, 1963, pp. 246–99.

Henderson, S. W., 'Concerning the Loaves: Comprehending Incomprehension in Mark 6.45–52', *JSNT*. 83, 2001, pp. 3–26.

Hendrickx, H., *The Miracle Stories of the Synoptic Gospels*. Harper & Row, San Francisco, 1987.

Hertig, P., 'The Jubilee Mission of Jesus in the Gospel of Luke: Reversal of Fortunes', *Missiology*. 26.2, 1998, pp. 167–79.

Hiebert, D. E., *Mark: A Portrait of a Servant*. Moody, Chicago, 1974.

Hodges, Z. C., 'The Angel at Bethesda – John 5.4', *BibS*. 136, 1979, pp. 25–39.

Hoffman, D. S., 'The Historical Jesus of Ancient Belief', *JETS*. 40.4, 1997, pp. 551–62.

Hogan, L. P., *Healing in the Second Tempel (sic) Period*. Vandenhoeck & Ruprecht, Göttingen, 1992.

Holleran, J. W., 'Seeing the Light: A Narrative Reading of John 9', *Ephemerides Theologicae Lovaniensis*. 69.1, 1993, pp. 5–26; 69.4, 1993, pp. 354–82.

Hooke, S. H., 'Jesus and the Centurion: Matthew 8. 5–10', *ExpTim*. 69, 1957/8, pp. 79–80.

Hooker, M. D., *A Commentary on the Gospel According to St. Mark*. Black, London, 1991.

Hopson, R. E., 'The Role of Faith in the Psychotherapeutic Context', *JRHlth*. 31.2, Summer 1992, pp. 95–105.

Horbury, W., 'The Temple Tax', in *Jesus and the Politics of His Day*. (eds) Bammel, E., Moule, C. F. D., Cambridge University Press, Cambridge, 1984, pp. 265–86.

Horsley, G. H. R., *New Documents Illustrating Early Christianity (NDIEC)*. The Ancient History Documentary Research Centre, MacQuarie University, 1987–.

Horsley, R. A., *Jesus and the Spiral of Violence*. Harper & Row, San Francisco, 1987.

Horsley, R. A., *Hearing the Whole Story: The Politics of Plot in Mark's Gospel*. Westminster Press, Louisville, 2001.

Howard, J. K., *Disease and Healing in the New Testament: An Analysis and Interpretation*. University Press of America, New York, 2001.

Hull, J. M., *Hellenistic Magic and the Synoptic Tradition*. SCM, London, 1974.

Hultgren, A., 'The Miracle Stories of the Gospels: The Continuing Challenge for Interpreters', *WW*. 29.2, 2009, pp. 129–35.

Hurtado, L., 'Miracles . . . Pagan and Christian', *Paraclete*. 4.4, 1970, pp. 13–16.

Huskinson, L., 'Deliverance and Exorcism in Pop Culture', in *Exorcism and Deliverance: Multi-disciplinary Studies*. (eds) Kay, W. K., Parry, R., Paternoster Press, Milton Keynes, 2011, pp. 181–202.

Hutter, M., 'Ein altorientalischer Bittegestus im Mt. 9, 20–22', *ZNW*. 75, 1984, pp. 133–5.

Iverson, K. R., *Gentiles in the Gospel of Mark*. T. & T. Clark, London, 2007.

Jenkins, A. K., 'The Case of Malchus's Ear: Narrative Criticism and John 18.1–12', *ExpTim*. 112.1, October 2000, pp. 8–11.

Jeter, H. P., 'Power . . . Present to Heal', *Paraclete*. 8.1, 1974, pp. 3–6.

Johns, C. B., 'Healing and Deliverance: A Pentecostal Perspective', in *Pentecostal Movements as an Ecumenical Challenge*. (eds) Moltmann, J., Kuschel, K-J., SCM, London, 1996, pp. 45–54.

Johns, L. L. and Miller, D. B., 'The Signs as Witnesses in the Fourth Gospel: Re-examining the Evidence', *CBQ*. 56.3, 1994, pp. 519–35.

Johnson, D. H., 'Preaching the Miracle Stories of the Synoptic Gospels', *TrinJourn*. 18.1, 1997, pp. 85–97.

Johnson, E. S., 'Mark 10.46–52: Blind Bartimaeus', *CBQ*. 40.2, 1978, pp. 191–204.

Johnson, J. E., 'Mark 8.22–26: The Blind Man from Bethsaida', *NTS*. 25, 1979, pp. 370–83.

Jones, L. P., *The Symbol of Water in the Gospel of John*. Sheffield Academic Press, Sheffield, 1997.

Juel, D., *Messianic Exegesis: Christological Interpretation of the Old Testament in Early Christianity*. Fortress Press, Philadelphia, 1988.

Juel, D., *Mark*. Augsburg, Minneapolis, 1990.

Kahl, W., *New Testament Miracle Stories in Their Religious-Historical Setting*. Vandenhoeck & Ruprecht, Göttingen, 1994.

Kalin, E. R., 'Matthew 9.18–26: An Exercise in Redaction Criticism', *CurTM*. 15, 1988, pp. 39–47.

Kallas, J., *The Significance of the Synoptic Miracles*. SPCK, London, 1961.

Kay, W. K., 'Deliverance and Exorcism in Psychological Perspective', in *Exorcism and Deliverance: Multi-disciplinary Studies*. (eds) Kay, W. K., Parry, R., Paternoster Press, Milton Keynes, 2011, pp. 139–55.

Kay, W. K. and Parry, R. (eds), *Exorcism and Deliverance: Multi-disciplinary Studies*. Paternoster Press, Milton Keynes, 2011.

Kazmierski, C. R., 'Evangelist and Leper: A Socio-Cultural Study of Mark 1.40–45', *NTS*. 38.1, 1992, pp. 37–50.

Kee, H. C., 'The Terminology of Mark's Exorcism Stories', *NTS*. 14, 1967/8, pp. 232–46.

Kee, H. C., *Miracles in the Early Christian World: A Study in Socio-historical Method*. Cambridge University Press, Cambridge, 1983.

Kee, H. C., *Medicine, Miracle and Magic in New Testament Times*. Cambridge University Press, Cambridge, 1986.

Keener, C. S., *A Commentary on the Gospel of Matthew*. Eerdmans, Grand Rapids, 1999.

Keener, C. S., *Gospel of John: A Commentary*. Hendrickson, Peabody, 2003.

Keener, C. S., *The Historical Jesus of the Gospels*. Eerdmans, Grand Rapids, 2009.

Keener, C. S., *Miracles: The Credibility of the New Testament Accounts*. Baker, Grand Rapids, 2011.

Keeranleri, G., 'The Gospel of Matthew: The Mighty Deeds of Jesus', *Vidajyoti*. 69.4, 2005, pp. 293–308.

Kelhoffer, J. A., *Miracle and Mission*. Mohr Siebeck, Tübingen, 2000.

Keller, E. and M., *Miracles in Dispute*. Fortress Press, Philadelphia, 1968.

Kern-Ulmer, B., 'The Depiction of Magic in Rabbinic Texts: The Rabbinic and the Greek Concept of Magic', *JSJ*. 27.3, 1996, pp. 289–303.

Kiev, A. (ed.), *Magic, Faith and Healing: Studies in Primitive Psychiatry Today*. Free Press, New York, 1964.

Kilgallen, J. J., '"I Have Not Found Such Faith in Israel" (Luke 7,9)', *MelTheol*. 49.2, 1998, pp. 19–24.

Kilgallen, J. J., 'The Obligation to Heal (Luke 13.10–17)', *Biblica*. 82.3, 2001, pp. 402–9.

Kingsbury, J. D., 'The Title "Son of David" in Matthew's Gospel', *JBL*. 95.4, 1976, pp. 591–602.

Kingsbury, J. D., 'Observations on the "Miracle Chapters" of Matthew 8–9', *CBQ*. 40, 1978, pp. 559–73.

Kingsbury, J. D., 'The Verb *akolouthein* (to follow) as an Index of Matthew's View of His Community', *JBL*. 97, 1978, pp. 56–73.

Kingsbury, J. D., *Conflict in Luke: Jesus, Authorities, Disciples*. Fortress Press, Minneapolis, 1991.

Klauck, H-J., *The Religious Context of Early Christianity*. T. & T. Clark, Edinburgh, 2000.

Kleist, J. A., 'The Gadarene Demoniacs', *CBQ*. 9, 1947, pp. 101–05.

Klutz, T. (ed.), *Magic in the Biblical World*. T. and T. Clark, London, 2003.

Klutz, T. (ed.), *The Exorcism Stories in Luke-Acts: A Sociostylistic Reading*. Cambridge University Press, Cambridge, 2004.

Knapp, S. A., 'He Could Do No Mighty Deed There . . . Mark 6.1–6', *Proceedings*. 12, 1992, pp. 155–66.

Koch, D. A., *Die Bedeutung der Wundererzählungen für die Christologie des Markusevangeliums*. De Gruyter, Berlin, 1976.

Kostenberger, A. J., *The Missions of Jesus and the Disciples According to the Fourth Gospel*. Eerdmans, Grand Rapids 1998.

Kottek, S. S., *Medicine and Hygiene in the Works of Flavius Josephus*. Brill, New York, 1994.

Kuthirakkattel, S., *The Beginning of Jesus' Ministry According to Mark's Gospel (1,14–3,6): A Redaction Critical Study*. Pontifical Biblical Institute, Rome, 1990.

Kvalbein, H., 'The Wonders of the End-Time: Metaphoric Language in 4Q251 and the Interpretation of Matthew 11.5 *par*', *JSP*. 18, 1998, pp. 87–110.

La Grand, J., 'The First of the Miracle Stories According to Mark (1.21–28)', *CurTM*. 20.6, 1993, pp. 479–84.

Ladd, G. E., *The Gospel of the Kingdom*. Eerdmans, Grand Rapids, 1959.

Lake, K., 'EMBRIMESAMENOS and ORGISTHEIS, Mk. 1.40–45', *HTR*. 16, 1923, pp. 19–26.

Lalleman, P. J., 'Healing by a Mere Touch as a Christian Concept', *TynBul*. 48.2, 1997, pp. 355–62.

Lane, W. L., *The Gospel According to Mark*. Marshall, Morgan & Scott, London, 1974.

Larson, B., *Luke*. Word, Waco, 1984.

Larson, E. L. and B. M., 'A Philosophy of Healing from the Ministry of Jesus', *FT*. 112, 1986, pp. 67–75.

Latourelle, R., *The Miracles of Jesus and the Theology of Miracles*. Paulist Press, New York, 1988.

Leeper, E. A., 'Exorcism in Early Christianity', PhD, Duke University, 1991.

Levine Amy-Jill, 'Discharging Responsibility: Matthean Jesus, Biblical Law, and Hemorrhaging Woman', in *Treasures Old and New: Contributions to Matthean Studies*. (eds) Bauer, D. R., Powell, M. A., Scholars Press, Atlanta, 1996, pp. 394–409.

Lewis, D., *Healing: Fiction, Fantasy or Fact?* Hodder & Stoughton, London, 1989.

Leyrer, D. P., 'Matthew 15.27 – The Canaanite Woman's Great Faith', *Wisconsin Lutheran Quarterly*. 96.3, 1999, pp. 218–27.

Lindars, B., *The Gospel of John*. Oliphants, London, 1972.

Lindars, B., 'Rebuking the Spirit: A New Analysis of the Lazarus Story of John 11', *NTS*. 38.1, 1992, pp. 89–104.

Loader, W., 'Challenged at the Boundaries: A Conservative Jesus in Mark's Tradition', *JSNT*. 63, 1966, pp. 45–61.

Loader, W., 'Son of David, Blindness, Possession, and Duality in Matthew', *CBQ*. 44, 1982, pp. 570–85.

Loader, W., 'The Historical Jesus Puzzle', *Colloquium*. 29.2, 1997, pp. 131–50.

Long, W. M., *Health, Healing and God's Kingdom: New Pathways to Christian Health Ministry in Africa*. Regnum, Oxford, 2000.

Louw, J. P., *Semantics of New Testament Greek*. Scholars Press, Atlanta, 1982.

Love, S. L., 'Jesus, Healer of the Canaanite Woman's Daughter in Matthew's Gospel: A Socio-scientific Inquiry', *BTB*. 32.1, 2002, pp. 11–20.

Lucas, E., 'The Significance of Jesus' Healing Ministry', in *Christian Healing*. Lynx, London, 1997, pp. 95–9.

Luz, U., *Matthew 8–20*. Fortress Press, Minneapolis, 2001.

Ma, W., 'The Presence of Evil and Exorcism in the Old Testament', in *Exorcism and Deliverance*. (eds) Kay, W., Parry, R., Paternoster Press, Milton Keynes, 2011, pp. 27–44.

McCasland, S. V., 'The Demonic "Confession" of Jesus', *Journal of Religion*. 24, 1944, pp. 33–6.

McCaughey, T., 'Paradigms of Faith in the Gospel of St. Luke', *ITQ*. 45, 1978, pp. 177–84.

McConvery, B., 'Ben Sira's "Praise of the Physician" (Sir. 38. 1–15) in the Light of Some Hippocratic Writings', *Proceedings of the Irish Biblical Association*. 21, 1998, pp. 62–87.

McHugh, J. F., *John 1–4: A Critical and Exegetical Commentary*. T. & T. Clark, Edinburgh, 2009.

McNeil, B., 'The Raising of Lazarus', *DR*. 92, 1974, pp. 269–75.

McNeile, A. H., *The Gospel According to St. Matthew*. Baker, Grand Rapids, 1980.

Malina, B. J., Rohrbaugh, R. L., *Social-science Commentary on the Synoptic Gospels*. Fortress Press, Minneapolis, 1992.

Mann, C. S., *Mark*. Doubleday, Anchor City, 1986.

Margalioth, M. (ed.), *Sepher-ha-Razim: The Book of Mysteries*. Scholars Press, Atlanta, 1983.

Marshall, C. D., *Faith as a Theme in Mark's Narrative*. Cambridge University Press, Cambridge, 1989.

Marshall, I. H., *The Gospel of Luke: A Commentary on the Greek Text*. Paternoster Press, Exeter, 1978.

Marshall, I. H., 'Jesus as Lord: The Development of the Concept', in *Eschatology and the New Testament*. (ed.) Gloer, W. H., Hendrickson, Peabody, 1988, pp. 129–45.

Matera, F. J., 'The Incomprehension of the Disciples and Peter's Confession', *Biblica*. 70, 1989, pp. 153–72.

May, D. M., 'The Straightened Woman (Luke 13.10–17): Paradise Lost and Regained', *PRS*. 23.3, 1997, pp. 245–58.

May, E., 'For Power Went Forth from Him . . . Lk. 6.19', *CBQ*. 14, 1952, pp. 93–103.

Mead, R. T., 'The Healing of the Paralytic: A Unit?', *JBL*. 80, 1961, pp. 348–54.

Meier, J. P., *A Marginal Jew*. Doubleday, Garden City, 1991.

Melinsky, M. A. H., *Healing Miracles*. Mowbray, London, 1968.

Menken, M. J. J., 'The Source of the Quotation from Isaiah 53.4 in Matthew 8.17', *NovT*. 39, 1997, pp. 313–27.

Menzies, R. P., 'A Pentecostal Perspective on "Signs and Wonders"', *Pneuma*. 17.2, 1995, pp. 265–78.

Menzies, R. P., 'Healing in the Atonement', in *Spirit and Power: Foundations of Pentecostal Experience*. (eds) Menzies, W. W. and Menzies, R. P., Zondervan, Grand Rapids, 2000, pp. 159–70.

Merz, A. 'Jesus als Wundertäter: Konturen, Perspectiven, Deutungen', *ZNW*. 1.1, 1998, pp. 40–7.

Metzger, B. M., *A Textual Commentary on the Greek New Testament*. Deutsches Bibelgesellschaft, Stuttgart, 1994.

Meyer, P. W., 'Seeing, Signs, and Sources in the Fourth Gospel', in *The Word in This World: Essays in New Testament Exegesis and Theology*. Westminster John Knox Press, Louisville, 2004, pp. 240–53.

Michaels, J. R., *The Gospel of John*. Eerdmans, Grand Rapids, 2010, pp. 277–8.

Miranda, V. A., 'A Cristogia dos Demonios', *VoxScrip*. 10.1, 2000, pp. 3–18.

Mirro, J. A., 'Bartimaeus: The Miraculous Cure', *BibT*. 20, 1982, pp. 221–5.

Mkole, J. C. L., 'A Liberating Women's Profile in Mk. 5.25–34', *ACS*. 13.2, 1997, pp. 36–47.

Montgomery, J. W., *Demon Possession: A Medical, Historical, Anthropological and Theological Symposium*. Bethany Fellowship, Minneapolis, 1976.

Morris, L., *The Gospel According to John*. Marshall, Morgan & Scott, London, 1972.

Morris, L., *The Gospel According to Matthew*. Eerdmans, Grand Rapids, 1992.

Morton, J. G., 'Christ's Diagnosis of Disease at Bethesda', *ExpTim*. 33, 1921–2, pp. 424–6.

Moule, C. F. D. (ed.), *Miracles*. Mowbray, London, 1965.

Mounce, R. H., *Matthew*. Hendrickson, Peabody, 1991.

Mourlon, P. B., 'Jesus Christ and Health: The Testimony of the Gospels', *LV*. 41.1, 1986, pp. 35–48.

Mullins, T. Y., 'Jesus, the "Son of David"', *Andrews University Seminary Studies*. 29, 1991, pp. 117–26.

Murphy-O'Connor, J., 'Péché et communauté dans le Nouveau Testament', *RB*. 74, 1967, pp. 182–193.

Mussner, F., *The Miracles of Jesus*. (tr.) Wimmer, A., Ecclesia Press, Shannon, 1970.

Myers, C., *Binding the Strong Man: A Political Reading of Mark's Story of Jesus*. Orbis Books, Maryknoll, 1988.

Naveh, J., Shaked, S., *Amulets and Magic Bowls: Aramaic Incantations in Late Antiquity*. Magnes Press, Jerusalem, 1985.

Neirynck, F., 'The Miracle Stories in the Acts of the Apostles: An Introduction', in *Les Actes des Apôtres*. (ed.) Kremer, J., Duculot, Gembloux, 1979, pp. 169–213.

Neusner, J., 'The Idea of Purity in Ancient Judaism', *JAAR*. 43, 1975, pp. 20–31.

Neusner, J., *Purity in Rabbinic Judaism: A Systemic Account*. Scholars Press, Atlanta, 1994.

Newmyer, S., 'Climate and Health: Classical and Talmudic Perspective', *Judaism*. 33.4, 1984, pp. 426–38.

Neyrey, J. H., 'The Thematic Use of Isaiah 42.1–4 in Matthew 12', *Biblica*. 63, 1982, pp. 457–73.

Neyrey, J. H., 'The Idea of Purity in Mark's Gospel', *Semeia*. 35, 1986, pp. 91–128.

Nicklas, T., Spittler, J. E., *Credible, Incredible: The Miraculous in the Ancient Mediterranean*. Mohr Siebeck, Tübingen, 2013.

Nicol, W., *The Semeia in the Fourth Gospel*. Brill, Leiden, 1972.

Niehaus, J., 'Old Testament Foundations: Signs and Wonders in Prophetic Ministry and the Substitutionary Atonement of Isaiah 53', in *The Kingdom and the Power*, (eds) Greig, G. S. and Springer, K., Regal, Ventura, 1995, pp. 41–54.

Nolland, J., *Luke 1–9.20*. Word, Dallas, 1989.

Nolland, J., *Luke 9.21–18.34*. Word, Dallas, 1993.

Nolland, J., *Luke 18.35–24.53*. Word, Dallas, 1993.

Novakovic, L., 'Jesus as the Davidic Messiah in Matthew', *HBT*. 19.2, 1997, pp. 148–91.

Novakovic, L., 'Miracles in Second Temple and Early Rabbinic Judaism', *The Cambridge Companion to Miracles*. (ed.) Twelftree, G. H., Cambridge University Press, Cambridge, 2011, pp. 95–112.

Oegema, G. S., *The Anointed and His People: Messianic Expectations from the Maccabees to Bar Kochba*. Sheffield Academic Press, Sheffield, 1998.

Olekamma, I. U., *The Healing of Blind Bartimaeus (Mk. 10, 46–52) in the Markan Context*. Peter Lang, Frankfurt, 1999.

Onwu, N., '"Don't Mention It": Jesus' Instruction to Healed Persons', *AJBS*. 1, 1986, pp. 35–47.

Onyinah, O., 'Deliverance as a Way of Confronting Witchcraft in Modern Africa: Ghana as a Case History', *AJPS*. 5.1, 2002, pp. 107–34.

O'Toole, R. F., 'Some Exegetical Reflections on Luke 13.10–17', *Biblica*. 73, 1992, pp. 84–107.

Overman, J. A., *Church and Community in Crisis: The Gospel According to Matthew*. Trinity Press, Valley Forge, 1996.

Page, S. H. T., *Powers of Evil*. Baker, Grand Rapids, 1995.

Pain, T., 'Jesus' Healing Ministry', *HW*. 4, Oct.–Dec. 1991, pp. 32–4.

Painter, J., 'John 9 and Interpretation of the Fourth Gospel', *JSNT*. 28, 1986, pp. 31–61.

Palmer, B., *Medicine and the Bible*. Paternoster Press, Exeter, 1986.

Park, E. C., *The Mission Discourse in Matthew's Interpretation*. Mohr Siebeck, Tübingen, 1995.

Patte, D., *The Gospel According to Matthew*. Fortress Press, Philadelphia, 1987.

Paul, A., 'La guérison de l'aveugle (des aveugles) de Jericho', *FV*. 69.3, 1970, pp. 44–69.

Pearson, M., *Christian Healing*. Hodder & Stoughton, London, 1996.

Penney, J. M., *The Missionary Emphasis of Lucan Pneumatology*. Sheffield Academic Press, Sheffield, 1997.

Percy, M., *Words, Wonders and Power*. SPCK, London, 1996.

Percy, M., 'The Gospel Miracles and Modern Healing Movements', *Theology*. 99.793, Jan.–Feb., 1997, pp. 8–17.

Pesch, R., 'Jairus (Mk. 5.22/Lk. 8.41)', *BZ*. 14, 1970, pp. 152–6.

Petts, D., 'Healing and the Atonement', PhD, University of Nottingham, 1993.

Pilch, J. J., 'The Health Care System in Matthew: A Social Science Analysis', *BTB*. 16.3, 1986, pp. 102–6.

Pilch, J. J., 'Understanding Biblical Healing: Selecting an Appropriate Model', *BTB*. 18, 1988, pp. 60–6.

Pilch, J. J., 'Sickness and Healing in Luke-Acts', *BibT*, 27.1, Jan. 1989, pp. 22–7.

Pilch, J. J., 'Sickness and Long Life', *BibT*. 33, Feb. 1995, pp. 94–8.

Pilch, J. J., *Healing in the New Testament: Insights from Medical and Mediterranean Anthropology*. Augsburg Fortress, Minneapolis, 2000.

Plumer, E., 'The Absence of Exorcisms in the Fourth Gospel', *Biblica*. 78.3, 1997, pp. 350–68.

Poon, W. C. K., 'Superabundant Table Fellowship in the Kingdom: The Feeding of the Five Thousand and the Meal Motif in Luke', *ExpTim*. 114.7, 2003, pp. 224–30.

Porter, S. E., 'Discourse Analysis and New Testament Studies: An Introductory Survey', in *Discourse Analysis and Other Topics in Biblical Greek*. (eds) Porter, S. E., Carson, D. A., Sheffield Academic Press, Sheffield, 1995, pp. 14–35.

Powers, J. E., '"Your Daughters Shall Prophesy": Pentecostal Hermeneutics and the Empowerment of Women', in *The Globalization of Pentecostalism*. (eds) Dempster, M. W., Klaus, B. D., Petersen, D., Regnum, Oxford, 1999, pp. 313–7.

Prasinos, S., 'Spiritual Aspects of Psychotherapy', *JRHlth*. 31.1, Spring 1992, pp. 41–52.

Price, R. M., 'Illness Theodicies in the New Testament', *JRHlth*. 25.4, Winter 1986, pp. 309–15.

Quesnell, Q., *The Mind of Mark: Interpretation and Method through the Exegesis of Mark 6,52*. Pontifical Biblical Institute, Rome, 1969.

Reimer, A. M., *Miracle and Magic: A Study in the Acts of the Apostles and the Life of Apollonius of Tyana*. Sheffield Academic Press, Sheffield, 2002.

Remus, H., *Pagan-Christian Conflict over Miracle in the Second Century*. Philadelphia Patristic Foundation, Cambridge, MA, 1983.

Remus, H., *Jesus the Healer*. Cambridge University Press, Cambridge, 1997.

Remus, H., '"Magic", Method, Madness', *Method and Theory in the Study of Religion*. 11.3, 1999, pp. 258–98.

Rhoads, D., 'Jesus and the Syrophoenician Woman in Mark: A Narrative-Critical Study', *JAAR*. 62, 1994, pp. 343–75.

Rich, A. T., 'Luke 5.26', *ExpTim*. 44, 1932–3, pp. 428–9.

Richardson, A., *The Miracle-Stories of the Gospels*. SCM, London, 1941.

Robbins, V., 'The Healing of Blind Bartimaeus (10.46–52) in the Marcan Theology', *JBL*. 92.72, 1973, pp. 224–43.

Robbins, V., 'By Land and Sea: The We-Passages and Ancient Sea Voyages', in *Perspectives on Luke-Acts*. (ed.) Talbert, C. H., ABPR, Danville, 1978, pp. 215–42.

Robbins, V., 'The Woman Who Touched Jesus' Garments: Socio-rhetorical Analysis of the Synoptic Accounts', *NTS*. 33, 1987, pp. 502–15.

Robin, A. de Q., 'The Cursing of the Fig Tree in Mark 11: A Hypothesis', *NTS*. 8.3, 1962, pp. 276–81.

Rosner, F., *Medicine in the Mishnah Torah of Maimonides*. Ktav, New York, 1984.

Ross, R., 'Was Jesus Saying Something or Doing Something?', *BibT*. 41.4, 1990, pp. 441–5.

Runge, S. E., *Discourse Grammar of the Greek New Testament.* Hendrickson, Peabody, 2011.

Ryrie, C. C., 'The Cleansing of the Leper', *BibS.* 113, July 1956, pp. 262–7.

Ryrie, C. C., 'An Act of Divine Healing', *BibS.* 113, Oct. 1956, pp. 353–60.

Sanders E. P., *Jesus and Judaism.* Fortress Press, Philadelphia, 1985.

Sanders E. P., *The Historical Figure of Jesus.* Penguin, New York, 1993.

Sanders, J. N., Mastin, B. A., *The Gospel According to St. John.* A. & C. Black, London, 1968.

Sanford, J. A., *Healing Body and Soul.* Gracewing, Leominster, 1992.

Satterthwaite, P. E., Hess, R. S., Wenham, G. J. (eds), *The Lord's Anointed: Interpretation of Old Testament Messianic Texts.* Paternoster Press, Carlisle, 1995.

Saucy, M., 'Miracles and Jesus' Proclamation of the Kingdom of God', *BibS.* 153, July–Sept. 1996, pp. 281–307.

Schnackenburg, R., *Jesus in the Gospels.* (tr.) Dean, O. C., Westminster Press, Louisville, 1995.

Schnackenburg, R., *The Gospel of Matthew.* (tr.) Barr, R., Eerdmans, Grand Rapids, 2002.

Schneiders, S. W., 'Death in the Community of Eternal Life: History, Theology, and Spirituality in John 11', *Interpretation.* 51, 1987, pp. 44–56.

Schürer, E., *The History of the Jewish People in the Age of Christ.* T. & T. Clark, London, 1986.

Schwartz, J., 'Dogs in Jewish Society in the Second Temple Period and in the Time of the Mishnah and the Talmud', *JJS.* 55.2, 2004, pp. 246–77.

Schweizer, E., *The Good News According to Matthew.* (tr.) Green, D. E., John Knox Press, Atlanta, 1975.

Scott, J. M., 'Matthew 15.21–28: A Test Case for Jesus' Manners', *JSNT.* 63, 1996, pp. 21–44.

Scott, M., *Healing Then and Now.* Word, Milton Keynes, 1993.

Seet, C., 'The Doctrine of Healing in the Atonement', *The Burning Bush.* 2.2, July 1996, pp. 93–9.

Seim, T. K., *The Double Message: Patterns of Gender in Luke-Acts.* T. & T. Clark, Edinburgh, 1994.

Selvidge, M., 'Mark 5.25–34 and Leviticus 15.19–20: A Reaction to Restrictive Purity Regulations', *JBL.* 103, 1984, pp. 619–23.

Selvidge, M., *Woman, Cult and Miracle Recital: A Redactional Critical Investigation of Mark 5.24–34.* Bucknell University Press, Lewisburg, 1990.

Senior, D., *Matthew.* Abingdon Press, Nashville, 1998.

Seybold, K., Mueller, U. B., *Sickness and Healing.* (tr.) Stott, D. W., Abingdon Press, Nashville, 1981.

Sharot, S., *Messianism, Mysticism and Magic: A Sociological Analysis of Jewish Religious Movements.* University of Carolina Press, Chapel Hill, 1982.

Sibinga, J., 'Eine literische Technik im Matthausevangelium', in *L'Evangile selon Matthieu: Rédaction et théologie.* (ed.) Didier, M., Duculot, Gembloux, 1972, pp. 99–105.

Sinclair, S. G., 'The Healing of Bartimaeus and Gaps in Mark's Messianic Secret', *SLJT*. 33.4, 1990, pp. 249–57.

Slusser, D. M., 'The Healing Narratives in Mark', *CC*. 87.19, 1970, pp. 597–9.

Smith, M., *Jesus the Magician*. Harper & Row, San Francisco, 1978.

Smith, S. H., 'Mark 3,1–6: Form, Redaction and Community Function', *Biblica*. 75.2, 1994, pp. 153–74.

Smith, S. M., 'The Function of the Son of David Tradition in Mark's Gospel', *NTS*. 42.4, 1996, pp. 523–39.

Sorensen, E., *Possession and Exorcism in the New Testament and Early Christianity*. Mohr Siebeck, Tübingen, 2002.

Staley, J. F., 'Stumbling in the Dark, Reaching for the Light: Reading Characters in John 5 and 9', *Semeia*. 53, 1991, pp. 55–80.

Stanislaus, L., 'Healing and Exorcism: Dalit Perspectives', *Vidyajoti*. 63.3, 1999, pp. 192–9.

Stanton, G. N., *Gospel Truth? New Light on the Gospels*. Trinity Press, Valley Forge, 1995.

Stein, R. H., *Luke*. Broadman Press, Nashville, 1992.

Stein, R. H., *Mark*. Baker Academic, Grand Rapids, 2008.

Steinhauser, M. G., 'The Form of the Bartimaeus Narrative (Mark 10, 46–52)', *NTS*. 32, 1986, pp. 583–95.

Sterling, G. E., 'Jesus as Exorcist: An Analysis of Matthew 17.14–20; Mark 9.14–29; Luke 9.37–43a', *CBQ*. 55.3, 1993, pp. 467–93.

Stibbe, M. W. G., 'A Tomb with a View: John 11.1–44 in Narrative-Critical Perspective', *NTS*. 40, 1994, pp. 38–54.

Strack, H. L., Billerbeck, P., *Kommentar zum Neuen Testament und Midrasch*. Beck, Munich, 1956.

Suggit, J. N., 'The Raising of Lazarus', *ExpTim*. 95, 1984, pp. 106–8.

Suhl, A., 'Der Davidssohn im Matthaeus-Evangelium', *ZNW*. 59, 1968, pp. 57–81.

Sweet, J. P. M., 'A Saying, a Parable, a Miracle', *Theology*. 76.125, 1973, pp. 125–33.

Syx, R., 'Jesus and the Unclean Spirit', *Louvain Studies*. 17, 1992, pp. 166–80.

Talbert, C. H., *Reading Luke*. SPCK, London, 1982.

Tannehill, R. C., *The Narrative Unity of Luke-Acts: A Literary Interpretation*. 2 vols, Fortress Press, Philadelphia, 1986, 1990.

Tannehill, R. C., *Luke*. Abingdon Press, Nashville, 1996.

Telford, G. B., 'Mark 1.40–45', *Interpretation*. 36.1, 1982, pp. 54–9.

Telford, W. R., *The Barren Temple and the Withered Tree*. JSOT Press, Sheffield, 1980.

Tenney, M. C., 'Topics from the Gospel of John – Part 2: The Meaning of the Signs', *BibS*. 132, April 1975, pp. 145–60.

Tenney, M. C., *John: The Gospel of Belief*. Eerdmans, Grand Rapids, 1982.

Theissen, G., *Miracle Stories of the Early Christian Tradition*. T. & T. Clark, Edinburgh, 1983.

Theissen G., Merz, A., *The Historical Jesus: A Comprehensive Guide*. (tr.) McDonagh, F., SCM, London, 1998.

Thiselton, A. C., 'The Supposed Power of Words in the Biblical Writings', *JTS*. 25, 1974, pp. 283–99.

Thiselton, A. C., 'Semantics and New Testament Interpretation', in *New Testament Interpretation*. (ed.) Marshall, I. H., Paternoster Press, Carlisle, 1992 (1977), pp. 76–84.

Thomas, J. C., '"Stop Sinning Lest Something Worse Come upon You": The Man at the Pool in John 5', *JSNT*. 59, 1995, pp. 3–20.

Thomas, J. C., *The Devil, Disease and Deliverance: Origins of Illness in New Testament Thought*. Sheffield Academic Press, Sheffield, 1998.

Thompson, M., 'Signs and Faith in the Fourth Gospel', *BBR*. 1, 1991, pp. 89–106.

Thompson, W. G., 'Reflections on the Composition of Matthew 8.1–9.34', *CBQ*. 33, 1971, pp. 368–87.

Tiede, D. L., *Luke*. Augsburg, Minneapolis, 1988.

Torgerson, H., 'The Healing of the Bent Woman: A Narrative Interpretation of Luke 13.10–17', *CurTM*. 32.3, 2005, pp. 176–86.

Torrance, T., 'The Giving of Sight to the Man Born Blind', *EvQ*. 9.1, 1937, pp. 74–82.

Trachtenberg, J., *Jewish Magic and Superstition: A Study in Folk Religion*. Atheneum, New York, 1987.

Tuckett, C. M., *Luke*. Sheffield Academic Press, Sheffield, 1996.

Turner, D. L., *Matthew*. Baker, Grand Rapids, 2000.

Turner, M. M. B., 'The Spirit and the Power of Jesus' Miracles in the Lucan Conception', *NovT*. 33, 1991, pp. 124–52.

Turner, N., *Grammatical Insights into the New Testament*. T. & T. Clark, London, 2004 (1965).

Tuzlak, A., 'Coins Out of Fishes: Money, Magic, and Miracle in the Gospel of Matthew', *StudRel*. 36.2, 2007, pp. 279–95.

Twelftree, G. H., *Christ Triumphant*. Hodder & Stoughton, London, 1985.

Twelftree, G. H., 'EI/DE . . . EGO EKBALLO TA DAIMONIA', in *Gospel Perpectives, Vol. 6: The Miracles of Jesus*. (eds) Wenham, D. and Blomberg, C. L., JSOT Press, Sheffield, 1986, pp. 361–400.

Twelftree, G. H., *Jesus the Miracle Worker*. InterVarsity Press, Downers Grove, 1999.

Twelftree, G. H., 'The Miracles of Jesus: Marginal or Mainstream?', *JSHJ*. 1, 2003, pp. 104–24.

Twelftree, G. H., 'Deliverance and Exorcism in the New Testament', in *Exorcism and Deliverance, Multi-disciplinary Studies*. (eds) Kay, W. K., Parry, R., Paternoster Press, Milton Keynes, 2011, pp. 45–68.

Twelftree, G. H., *Paul and the Miraculous*. Baker, Grand Rapids, 2013, pp. 39–42, 49–104.

Tyson, J. B., 'The Blindness of the Disciples in Mark', *JBL*. 80, 1961, pp. 261–8.

Ukpong, J. S., 'Leprosy: Untouchables of the Gospel of Today', *Concilium*. 1997/5, 67–72.

Umeagudosu, M. A., 'The Healing of the Gerasene Demoniac from a Specifically African Perspective', *ACS*. 12.4, 1996, pp. 30–7.

Uth, D. F. 'An Eschatological Interpretation of the Synoptic Miracles in the Mission and Message of Jesus', PhD, Southwestern Baptist Theological Seminary, 1991.

Van Aarde, A., 'Understanding Jesus' Healings', *Scriptura*. 74, 2000, pp. 223–36.

Van Cangh, J-M., 'Miracles grecs, rabbiniques et evangéliques', in *Miracles and Imagery in Luke and John*. Peeters, Leuven, 2008, pp. 213–36.

Van den Eynde, S., 'When a Teacher Becomes a Student: The Challenge of the Syrophoenician Woman (Mark 7.24–31)', *Theology*. 103.814, 2000, pp. 274–9.

Van der Loos, H., *The Miracles of Jesus*. Brill, Leiden, 1965.

Van der Toorn, K., Becking, B., van der Horst, P. W. (eds), *Dictionary of Deities and Demons in the Bible*. Brill, Leiden, 1995.

Van Eck, E. and van Aarde, A. G., 'Sickness and Healing in Mark: A Social Scientific Interpretation', *Neotestamentica*. 27.1, 1993, pp. 27–54.

Van Tilborg, S., *Imaginative Love in John*. Brill, Leiden, 1993.

Vannorsdall, J., 'Mark 2.1–12', *Interpretation*. 36.1, 1982, pp. 58–63.

Veersteg, P., 'Deliverance and Exorcism in Anthropological Perspective', in *Exorcism and Deliverance: Multi-disciplinary Studies*. (eds) Kay, W. K., Parry, R., Paternoster Press, Milton Keynes, 2011, pp. 120–38.

Vermes, G., *The Religion of Jesus the Jew*. Fortress Press, Minneapolis, 1993.

Vinson, R. B, *Luke*. Smyth and Helwyn, Macon, 2008.

Vledder, J. E., *Conflict in the Miracle Stories: A Socio-Exegetical Study of Matthew 8 and 9*. Sheffield Academic Press, Sheffield, 1997.

Vogel, A. A., *God, Prayer and Healing*. Fowler Wright Books, Leominster, 1995.

Vogels, W, 'A Semiotic Study of Luke 7.11–17', *Église et Théologie*. 14, 1983, pp. 273–92.

Vogtle, A., 'The Miracles of Jesus against Their Contemporary Background', in *Jesus in His Time*. (ed.) Schultz, H. J., SPCK, London, 1971, pp. 96–105.

Wacker, G., 'Wimber and Wonders: What about Miracles Today?', *Reformed Journal*. 37, April 1987, pp. 16–22.

Waetjen, H. C., *A Reordering of Power: A Socio-political Reading of Mark's Gospel*. Fortress Press, Minneapolis, 1989.

Wahlberg, R. C., *Jesus Freed the Woman*. Paulist Press, New York, 1978.

Wahlen, C., *Jesus and the Impurity of Spirits in the Synoptic Gospels*. Mohr Siebeck, Tübingen, 2004.

Wainwright, E., *Towards a Feminist Critical Reading of the Gospel*. De Gruyter, Berlin, 1991.

Walker, P. 'A First-Century Sermon', in *The New Testament in Its First Century Setting*. (eds) Williams, P. J., Clarke, A. D., Head, P. M., Instone-Brewer, D., Eerdmans, Cambridge, 2004, pp. 225–35.

Wall, L., 'Jesus and the Unclean Woman: How a Study in Mark's Gospel Sheds Light on the Problem of Obstetric Fistulas', *Christianity Today.* January 2010, pp. 48–52.

Warrington, K., 'The Use of the Name (of Jesus) in Healing and Exorcism with Particular Reference to the Teachings of Kenneth Hagin', *JEPTA.* 17, 1997, pp. 16–36.

Warrington, K., 'Healings by Jesus in Luke and in Acts: Pedagogical and Paradigmatic Explorations', *Evangelical Theological Society Conference.* Boston, MA, November, 1999.

Warrington, K., 'The Role of Jesus in the Healing Praxis and Teaching of British Pentecostalism: A Re-Examination', *Pneuma.* 25.1, 2003, pp. 66–92.

Warrington, K., *Healing and Suffering: Biblical and Pastoral Reflections.* Paternoster Press, Carlisle, 2005.

Weissenrieder, A., *Images of Illness in the Gospel of Luke.* Mohr Siebeck, Tübingen, 2003.

Wells, L., *The Greek Language of Healing from Homer to New Testament Times.* De Gruyter, Berlin, 1998.

Wenham, D. and Blomberg, C. L., *Gospel Perspectives, Vol. 6: The Miracles of Jesus.* JSOT Press, Sheffield, 1986.

Wenham, G., 'Christ's Healing Ministry and His Attitude to the Law', in *Christ the Lord.* (ed.) Rowdon, H. H., IVP, Leicester, 1982, pp. 115–26.

Wheatley-Irving, L., 'The Miracles of the Messiah and Peter's Confession (Mark 7.31–9.1)', *Proceedings.* 12, 1992, pp. 145–53.

Wiebe, P. H., 'Deliverance and Exorcism in Philosophical Perspective', in *Exorcism and Deliverance: Multi-disciplinary Studies.* (eds.) Kay, W. K., Parry, R., Paternoster Press, Milton Keynes, 2011, pp. 156–80.

Wilkinson, J., 'A Study of Healing in the Gospel According to John', *SJT.* 20.4, 1967, pp. 442–61.

Wilkinson, J., 'The Case of the Bent Woman', *EvQ.* 49, 1977, pp. 195–205.

Wilkinson, J., *Health and Healing.* Handsel Press, Edinburgh, 1980.

Williams, D. T., 'Why the Finger?', *ExpTim.* 115.2, November 2003, pp. 45–9.

Wink, W., 'Mark 2.1–12', *Interpretation.* 36, 1982, pp. 58–63.

Wink, W., *Unmasking the Powers: The Invisible Forces That Determine Human Existence.* Fortress Press, Philadelphia, 1986.

Wink, W., *The Powers That Be: Theology for a New Millennium.* Doubleday, New York, 1998.

Wire, A. C., 'The Structure of the Gospel Miracle Stories and Their Tellers', *Semeia.* 11, 1978, pp. 83–113.

Witherington, B. III., *Women in the Ministry of Jesus: A Study of Jesus' Attitudes to Women and Their Roles as Reflected in His Earthly Life.* Cambridge University Press, Cambridge, 1984.

Witherington, B. III., *John's Wisdom.* Lutterworth Press, Cambridge, 1995.

Witherington, B. III., 'Salvation and Health in Christian Antiquity: The Soteriology of Luke-Acts in Its First-Century Setting', in *Witness to the Gospel: The Theology of Acts.* (eds) Marshall, I. H., Peterson, D., Eerdmans, Grand Rapids, 1998, pp. 145–66.

Witkamp, L. T., 'The Use of Traditions in John 5.1–18', *JSNT*. 25, 1985, pp. 22–5.

Wojciechowski, M., 'The Touching of the Leper (Mk. 1.40–45)', *BZ*. 33, 1989, pp. 114–19.

Woods, E. J., *The 'Finger of God' and Pneumatology in Luke-Acts*. Sheffield Academic Press, Sheffield, 2001.

Wright, A. T., *The Origins of Evil Spirits: The Reception of Genesis 6.1–4 in Early Jewish Literature*. Mohr Siebeck, Tübingen, 2005.

Wright, N. T., *Jesus and the Victory of God*. SPCK, London, 1996.

Wright, N. T., *How God Became King: The Forgotten Story of the Gospels*. SPCK, London, 2012.

Yamauchi, E., 'Magic or Miracle? Diseases, Demons and Exorcisms', in *Gospel Perspectives, Vol. 6*. (eds) Wenham, D., Blomberg, C. L., JSOT Press, Sheffield, 1986, pp. 89–183.

Yeung, M. W., *Faith in Jesus and Paul*. Mohr Siebeck, Tübingen, 2002, pp. 67–97.

York, J. O., *The Last Shall Be First: The Rhetoric of Reversal in Luke*. Sheffield Academic Press, Sheffield, 1991.

Index of biblical texts

Index of subjects

Keith Warrington (BA, MPhil, PhD) was, until autumn 2013, Vice-Principal and Director of Doctoral Studies at Regents Theological College, Malvern, UK, and, for 30 years, a lecturer in New Testament studies. As well as continuing to lecture at Regents, he now spends much of his time teaching in the UK and abroad, as well as being engaged in a programme entitled Word and Spirit, which exists to help believers engage with the Bible in ways that are transformative and enjoyable.

He is an editor of the Studies in Charismatic and Pentecostal Issues series (Paternoster Press). He has contributed to many journals, and his books include *Pentecostal Perspectives* (Paternoster Press, 1998), *God and Us: A life-changing adventure* (Scripture Union, 2003), *Discovering the Holy Spirit in the New Testament* (Hendrickson/Baker, 2005), *Healing and Suffering: Biblical and pastoral reflections* (Paternoster Press, 2005), *Pentecostal Theology: A theology of encounter* (T. & T. Clark, 2009), *The Message of the Holy Spirit* (IVP, 2009), *Discovering Jesus in the New Testament* (Hendrickson/Baker, 2009) and *A Biblical Theology of the Holy Spirit* (SPCK, 2014).

He is married to Judy and they have two married children, Luke and Anna-Marie, and four grand-daughters. In his professional life, he most enjoys the opportunity to explore God with people who really want to learn – a great privilege.